新视野

初级商务汉语口语

主　　编　王晓华

浙江工商大學出版社 ZHEJIANG GONGSHANG UNIVERSITY PRESS | 杭州

图书在版编目(CIP)数据

新视野初级商务汉语口语 / 王晓华主编. — 杭州 ：浙江工商大学出版社，2019.8

ISBN 978-7-5178-3265-2

Ⅰ. ①新… Ⅱ. ①王… Ⅲ. ①商务—汉语—口语—对外汉语教学—教材 Ⅳ. ①H195.4

中国版本图书馆 CIP 数据核字(2019)第 119196 号

新视野
初级商务汉语口语
主　编　王晓华

责任编辑　沈明珠　张晶晶
封面设计　林朦朦
责任印制　包建辉
出版发行　浙江工商大学出版社
(杭州市教工路 198 号　邮政编码 310012)
(E-mail:zjgsupress@163.com)
(网址:http://www.zjgsupress.com)
电话:0571-81902049,88831806(传真)
排　　版　杭州朝曦图文设计有限公司
印　　刷　杭州高腾印务有限公司
开　　本　850mm×1168mm　1/16
印　　张　28.25
字　　数　637 千
版 印 次　2019 年 8 月第 1 版　2019 年 8 月第 1 次印刷
书　　号　ISBN 978-7-5178-3265-2
定　　价　98.00 元(共 3 册)

序 言

随着我国综合国力的不断增强,"汉语热"在不断升温。汉语学习热度成为体现中国软实力的晴雨表,商务汉语的应运而生并蓬勃发展就是明证。商务汉语教学是特殊目的汉语教学,也称专用汉语教学。商务汉语课程是为具有一定汉语基础的非母语学习者开设的专业语言课程,所用教材是以商务知识为背景的汉语语言教材。本系列教材为汉语初学者提供与商务活动相关的口语学习内容,注重将日常口语交流与商务情境相结合,旨在让学生学习该课程后,能用汉语解决日常学习、生活中的基本问题,也能在商务场合进行简单的口语交流。本书特点鲜明:

第一,实用性突出。教材既有初来乍到的留学生需要的信息,如报到、住宿、逛街等;又有简单的商务活动表达范例,如宴请、酒会、接机、实习等;还有绕不开的学校生活,比如查成绩、咨询课程、换宿舍、交学费等。

第二,时代感突出。教材中对话内容紧紧抓住时代脉搏,围绕中国社会经济的若干问题展开,比如义乌小商品市场、共享经济、电子支付、网购,还有关于杭州G20峰会的话题。

第三,实践性突出。在人物安排上,有来自不同生源国的学生,使学习者获得亲切感和认同感。在话题上,涉及了不同国家的学生所关心的不同领域。在练习设计中,更是以功能为导向,课堂练习和课后练习都围绕口语实践展开,强调学以致用,这个是商务汉语口语学习的最终目标。

本教材使用对象分别为已经完成大约2个月、3个月、4个月强化学习的非汉语母语学习者,也就是累计学习汉语120—400学时的汉语学习者。语言难度设定为HSK1—3级之间,基本上就是HSK初级水平,或者BCT1级水平。本系列教材为包含商务元素的口语教材,共三册,每册使用相同主题结构,但在话题选取、词汇使用等方面体现难易层次差别。根据每学期教学周数量,每册设置15课。根据学生水平,每一课设置2篇话题类似但难度有所不同的课文。

本系列教材的编写者都是多年从事对外汉语教学和商务汉语教学的一线教师。主编王晓华老师早年毕业于华东师范大学对外汉语专业,有近30年高校教龄,负责全套教材的话题设计、例课编写、难点把控、出版策划及最后终审工作。各分册主编分别由王晓慧老师、刘杰老师和孙鹏飞老师担任。本系列教材特别邀请了北京语言大学张旺熹副校长、暨南大学宗世海教授、澳大利亚标准中文学校校长李复新博士和浙江工商大学国际教育学院姜波院长担任编辑指导委员会委员。本系列教材的配套语音材料由本院刘杰、孙蕾、吴雅云、俞洁慧、李峰安、金利川、张颖、高璐、吴鸣琴和龚思老师共同录制,在此一并表示感谢。

由于水平和经验有限,编写时间也较为仓促,难免有不足之处,欢迎大家批评指正。

编者

2019年6月

Ⅰ The Users

The series of textbooks are intended for non-native Chinese learners who have learnt an intensive Chinese course as a second language for approximately 2 months , 3 months and 4 months. It is also commonly available to the learners who have cumulatively learned Chinese over 150—400 hours. (One or one and a half terms' long-term Chinese course and short-term spoken Chinese course are both suitable to use the textbooks.) The level of this textbooks is similar to the level of HSK 1—3, the primary level of HSKK, and the level of the BCT 1.

As far as we know, most of the students are beginners or low Chinese proficiency learners. Those high-level business Chinese textbooks are totally not suitable for them. Therefore, we forcus on the compilation of primary level of oral Chinese textbooks which can combine the daily communication with business situations.

Our students will have the ability to solve the simple problems in learning Chinese and daily life by taking this course. Moreover, they can apply what they have learnt to make a practical communication in business situations.

Ⅱ The Main Attribute

This textbooks are short-term spoken Chinese textbooks which contain elements of business. We plan to compile three volumes of textbooks which share the same thematic structure. However, in terms of topic and vocabulary, we do make a difference in level 1, level 2 and level 3.

Ⅲ The Basic Structure

According to the quantity of teaching week, 15 lessons can be set of one term for each volume. Because the level of student is limited, the content of each lesson should be appropriate. Therefore, two texts are in similar topic, but with different level.

编辑指导委员会

语法术语及缩略语参照表

Abbreviation of Grammar Terms

Grammar Terms in Chinese	Grammar Terms in Pinyin	Grammar Terms in English	Abbreviations
名词	míng cí	noun	*n.*
形容词	xíng róng cí	adjective	*adj.*
动词	dòng cí	verb	*v.*
助动词	zhù dòng cí	auxiliary	*aux.*
量词	liàng cí	measure word	*mw.*
代词	dài cí	pronoun	*pron.*
副词	fù cí	adverb	*adv.*
介词	jiè cí	preposition	*prep.*
连词	lián cí	conjunction	*conj.*
助词	zhù cí	particle	*part.*
拟声词	nǐ shēng cí	onomatopoeia	*onom.*
叹词	tàn cí	interjection	*int.*
成语	chéng yǔ	idiom	*idm.*
名词短语	míng cí duǎn yǔ	noun phrase	*NP*
动词短语	dòng cí duǎn yǔ	verb phrase	*VP*
形容词短语	xíng róng cí duǎn yǔ	adjectival phrase	*AP*
动宾结构	dòng bīn jié gòu	verb-object	*VO*
动补结构	dòng bǔ jié gòu	verb-complement	*VC*

人物身份介绍

Introduction of the Main Characters in the Book

Mǎ kè
1.马克

男,英国人,工商大学留学生。学习努力,非常喜欢学习汉语和中国文化。Mark is a student from UK in Gongshang University. He works hard and like to learn Chinese and Chinese culture.

Ān nà
2.安娜

女,俄罗斯留学生,爱好唱歌、跳舞。她在另一所大学学习酒店管理专业,跟马克、玛丽都是朋友。Anna is a Russian student and she likes singing and dancing. She is studying Hotel Management in another university. She, Mark and Mary are good friends.

Mǎ lì
3.玛丽

女,南非人,工商大学留学生。热情,热爱运动、旅行。Mary is a student from South Africa in Gongshang University. She is very enthusiastic and loves sports and traveling.

Měi líng
4.美玲

女,印尼人,工商大学留学生。对中国商务很感兴趣,在陈龙的公司里实习,希望毕业以后从事印中贸易。Meiling is an Indonesian student in Gongshang University. She is interested in Chinese business. She is doing her intership in Chen Long's company and hopes to do trade between the two countries after her graduation.

Mǎ lǎo shī
5.马老师

男,工商大学汉语老师。Teacher Ma works in Gongshang University. He teaches Chinese.

Lǐ Míng
6.李明

男,中国学生。Li Ming is a Chinese student.

Ā màn
7.阿曼

男,哈萨克斯坦人,中文不错,在爸爸的公司担任经理。Aman is from Kazakhstan and working in his father's company as a manager. He speaks Chinese well.

Dà wèi
8.大卫

男,美国人,在一家外贸公司工作。David is an American and works in a foreign trade company.

Zhāng Lì
9. 张 丽

女,中国人,在阿曼爸爸公司工作,是阿曼的同事。Zhang Li is a Chinese girl and works in Arman's father's company.

Chén Lóng
10. 陈 龙

男,中国人,大卫的同事。Chen Long is a Chinese young man and works together with David.

wáng lǎo shī
11. 王 老师

男,工商大学汉语老师。Teacher Wang works in Gongshang University. He teaches Chinese.

Ā bù lái
12. 阿布来

男,哈萨克斯坦人,工商大学留学生。平时在爸爸的中国公司兼职。Abylai is from Kazakhstan. He is an international student in GongShang University, also works part-time in his father's Chinese company.

Nà tǎ shā
13. 娜塔莎

女,津巴布韦人,工商大学留学生。热情,热爱运动、旅行、参加各种活动。Natasha is from Zimbabwe. She is an international Student in GongShang University. She is enthusiastic, and she loves sports, traveling and participating in various activities.

Ài lín
14. 艾琳

女,泰国人,工商大学留学生。对中国商务很感兴趣,希望毕业以后从事泰中贸易。Ailin is from Thailand. She is an international Student in Gongshang University. She is interested in Chinese business and hopes to engage in Thai-Chinese trade after graduation.

Jīn Míng xué
15. 金 明 学

男,韩国留学生,热情好客。Jin Mingxue is from South Korea. He is hospitable.

Kǎ kǎ
16. 卡卡

男,巴西留学生,喜欢踢足球。Kaka is from Brazil. He likes playing football.

新视野

初级商务汉语口语(1)

主　　编　王晓华
本册主编　王晓慧
本册编写　王晓慧　吴雅云　傅翠娟　吴鸣琴

学习指南

Guide to the Lessons

课数 Lessons	语法项 Grammar Items	功能项 Functional Items
第1课　这是我的名片	1. A 还是 B? 2. 如果……,(就)…… 3. 能愿动词"可以" 4. "吧"表示猜测语气 5. 跟 + …… + *v*. 6. 派 + …… + *v*. 7. 先 + *v*. 8. 动词重叠	1. 酒会上相互介绍身份(职位、专业)等基本信息 2. 公务会面,互递名片
第2课　几点到北京	1. 下…… 2. *v*. + 一下 3. *v*. + 时间段 4. 能愿动词 "想" 5. 请 + sb. + *v*. 6. 时间 + 地点 + *v*.	1. 时间、日期表达 2. 邀请他人
第3课　明天天气不好	1. 还 + *v*. 2. A 比 B + *adj*. 3. 真…… 4. 不 + *adj*.1 + 不 + *adj*.2 5. 能愿动词"应该" 6. *adj*. + 一点儿	1. 谈论天气 2. 根据天气讨论安排
第4课　去购物中心看看	1. 有的……有的…… 2. sentence + "吧" 3. 什么都…… 4. 再 + *v*. 5. 用…… + *v*.	1. 讨论去哪儿购物 2. 完成简单的购物任务
第5课　你住哪个小区	1. "楼"的两种意思 2. 以前 3. "哪"的用法 4. A 离 B…… 5. "的"字短语 6. *v*. + 到(趋向补语) 7. sb. + 那儿	1. 住址表达 2. 介绍住址、学校、公司地址

续 表

课数 Lessons	语法项 Grammar Items	功能项 Functional Items
第 6 课　我去浙江工商大学	1. 了 2. 给 3. 怎么 + *v*. 4. ……路，……号线 5. ……站 6. 先……然后…… 7. 就	1. 打车 2. 弄清去某地的路线
第 7 课　你吃饭了吗	1. 好久不见 2. 祝你生日快乐 3. 还 4. "了"置于句尾 5. 最 + *adj*. 6. ……的话	1. 讨论去哪儿吃 2. 饭店点菜
第 8 课　这个周末你干什么	1. 干什么 2. 对……好 3. *v*. 不 *v*. 4. 能愿动词 "要" 5. 多 + *v*. 6. 日期与时间的表达 7. 能愿动词"会" 8. 几	1. 兴趣爱好的表达 2. 简单讨论业余生活
第 9 课　家人和职业	1. 口 2. 真……啊 3. 是……的 4. 当 + 职业 5. 在 + *v*. 6. 家 7. 或者	1. 介绍家庭成员 2. 介绍他人职业等方面
第 10 课　1 美元换多少人民币	1. *v*. + 好 2. 数字读法 3. 帮 + sb. + *v*.	1. 换钱 2. 取钱
第 11 课　我带您去酒店	1. 带 + sb. + 去 2. 是来 + purpose + 的 3. *v*. + 的 + *n*. 4. 看起来	1. 招待朋友住宿 2. 办理宾馆入住

续 表

课数 Lessons	语法项 Grammar Items	功能项 Functional Items
第 12 课 每天都有好多工作	1. *adj*. + 不 + *adj*. 2. 挺 + *adj*. + 的 3. 好 + *adj*. 4. 快(要)……了/要……了 5. *v*. + 了 + 时间 + (O) 6. 能愿动词“能”	1. 简单谈论工作 2. 工作经历介绍
第 13 课 假期安排	1. *v*. + 得 + 程度补语 2. 又 3. 什么 + in + 吗 4. 时段 + 就 + *v*. 5. 一……就……	1. 询问假期时间 2. 讨论假期安排
第 14 课 你租的房子怎么样	1. 比较 + *adj*. 2. ……怎么样 3. 可能 4. *v*. + 一 + *v*. 5. 但是 6. 所以	1. 谈论房间 2. 租房
第 15 课 成绩出来了吗	1. 别 + *v*. 2. 量词“张”“门”	1. 询问上课安排 2. 查询成绩

mù lù
目录

1 这是我的名片
This is my name card

话题导学
Guidance

1. 你的专业是什么?
   What is your major?
2. 你知道哪些职业的汉语名称?
   Do you know how to say the job occupations in Chinese?
3. 第一次跟人见面的时候,怎么用汉语打招呼?
   How do you greet each other in Chinese when you first meet someone?

生词学习(一)
New words I

1. 还是 (hái shì) *conj.* or(used in questions) 学生还是老师;你还是他
2. 外贸 (wài mào) *n.* foreign trade 做外贸;外贸公司
3. 公司 (gōng sī) *n.* company 去公司;那个公司
4. 名片 (míng piàn) *n.* name card 我的名片;给你名片
5. 哦 (ò) *interj.* oh(expressing realization and understanding) 哦,是这样
6. 经理 (jīng lǐ) *n.* manager 是经理;公司经理
7. 专业 (zhuān yè) *n.* major 什么专业;他的专业
8. 国际商务 (guó jì shāng wù) *n.* international business 学习国际商务课程
9. 如果 (rú guǒ) *conj.* if; in case 如果来;如果不去
10. 问 (wèn) *v.* ask 问我;问什么

wèn tí
11. 问题 *n.* question; problem 有问题;一个问题

kě yǐ
12. 可以 *aux.* can(indicating permission) 可以问;可以去

专有名词(Proper noun)

zhè jiāng gōng shāng dà xué
浙江工商大学 Zhejiang Gongshang University

课文(一) 相识在酒会上
Text A Meeting people at a banquet

Ā màn Nǐ hǎo Wǒ jiào Ā màn
阿曼:你好!我叫阿曼。

Mǎ lì Nǐ hǎo wǒ jiào Mǎ lì Hěn gāo xìng rèn shí nǐ
玛丽:你好,我叫玛丽。很高兴认识你!

Ā màn Nǐ zài zhèr gōng zuò hái shì liú xué
阿曼:你在这儿工作还是留学?

Mǎ lì Wǒ shì liú xué shēng zài Zhè jiāng gōng shāng dà xué xué xí Nǐ ne
玛丽:我是留学生,在浙江工商大学学习。你呢?

Ā màn Wǒ zài wài mào gōng sī gōng zuò zhè shì wǒ de míng piàn
阿曼:我在外贸公司工作,这是我的名片。

Mǎ lì Xiè xie Ò nǐ shì jīng lǐ a
玛丽:谢谢!哦,你是经理啊!

Ā màn Nǐ zài dà xué lǐ xué shén me zhuān yè
阿曼:你在大学里学什么专业?

Mǎ lì Guó jì shāng wù Rú guǒ yǒu wèn tí kě yǐ wèn nǐ ma
玛丽:国际商务。如果有问题,可以问你吗?

Ā màn Kě yǐ a
阿曼:可以啊!

根据课文(一)回答问题
Answer these questions according to the Text A

1. 玛丽在什么大学学习?
2. 玛丽学习什么专业?
3. 阿曼做什么工作?

生词学习(二)
New words II

gēn
1. 跟 *prep.* with; towards 跟你去;跟我来

2. 第 (dì) *n.* (used before integers to indicate order) 第一;第二
3. 次 (cì) *n.* time 一次;第一次
4. 见面 (jiànmiàn) *v.* meet with 跟他见面;见一次面
5. 指教 (zhǐjiào) *v.* / *pol.* (used to ask sb. to give advice or comments) 多指教;谢谢指教
6. 派 (pài) *v.* distribute; dispatch; appoint 派他来;派我去
7. 谈 (tán) *v.* talk 跟你谈;谈什么
8. 先 (xiān) *adv.* first 先去;先吃
9. 一起 (yì qǐ) *adv.* together 一起看;一起做
10. 材料 (cái liào) *n.* material; information 公司材料;看材料
11. 行 (xíng) *v.* be alright; will do 不行;行啊

课文(二) 公务会面
Text B A business meeting

陈龙和张丽因为公务,在咖啡馆第一次见面。

Chen Long and Zhang Li arrange their first meeting in a cafe for business.

Chén Lóng Nín hǎo Qǐngwèn nín shì Zhāng Lì ma
陈 龙:您好!请问您是张丽吗?

Zhāng Lì Nín hǎo Wǒ shì Nín shì Chén xiānsheng ba
张 丽:您好!我是。您是陈先生吧?

Chén Lóng Duì hěn gāoxìng gēn nín jiànmiàn zhè shì wǒ de míngpiàn
陈 龙:对,很高兴跟您见面,这是我的名片。

Zhāng Lì Qǐng zuò qǐng zuò Zhè shì wǒ de míngpiàn
张 丽:请坐请坐!这是我的名片。

Chén Lóng Xiè xie Jīn tiān dì yī cì jiànmiàn qǐng duō zhǐ jiào
陈 龙:谢谢!今天第一次见面,请多指教!

Zhāng Lì Nín tài kè qì le Wǒ men jīng lǐ jīn tiān yǒu shì pài wǒ lái gēn nín tán
张 丽:您太客气了。我们经理今天有事,派我来跟您谈。

Chén Lóng Hǎo de méi wèn tí Wǒ men xiān yì qǐ kàn kan cái liào
陈 龙:好的,没问题。我们先一起看看材料。

Zhāng Lì Xíng
张 丽:行。

根据课文(二)回答问题
Answer these questions according to the Text B

1. 陈龙和张丽认识吗?
2. 陈龙和张丽见面后,交换(jiāohuàn,exchange)了什么?
3. 为什么是张丽来跟陈龙见面?

语言点
Language points

1. A还是B?

你在这儿工作还是留学?

Are you working here or studying (as a foreign student) here?

"还是"表示选择,用在问句里。

"还是" is used in a question to express selection among several choices.

(1)你是学生还是老师?

(2)你说英文还是中文?

(3)你今天来还是明天来?

2. 如果……,(就)……

如果有问题,可以问你吗?

If I have any questions during study can I ask you?

"如果"表示假设某种情况,常用在两个分句中的前一个分句中。

"如果" means if, in case. The clause with "如果" is often put in the previous sentence.

(1)如果有问题,我可以帮(bāng,to help)你。

(2)如果你去,我也去。

(3)如果不喜欢,就不买。

3. 能愿动词"可以"

如果有问题,可以问你吗?

May I ask you if I've got any questions?

"可以"表示能够,或表示许可。

"可以" means something can or may be done, or indicates permission.

(1)这儿可以坐吗?

(2)你可以看一下吗?

(3)我们明天见面,可以吗?

4. “吧”表示猜测语气

您是陈先生吧？

You are Mr. Chen, right?

“吧”用在句尾，表示疑问，带有“猜测”的意思。

“吧” is used at the end of a sentence, to imply doubt or supposition.

(1)您是王老师吧？

(2)这是张经理吧？

(3)您是他的老师吧？

5. 跟＋……＋v.

很高兴跟您见面。

It's very nice to meet you.

“跟”字短语用在动词前面，引入动作的对象，有“和”的意思，也有“对”的意思。

“跟……” is used before a verb to indicate accompaniment, relationship, involvement, etc. It can mean “with, towards.”

(1)我跟他说吧。

(2)我跟你一起去。

(3)你跟同学们介绍一下。

6. 派＋……＋v.

我们经理今天有事，派我来跟您谈。

Our manager is not available today, so he dispatched me to come to talk with you.

“派”的意思是比较正式地安排、派遣、分配。

“派”means to dispatch or appoint officially.

(1)经理派他去上海。

(2)公司派我来这儿工作。

(3)学校派了一位老师去那儿。

7. 先＋v.

我们先一起看看材料。

Let's read the materials together first.

“先”的意思是 first，但在句中的位置与 first 不同，它一般用于动词短语前面，而非主语前或者句末，除非是用于强调不同主语顺序的情况。

Different from the English word “first”,“先” is often used before a verb phrase instead of the subject, also not at the end of a sentence. Unless used to indicate the order of different subjects, it may be put before a subject.

(1)你们先见面谈谈。

(2)你先去吧。

(3)先留学,再(zài,then)工作。

8. 动词重叠

我们先一起看看材料。

First let's take a look at the materials together.

动词重叠表示尝试、建议,含有动作持续时间短的意味。

The reduplication of a verb means trying, or giving suggestions to others. It indicates that the action will not last for a long time.

(1)你先来看看吧。

(2)这是什么歌(gē, song),我听听。

(3)如果有问题,可以问问他。

核心句 Key sentences

1. 这是我的名片。
2. 如果有问题,可以问你吗?
3. 您是陈先生吧?
4. 第一次见面,请多指教!
5. 您太客气了。
6. 好的,没问题。

综合练习 Comprehensive exercises

(一)熟读短语 Read the following phrases

1. 外贸公司　一家公司　什么公司　在公司
2. 我的名片　一张名片　给你名片　没有名片
3. 李经理　张经理　公司经理　谁是经理
4. 问我　问你　问谁　我问你　问问题
5. 可以问　可以吃　可以去　可以看
6. 跟你见面　跟你谈　跟他一起
7. 第一次　第一个　第一天　第一本
8. 一起去　一起看看　一起吃饭　跟你一起

(二)选词填空 Choose a suitable word for each sentence

公司　专业　如果　问题　还是

1. 他在外贸________工作。
2. 玛丽的________是国际商务。
3. ________我有问题,可以问你吗?
4. 今天的工作有________吗?
5. 他在这儿工作________学习?

见面　派　经理　一起　指教

1. 很高兴跟您________。
2. 对不起,我们________今天有事。
3. 经理________我来跟您谈。
4. 第一次见面,请多________。
5. 我们________看看材料吧。

(三)替换练习 Substitution drills

1. 你在这儿工作还是留学?

　　是学生　　老师
　　明天工作　　休息
　　学习汉语　　英语

2. 我在工商大学学习。

　　外贸公司工作
　　义乌(Yìwū, name of a city)做外贸
　　商店买东西

3. 如果有问题,可以问你吗?

　　有问题　　找你
　　听不懂　　问你
　　不喜欢　　不吃

4. 您是陈先生吧?

　　王老师
　　大卫的朋友
　　王经理

5. 经理派我来跟您谈。

　　经理　我去那个公司
　　学校　王老师去北京开会
　　公司　小张来跟我见面

(四)完成对话 Complete the following dialogues

1. A:你在这儿工作还是留学?

B:我是留学生,在________________。你呢?(大学、学习)

A:我在________________。(公司、工作)

2. A:我在________________,这是我的名片。(公司、工作)

B:谢谢!哦,您是________________啊!

3. A:我是陈龙,很高兴跟您________________。

B:请坐请坐!今天第一次见面,请________________!(指教)

4. A:我们经理今天有事,派我________________。(跟、谈)

B:没问题,我们先看看材料吧。

(五)课堂活动 In-class exercises

1. 看图说话 Talk about the pictures

请根据图片说出简短的句子或对话。Try to make brief sentences or dialogues according to each picture.

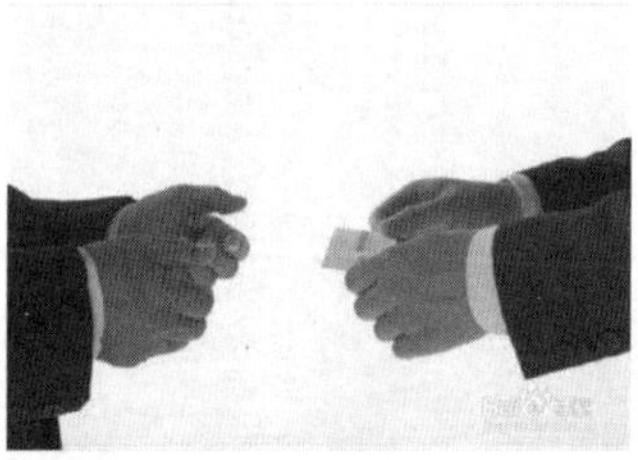

2. 角色扮演 Role-play

你在一次酒会中认识了一个新朋友,你们互相介绍自己。请尽量使用所给的词语或句型。You get to know a new friend in a banquet, and you two are introducing yourselves to each other. Please try to use the given words or phrases as many as possible.

高兴　认识　A还是B　留学　专业　公司　名片　第一次　请多指教

(六)课后练习 After-class exercises

采访3个人,简单记录他们的情况(学习或工作),在下一次课上跟同学们做介绍,介绍时需要包含基本的信息。Please interview three people and write down some basic information about them. Try to introduce them next class.

序号(Number)	姓名(Name)	他/她的职业(Profession)	他/她在哪儿学习/工作
例(Example)	玛丽	留学生	浙江工商大学
1			
2			
3			

课文翻译 Translation of texts

Text A　Meeting people at a banquet

Aman: Hi! I'm Aman.

Mary: Hi, I'm Mary. Nice to meet you!

Aman: Are you working or studying here?

Mary: I'm a foreign student studying in Zhejiang Gongshang University. What about you?

Aman: I'm working in an international trade company. Here is my name card.

Mary: Thanks! Oh, you are the manager.

Aman: What is your major in the university?

Mary: International Business. If I have any questions during study can I ask you?

Aman: Sure!

Text B　A business meeting

Chen Long: Excuse me, are you Ms. Zhang Li?

Zhang Li: Yes, I am. You're Mr. Chen, right?

Chen Long: Yes. It's nice to meet you. Here is my name card.

Zhang Li: Please take a seat! And this is my name card.

Chen Long: Thanks! Today is our first meeting and I'm looking forward to any advice you might have.

Zhang Li: You're welcome. Our manager is not available today, so he sent me to talk to you first.

Chen Long: OK, no problem. First let's read the materials together.

Zhang Li: Alright.

2 几点到北京
When will we arrive in Beijing?

话题导学 Guidance

1. 你是什么时候来中国的？
   When did you come to China?
2. 从你的城市坐飞机到北京要多长时间？
   How long does it take from your city to Beijing by plane?
3. 星期六是几月几号？
   What's the date of this coming Saturday?
4. 别人请你吃饭，你怎么回答？
   What will you say when someone is inviting you to have meal together?

生词学习(一) New words I

1. 时候	shí hòu	*n.* time	什么时候；那个时候
2. 开会	kāi huì	*v.* have a meeting	在开会；去开会
3. 下	xià	*n.* next	下一个；下一次
4. 星期	xīng qī	*n.* week	一个星期；下星期
5. 机票	jī piào	*n.* plane ticket	买机票；没有机票
6. 可能	kě néng	*adj.* likely; possible	可能去；不可能
7. 飞机	fēi jī	*n.* plane	坐飞机；飞机票
8. 到	dào	*v.* arrive(at/in); reach	到北京；几点到
9. 大概	dà gài	*adv.* probably; approximately	大概5点；大概10个人

fēi
10. 飞 *v.* fly　　飞几个小时;几点飞

xiǎo shí
11. 小时 *n.* hour　　一个小时;几个小时

专有名词 Proper noun

Běi jīng
北京　Beijing(the capital of China)

课文(一)　出差的安排
Text A　Talk about the schedule of a business trip

Ā màn　Zhāng Lì　wǒ men shén me shí hòu qù Běi jīng kāi huì
阿曼：张丽,我们什么时候去北京开会?

Zhāng Lì　Wǒ men xià xīng qī qù
张丽：我们下星期去。

Ā màn　Jī piào shì jǐ hào de
阿曼：机票是几号的?

Zhāng Lì　Bā hào　xīng qī sān
张丽：八号,星期三。

Ā màn　Shàng wǔ hái shì xià wǔ　Xià xīng qī sān shàng wǔ　wǒ kě néng yǒu shì
阿曼：上午还是下午?下星期三上午,我可能有事。

Zhāng Lì　Wǒ kàn yí xià shí jiān　Wǒ men zuò xià wǔ sān diǎn de fēi jī qù
张丽：我看一下时间。我们坐下午三点的飞机去。

Ā màn　Hǎo　Wǒ men jǐ diǎn dào Běi jīng
阿曼：好。我们几点到北京?

Zhāng Lì　Wǔ diǎn dào Běi jīng　Dà gài fēi liǎng gè xiǎo shí
张丽：五点到北京。大概飞两个小时。

Ā màn　Hǎo de　wǒ zhī dào le　xiè xie nǐ
阿曼：好的,我知道了,谢谢你。

根据课文(一)回答问题
Answer these questions according to the Text A

1. 阿曼去北京做什么?
2. 阿曼和张丽星期几去北京?
3. 飞到北京要几个小时?

生词学习(二)
New words II

xiǎng
1. 想 *aux.* want to　　想去;想吃

bāngzhù
2. 帮助 v./n. help;favor 帮助他;你的帮助

bié de
3. 别的 adj. other 别的人;别的时间

ān pái
4. 安排 v./n. arrange;arrangement 有安排;什么安排

kòng
5. 空 n. unoccupied space or time 有空;没空

lǜ chá
6. 绿茶 n. green tea 喝绿茶;一杯绿茶

fàndiàn
7. 饭店 n. restaurant 什么饭店;在饭店

zěn me yàng
8. 怎么样 pron. how about...; what about... 明天怎么样;6 点怎么样

课文(二) 请人吃饭
Text B Invite someone to have a meal together

美玲想请陈龙吃饭,感谢他在实习时给予的帮助。

Meiling wants to invite Chen Long to have a meal together to thank him for his help when she is doing internship in the company.

Měi líng Nín hǎo Chén xiān sheng Wǒ shì Měi líng
美玲:您好,陈先生。我是美玲。

Chén Lóng Měi líng nǐ hǎo Yǒu shì ma
陈龙:美玲你好!有事吗?

Měi líng shí èr yuè sān shí hào wǎn shang wǒ xiǎng qǐng nín chī fàn xiè xie nín bāng zhù wǒ
美玲:十二月三十号晚上我想请您吃饭,谢谢您帮助我。

Chén Lóng Ò nǐ tài kè qi le shí èr yuè sān shí hào shì xīng qī jǐ
陈龙:哦,你太客气了!十二月三十号是星期几?

Měi líng Shì xīng qī liù Nín yǒu méi yǒu bié de ān pái
美玲:是星期六。您有没有别的安排?

Chén Lóng Wǒ xiǎng yí xià Méi wèn tí wǒ yǒu kòng
陈龙:我想一下。没问题,我有空。

Měi líng Tài hǎo le nà wǎn shang liù diǎn zài Lǜ chá fàn diàn chī fàn zěn me yàng
美玲:太好了,那晚上六点在绿茶饭店吃饭,怎么样?

Chén Lóng Xíng xīng qī liù jiàn
陈龙:行,星期六见!

根据课文(二)回答问题
Answer these questions according to the Text B

1. 为什么美玲想请陈龙吃饭?

2. 陈龙星期六有时间吗?

3. 他们6点在哪儿吃饭?

语言点
Language points

1. 下……

我们下星期去。

We will go next week.

"下"表示次序或时间在后。

"下" indicates the order or time is later, next.

(1)下次再见。

(2)下星期去那个公司工作。

(3)你可以下个月来。

2. *v.* +一下

我看一下时间。

Let me check the time.

"*v.* +一下"是汉语口语中的常用结构,用法类似于"*v.* + *v.*"结构,表示"尝试、建议"的意思,含有动作持续时间短的意味。

"*v.* +一下" is used very frequently in speaking Chinese. Similar to "*v.* + *v.*"; It also means trying, or giving suggestions to others. It indicates that the action will not last for a long time.

(1)我先看一下你的材料。

(2)请问一下,这是什么公司?

(3)你可以跟他谈一下。

3. *v.* +时间段

大概飞两个小时。

It will fly for two hours approximately.

该结构表示动作持续的时间,动词后不可以用时间点,必须用表示时间段的词语或短语。如果动词带有宾语,完整结构为:

This structure indicates the duration of an action. Certain time period shall be used after the verb, instead of a specific time. If there is an object after the verb, the complete structure shall be:

v. + *o.* + *v.* + time period

你看材料看几个小时? How long will you read the material?

v. + time period + O.

你看几个小时材料? How long will you read the material?

该结构用于描述一般的情况或即将发生的情况。如果表示动作已完成,动词后需加"了"。

This structure is used to describe a normal situation or a situation that will take place in the future. "了" is needed after the verb if it indicates the action is completed already.

(1)你大概去几天?

(2)我们开会开两个小时。

(3)我每天睡(shuì, to sleep)七个小时。

(4)你去了几天?

(5)我们开会开了两个小时。

(6)我昨天睡了七个小时。

4. 能愿动词"想"

12 月 30 号晚上我想请您吃饭。

I'd like to invite you to have dinner with me in the evening of Dec. 30.

"想"有不同的意思,作为能愿动词,它的意思是某人希望做什么事,后面一般加动词或动词短语。它的语气没有"要"那么强,而且不像"要"一样可以加名词短语,表示某人要什么东西。

"想" has different meaning, and as an auxiliary verb, it means someone wants to do something. A verb or verb phrase shall be used after it. The tone of "想" is not as strong as "要", which also means "want". A noun or noun phrase can also be used after "要", instead of "想", to mean someone wants something.

(1)我想去他的公司看看。

(2)你想在哪儿吃饭?

(3)他想买几号的机票?

5. 请 + sb. + *v.*

12 月 30 号晚上我想请您吃饭。

I'd like to invite you to have dinner with me in the evening of Dec. 30.

"请"用在该结构中表示邀请别人做什么,或有礼貌地让别人做什么。

This structure indicates inviting someone to do something, or asking someone to do something politely.

(1)明天请你吃饭,怎么样?

(2)请张经理一起去开会吧!

(3)请你看一下我们公司的材料。

6. 时间＋地点＋*v.*

那晚上6点在绿茶饭店吃饭。

Then let's have dinner in the Green Tea Restaurant at 6 p.m.

在汉语里，用于表示动作发生时间和地点的词或短语一般用于动词短语之前，时间短语一般用于地点短语之前，也可放在主语前面。

The structure which indicates the time and location of an action, is usually put before the verb phrase. The time phrase often appears first, and it can be put before the phrase of location, or before the subject of a sentence.

(1)我下午两点在公司开会。

(2)明天10点我们在咖啡馆(kā fēi guǎn, cafe)见面。

(3)下星期他在哪儿工作？

核心句 Key sentences

1. 我们下星期去。
2. 我们五点到北京。
3. 谢谢您帮助我。
4. 您有没有别的安排？
5. 你太客气了。
6. 星期六见！

综合练习 Comprehensive exercises

(一)熟读短语 Read the following phrases

1. 什么时候　有的时候　有空的时候
2. 下星期　下星期三　下个月　下一个
3. 可能有事　可能有空　可能不去　可能不来
4. 到家　到北京　到哪儿　到学校　到了
5. 大概两个小时　大概一个星期　大概三天　大概十人　大概五点
6. 帮助我　帮助他　帮助别人　你的帮助　大家的帮助
7. 别的人　别的地方　别的学校　别的饭店　别的车
8. 有安排　明天的安排　下星期的安排　上课的安排

(二)组词成句 Use the words to construct sentences

1. 五点　北京　飞机　大概　到

2. 星期三 可能 我 下午 有事

____

3. 帮助 我 您 谢谢

____

4. 安排 有 别的 没有 您

____

5. 6点 晚上 吃饭 在 绿茶饭店

____

(三)替换练习 Substitution drills

1. 下星期三上午,我可能有事。

   明天下午　　　有课

   这个星期六　　没有时间

   下星期一上午　有会议

2. 我们几点到北京?

   你们　到学校

   他们　上课

   你　　去公司

3. 大概飞两个小时。

   走一个小时

   住一个星期

   开两天(会)

4. 晚上6点在绿茶饭店吃饭。

   中午12点在食堂

   明天晚上在我家

   下午5点在小饭馆

5. 星期六见!

   明天上午

   下星期

   晚上7点

(四)完成对话 Complete the following dialogues

1. A:我们________________去北京?(时候)

   B:我们________________去。(星期)

2. A:我们几点到那儿?

   B:大概______________到。(点)

3. A:机票是几号的?

B:________月________号,星期________。

4. A:我想星期六晚上请你吃饭。

B:哦,你____________________________!(客气)

5. A:我们什么时候在绿茶饭店吃饭?

B:下星期________晚上 ________点。

(五)课堂活动 In-class exercises

1. 看图说话 Talk about the pictures

请根据图片说出简短的句子或对话。Make brief sentences or dialogues according to each picture.

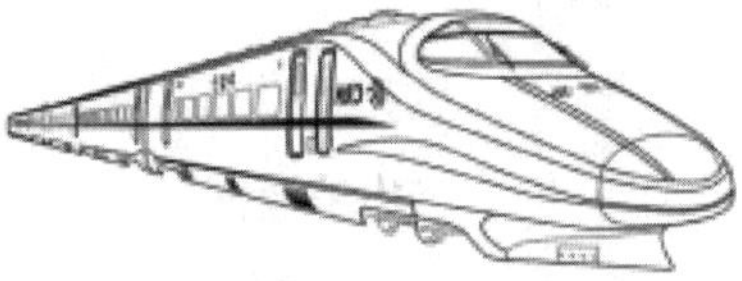

2. 角色扮演 Role-play

(1)A 问 B 他们买的飞机票是什么时候的,要飞多长时间。请使用以下词语或词组表达。A asks B about their flight departure date and how long it will take. Try to use the following words or phrases.

……月……号　星期　还是　可能　大概　小时

(2)A 想请 B 吃饭,他们商量吃饭的时间。A intends to invite B to have a meal together and they are discussing about the time.

请　晚上　安排　有空　怎么样

(六)课后练习 After-class exercises

用中文邀请你的朋友一起吃饭,或去买东西,或去购物中心,或喝咖啡,等等。先问别人有没有时间,然后商量一下约什么时间。Invite your friends to have a meal together, or go shopping, or stroll around the shopping mall, or have coffee, etc. Find out whether your friends have time and then fix a time with them.

序号	朋友的名字	去哪儿	几月几号	星期几	几点
1					
2					

课文翻译 Translation of texts

Text A　The schedule of a business trip

Aman: Hi, Zhang Li, when will we go to attend the meeting in Beijing?

Zhang Li: We will go next week.

Aman: What's the date of our plane ticket?

Zhang Li: 8th, Wednesday.

Aman: Is it in the morning or afternoon? I may not be available next Wednesday morning.

Zhang Li: Let me check the time. We will take flight at 3 p. m.

Aman: OK. What time will we arrive in Beijing?

Zhang Li: We will get there at 5 p. m. It will take around two hours.

Aman: OK. Thank you.

Text B　Invite someone to have a meal together

Meiling: Hello, Mr. Chen. This is Meiling.

Chen Long: Hi Meiling! How can I help you?

Meiling: I'd like to invite you to dinner on December 30th. Thank you for helping me in my work.

Chen Long: Oh, that's very nice of you! What day is December 30th?

Meiling: It's Saturday. Do you have other arrangements at that time?

Chen Long: Let me see. No problem. I'm available.

Meiling: Great. Then let's meet at the Green Tea Restaurant at 6 p. m. Is that OK for you?

Chen Long: Yes. See you on Saturday!

3 明天天气不好
The weather is not nice tomorrow

话题导学 Guidance

1. 你习惯中国的气候吗?
   Are you used to the climate in China?
2. 在中国,你喜欢哪个季节?
   Which season do you prefer in China?
3. 你的国家有几个季节?
   How many seasons are there in your country?
4. 你去过广州吗? 广州冬天的天气怎么样?
   Have you been to Guangzhou? If you've been there, how do you like the winter weather in that city?

生词学习(一) New words I

1. lěng 冷 *adj.* cold — 太冷了;冷吗
2. xià yǔ 下雨 *v.* rain — 不下雨;下大雨
3. hái 还 *adv.* also; in addition — 明天很冷,还下雨
4. guā fēng 刮风 *v.* blow the wind — 在刮风;刮大风
5. dù 度 *n.* degree — 20度;几度
6. bǐ 比 *prep.* than; to(used to compare) — 比昨天冷;比你大
7. dī 低 *adj.* low — 很低;气温低
8. zhēn 真 *adv.* really; so — 真冷;真好
9. dōng tiān 冬天 *n.* winter — 冬天冷;没有冬天

xià tiān
10. 夏天 *n.* summer 喜欢夏天

yóu yǒng
11. 游泳 *v.* swim 去游泳；想游泳

chūn tiān
12. 春天 *n.* spring 春天很美

bú cuò
13. 不错 *adj.* good; nice 天气不错；中文不错

rè
14. 热 *adj.* hot 冷热；不热

cháng cháng
15. 常常 *adv.* often; frequently 常常下雨；常常刮风

fāng biàn
16. 方便 *adj.* convenient 很方便；坐车方便

课文(一) 谈论天气
Text A Talk about the weather

玛丽和美玲都不习惯杭州的冬天。

Both Mary and Meiling are not used to the winter in Hangzhou.

Mǎ lì Tài lěng le Měi líng míng tiān tiān qì zěn me yàng
玛丽：太冷了，美玲，明天天气怎么样？

Měi líng Wǒ kàn yí xià shǒu jī Míng tiān xià yǔ hái guā fēng
美玲：我看一下手机。明天下雨，还刮风。

Mǎ lì Duō shǎo dù
玛丽：多少度？

Měi líng Wǔ dù bǐ jīn tiān dī
美玲：5度，比今天低。

Mǎ lì Míng tiān bǐ jīn tiān lěng Wǒ zhēn bù xǐ huān dōng tiān
玛丽：明天比今天冷。我真不喜欢冬天。

Měi líng Wǒ yě bù xǐ huān Wǒ xǐ huān xià tiān kě yǐ qù yóu yǒng
美玲：我也不喜欢。我喜欢夏天，可以去游泳。

Mǎ lì Chūn tiān yě bú cuò bù lěng bú rè
玛丽：春天也不错，不冷不热。

Měi líng Kě shì Háng zhōu de chūn tiān cháng cháng xià yǔ bú tài fāng biàn
美玲：可是杭州的春天常常下雨，不太方便。

根据课文(一)回答问题
Answer these questions according to the Text A

1. 明天天气好吗？
2. 根据天气预报，明天比今天冷吗？

3. 美玲喜欢什么季节?

生词学习(二) New words II

1.	tīng 听₁ *v.* listen	听他说;听音乐
2.	bú yòng 不用 *adj.* need not	不用买;不用做
3.	dài 带 *v.* bring; take	带什么;带钱
4.	yī fu 衣服 *n.* clothes	很多衣服;冬天的衣服
5.	zuì jìn 最近 *n.* recent time;lately	最近很冷;最近常下雨
6.	jiā 家₁ *n.* home	回家;我家
7.	chū qù 出去 *v.* go out	出去看看;常常出去
8.	wánr 玩儿 *v.* play	喜欢玩儿;出去玩儿
9.	yù bào 预报 *n.* forcast	天气预报
10.	zhōu mò 周末 *n.* weekend	这个周末;周末有空
11.	tíng 停 *v.* stop	停车;雨停了
12.	shì zhōng xīn 市中心 *n.* city center	去市中心
13.	yīng gāi 应该 *aux.* should; ought to	应该出去;应该帮助
14.	xī wàng 希望 *v./n.* hope	希望天气好;希望不下雨

专有名词 Proper noun

Guǎngzhōu 广州 Guangzhou(a city in China)

课文(二) 广州的天气 Text B The weather in Guangzhou

阿曼要去广州出差,他向张丽了解当地的天气情况。

Aman is going to Guangzhou for business. He is asking about the weather there from Zhang Li.

Ā màn Xīng qī sì wǒ yào qù Guǎng zhōu nàr dōng tiān lěng bù lěng
阿曼：星期四我要去广州，那儿冬天冷不冷？
Zhāng Lì Wǒ de gē ge zài Guǎng zhōu gōng zuò tīng tā shuō bú tài lěng
张丽：我的哥哥在广州工作，听他说不太冷。
Ā màn Hǎo de nà wǒ bú yòng dài tài duō yī fu
阿曼：好的，那我不用带太多衣服。
Zhāng Lì Wǒ gē ge shuō zuì jìn Guǎng zhōu cháng cháng xià yǔ
张丽：我哥哥说，最近广州常常下雨。
Ā màn Méi guān xì wǒ qù kāi huì zài kàn liǎng jiā gōng sī bù chū qù wánr
阿曼：没关系，我去开会，再看两家公司，不出去玩儿。
Zhāng Lì Wǒ kàn le tiān qì yù bào zhōu mò méi yǒu yǔ
张丽：我看了天气预报，周末没有雨。
Ā màn Rú guǒ yǔ tíng le wǒ qù shì zhōng xīn zǒu zǒu
阿曼：如果雨停了，我去市中心走走。
Zhāng Lì Nǐ dì yī cì qù Guǎng zhōu yīng gāi qù shì zhōng xīn kàn kan
张丽：你第一次去广州，应该去市中心看看。
Ā màn Xī wàng tiān qì hǎo yì diǎnr
阿曼：希望天气好一点儿。

根据课文(二)回答问题
Answer these questions according to the Text B

1. 最近广州天气怎么样？
2. 阿曼去广州玩儿吗？
3. 阿曼去不去广州的市中心？

语言点
Language points

1. 还 + *v.*

明天下雨，还刮风。

It will rain, and also blow wind tomorrow.

"还"有多种意思，在这儿，"还"表示在某个范围之外有所补充。

"还" has different meanings. Here, "还" means even more than a certain scope, also, in addition.

(1)明天很冷，还下雨。

(2)你还想买什么？

(3)在中国，他想去长城(Chángchéng, the Great Wall)，还想看看西湖(Xīhú, the West Lake)。

2. A比B+*adj*.

明天比今天冷。

Tomorrow will be colder than today.

汉语中的比较句结构与英语有较大的不同,先列两个比较的对象,再列形状或程度上的差别。另外,具体描述差别大小的词或短语需放置在形容词后。

The structure of comparative sentences in Chinese is quite different from English. In Chinese, the comparison parts are listed first, then comes the difference of properties. Modifiers that indicate the degree of the difference shall be put after the adjective.

(1)今天比昨天热。

(2)今天比昨天热一点儿。

(3)广州比杭州大吗?

(4)哥哥比我大三岁(suì, year of age)。

3. 真……

我真不喜欢冬天。

I really don't like winter.

"真"用在形容词或表示心理活动的动词前面,表示"的确",表达说话人的比较强烈的感情。一般用"真"表示程度很深,有加强肯定语气的作用。常用于口语。

"真" is used to modify an adjective or a mental action verb. It means "indeed""truly", indicating the strong emotion of the speaker. It shows high degree and takes an affirmative tone. "真" is usually used in spoken Chinese.

(1)这儿的春天真美!

(2)我真喜欢这儿!

(3)天气很好,我真想出去玩儿!

4. 不+*adj*.1+不+*adj*.2

春天也不错,不冷不热。

Spring is also nice. It's neither cold nor hot.

这个结构一般表示程度不高不低,正合适,令人满意。两个形容词互为反义。

This structure means "neither...nor...". It indicates a suitable and satisfying degree, which is neither too high nor too low. Usually the two adjectives are of opposite meanings.

(1)这件衣服不大不小。

(2)今天的作业不多不少。

(3)裤子(kùzi, pants)不长(cháng,long)不短(duǎn, short),很好。

5. 能愿动词"应该"

你第一次去广州，应该去市中心看看。

It's your first time to Guangzhou, so you definitely should visit the city center.

"应该"意思是某人理所当然地做某事。

"应该" means someone should or ought to do something, as a matter of course.

(1)你应该出去走走。

(2)学习汉语应该多说。

(3)如果来杭州，应该去西湖看看。

6. *adj*. +一点儿

希望天气好一点儿。

I wish the weather will be better.

"一点儿"用于形容词后，意思是"稍微，略微"，有程度上进行比较的意思。

When used after an adjective, "一点儿" means comparison in degree and it indicates a little difference.

(1)今天比昨天冷一点儿。

(2)这件衣服大一点儿。

(3)可以便宜(pián yi, cheap)一点儿吗?

核心句 Key sentences

1. 明天比今天冷。
2. 我真不喜欢冬天。
3. 春天也不错，不冷不热。
4. 最近广州常常下雨。
5. 你第一次去广州。
6. 希望天气好一点儿。

综合练习 Comprehensive exercises

(一)熟读短语 Read the following phrases

1. 常常下雨　常常刮风　常常去图书馆　常常去上海　常常学习
2. 听他说　听老师说　听朋友说　你听我说　听不懂　听不见
3. 不用谢　不用带　不用去　不用买　不用看　不用做
4. 带衣服　带钱　带书　带什么　我带你去

5. 雨停了　车停了　停车　停一下

6. 希望天气好　希望雨停　希望你去　希望你高兴

(二)选词填空 Choose a suitable word for each sentence

真　比　方便　游泳　不错

1. 明天将会_________今天冷。

2. 我喜欢夏天,可以去_________。

3. 这儿常常下雨,不太_________。

4. 春天的天气_________,不冷不热。

5. 我_________不喜欢冬天。

希望　停　出去　不用　预报

1. 广州不太冷,你_________带很多衣服。

2. 我去开会,不_________玩儿。

3. 如果雨_________了,我去市中心走走。

4. _________天气好一点儿。

5. 我看了天气_________,周末没有雨。

(三)替换练习 Substitution drills

1. 明天比今天冷。

　今天　昨天热

　北京　杭州冷

　上海　杭州大

2. 我真不喜欢冬天。

　不喜欢夏天

　喜欢吃饺子

　喜欢杭州

3. 春天不　　冷不热。

　这件衣服　大　小

　今天的作业　多　少

　裤子　长　短

4. 杭州的春天常常下雨。

　北京　秋天　刮风

　北方　冬天　下雪

　这儿　夏天　很热

5. 我去开会,再看两家公司。

　去银行　去买点东西

　要两本书　买一些(yì xiē,some)笔

6. 你第一次去广州，应该去市中心看看。

    来杭州　　去西湖看看

    来中国　　吃一吃中国菜

    去北京　　去长城走走

7. 希望天气好一点儿。

    那儿的东西便宜一点儿

    房间大一点儿

    我的汉语好一点儿

(四)完成对话 Complete the following dialogues

1. A:明天天气怎么样?

    B:明天__________,还__________。(下雨,刮风)

2. A:今天冷还是明天冷?

    B:__________比__________ ________。(A 比 B *adj*.)

3. A:你喜欢冬天吗?

    B:不喜欢,我喜欢__________,______________(explain the reason).

4. A:杭州的春天怎么样?

    B:____________________________。(常常)

5. A:这是我第一次来广州。

    B:哦,那你应该________________________。(市中心,看)

(五)课堂活动 In-class exercises

1. 看图说话 Talk about the pictures

    请根据图片说出简短的句子。Try to make brief sentences according to each picture.

2. 角色扮演 Role-play

(1)A 和 B 讨论什么季节去某个城市比较好,比如杭州、上海、广州、北京、西安等。简单说一下为什么。A and B are discussing about when might be the best season to go to a city like Hangzhou, Shanghai, Guangzhou, Beijing, Xi'an, etc. Try to explain why.

冷　热　常常　方便　冬天　春天　夏天　秋天　下雨　刮风

(2) A 要去上海出差,问 B 上海的天气怎么样。A is going to have a business trip in Shanghai, and he is asking B about the weather there.

下雨　冷　热　不太　带　出去

(六)课后练习 After-class exercises

采访你的一个朋友,跟他/她了解所在城市的四季气候,简单地做一下记录。Interview one of your friends and ask about the climate in his or her city. Try to write down the information you get.

	大概几度	常常下雨吗	常常刮风吗	其他(qítā,other)
春天				
夏天				
秋天				
冬天				

课文翻译 Translation of texts

Text A　Talk about the weather

Mary: It's so cold, Meiling. How is the weather tomorrow?

Meiling: Let me check on the phone. It's going to rain tomorrow, and also windy.

Mary: What's the temperature?

Meiling: 5℃, lower than today.

Mary: Oh, so it's going to be colder tomorrow. I really don't like winter.

Meiling: Me neither. I prefer summer. It's a good time to go swimming.

Mary: Spring is also very nice. It's neither too cold nor too hot.

Meiling: But it often rains in spring in Hangzhou. It's a little inconvenient.

Text B　The weather in Guangzhou

Aman: I'm going to Guangzhou on Thursday. Is it cold there in winter?

Zhang Li: My older brother works there; according to him it's not very cold in winter.

Aman: OK, then I don't need to take too many clothes.

Zhang Li: My brother said, it often rains recently (in Guangzhou).

Aman: It's OK。I'm going to take a meeting, and then to visit two companies. I'm not going sightseeing.

Zhang Li: I checked the weather forecast. It won't rain in the weekend.

Aman: If the rain stops, I will take a wolk in the city center.

Zhang Li: It's your first time going there. You definitely should visit the city center.

Aman: I hope the weather will be better.

4 去购物中心看看
Let's go to the shopping center

话题导学 Guidance

1. 你喜欢去哪儿买衣服?
   Where do you usually buy clothes?
2. 网上的东西怎么样?
   How are the products on line?
3. 中国的超市怎么样?
   What do you think about the supermarkets in China?
4. 如果需要招待客人,你会准备什么?
   What would you prepare to entertain the guests?

生词学习(一) New words I

1. 面试 (miàn shì)	*v.* interview	有面试;明天面试
2. 新 (xīn)	*adj.* new	新工作;新公司
3. 网 (wǎng)	*n.* internet	网上有;在网上看
4. 上网 (shàng wǎng)	*v.* surf the internet	上网买;常常上网
5. 有的 (yǒu de)	some(part of a group or things)	有的时候;有的衣服
6. 质量 (zhì liàng)	*n.* quality	质量好;质量不错
7. 购物中心 (gòu wù zhōng xīn)	*n.* shopping center	去购物中心
8. 打折 (dǎ zhé)	*v.* have discount	打折吗;打几折
9. 大衣 (dà yī)	*n.* overcoat;topcoat	买大衣;新大衣

课文(一) 准备面试服装
Text A Get suitable clothes for a job interview

Ān nà Mǎ lì wǒ yǒu yí gè miàn shì xiǎng mǎi yí jiàn xīn yī fú
安娜：玛丽，我有一个面试，想买一件新衣服。

Mǎ lì Nǐ kě yǐ shàng wǎng kàn kan
玛丽：你可以上网看看。

Ān nà Wǎng shàng de yī fu hěn duō yǒu de zhì liàng bú tài hǎo
安娜：网上的衣服很多，有的质量不太好。

Mǎ lì Nǐ yě kě yǐ qù gòu wù zhōng xīn kàn kàn nàr cháng cháng dǎ zhé
玛丽：你也可以去购物中心看看，那儿常常打折。

Ān nà Hǎo a xiān qù nàr kàn kan Nǐ xiǎng bù xiǎng mǎi yī fu
安娜：好啊，先去那儿看看。你想不想买衣服？

Mǎ lì Tiān qì hěn lěng wǒ yě xiǎng mǎi dà yī yì qǐ qù ba
玛丽：天气很冷，我也想买大衣，一起去吧。

Ān nà Míng tiān shì zhōu mò wǒ men shàng wǔ qù zěn me yàng
安娜：明天是周末，我们上午去，怎么样？

Mǎ lì Hǎo Wǒ men shí diǎn qù ba
玛丽：好！我们十点去吧。

根据课文(一)回答问题
Answer these questions according to the Text A

1. 安娜为什么要买新衣服？
2. 安娜喜欢上网买衣服吗？
3. 购物中心的衣服打折吗？
4. 玛丽去买什么？

生词学习(二)
New words II

chāo shì
1. 超市 *n.* supermarket 大超市；哪个超市

yì xiē
2. 一些 *n.* some 一些东西；一些时间

jiǔ
3. 酒 *n.* wine; alcohol; drink 喝酒；什么酒

hóng jiǔ
4. 红酒 *n.* red wine 喝红酒；买红酒

pí jiǔ
5. 啤酒 *n.* beer 喝啤酒；买啤酒

6. ná 拿 *v.* get; take —— 拿啤酒;拿钱

7. píng 瓶 *n.* bottle —— 一瓶酒;两瓶水

8. tīng 听$_2$ *n.* tin; can(measure word) —— 一听可乐;一听啤酒

9. tóng shì 同事 *n.* colleague —— 我的同事;两个同事

10. guǒ zhī 果汁 *n.* fruit juice —— 买果汁;什么果汁

11. shuǐ guǒ 水果 *n.* fruit —— 很多水果;水果店

12. jiàn kāng 健康 *adj.* healthy —— 身体健康

13. líng shí 零食 *n.* snack —— 吃零食;一些小零食

14. dàn gāo 蛋糕 *n.* cake —— 一个蛋糕;生日蛋糕

15. mén kǒu 门口 *n.* doorway; entrance —— 超市门口;公司门口

16. fù qián 付钱 *v.* pay money —— 谁付钱;怎么付钱

课文(二) 准备冷餐会
Text B Prepare for a buffet party

Chén Lóng Zhè chāo shì hěn dà shén me dōu yǒu
陈　龙:这超市很大,什么都有。

Dà wèi Wǒ men xiān kàn kan jiǔ Mǎi yì xiē hóng jiǔ pí jiǔ zěn me yàng
大卫:我们先看看酒。买一些红酒、啤酒,怎么样?

Chén Lóng Bú cuò ná wǔ píng hóng jiǔ shí tīng pí jiǔ ba Kě néng yǒu de tóng shì bù hē jiǔ
陈　龙:不错,拿五瓶红酒、十听啤酒吧。可能有的同事不喝酒。

Dà wèi Nà wǒ men ná sān píng guǒ zhī
大卫:那我们拿三瓶果汁。

Chén Lóng Mǎi shén me chī de ne zhèr de shuǐ guǒ bú cuò
陈　龙:买什么吃的呢?这儿的水果不错。

Dà wèi Hǎo a shuǐ guǒ hěn jiàn kāng dà jiā dōu xǐ huān
大卫:好啊,水果很健康,大家都喜欢。

Chén Lóng Zài mǎi yì xiē xiǎo líng shí
陈　龙:再买一些小零食。

Dà wèi Hái yào mǎi yí ge dàn gāo Wǒ men qù mén kǒu de dàn gāo diàn kàn kan
大卫:还要买一个蛋糕。我们去门口的蛋糕店看看。

Chén Lóng　Nà ge dàngāo diàn bú cuò　Hěn duō tóng shì xǐ huān zài nàr mǎi
陈　龙：那个蛋糕店不错。很多同事喜欢在那儿买。

Dà wèi　Hǎo de　wǒ xiān yòng shǒu jī fù qián
大卫：好的，我先用手机付钱。

根据课文(二)回答问题
Answer these questions according to the Text B

1. 他们买了什么喝的东西？
2. 他们买了什么吃的东西？
3. 门口的蛋糕店怎么样？
4. 他们怎么付钱？

语言点
Language points

1. 有的……有的……

网上的衣服很多，有的质量不太好。

There are lots of clothes sold on line. Some of them are of poor quality.

这个结构表示人或事物中的一部分，常叠用。

This structure is used to mean part of a group of people or things and often used repeatedly.

(1)有的贵，有的便宜。

(2)有的喜欢红酒，有的喜欢啤酒。

2. sentence + "吧"

我们十点去吧。

Let's go at 10:00.

"吧"用于句末，表示商量、提议、请求、命令等不同语气。具体语气跟语境和说话人的语气相关。

"吧" is used at the end of a sentence to imply soliciting one's advice, suggestion, request or mild command. The tone of the sentence with "吧" is also decided by the context and speaker's attitude.

(1)咱们走吧！

(2)你先想想吧！

(3)我们一起吃个饭吧！

3. 什么都……

这超市很大,什么都有。

It's a big supermarket and you can find anything here.

"什么"在这儿表示"任何东西"的意思,后面常跟"都""也"等。

Here,"什么" means anything, followed by "都""也".

(1)他什么都吃。

(2)什么都可以买。

(3)这儿什么也没有。

4. 再+*v.*

再买一些小零食。

(Let's buy some fruit)Then buy some snacks.

"再"有多种意思,在这儿表示一个动作发生在另一个动作之后。

"再" has different meanings. In this lesson it indicates one action taking place after the completion of another.

(1)先学汉语,再学专业。

(2)我先问问他,再买机票。

(3)今天我先跟你谈,明天经理再跟你见面。

5. 用……+*v.*

我先用手机付钱。

I will pay by phone first.

这个结构表示使用某种方式、工具等来做某事。

This structure means using certain ways or tools to do sth.

(1)请用中文说。

(2)现在很多地方可以用手机付钱。

(3)在中国,人们用人民币(rénmínbì,RMB, China Yuan)买东西。

核心句 Key sentences

1. 你可以上网看看。
2. 那儿常常打折。
3. 我也想买大衣,一起去吧。
4. 拿五瓶红酒、十听啤酒吧。
5. 我先用手机付钱。

综合练习
Comprehensive exercises

(一)熟读短语 Read the following phrases

1. 新衣服　新手机　新书　新朋友　新车　很新　新的
2. 网上有　网上买　网上看看　网上聊天
3. 质量很好　质量不太好　质量怎么样　东西的质量
4. 常常打折　打折吗　打几折　打不打折
5. 一些酒　一些水果　一些零食　一些同事　一些时间
6. 一瓶酒　一瓶果汁　一瓶水　买几瓶
7. 一听啤酒　一听可乐　一听汽水(qì shuǐ,soda)
8. 超市门口　学校门口　家门口　小区门口　教室门口
9. 用手机付钱　怎么付钱　在哪儿付钱　用现金付钱　用银行卡付钱

(二)组词 Make words

网:__________　酒:__________　市:__________　果:__________
面:__________　打:__________　天:__________　衣:__________

(三)组句 Use the following words to construct sentences

1. 衣服　新　一件　买　我　想

____

2. 质量　好　衣服　不太　的

____

3. 打折　购物　中心　常常

____

4. 拿　果汁　三瓶　我们　吧

____

5. 付钱　手机　用　我　先

____

(四)替换练习 Substitution drills

1. 你可以<u>上网看看</u>。

　　去购物中心看看
　　去办公室问问
　　去银行问问

2. 我也想<u>买大衣</u>,一起去吧。

　　吃面条
　　看电影
　　去买票

3. 我们上午去,怎么样?

星期三去

九点见面

买一些酒

4. 水果很健康,大家都喜欢。

东西不贵

衣服很漂亮

蛋糕很不错

5. 我用手机 付钱。

中文 回答

筷子(kuàizi, chopsticks) 吃饭

手机 上网

(五)完成对话 Complete the following dialogues

1. A:我想买一件新衣服。

B:你可以________________。(购物中心)

A:你去不去?

B:我也____________,一起__________。(买,去,吧)

2. A:购物中心的衣服怎么样?

B:不错,也常常__________。

3. A:我想上网买衣服。

B:网上的衣服______________________。(多,质量)

4. A:我们买什么喝的?

B:可以买________红酒,________啤酒,________果汁。(瓶,听)

5. A:大家喜欢吃什么?我不知道买什么。

B:可以买一些____________,再买________________。

6. A:我没带很多钱。

B:没关系,我们可以__________付钱。(用)

(六)课堂活动 In-class exercises

1. 看图说话 Talk about the pictures

请根据图片说出简单的句子。Try to make brief sentences according to each picture.

2. 角色扮演 Role-play

(1)A和B讨论去哪儿买衣服,A觉得去购物中心买好,B觉得在网上买好,最后他们要决定去哪儿买。A and B are talking about where to buy clothes. A prefers to go to the shopping center, while B thinks it's better to buy clothes on line. At last they need to make a decision.

质量　方便　打折　便宜　很多　看看　一起　怎么样

(2)为了准备会议的茶歇(tea break),公司需要买一些食物和饮料。A和B一起去超市挑选。A and B are going to the supermarket to get some food and drinks for the tea break of a meeting in the company.

瓶　包　水果　零食　蛋糕　咖啡　茶

(七)课后练习 After-class exercises

采访几个朋友,问问他们喜欢网购还是去店里买,再问一问原因。Interview some friends and get to know if they prefer online shopping or going to the shops. Try to get the reasons.

	喜欢网购还是去店里买	原因
朋友1		
朋友2		
朋友3		
朋友4		

课文翻译 Translation of texts

Text A　Get suitable clothes for a job interview

Anna：Hi, Mary, I have an interview, so I want to buy a new clothes.

Mary：You can take a look on the internet.

Anna：There are lots of clothes on line, but some are not good quality.

Mary：You can also go to the shopping center; there are often discounts and promotions.

Anna：OK, I will go there and take a look first. Do you want to buy some clothes?

Mary：It's quite cold, so I also want to get a new overcoat. Let's go together.

Anna：It's the weekend tomorrow. How about we go in the morning?

Mary：OK! Let's go at 10:00.

Text B　Prepare for a buffet party

Chen Long：This supermarket is (pretty) big. You can find anything here.

David：Let's take a look at some wine first. Let's get some wine and beer?

Chen Long：OK. Let's get five bottles of wine and ten cans of beer. Some colleagues may not drink alcohol.

David：Then let's get three bottles of juice.

Chen Long：What food shall we buy? The fruit here is pretty good.

David：Good idea. Fruit is healthy and everyone likes it.

Chen Long：We can also buy some snacks.

David：And a cake. We can take a look at the cake shop just outside the supermarket.

Chen Long：It's a good one. Many colleagues like to buy cakes there.

David：Alright, first let me pay by phone.

5 你住哪个小区
Which residential district do you live in?

话题导学 Guidance

1. 你住学校宿舍还是校外?
   Do you live in the school dormitory or outside of the school?
2. 你住在几号楼?
   What's your building number?
3. 你知道怎么用中文写你家地址吗?
   Do you know how to express your address in Chinese?

生词学习(一) New words I

1. 宿舍 (sù shè) *n.* dormitory — 我的宿舍;在宿舍
2. 楼 (lóu) *n.* floor; building — 宿舍楼;几楼
3. 以前 (yǐ qián) *n.* before; ago — 上课以前;吃饭以前
4. 住 (zhù) *v.* live — 住在宿舍;住在几楼
5. 外面 (wài miàn) *n.* outside — 学校外面;住在外面
6. 搬 (bān) *v.* move — 搬东西;搬出去
7. 搬家 (bān jiā) *v.* move house — 我搬家;帮朋友搬家
8. 小区 (xiǎo qū) *n.* residential district — 小区门口;小区外面
9. 南边 (nán biān) *n.* southside — 大学南边;马路南边
10. 离 (lí) *v.* be away from — 离宿舍近;离公司近

jìn
11. 近 *adj.* close; near 很近;不太近

课文(一) 住在校外
Text A Live outside of school

马克刚从学校宿舍搬到了校外。

Mark just moved out of the school dormitory.

Ān nà Mǎ kè nǐ de sù shè zài jǐ hào lóu
安娜:马克,你的宿舍在几号楼?

Mǎ kè Yǐ qián wǒ zhù zài shí yī hào lóu bā lóu xiàn zài zhù zài wài miàn
马克:以前我住在十一号楼八楼,现在住在外面。

Ān nà Shì ma Nǐ bān dào wài miàn le
安娜:是吗?你搬到外面了?

Mǎ kè Duì wǒ bān jiā le
马克:对,我搬家了。

Ān nà Nǐ zhù nǎ gè xiǎo qū
安娜:你住哪个小区?

Mǎ kè Huā yuán xiǎo qū zài xué xiào nán bian
马克:花园小区,在学校南边。

Ān nà Bú cuò lí xué xiào hěn jìn
安娜:不错,离学校很近。

Mǎ kè Yǒu kòng de shí hòu kě yǐ qù wǒ jiā wánr
马克:有空的时候,可以去我家玩儿。

Ān nà Tài hǎo le xiè xie a
安娜:太好了,谢谢啊!

根据课文(一)回答问题
Answer these questions according to the Text A

1. 以前马克住在几号楼?
2. 现在马克的家离学校远吗?
3. 马克住在学校南边还是北边?

生词学习(二)
New words II

hóng sè
1. 红色 *n.* red color 红色的大衣;红色还是白色

jì
2. 寄 *v.* send 寄东西;寄到哪儿

qū
3. 区 *n.* district 什么区;哪个区

lù
4. 路₁ *n.* road; street 马路;走路

tián
5. 填 *v.* fill in 填名字;填手机号

shōuhuò rén
6. 收货人 *n.* consignee 谁是收货人;收货人的名字

xìngmíng
7. 姓名 *n.* name; fullname 我的姓名;问姓名

hàomǎ
8. 号码 *n.* number 手机号码;房间号码

zì jǐ
9. 自己 *n.* oneself 自己填;自己去

zuì hòu
10. 最后 *n.* at last 到最后;最后一个

diǎn
11. 点₁ *v.* click 点一下;点哪儿

què rèn
12. 确认 *v.* confirm 确认一下;确认时间

专有名词(Proper noun)

Pǔdōng
浦东 Pudong(name of a district in Shanghai)

课文(二) 填网购地址
Text B Fill in the address for online shopping

Mǎ lì Wǒ yào mǎi zhè ge hóng sè de
玛丽:我要买这个,红色的。

Lǐ míng Hǎo jì dào nǎr
李明:好,寄到哪儿?

Mǎ lì Jì dào wǒ dì di nàr tā zài shàng hǎi
玛丽:寄到我弟弟那儿,他在上海。

Lǐ míng Hǎo de zài Shàng hǎi shén me qū shén me lù
李明:好的,在上海什么区,什么路?

Mǎ lì Pǔ dōng qū Dōng hǎi lù sān bǎi hào Dà míng gōng sī
玛丽:浦东区,东海路三百号,大明公司。

Lǐ míng Zhèr tián shōu huò rén de xìngmíng shǒu jī hào mǎ
李明:这儿填收货人的姓名,手机号码。

Mǎ lì Zhè ge wǒ zì jǐ tián xiè xie
玛丽:这个我自己填,谢谢!

Lǐ míng Hǎo de Zuìhòu nǐ diǎn yí xià quèrèn
李明：好的。最后，你点一下“确认”。

根据课文(二)回答问题
Answer these questions according to the Text B

1. 玛丽给谁买东西？
2. 玛丽的弟弟在什么公司工作？
3. 玛丽的弟弟的公司在上海哪儿？
4. 上网买东西，怎么填收货人的信息(xìnxī, information)？

语言点
Language points

1. “楼”的两种意思

你的宿舍在几号楼？

Which building is your dormitory?

“楼”在本文中意思是楼层，与“层”同义，该词本义是“楼房”，即两层以上的房屋。一般意思为“楼房”时，会在数字后面加“号”以表示楼号，如：2号楼。

“楼”means floor in this lesson, and it’s similar to another Chinese character “层”. The original meaning of “楼” is storied building. When it means building, the word “号” shall be used after the number, for example.

(1)我的宿舍在4号楼10楼。

(2)你住几楼？

2. 以前

以前我住在十一号楼八楼，现在住在外面。

I used to live on the 8th floor in Building 11 before, and now I’m living outside (of school).

“以前”有两种用法，一种是单用，常用于“以前……现在……”的句式中；一种是用于“……以前”句式中，表示在做某事之前或某个时间之前。

“以前” is used in two different ways. It can be used alone in a clause, and often used in the sentence structure “以前……现在……”. It is also often used in the structure“……以前”, indicating before doing something specifically, or before certain time.

(1)以前我在北京工作，现在搬到杭州了。

(2)以前我去购物中心买东西，现在常常在网上买。

(3)来中国以前，我不会说中文。

3. “哪”的用法

你住哪个小区?

Which living district do you live in?

与英语不同,汉语里用“哪”表示哪个对象的时候,需要根据对象的不同加不同的量词。

Different from English, a suitable measure word shall be put after “哪” when it means the object pointed.

(1)哪本书?

(2)哪位老师?

(3)哪个公司?

(4)哪瓶水?

4. A 离 B……

离学校很近。

My place is quite close to the school.

“离”表示两个对象在空间或时间上的距离。结构上,“离”用于两个对象之间,在一定语境中,第一个对象可以省略。请注意与“从”的区别。

“离” indicates the space distance or time interval. It is used in the structure “A 离 B……”, and A can be omitted in certain context. Notice the difference from “从”.

(1)小区离学校很近。

(2)杭州离上海不远。

(3)现在离上课还有一个小时。

5. “的”字短语

我要买这个,红色的。

I want to buy this one, the red one.

“的”用在各种词性的词后面,变成名词性质的“的”字短语。在口语中经常使用,有简短表达的用途。

“的” can be put after different types of words, and once a word is followed by “的”, it will become a noun phrase. It is used very common in spoken Chinese and make a speech briefer.

(1)这是我的宿舍,那是我同学的。

(2)明天的票没有了,我买后天的。

(3)大的给你,小的给我。

6. *v.* + 到(趋向补语)

寄到我弟弟那儿。

Send it to my younger brother's place.

动词后面加"到",表示由于这个动作,人或物的位置从一处换到了另一处。

The complement "到" used after a verb, indicates the position of certain things or person is changed from one place to another place because of the action, which also indicates the complement of the action.

(1)我搬到外面了。

(2)这个寄到哪儿?

(3)你走到学校门口了吗?

7. sb. +那儿

寄到我弟弟那儿。

Send it to my younger brother's place.

"那儿"用在人名或人称代词后面,表示该人所在的地方。

"那儿" used after the name of a person or a pronoun, indicates the place of the person.

(1)我去他那儿看看。

(2)我常常去大卫那儿玩儿。

(3)他在经理那儿。

核心句 Key sentences

1. 以前我住在十一号楼八楼。
2. 你搬到外面了?
3. 不错,离学校很近。
4. 有空的时候可以去我家玩儿。
5. 在上海什么区,什么路?
6. 这个我自己填。
7. 你点一下"确认"。

综合练习 Comprehensive exercises

(一)熟读短语 Read the phrases or words

1. 几楼　八楼　楼上　楼下
2. 住在宿舍　住在几楼　住在哪儿　住在外面　住在什么小区
3. 搬家　搬到外面　搬东西　搬出去　搬进来
4. 学校南边　图书馆南边　超市南边　公园南边

5. 寄东西　寄衣服　寄到哪儿　寄到上海　寄给妈妈
6. 填一下　填姓名　填号码　填什么　怎么填
7. 手机号码　电话号码　房间号码　护照(hù zhào, passport)号码
8. 自己去　自己填　自己做　自己看

(二)选词填空 Choose a suitable word for each sentence

离　以前　搬　宿舍　南边

1. 我的小区________学校很近。
2. 你的________在几号楼?
3. 最近我________家了。
4. ________我住在11号楼,现在住在外面。
5. 花园小区在学校的________。

寄　填　最后　自己　路

1. 请在这儿________姓名和手机号码。
2. 衣服________到哪儿?
3. 谢谢你,我可以________填。
4. 买好衣服,________你点一下“确认”。
5. 他住在上海什么区什么________?

(三)替换练习 Substitution drills

1. 我住在<u>11</u>号楼<u>8</u>楼。

4	9
5	2

2. 以前<u>我住在宿舍</u>,现在<u>住在外面</u>。

我在北京	我在杭州
我们不认识	我们是好朋友
我不喜欢上网	常常上网

3. <u>花园小区</u>离<u>学校</u>很<u>近</u>。

杭州	义乌	近
杭州	广州	远
银行	大学	近

4. <u>上海浦东区</u>　<u>东海路</u>　<u>300</u>号。

上海静安(ShànhǎiJìnggān)	南京(Nánjīng)	100
杭州江干(Jiānggān)	文泽(Wénzé)	20
杭州西湖	文一(Wényī)	180

5. 这个我自己填,谢谢!

做

写

看

(四)完成对话 Complete the following dialogues

1. A:你的宿舍在几号楼?

B:我住在______________。

A:你住八楼吗?

B:不,我_____________________。

2. A:你住在宿舍还是外面?

B:昨天我搬家了,现在不住宿舍,我________________。

3. A:你住的小区在哪儿?

B:在学校_______边,离学校___________。(近)

4. A:你的东西寄到哪儿?

B:寄到_______。我弟弟在那儿工作。

A:好,什么_______? 什么_________?

B:浦东区,东海路 300 号。

5. A:这儿填什么?

B:填你的姓名和_________________。(号码)

(五)课堂活动 In-class exercises

1. 看图说话 Talk about the pictures

根据图片说出简短的对话。Make brief dialogues according to each picture.

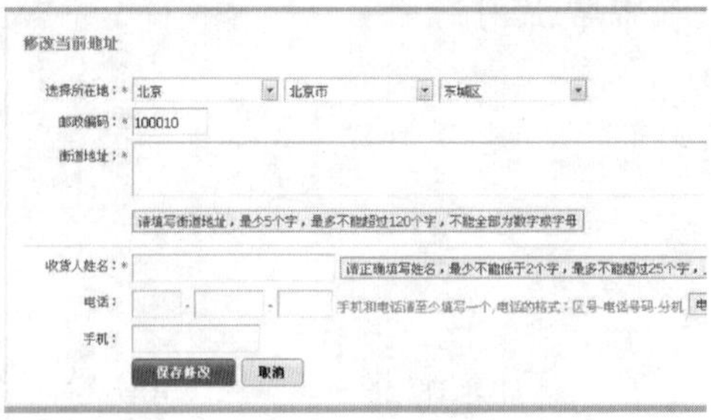

2. 角色扮演 Role-play

(1)A 和 B 都是大一的新同学,他们问对方住在哪儿。一个人住在宿舍,一个人住在学校外面。Both A and B are freshmen in the university. They are asking each other about where they're living. One is living in the school dormitory and the other is living outside of school. Try to use the following words.

楼　号　外面　小区　南边　离　远/近　不错　玩儿

(2)A 让 B 帮他在网上买东西给朋友,B 问 A 寄到什么地址。A asks B to help him to buy something online for his friend. B needs to know the address of the receiver. Try to use the following words and phrases.

寄到　……区……路……号　收货人　填　姓名　手机号码

(六)课后练习 After-class exercises

你会用中文写一个学校或公司的地址吗?Can you write the address of a school or a company in Chinese?

课文翻译 Translation of texts

Text A　Living outside of school

Anna：Mark, which building is your dormitory at?

Mark：I used to live on the 8th floor in Building 11, but now I live outside of school.

Anna：Really? You've moved out?

Mark：Yes, I moved.

Anna：Which residential district are you living in now?

Mark：Garden district. It's to the south of school.

Anna：Good, It's close to school.

Mark：You can visit my place when you are free.

Anna：Great! Thanks!

Text B　Fill in the address for online shopping

Mary：I want to buy this one, the red one.

Li Ming：OK. Where will it be sent to?

Mary：To my younger brother. He is in Shanghai.

Li Ming：OK. Which district and road in Shanghai?

Mary：Pudong Dictrict, Donghai Road, No. 300. Daming Company.

Li Ming：Here fill in the consignee's name and phone number.

Mary：That I can fill by myself. Thanks!

Li Ming：OK. Lastly, click "confirm".

⑥ 我去浙江工商大学
I'm going to Zhejiang Gongshang University

话题导学
Guidance

1. 你常常外出吗？
   Do you often go out?
2. 你外出时，常常选择什么交通方式？
   What kind of transportation do you usually choose?
3. 在中国，你乘坐过出租车吗？
   Have you ever taken a taxi in China?

生词学习（一）
New words I

1. zuò 坐	*v.* sit; travel by	坐出租车；坐地铁
2. chū zū chē 出租车	*n.* taxi	坐出租车；出租车司机
3. shī fu 师傅	*n.* master (a title for showing respect for skilled men)	我的师傅；出租车师傅
4. sī jī 司机	*n.* driver; engine driver	谁是司机；出租车司机
5. qù 去	*v.* go	去学校；去图书馆；去银行换钱
6. le 了	*part.* used after a verb or an adjective to indicate completion of the work or change	到了；吃了
7. gěi 给	*v.* give	给我一本书；给你钱
8. fā piào 发票	*n.* invoice; bill; receipt	给我发票；一张发票

课文（一）　坐出租车
Text A　Take a taxi

马克坐出租车去浙江工商大学。

Mark goes to Zhejiang GongshangUniverisity by taxi.

Mǎ kè　Shī fu　wǒ qù Zhèjiānggōngshāng dà xué
马克:师傅,我去浙江工商大学。

Sī jī　Hǎo de
司机:好的。

十分钟以后。

After ten minutes.

Sī jī　Nǐ hǎo　Zhèjiānggōngshāng dà xué dào le
司机:你好,浙江工商大学到了。

Mǎ kè　Xiè xie　Duō shǎo qián
马克:谢谢! 多少钱?

Sī jī　Sān shí kuài qián
司机:三十块钱。

Mǎ kè　Hǎo de　gěi nǐ qián　Qǐng gěi wǒ fā piào
马克:好的,给你钱。请给我发票。

根据课文(一)回答问题
Answer these questions according to the Text A

1. 马克去哪儿?
2. 马克怎么去浙江工商大学?
3. 马克坐出租车用了多少钱?
4. 马克想要什么?

生词学习(二)
New words II

1.	zěn me 怎么 *pron.* how to...	怎么去;怎么写;怎么说
2.	huì yì 会议 *n.* conference; meeting	国际会议;汉语会议
3.	zhōng xīn 中心 *n.* center	会议中心;市中心
4.	zhī dào 知道 *v.* know; realize	知道这个;不知道;你知道吗
5.	lù 路$_2$ *n.* road; route(of bus)	10 路;370 路;几路
6.	gōnggòng qì chē 公共汽车 *n.* public bus	10 路公共汽车;坐公共汽车
7.	dì tiě 地铁 *n.* subway	地铁 1 号线;坐地铁

hào
8. 号 *n.* (serial)number 1号;2号;几号

xiàn
9. 线 *n.* line 1号线;2号线;几号线

dōng
10. 东 *n.* east 东边;东站;东方

zhàn
11. 站 *n.* station 公共汽车站;地铁站;杭州东站

rán hòu
12. 然后 *conj.* afterwards; then 我先去银行,然后去超市

huàn
13. 换 *v.* change; exchange 换钱;换车;换地铁4号线

shì mín
14. 市民 *n.* citizen 杭州市民;市民中心;市民卡(kǎ,card)

xià chē
15. 下车 *v.* get off 在哪儿下车;我要下车

jiù
16. 就 *adv.* exactly; precisely 就是我;就在旁边

páng biān
17. 旁边 *n.* side 图书馆旁边;在你旁边

专有名词(Proper noun)

Háng zhōu dōng zhàn
杭州东站 Hangzhou East Railway Station

课文(二) 问路
Text B Ask for the direction

玛丽不知道怎么去杭州国际会议中心,她问路人。

Mary wants to know how to get to Hangzhou International Conference Centre, and she is asking the pedestrians.

Mǎ lì Nín hǎo Qǐng wèn zěn me qù Háng zhōu guó jì huì yì zhōng xīn
玛丽:您好!请问怎么去杭州国际会议中心?

Lù rén jiǎ Duì bu qǐ wǒ bù zhī dào
路人甲:对不起,我不知道。

Mǎ lì Méi guān xi
玛丽:没关系。

Mǎ lì Nín hǎo Qǐng wèn nín zhī dào zěn me qù Háng zhōu guó jì huì yì zhōng xīn ma
玛丽:您好!请问,您知道怎么去杭州国际会议中心吗?

Lù rén yǐ Zhī dào Nǐ kě yǐ zuò liù shí bā lù gōng gòng qì chē Nǐ yě kě yǐ zuò dì tiě xiān zuò
路人乙:知道。你可以坐六十八路公共汽车。你也可以坐地铁,先坐

dì tiě yī hào xiàn dào Háng zhōu dōng zhàn rán hòu huàn dì tiě sì hào xiàn dào Shì mín zhōng xīn zhàn xià chē
地铁1号线到杭州东站，然后换地铁4号线，到市民中心站下车。

Mǎ lì Shì mín zhōng xīn zhàn
玛丽：市民中心站？

Lù rén yǐ Shì de Háng zhōu guó jì huì yì zhōng xīn jiù zài Shì mín zhōng xīn zhàn de páng biān
路人乙：是的。杭州国际会议中心就在市民中心站的旁边。

Mǎ lì Hǎo de xiè xie nín
玛丽：好的，谢谢您！

Lù rén yǐ Bú kè qi
路人乙：不客气。

根据课文(二)回答问题
Answer these questions according to the Text B

1. 玛丽去哪儿？
2. 玛丽知道怎么去杭州国际会议中心吗？
3. 谁知道怎么去杭州国际会议中心？
4. 怎么去杭州国际会议中心？

语言点
Language points

1. 了

"了"用于动词或形容词之后，表示动作或变化已经完成。

"了" is a particle used after a verb or an adjective to indicate completion of the work or change.

(1)我们到了。

(2)我吃了。

(3)我的爸爸去了中国。

(4)树叶红了。

2. 给

"给"的意思是"给予"或"传递"，可用于"给某人某物"的结构中。

"给"means "to give", which could be used in the structure of "give sb. sth.".

(1)给我一杯水。

(2)给你钱。

(3)请给我发票。

(4)老师给了我一本书。

3. 怎么+v.

"怎么+v."用于询问怎样做某事。

怎么+v. is used to ask how to do something.

例如,在这篇课文中,"怎么去"可用于询问地址。与"……在哪儿"句型相比,该句型更侧重于询问达到目的地的方式。

For example, in this lesson (Text B), "怎么去" could be used to ask for directions (how to get to some place). Compared with "where is...", this expression more focuses on asking how to arrive at the place.

(1)怎么去超市?

(2)怎么去学校?

(3)怎么去商场(shāngchǎng, shopping mall)?

4.……路,……号线

"……路"用于表达公交车的路线安排,"……号线"用于表达地铁的路线规划。

"……路" is used to express the bus number, while the "……号线" is used to express the subway train number.

(1)68 路公共汽车

(2)地铁 1 号线

5. ……站

"……站"用于表达站点名称。这个站点可以是公共汽车站、地铁站,也可以是火车站、高铁站。

"……站" is used to express the station's name. It could be the station of bus or subway; it could also be the station of train or high-speed railway.

(1)浙江工商大学站

(2)杭州东站

(3)北京站

6. 先……然后……

"先……然后……"常用于表达两个或多个动作依时间顺序发生,先发生的动作可能是后发生动作的前提和基础。

"先……然后……", which means "first do sth., then do sth.", is usually used to express the actions happen in order. Sometimes, the action happens first is the premise of the other action.

(1)我先去学校,然后去银行。

(2)你先坐地铁1号线,然后换地铁4号线。

(3)每天早上,我先运动(yùndòng,do sports),然后吃早饭。

7. 就

"就"用于"是"或者"在"前面时,常常用来加强肯定语气。

When "就" is used before "是" or "在", it is usually an emphasis on affirmation mode.

(1)他就是马克。

(2)这就是我们学校。

(3)杭州国际会议中心就在市民中心站的旁边。

(4)超市就在学校的旁边。

核心句 Key sentences

1. 我去浙江工商大学。
2. 浙江工商大学到了。
3. 请问怎么去杭州国际会议中心?
4. ——对不起,我不知道。

   ——没关系。
5. 你先坐地铁1号线到杭州东站,然后换地铁4号线到市民中心站下车。
6. 杭州国际会议中心就在市民中心站的旁边。

综合练习 Comprehensive exercises

(一)熟读短语 Read the following phrases

1. 坐出租车　坐公交车　坐地铁
2. 去浙江工商大学　去杭州国际会议中心　去市民中心　去火车东站
3. 浙江工商大学到了　杭州国际会议中心到了　市民中心到了　火车东站到了
4. 请给我发票　请给我一杯水　请给我30块钱
5. 怎么去浙江工商大学　怎么去杭州国际会议中心　怎么去市民中心　怎么去火车东站
6. 工商大学站　杭州站　杭州东站　市民中心站
7. 先坐地铁1号线,然后坐地铁4号线　先坐12路,然后坐370路

   先去超市,然后回宿舍　先学习汉语,然后休息(xiūxi,take a rest)

(二)选词填空 Choose a suitable word for each sentence

坐　给　去　知道　在　换

1. 司机师傅,我________浙江工商大学。

2. 你先________地铁1号线到杭州东站，然后________地铁4号线到市民中心站下车。
3. 杭州国际会议中心就________市民中心站的旁边。
4. 你好，请________我一杯水。
5. 请问，你________浙江工商大学在哪儿吗？

（三）替换练习 Substitution drills

1. 马克坐出租车去浙江工商大学。

   公交车　市民中心
   地铁　杭州东站

2. 请给我　发票。

   马克　一本汉语书
   她　一杯可乐

3. 请问，怎么去杭州国际会议中心？

   浙江工商大学
   杭州东站
   市民中心

4. 你先坐地铁1号线，然后坐地铁4号线。

   坐公交车　坐地铁
   坐35路公交车　坐地铁1号线
   去图书馆　去银行

5. 杭州国际会议中心就在市民中心站的旁边。

   马克　玛丽　旁边
   超市　学校　东边
   图书馆　学校　里边

（四）完成对话 Complete the following dialogues

1. A：你好，浙江工商大学到了。
   B：谢谢！____________？（多少）
   A：三十块钱。
   B：好的，____________。请给我发票。（谢谢）
2. A：您好！请问怎么去杭州国际会议中心？
   B：对不起，____________。（知道）
   A：____________。
3. A：您好！请问，杭州国际会议中心____________？（怎么）
   B：你可以坐地铁去。____。（先……然后……）

（五）课堂活动 In-class activities

1. 看图说话 Talk about the pictures

   请根据图片说出简短的句子。Try to make brief sentences according to each picture.

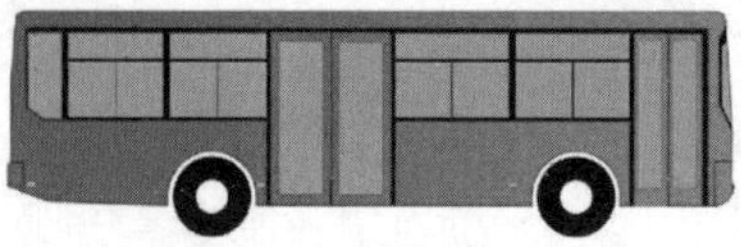

2. 角色扮演 Role-play

(1)两个同学为一组,练习坐出租车。

Please two students in a group practice taking a taxi.

(2)两个或三个同学为一组,练习问路。

Please two or three students in a group practice asking for directions.

(六)课后练习 After-class exercises

请说一说在杭州你想去哪儿,怎么去。Please talk about where you want to visit in Hangzhou and how you arrive there.

课文翻译 Translation of texts

Text A Take a taxi

Mark: Driver, I want to go to Zhejiang Gongshang University.

Driver: OK.

(After ten minutes)

Driver: Hello, here we are.

Mark: Thank you. How much?

Driver: 30 *Yuan*.

Mark: OK, here you are. Please give me an invoice.

Text B Ask for directions

Mary: Hello! May I ask how to get to the Hangzhou International Conference Center?

Pedestrian A: Sorry. I don't know.

Mary: It's OK.

Mary: Hello. May I ask if you know how to get to the Hangzhou International Conference Center?

Pedestrian B: Sure. You can take bus No. 68. You can also get there by subway, first take subway line No. 1 to Hangzhou East Station, and then transfer to line No. 4 to get off at the Civic Center Station.

Mary: Civic Center Station?

Pedestrian B: Yes. Hangzhou International Conference Center is next to the Civic Center Station.

Mary: OK. Thank you!

Pedestrian B: You're welcome.

7 你吃饭了吗

Have you eaten?

话题导学 Guidance

1. 你今天吃早饭了吗?
   Did you eat breakfast today?
2. 你常常去哪儿吃饭?
   Where do you usually have a meal?
3. 你喜欢吃中国菜吗? 你喜欢吃什么中国菜?
   Do you like Chinese Cuisine? What is your favorite?

生词学习(一) New words I

1. liáo tiānr 聊天儿 *v.* chat —— 在宿舍聊天儿;聊聊天儿
2. hǎo jiǔ bú jiàn 好久不见 long time no see(a greeting when haven't seen someone for a while) —— 真的好久不见了;他俩好久不见了
3. tīng shuō 听说 *v.* have heard of something —— 听说你去了中国;听说你汉语很好
4. zuó tiān 昨天 *n.* yesterday —— 昨天晚上;昨天我在上海
5. shēng rì 生日 *n.* birthday —— 你的生日;生日蛋糕
6. zhù 祝 *v.* wish —— 祝你生日快乐;祝你新年快乐
7. kuài lè 快乐 *adj.* happy —— 生日快乐;新年快乐
8. méi yǒu 没(有) *v.* did not —— 没有吃饭;没有去上海
9. zhǔn bèi 准备 *v.* prepare; plan —— 准备学习汉语;准备去餐厅吃饭
10. yuán gōng 员工 *n.* staff; employee —— 公司员工;员工餐厅

cān tīng
11. 餐厅 *n.* canteen　　学生餐厅;餐厅在哪儿

课文(一)　同事聊天儿
Text A　Chat between colleagues

Chén Lóng　Nǐ hǎo　dà wèi　hǎo jiǔ　bú jiàn
陈　龙:你好,大卫,好久不见。

Dà wèi　Hǎo jiǔ　bú jiàn　Nǐ　zuì　jìn hǎo ma
大卫:好久不见。你最近好吗?

Chén Lóng　Wǒ hěn hǎo　Tīng shuō zuó tiān shì　nǐ　de shēng　rì　zhù　nǐ　shēng　rì　kuài　lè
陈　龙:我很好。听说昨天是你的生日,祝你生日快乐!

Dà wèi　Xiè xie　Nǐ　chī　fàn　le　ma
大卫:谢谢!你吃饭了吗?

Chén Lóng　Hái méi yǒu　Nǐ　ne
陈　龙:还没有。你呢?

Dà wèi　Wǒ　yě　méi yǒu　Wǒ zhǔn bèi　qù　yuán gōng cān tīng chī　fàn　zán men　yì　qǐ　qù　ba
大卫:我也没有。我准备去员工餐厅吃饭,咱们一起去吧!

Chén Lóng　Hǎo　a
陈　龙:好啊。

根据课文(一)回答问题
Answer these questions according to the Text A

1. 陈龙和大卫是什么关系?
2. 陈龙和大卫常常见面吗?
3. 陈龙和大卫吃饭了吗?

生词学习(二)
New words II

diǎn
1. 点$_2$ *v.* order　　点菜;点外卖

cài
2. 菜 *n.* vegetable; dish　　中国菜;什么菜

fèn
3. 份 *mw.* set(often used for dishes, jobs...)　　一份菜;一份面条;一份工作

xī hóng shì
4. 西红柿 *n.* tomato　　西红柿炒鸡蛋;吃西红柿

chǎo
5. 炒 *v.* fry; stir fry　　炒饭;炒鸡蛋

jī dàn
6. 鸡蛋 *n.* (hen's)egg　　一个鸡蛋;买鸡蛋

suān
7. 酸 *adj.* sour 太酸了;很酸

tián
8. 甜 *adj.* sweet 太甜了;很甜

hǎo chī
9. 好吃 *adj.* delicious 太好吃了;很好吃

tè bié
10. 特别 *adv.* special; unusual; particular 特别好;特别漂亮

kǎo
11. 烤 *v.* roast 烤鸭;烤面包

yā
12. 鸭 *n.* duck 烤鸭;小鸭子

zuì
13. 最 *adv.* most 最好;最大

shí jiān
14. 时间 *n.* time 有时间;什么时间;多长时间

de huà
15. 的话 in terms of; if 有时间的话;这样的话

课文(二) 餐厅点餐
Text B Order food in the canteen

Dà wèi Nǐ xiǎng diǎn shén me cài
大卫:你想点什么菜?

Chén Lóng Wǒ xiǎng diǎn yí fèn xī hóng shì chǎo jī dàn
陈龙:我想点一份西红柿炒鸡蛋。

Dà wèi Wǒ yě xǐ huān xī hóng shì chǎo jī dàn suān suān tián tián de hěn hǎo chī
大卫:我也喜欢西红柿炒鸡蛋,酸酸甜甜的,很好吃。

Chén Lóng Nǐ xǐ huān chī zhōng guó cài ma
陈龙:你喜欢吃中国菜吗?

Dà wèi Xǐ huān Zhōng guó cài hěn hǎo chī tè bié shì Běi jīng kǎo yā
大卫:喜欢。中国菜很好吃,特别是北京烤鸭。

Chén Lóng Wǒ zuì xǐ huān de jiù shì Běi jīng kǎo yā Yǒu shí jiān de huà wǒ men yì qǐ qù chī běi jīng kǎo yā ba
陈龙:我最喜欢的就是北京烤鸭。有时间的话,我们一起去吃北京烤鸭吧!

Dà wèi Hǎo a
大卫:好啊。

根据课文(二)回答问题
Answer these questions according to the Text B

1. 陈龙想点什么菜?

2. 大卫喜欢吃中国菜吗?

3. 大卫喜欢吃什么中国菜?

4. 陈龙喜欢吃什么中国菜?

语言点 Language points

1. 好久不见

"好久不见"用于相识的人在长久分别之后再次见面,可用于打招呼。

"好久不见" is used in the situation of people meet again after a long separation. It's a way of greeting.

2. 祝你生日快乐

"祝你生日快乐"是生日的祝福语。"祝你……"是常用的祝福语结构。

"祝你生日快乐" is an expression of birthday blessings. "祝你……" is usually used to express blessings. For example,

(1)祝你新年快乐!

(2)祝你考试(kǎoshì, exam)顺利(shùnlì, smoothly)!

(3)祝你一路顺风(yílùshùnfēng, have a good jounney)!

3. 还

"还"用于谓词之前,表示没有发生变化。

"还" used before a predicate, which can indicate no change of certain situation.

(1)我还没有吃中饭。

(2)大卫还在图书馆。

(3)天还不冷。

4. "了"置于句尾

你吃饭了吗?

语气助词"了"置于句尾,如表示事情的发生、动作的完成、情况的出现、状态的变化等。否定形式为:"没有 + *v*.", 句尾不用"了"。"还没有 + *v*."含有即将开始或完成的意思。

The particle "了" is used at the end of a sentence, can indicate different meanings, such as the happening of something, the completion of an action, the emergence of a situation, and the change of a state, etc.

The negative form is "没有 + *v*.", without "了" in the end.

And the structure "还没有 + *v*." indicates an action will begin or be completed later.

(1)我跟他见面了。/我没有跟他见面。/我还没有跟他见面。

(2)外面下雨了。/外面没有下雨。/外面还没有下雨。

(3)他去办公室(bàngōngshì,office)了。/他没有去办公室。/他还没有去办公室。

5. 最 + *adj*.

"最"放在形容词前,表示极端的程度。

"最" is used before an adjective to express an extreme degree.

(1)我最喜欢的就是火锅。

(2)大卫的汉语最好。

(3)中国的人口(rénkǒu,population)最多。

6. ……的话

"的话"常置于句末,用来表达假设的语气,可用于"如果……的话"结构。

"的话" is used at the end of the sentence to express a subjunctive mood. It could be used in the structure of "如果……的话".

(1)有时间的话,我们一起去吃火锅吧!

(2)如果你今天晚上有时间的话,我们一起吃晚饭吧。

"的话"还可与"就"搭配,用于"(如果)……的话,就……"结构。

"的话" could also be used with "就" in the structure of "(如果)……的话,就……".

(3)明天没课的话,我就去图书馆。

在口语中,"的话"也可表示语气上的停顿。

In spoken Chinese, "的话" could also express a pause in the mood.

核心句 Key sentences

1. 好久不见。
2. 你最近好吗?
3. 祝你生日快乐!
4. 你吃饭了吗?
5. 我准备去员工餐厅吃饭,咱们一起去吧!
6. 中国菜很好吃,特别是北京烤鸭。
7. 有时间的话,我们一起去吃北京烤鸭吧!

综合练习 Comprehensive exercises

(一)熟读短语 Read the following phrases or sentences

1. 听说昨天是你的生日　听说你去中国留学了　听说明天没有课
2. 祝你生日快乐　祝你新年快乐　祝你身体健康
3. 你吃饭了吗　你今天学习汉语了吗　你下课了吗
4. 准备去吃饭　准备学习汉语　准备睡觉
5. 喜欢什么菜　喜欢中国菜　喜欢谁　喜欢哪儿
6. 最喜欢　最好　最新　最近(jìn, close/near)
7. 有时间的话　你喜欢的话　你来中国的话

(二)选词填空 Choose a suitable word for each sentence

听说　特别　祝　准备　的话

1. ________你新年快乐。
2. ________你在学习汉语。
3. 我很喜欢中国语言和文化,________是汉字。
4. 明天不下雨________,咱们就去超市买东西。
5. 我________去中国学习汉语。

(三)替换练习 Substitution drills

1. 听说<u>昨天是你的生日</u>。
   明天有汉语课
   你住在学校宿舍
   你在工商大学学习汉语
2. 祝你<u>生日</u>快乐!
   新年(xīnnián, new year)
   春节(Chūnjié, the Chinese Spring Festival)
   节日(jiérì, festival)
3. 我想点<u>一份西红柿炒鸡蛋</u>。
   一杯咖啡
   一个披萨(pīsà, pizza)
   一个汉堡(hànbǎo, hamburger)和一份(fèn, a set of)薯条(shǔtiáo, French fries)
4. <u>有时间</u>的话,　<u>我们一起去吃火锅吧</u>!
   你喜欢　就送给你吧
   你明天有时间　来学校找我

汉字不好　　　　要多练习(liànxí, practice)

(四)完成对话 Complete the following dialogues

1. A: 你好,大卫,好久不见。
   B: ________。你最近好吗?
   A: ________。
2. A: 听说昨天是你的生日,________________!(祝)
   B: 谢谢!
3. A: 你吃饭了吗?
   B: ________。你呢?(还)
   A: 我也没有。我准备去员工餐厅吃饭,咱们一起去吧!
4. A: 你想点什么菜?
   B: ________________________________。
5. A: 你喜欢吃中国菜吗?
   B: ________。中国菜很好吃,特别是________。
   A: 我也喜欢吃北京烤鸭。

(五)课堂活动 In-class activities

1. 看图说话 Talk about the pictures

(1)根据图片,说一说你去哪儿吃饭? Where do you eat? Try to make sentences according to each picture.

(2)根据图片,说一说你今天吃了什么?味道怎么样? What did you eat? How does it taste? Try to make sentences according to each picture.

2. 说一说你们喜欢的中国菜。Please talk about your favorite Chinese dish.
3. 角色扮演 Role-play

   两个或三个同学为一组,练习点菜。Two or three students in a group practice ordering the dishes.

(六)课后练习 After-class exercises

你喜欢吃中国菜吗?请说一说你最喜欢的中国菜。Do you like Chinese food? Please tell your friends about your favorite Chinese food.

课文翻译 Translation

Text A　Chat between colleagues

Chen Long: Hello, David. Long time no see.

David: Haven't seen you for a long time. How are you?

Chen Long: I'm fine. I heard yesterday was your birthday. Happy Birthday!

David: Thanks! Have you eaten?

Chen Long: Not yet. And you?

David: Me neither. I am going to the staff canteen to have meal. Let's go together!

Chen Long: OK.

Text B　Order food in the canteen

David: What dish do you want to order?

Chen Long: I want scrambled eggs with tomatoes.

David: I like scrambled eggs with tomatoes too. It's sweet and sour, and very delicious.

Chen Long: Do you like Chinese food?

David: Yeah. Chinese food is delicious, especially Beijing roast duck.

Chen Long: My favorite dish is exactly Beijing roast duck. When you're free let's go to eat Beijing roast duck.

David: OK.

8 这个周末你干什么
What will you do this coming weekend?

话题导学 Guidance

1. 你的学习忙不忙?
   Are you busy with your study?
2. 周末你常常做什么?
   What do you often do on the weekend?
3. 你喜欢什么运动或活动?
   What sports or activities do you like?

生词学习(一) New words I

1. 干 gàn	*v.* do; work	干什么;干活
2. 打算 dǎ suàn	*v.* plan to; intend to	打算学习;有什么打算
3. 加班 jiā bān	*v.* work overtime; work extra hours	打算加班
4. 打 dǎ	*v.* play(ball games)	打篮球;打网球
5. 篮球 lán qiú	*n.* basketball	篮球运动员;打篮球
6. 对 duì	*prep.* for; to; as for	对身体好;对学习好
7. 身体 shēn tǐ	*n.* body	身体好;身体怎么样
8. 要 yào	*v.* need; want	要学习;要加班
9. 运动 yùn dòng	*v./n.* exercise; sport	篮球运动;做运动
10. 运动场 yùn dòng chǎng	*n.* sports ground; playground	篮球运动场;足球运动场

课文(一) 周末的安排
Text A Arrangements for the weekend

Chén lóng Dà wèi zhè ge zhōu mò nǐ gàn shén me
陈龙：大卫，这个周末你干什么？

Dà wèi Wǒ dǎ suàn shàng wǔ qù gōng sī jiā bān xià wǔ qù dǎ lán qiú
大卫：我打算上午去公司加班，下午去打篮球。

Chén lóng Wǒ yě xǐ huān dǎ lán qiú dǎ lán qiú duì shēn tǐ hěn hǎo
陈龙：我也喜欢打篮球，打篮球对身体很好。

Dà wèi Nǐ zhōu mò yǒu shí jiān ma Yào bú yào yì qǐ dǎ lán qiú
大卫：你周末有时间吗？要不要一起打篮球？

Chén lóng Hǎo a wǒ yě yào duō yùn dòng
陈龙：好啊，我也要多运动。

Dà wèi Nà zán men zhè ge xīng qī liù xià wǔ liǎng diǎn lán qiú yùn dòng chǎng jiàn
大卫：那咱们这个星期六下午两点篮球运动场见。

根据课文(一)回答问题
Answer these questions according to the Text A

1. 大卫这个周末打算干什么？
2. 陈龙喜欢打篮球吗？为什么？
3. 大卫和陈龙这个周末打不打篮球？

生词学习(二)
New words II

xià 1. 下	*n.* next; latter; second	下个月；下星期
zú qiú 2. 足球	*n.* football; soccer	足球运动员；踢足球
bǐ sài 3. 比赛	*n.* game; competition	足球比赛；篮球比赛
bù mén 4. 部门	*n.* department; section	财务部门；哪个部门
huì 5. 会	*aux.* can; be able to; will(indicate possibility)	会说汉语；会写汉字
cān jiā 6. 参加	*v.* join; attend	参加比赛；参加会议
cái wù bù 7. 财务部	*n.* accounting department	公司财务部
jǐ 8. 几$_1$	*num.* several; some	几个朋友；几块钱

liàn xí
9. 练习 v. exercise; practice 练习汉字

lái
10. 来 v. come 来学校;来踢球;来玩儿

tī
11. 踢 v. play(football or soccer) 踢足球

补充词语(Supplementary vocabulary)

yóu yǒng
1. 游泳 v. swim 喜欢游泳;会游泳

pǎo bù
2. 跑步 v. run 常常跑步

pá shān
3. 爬山 v. climb the mountains 爬爬山

chàng gē
4. 唱歌 v. sing 喜欢唱歌;常常唱歌

tiào wǔ
5. 跳舞 v. dance 喜欢跳舞;常常跳舞

课文(二) 足球比赛
Text B Football match

陈龙和大卫的公司下周末有足球比赛。

Chen Long and David's company has a football match next weekend.

Dà wèi Chén Lóng xià zhōu mò gōng sī de zú qiú bǐ sài nǐ men bù mén huì cān jiā ma
大卫:陈龙,下周末公司的足球比赛你们部门会参加吗?

Chén Lóng Cān jiā nǐ men cái wù bù ne
陈龙:参加!你们财务部呢?

Dà wèi Wǒ men yě huì cān jiā
大卫:我们也会参加。

Chén Lóng Zhè ge zhōu mò wǒ hé jǐ ge péng yǒu dǎ suàn yì qǐ liàn xí nǐ yào bú yào lái
陈龙:这个周末我和几个朋友打算一起练习,你要不要来?

Dà wèi Hǎo a Nǐ men zài nǎr liàn xí
大卫:好啊。你们在哪儿练习?

Chén Lóng Zhè ge zhōu liù xià wǔ sān diǎn zài Gōng shāng dà xué de yùn dòng chǎng
陈龙:这个周六下午三点,在工商大学的运动场。

Dà wèi Hǎo de Zhōu mò jiàn
大卫:好的。周末见!

Chén Lóng Zhōu mò zài jiàn
陈龙:周末再见!

根据课文(二)回答问题
Answer these questions according to the Text B

1. 陈龙和大卫的公司下个周末有什么活动?
2. 大卫是公司哪个部门的员工?
3. 大卫会不会参加这次的足球比赛?
4. 他们在哪儿练习?

语言点
Language points

1. 干什么

"干什么"常用于口语,用于询问"做什么"。

"干什么" is usually used in spoken Chinese for asking "doing what".

(1)你在干什么?

(2)这个周末你干什么?

2. 对……好

"对……好"用于表示对某人或某事有好处或有帮助,反之则用"对……不好"。

"对……好" is used to indicate being good for something or somebody. It's antonym is "对……不好".

(1)打篮球对身体很好。

(2)我的朋友们对我都很好。

(3)喝酒对身体不好。

3. *v*.不 *v*.

"*v*.不 *v*."是一个正反问句,这种结构强调语义的选择性,需要答话者做出肯定或否定的选择。

"*v*. 不 *v*." (*v*.-not-*v*. question) is an affirmative-negative question structure. This structure could emphasize the selectivity of semantics, which needs the respondent make an affirmative or negative choice.

(1)你吃不吃中国菜?

(2)你说不说汉语?

(3)你要不要来?

4. 能愿动词"要"

"要"是一个能愿动词,用于表达"想""打算""需要"等主观意愿。

"要" is an auxiliary verb to express the subjective will of "want to","plan to" or "need to".

(1)你这个周末要不要来我们学校玩儿?

(2)你要不要喝咖啡?

(3)明天要不要上课?

5. 多 + *v*.

"多"用于动词前,表示比原来的数量有所增加。

"多" is used before a verb to indicate more than the required.

(1)你要多练习汉语。

(2)你要多听汉语歌。

(3)你要多去图书馆。

6. 日期与时间的表达

用汉语表达日期与时间的时候,常常从大的时间陈述到小的时间,即×年－×月－×日－星期×－早上/上午/中午/下午/晚上－×时/点－×分。例如,2018 年 6 月 1 日星期五早上 8 点 18 分。

In Chinese, the date and time is often expressed in the following order, "2018 年 6 月 1 日星期五早上 8 点 18 分"(8:18 a.m., Friday, 1st of June, 2018).

7. 能愿动词"会"

"会"是一个能愿动词,除了表示有某方面的能力之外,还可表达可能性。

"会" is an auxiliary verb. Besides indicating someone has the ability or skill to do something, it can also be used to express the possibility.

(1)下周末公司的足球比赛你们部门会参加吗?

(2)我下个月会去中国。

(3)明天会下雨。

8. 几

"几"用于陈述句表示不确定的数量。

"几" is used in declarative sentence to indicate an indeterminate number (usually not too many).

(1)你可以借(jiè, to lend)我几块钱吗?

(2)我约(yuē, to arrange; to date)了几个中国朋友一起吃饭,你一起来吧。

(3)汉字太难写，我就(jiù, just)会写几个汉字。

(4)这几天你去哪儿了？

核心句
Key sentences

1. 周末你打算干什么？
2. 打篮球对身体好。
3. 你周末有时间吗？
4. 要不要一起打篮球？
5. 我也要多运动。
6. 咱们这个星期六下午 2 点篮球运动场见。
7. 这个周末我和几个朋友打算一起练习，你要不要来？

综合练习
Comprehensive exercises

(一)熟读短语 Read the following phrases

1. 打算去公司加班　打算学习汉语　打算参加比赛
2. 打篮球　踢足球　跑步　游泳
3. 爬什么山　跳什么舞　唱什么歌
4. 足球比赛　篮球比赛　唱歌比赛　游泳比赛
5. 要不要　去不去　学不学　吃不吃　来不来
6. 参加比赛　参加学习　参加练习

(二)选词填空 Choose a suitable word for each sentence

要　打算　参加　练习　运动

1. 唉，今天又________加班。
2. 我明天会________比赛。
3. 多________对身体好。
4. 你要多________写汉字。
5. 我________下个月去中国旅行。

(三)替换练习 Substitution drills

1. 我喜欢<u>打篮球</u>。

　　踢足球

　　游泳

　　唱歌

　　跳舞

2. 你要不要 打篮球?

去不去 超市

喝不喝 咖啡

想不想 去图书馆

会不会 说汉语

3. 打篮球 对身体 很好。

我的哥哥 我 很

踢足球 身体 很

抽烟(chōuyān,smoke) 身体 不

4. 我要多运动。

练习汉语

去图书馆

跟你聊天儿

(四)完成对话 Complete the following dialogues

1. A: 这个周末你干什么?

B: ________________。(加班,打篮球)

2. A: 你喜欢打篮球吗?

B: 喜欢,打篮球________________。(对……好)

A: 是的。

3. A: 这个周末我去工商大学的运动场踢足球,你________? (*v*.不 *v*.)

B: 好啊。周末见。

(五)请为下列动词搭配合适的宾语 Please add the proper words for the following verbs

1. 唱 chàng
2. 跑 pǎo
3. 跳 tiào
4. 踢 tī
5. 打 dǎ
6. 爬 pá

(六)课堂活动 In-class activities

1. 看图说话 Talk about the pictures

根据图片,说一说你喜欢的运动或活动。Please talk about your favorite sports or activities according to the pictures.

2. 请说一说你的兴趣爱好。Try to introduce your hobbies.

(七)课后练习 After-class exercises

问问你的室友或同学,这个周末他(她)打算干什么?他(她)喜欢什么运动或活动?Please ask your roommate or classmate what he or she is going to do this weekend. What sports or activities does he or she like?

课文翻译 Translation of the texts

Text A　Arrangements for weekend

Chen Long: David, what do you plan to do this weekend?

David: I plan to go to the company to work overtime in the morning, and I will play basketball in the afternoon.

Chen Long: I like to play basketball too. It's good for the health.

David: Do you have time this weekend? How about joining us?

Chen Long: That's good. I need more exercises as well.

David: Then let's meet at the basketball court at 2 p.m. this Saturday.

Text B　Football match

David: Chen Long, will your department join the the company's football game next weekend?

Chen Long: Yes! What about the finance department?

David: We will be there as well.

Chen Long: I'm going to practice with some friends this weekend. Would you like to come?

David: OK. Where do you play?

Chen Long: 3 p. m. in this Saturday afternoon, at the basketball court of Zhejiang Gongshang University.

David: OK. See you on the weekend.

Chen Long: See you on the weekend.

9 家人和职业
Family members and occupations

话题导学
Guidance

1. 你家有几口人?
   How many people are there in your family?
2. 你有兄弟姐妹吗?
   Do you have any brothers and sisters?
3. 你的家人做什么工作?
   What do your family members do?

生词学习(一)
New words I

1. 有 (yǒu)	*v.* have	有书;有汉语课
2. 几$_2$ (jǐ)	*pron.* how many	几个人? 几本书?
3. 口 (kǒu)	*mw.* measure word (for family members)	三口人;五口人;几口人
4. 爷爷 (yé ye)	*n.* grandpa	我的爷爷;爷爷在哪儿
5. 奶奶 (nǎi nai)	*n.* grandma	谁的奶奶;爷爷和奶奶
6. 爸爸 (bà ba)	*n.* dad	他的爸爸;爸爸的爸爸是爷爷
7. 妈妈 (mā ma)	*n.* mom	她的妈妈;爸爸和妈妈
8. 哥哥 (gē ge)	*n.* elder brother	我的哥哥;几个哥哥
9. 姐姐 (jiě jie)	*n.* elder sister	我的姐姐;三个姐姐
10. 弟弟 (dì di)	*n.* younger brother	姐姐和弟弟;一个弟弟

zhēn
11. 真 *adv.* really; truly; indeed 真好;真漂亮啊

zhǐ
12. 只 *adv.* only 只说汉语;只有一本书

mèimei
13. 妹妹 *n.* younger sister 兄妹;姐妹;谁的妹妹

hái zi
14. 孩子 *n.* child 一个孩子;很多孩子

duì
15. 对 *adj.* right; correct 很对;你是对的

课文(一) 家人
Text A Family members

李明和玛丽正在讨论他们的家人。

Li Ming and Mary are talking about their family members.

Lǐ Míng Mǎ lì nǐ jiā yǒu jǐ kǒu rén
李明:玛丽,你家有几口人?

Mǎ lì Wǒ jiā yǒu bā kǒu rén yé ye nǎi nai bà ba mā ma gē ge jiě jie dì di hé wǒ
玛丽:我家有八口人——爷爷、奶奶、爸爸、妈妈、哥哥、姐姐、弟弟和我。

Lǐ Míng Zhēn hǎo a
李明:真好啊!

Mǎ lì Nǐ ne
玛丽:你呢?

Lǐ Míng Wǒ jiā zhǐ yǒu sān kǒu rén bà ba mā ma hé wǒ wǒ hěn xiǎng yǒu yí ge mèimei
李明:我家只有三口人,爸爸、妈妈和我。我很想有一个妹妹。

Mǎ lì Nǐ jiā zhǐ yǒu yí ge hái zi ma
玛丽:你家只有一个孩子吗?

Lǐ Míng Duì
李明:对。

根据课文(一)回答问题
Answer these questions according to the Text A

1. 玛丽家有几口人?他们是谁?
2. 李明家有几口人呢?
3. 李明家只有一个孩子,对吗?

生词学习(二)
New words II

zuò
1. 做 *v.* do 做什么;做作业

gōng zuò
2. 工作 *n.* work; job　　做什么工作；工作很好

mào yì
3. 贸易 *n.* trade; commerce　　国际贸易；对外贸易

zhōng xué
4. 中学 *n.* middle school　　第一中学；哪个中学；中学生

dāng
5. 当 *v.* work as; serve as　　当老师；当医生

xiàn zài
6. 现在 *n.* now; at present　　现在几点

shí xí
7. 实习 *v.* do fieldwork; do internship　　去公司实习；实习生

liú
8. 留 *v.* stay; remain　　留在中国；留下来

yǐ hòu
9. 以后 *adv.* afterwards; later　　来中国以后；下班以后

lǜ shī
10. 律师 *n.* lawyer　　他是律师；当律师

huò zhě
11. 或者 *conj.* or　　当医生或者当老师；去图书馆或者去超市

课文(二) 谈论职业
Text B Talk about occupations

美玲和玛丽在谈论家人的工作。

Meiling and Mary are talking about their family members' occupations.

Měi líng　Mǎ lì　nǐ de bà ba mā ma zuò shén me gōng zuò
美玲：玛丽，你的爸爸妈妈做什么工作？

Mǎ lì　Wǒ de bà ba shì gōng sī jīng lǐ　shì zuò guó jì mào yì de　mā ma méi yǒu gōng zuò　Nǐ de bà ba mā ma ne
玛丽：我的爸爸是公司经理，是做国际贸易的。妈妈没有工作。你的爸爸妈妈呢？

Měi líng　Wǒ de bà ba zài fàn diàn gōng zuò　wǒ de mā ma zài zhōng xué dāng lǎo shī
美玲：我的爸爸在饭店工作，我的妈妈在中学当老师。

Mǎ lì　Tīng shuō nǐ zài shí xí
玛丽：听说你在实习？

Měi líng　Shì de　wǒ xiàn zài zài yì jiā Zhōng guó gōng sī shí xí
美玲：是的，我现在在一家中国公司实习。

Mǎ lì　Nǐ dǎ suàn liú zài Zhōng guó gōng zuò ma
玛丽：你打算留在中国工作吗？

Měi líng　Duì　wǒ xiǎng liú zài Háng zhōu　Nǐ yǐ hòu xiǎng zuò shén me gōng zuò
美玲：对，我想留在杭州。你以后想做什么工作？

Mǎ lì　Wǒ xiǎng dāng lǜ shī huò zhě lǎo shī
玛丽：我想当律师或者老师。

根据课文(二)回答问题
Answer these questions according to the Text B

1. 玛丽的爸爸做什么工作？
2. 美玲的妈妈做什么工作？
3. 美玲在哪儿实习？
4. 玛丽以后想做什么工作？

语言点
Language points

1. 口

量词“口”用于“数＋口＋人”结构，表达家人的数量。

“口” is a measure word, and is used in the structure of “num. ＋口＋人” for family members.

(1)我家只有三口人。

(2)玛丽家有八口人。

2. 真……啊

“真……啊”用于表达感叹的语气。

“真……啊” is used to a express exclamation mood.

(1)我今天真高兴啊！

(2)这个书真贵啊！

(3)真幸福啊！

3. 是……的

“是……的”表示强调，可以强调人物、时间、地点、事件等。

“是……的” is used for emphasis. It could emphasize the person, time, location, event, and so on.

(1)我爸爸是做国际贸易的。(emphasize the occupation)

(2)我是上个星期回来的。(emphasize the time)

(3)大卫和李明是在中国认识的。(emphasize the location)

4. 当＋职业

“当＋职业”用于表达所从事的工作或职业。

"当 + occupation" is used to indicate one's profession. It is also correct to say "做 + occupation".

(1)我的妈妈在中学当老师。

(2)毕业(bìyè, graduation)以后我想当律师。

5. 在 + *v*.

"在 + *v*."表示正在进行的动作或存在的状态。

In "在 + *v*." structure, "在" is used before a verb to indicate an action which is in progress or a condition already in existence.

(1)听说你在实习?

(2)我在看电影。

(3)你在干什么?

6. 家

"家"用于数词(或指示代词)和名词之间时,是一个量词,常用于餐厅或企业等。

In the structure of "*numeral/demonstrative pron.* + 家 + *n*.", "家" is a measure word used for restaurant, company and so on.

(1)一家中国公司

(2)这家餐厅

(3)一家超市

7. 或者

"或者"用于陈述句中,表示选择。

"或者" is used in a declarative sentence to indicate a choice (A or B).

(1)我想当律师或者老师。

(2)我打算明天或者后天去北京。

核心句 Key sentences

1. 你家有几口人?
2. 真好啊!
3. 我家只有三口人,爸爸、妈妈和我。
4. 你的爸爸、妈妈做什么工作?
5. 我的爸爸是做国际贸易的。
6. 我现在在一家中国公司实习。

7. 我想当律师或者老师。

综合练习 Comprehensive exercises

(一)熟读短语 Read the following phrases

1. 三口人　五口人　八口人
2. 有三口人　有汉语书　有钱　有中国朋友
3. 真好啊!　真大啊!　真漂亮啊!
4. 当老师　当律师　当经理　当医生　当什么
5. 外贸公司　一家公司　什么公司
6. 只有一个孩子　只喝咖啡　只去超市　只买书

(二)请用下列词语组句 Make sentences with the following words

1. 你　人　家　几　口　有

____

2. 我　一　孩子　个　只有　家

____

3. 我　实习　在　一　公司　中国　家　现在

____

4. 律师　老师　我　想　当　或者

____

(三)替换练习 Substitution drills

1. 我家有三口人。
   四口人
   五口人
   八口人
2. 我家只有一个孩子。
   我　十块钱
   今天　汉语课
   我　两个中国朋友
3. 我在公司当经理。
   中学　老师
   中国　律师
4. 我想当老师或者律师。
   学　汉语　日语
   喝　咖啡　可乐(kě lè,coke)

吃　饺子(jiǎo zi, dumplings)　　炒饭(chǎo fàn, fried rice)

(四)完成对话 Complete the following dialogues

1. A: 你家有几口人?

   B: ____。(……口人)

2. A: 你家只有一个孩子吗?

   B: ____。

3. A: 你的爸爸、妈妈做什么工作?

   B: ____。

   (律师/老师/医生(yī shēng, doctor)/在公司工作……)

4. A: 你以后打算留在中国工作吗?

   B: ____。

5. A: 你以后想做什么工作?

   B: ____。(当)

(五)课堂活动 In-class activities

1. 看图说话 Talk about the pictures

   (1)根据图片,介绍你的家人。Introduce the family members according to the pictures.

   (2)根据图片,介绍下列职业。Try to introduce the following occupation according to the pictures.

2. 请介绍你的家人以及他们从事的工作。Please try to introduce your family members and their occupations.

(六)课后练习 After-class exercises

请问一问你的室友或者同学,他(她)家有几口人?他们做什么工作?Please ask your roommates or classmates how many family members they have. What jobs do they do?

课文翻译 Translation of the texts

Text A　Family members

Li Ming：Mary, how many people are there in your family?

Mary：There are eight people in my family：grandfather, grandmother, father, mother, elder brother, elder sister, younger brother and I.

Li Ming：Nice!

Mary：How about you?

Li Ming：There are only three family members in my family：father, mother and I. I really want to have a younger sister.

Mary：You are the only child(in your family)?

Li Ming：Yeah.

Text B　Talk about occupations

Meiling：Mary, what do your parents do?

Mary：My father is a manager in an international trade company. My mother doesn't work. How about your parents?

Meiling：My father is working in a restaurant, and my mother is a teacher in a secondary school.

Mary：I heard you are doing an internship.

Meiling：Yes. I am doing an internship in a Chinese company now.

Mary：Do you plan to work in China?

Meiling：Yes, I want to stay in Hangzhou. What work do you want to do in the future?

Mary：I want to be a lawyer or a teacher.

10 1 美元换多少人民币

How much RMB can be changed for 1 US dollar?

话题导学 Guidance

1. 离你宿舍最近的是哪家银行？
   Which bank is the closest to your dormitory?
2. 你平常去哪里取钱？
   Where do you usually withdraw money?
3. 100 欧元可以兑换多少元人民币？
   How much RMB can you exchange for 100 Euros?

生词学习(一) New words I

1. qǔ 取 *v.* take, withdraw (money) — 取东西；取钱
2. shāng wù 商务 *n.* business affairs; commerce — 商务酒店；商务会议
3. yín háng kǎ 银行卡 *n.* bank card — 带银行卡；申请银行卡
4. hù zhào 护照 *n.* passport — 带护照；护照号码
5. shū rù 输入 *v.* input — 输入密码；输入名字
6. mì mǎ 密码 *n.* password — 银行卡密码；手机密码
7. gěi 给 *v.* give sth. to sb. — 给你；给同学；给钱
8. děng 等 *v.* wait(for sb.) — 等一下；等我

课文(一) 在银行取钱 Text A Withdraw money in the bank

Yín háng yuán gōng Xiān sheng nín hǎo
银行员工：先生，您好！

Ā màn Nín hǎo Wǒ xiǎng qǔ qián Míng tiān wǒ yào qù cān jiā shāng wù huì yì
阿曼：您好！我想取钱。明天我要去参加商务会议。

Yín háng yuán gōng Qǐng gěi wǒ nín de yín háng kǎ hé hù zhào
银行员工：请给我您的银行卡和护照。

Ā màn Gěi nín
阿曼：给您。

Yín háng yuán gōng Xiè xie Nín xiǎng qǔ duō shǎo qián
银行员工：谢谢！您想取多少钱？

Ā màn Sān qiān yuán
阿曼：三千元。

Yín háng yuán gōng Qǐng děng yí xià qǐng shū rù mì mǎ
银行员工：请等一下，请输入密码。

Ā màn Hǎo de
阿曼：好的。

Yín háng yuán gōng Zhè shì sān qiān yuán Qǐng ná hǎo nín de yín háng kǎ hé hù zhào Zài jiàn
银行员工：这是三千元。请拿好您的银行卡和护照。再见！

Ā màn Xiè xie nín Zài jiàn
阿曼：谢谢您！再见！

根据课文(一)回答问题
Answer these questions according to the Text A

1. 阿曼今天去哪里了？
2. 阿曼为什么要取钱？
3. 阿曼取了多少钱？

生词学习(二)
New words II

rén mín bì
1. 人民币 *n.* RMB; Chinese currency 有人民币；用人民币

měi yuán
2. 美元 *n.* US dollar 用美元；100 美元

duì huàn
3. 兑换 *v.* exchange 兑换美元；兑换人民币

wài bì
4. 外币 *n.* foreign money 兑换外币；什么外币

shì chǎng
5. 市场 *n.* market 逛市场；中国市场

xū yào
6. 需要 *v.* need; require 需要喝水；需要帮忙

wàn
7. 万 *n.* ten thousand 一万;五万

shāo děng
8. 稍 等 *v.* wait a minute(in a formal way) 稍等一下;稍等一会儿

fēi cháng
9. 非 常 *v.* very, extremely 非常快;非常不错

课文(二) 兑换外币
Text B Exchange foreign currency

大卫在银行用美元兑换人民币。他想去小商品市场看看。

David exchanges some US dollars for Chinese RMB in the bank. He is going to the small commodity market.

Yín háng yuán gōng Nín hǎo Wǒ néng bāng nín zuò shén me ma
银行员工:您好!我能帮您做什么吗?

Dà wèi Nín hǎo Wǒ yào yòng měi yuán huàn rén mín bì
大卫:您好!我要用美元换人民币。

Yín háng yuán gōng Hǎo de Nín xū yào duō shǎo rén mín bì
银行员工:好的。您需要多少人民币?

Dà wèi Sān wàn yuán Jīn tiān yì měi yuán duì huàn duō shǎo rén mín bì
大卫:三万元。今天一美元兑换多少人民币?

Yín háng yuán gōng Liù diǎn bā èr yuán Qǐng gěi wǒ nín de yín háng kǎ hé hù zhào
银行员工:六点八二元。请给我您的银行卡和护照。

Dà wèi Gěi nín
大卫:给您。

Yín háng yuán gōng Qǐng nín tián yí xià xìng míng hé hù zhào hào mǎ
银行员工:请您填一下姓名和护照号码。

Dà wèi Hǎo de Qǐng bāng wǒ huàn wǔ qiān měi yuán
大卫:好的。请帮我换五千美元。

Yín háng yuán gōng Kě yǐ qǐng shāo děng
银行员工:可以,请稍等。

10分钟后。

After 10 minutes.

Yín háng yuán gōng Xiān sheng zhè shì nín de qián Qǐng ná hǎo
银行员工:先生,这是您的钱。请拿好!

Dà wèi Fēi cháng gǎn xiè nín
大卫:非常感谢您!

Yín háng yuán gōng Bú kè qi
银行员工:不客气!

根据课文(二)回答问题
Answer these questions according to the Text B

1. 大卫想去哪里看看?
2. 大卫去银行做什么?
3. 大卫需要多少人民币?

语言点
Language points

1. *v.* +好

"*v.* +好"用在祈使句里,表示说话人要求或提醒听者做好某件事。

When "*v.* +好" is used in an imperative sentence, it expresses that the speaker asks or reminds the listener to do something well and smoothly.

(1)请写好你的作业。

(2)请坐好!

(3)请收好!

2. 数字读法

100:一百　1000:一千(qiān, thousand)　10000:一万

"100, 1000 and 10000" is read "yìbǎi, yìqiān and yíwàn" separately in Chinese.

(1)130 元:一百三十元

(2)8000 元:八千元

(3)30000 元:三万元

(4)5.20 : 五点二

3. 帮 + sb. + *v.*

"帮 + sb. + *v.*"表示某人帮助另一个人做某事。

"帮 + sb. + *v.*" is used to express that someone helps another one do something.

(1)我帮你买牛奶。

(2)她帮我拿箱子(xiāngzi, box/case)。

(3)她帮妈妈照顾(zhàogù, take care of)小妹妹。

核心句
Key sentences

1. 请给我您的银行卡和护照。

2. 您想取多少钱?

3. 请输入密码!

4. 您办什么业务?

5. 您需要多少人民币?

6. 请您填一下姓名和护照号码。

综合练习 Comprehensive exercises

(一)熟读短语 Read the following phrases

(1)取钱　取衣服　取书　取东西

(2)给我护照　给我发票　给我钱　给我人民币

(3)拿好护照　拿好银行卡　拿好钱　拿好箱子　拿好手机　拿好物品

(4)准备进货　准备出门　准备考试　准备上课

(5)需要人民币　需要护照　需要门票　需要水果　需要书本

(6)填一下　等一下　说一下　听一下　看一下　让(ràng, step aside)一下

(二)连词成句 Use the words to construct sentences

1. 钱　你　我　换　帮

____

2. 你　给　的　我　请　学生证

____

3. 好　护照　拿　和　你　请　银行卡

____

4. 的　我　护照　你　需要

____

5. 一下　你　请　表格　填写

____

(三)替换练习 Substitution drills

1. 请给我您的<u>银行卡和护照</u>!

学生卡

机票

号码

2. 明天我要去参加商务会议。

汉语培训(péixùn, training)

足球比赛(bǐsài, match)

生日晚会 (wǎnhuì, evening party)

3. 您可以帮我取钱吗?

换钱

买一瓶水

买车票(piào, ticket)

4. 您办什么业务?

手续(shǒuxù, procedure)

签证 (qiānzhèng, visa)

银行卡

5. 您需要多少人民币?

美元

时间

钱

6. 请您填一下姓名和护照号码!

地址

收货人

电话号码

(四)完成对话 Complete the following dialogues

1. A:先生,您好!

B:您好！我想取钱。明天我要去________________。(参加)

A:请给我您的银行卡和___________!

B:好的。

2. A:您好!

B:您好！我要用美元__________。(换)

A:好的。您需要多少人民币?

B:一万人民币。

3. A:请您_______姓名和护照号码!

B:好的。请帮我换五千美元。

A:可以。请_______!(等)

(五)课堂活动 In-class activities

1. 看图说话 Talk about the pictures

请根据图片说出简短的句子。Try to make brief sentences according to each picture.

2. 角色扮演 Role-play

你去银行取钱并和一位银行员工交谈。请尽量使用所给的词语或句型。You talk with a bank staff when you go to withdraw money in the bank. Please try to use the given words or phrases as many as possible.

取钱　银行卡　护照　输入　密码　请给我　请拿好　请填写

(六)课后作业 After-class exercises

采访3个人,简单记录他们去银行取钱或换钱的基本情况。在下节课向同学们介绍情况。Please interview three people and write down some basic information about withdrawing or exchanging money in the bank. Try to introduce the information to your classmates in your next class.

序号	姓名	他/她	他/她在哪个银行取钱/换钱
例	安娜	留学生	她在工商银行取钱
1			
2			
3			

课文翻译 Translation of texts

Text A　Withdraw money in the bank

Bank staff：Hello, Sir!

Arman：Hello! I would like to withdraw money. I will have a business meeting tomorrow.

Bank staff：Your bank card and passport, please.

Arman：Here you are.

Bankstaff：Thank you! How much do you want to withdraw?

Arman：3,000 yuan.

Bank staff：Please wait a minute. Please enter your password.

Arman：OK.

Bank staff：Here is 3,000 yuan, and please take your bank card and passport. Goodbye!

Arman：Thank you! Goodbye!

Text B　Exchange foreign currency

Bank staff：Hello,Sir! What can I do for you?

David：Hello! I want to exchange US dollars for Chinese *yuan*.

Bank staff：OK! How much RMB do you want?

David：Thirty thousand yuan. What is the exchange rate of USD to RMB today?

Bank staff：6.82 RMB for every dollar. May I have your passport and bank card please?

David：Here you are.

Bank staff：Please fill in your name and passport number!

David：Okay. I would like to exchange 5,000 US dollars.

Bank staff：OK! Please wait a minute!

(10 minutes later)

Bank staff：Here is your money, Sir! Please take care!

David：Thank you very much!

Bank staff：You are welcome!

11 我带您去酒店
Let me take you to the hotel

话题导学 Guidance

1. 你一般会通过哪种方式预订酒店？
   In which way do you usually book a hotel?
2. 你喜欢住哪种酒店房间？
   What kind of hotel room do you prefer?
3. 当你住商务酒店时，你最需要哪些服务？
   What services do you need most when staying in a business hotel?

生词学习(一) New words I

1. 已经 (yǐ jīng) *adv.* already　　已经看了；已经来了
2. 预订 (yù dìng) *v.* book; make a reservation　　预订酒店；预订机票
3. 酒店 (jiǔ diàn) *n.* hotel　　一家酒店；住酒店
4. 麻烦 (má fan) *v.* bother; trouble　　麻烦您；麻烦朋友
5. 看起来 (kàn qǐ lái) *v.* look　　看起来很好；看起来不错
6. 办理 (bàn lǐ) *v.* deal with; handle　　办理银行卡；办理护照
7. 手续 (shǒu xù) *n.* procedures　　办理手续；什么手续

课文(一) Text A　安排朋友住宿 Arrange accommodation for a friend

张丽带大卫到预订好的商务酒店。

Zhang Li takes David to the business hotel reserved.

Zhāng Lì　Dà wèi nín hǎo　Wǒ yǐ jīng bāng nín yù dìng le shāng wù jiǔ diàn
张丽：大卫您好！我已经帮您预订了商务酒店。

Dà wèi　Tài hǎo le　Xiè xie nín
大卫：太好了！谢谢您！

Zhāng Lì　Wǒ kāi chē dài nín qù jiǔ diàn　Nín shì yí gè rén lái cān jiā shāng wù huì yì de ma
张丽：我开车带您去酒店。您是一个人来参加商务会议的吗？

Dà wèi　Shì de　Má fan nín le
大卫：是的。麻烦您了。

15分钟后。

After 15 minutes.

Zhāng Lì　Dà wèi　nín zhù de jiǔ diàn dào le
张丽：大卫，您住的酒店到了。

Dà wèi　Jiǔ diàn kàn qǐ lái hěn bú cuò
大卫：酒店看起来很不错！

Zhāng Lì　Qǐng gěi wǒ hù zhào　wǒ bāng nín bàn lǐ shǒu xù
张丽：请给我护照，我帮您办理手续。

Dà wèi　Hǎo de　Xiè xie nín
大卫：好的！谢谢您！

根据课文（一）回答问题
Answer these questions according to the Text A

1. 张丽要带大卫去哪里？
2. 大卫要来参加什么会议？
3. 张丽要帮大卫做什么事？

生词学习（二）
New words II

1.	shēn fèn zhèng 身份证	*n.* ID card	拿身份证；带身份证
2.	shāng wù fáng 商务房	*n.* business room	订商务房
3.	ān jìng 安静	*adj.* quiet	安静的房间；安静的孩子
4.	xǐ yī 洗衣	*v.* wash clothes	洗衣房；洗衣服务
5.	fú wù 服务	*n.* service	酒店服务；服务很好
6.	sòng cān 送餐	*v.* deliver meals	送餐服务；酒店送餐

fáng kǎ
7. 房卡 *n.* room card 一张房卡;酒店房卡

rù zhù
8. 入住 *v.* check-in 入住酒店;入住手续

yú kuài
9. 愉快 *adj.* pleased; happy 祝你入住愉快

课文(二) 办理宾馆入住
Text B Hotel check in

陈龙前往预订好的商务酒店并办理入住手续。

Chen Long went to the business hotel reserved and checked-in.

Jiǔ diàn yuán gōng Xiān sheng wǎn shàng hǎo Qǐng wèn nín yǒu yù dìng ma
酒店员工:先生,晚上好!请问您有预订吗?

Chén Lóng Wǎn shàng hǎo Wǒ yù dìng le Wǒ shì Chén Lóng Zhè shì wǒ de shēn fèn zhèng hé Dà wèi de hù zhào
陈龙:晚上好!我预订了。我是陈龙。这是我的身份证和大卫的护照。

Jiǔ diàn yuán gōng Nín yù dìng le liǎng jiān shāng wù fáng duì ba
酒店员工:您预订了两间商务房,对吧?

Chén Lóng Duì de Wǒ men yào liǎng jiān ān jìng de shāng wù fáng
陈龙:对的。我们要两间安静的商务房。

Jiǔ diàn yuán gōng Kě yǐ Qǐng děng yí xià
酒店员工:可以。请等一下!

Chén Lóng Nǐ men yǒu xǐ yī fú wù ma
陈龙:你们有洗衣服务吗?

Jiǔ diàn yuán gōng Yǒu de Zhè shì xǐ yī fú wù de lián xì diàn huà
酒店员工:有的。这是洗衣服务的联系电话。

Chén Lóng Hǎo de Nǐ men yě yǒu sòng cān fú wù ma
陈龙:好的。你们也有送餐服务吗?

Jiǔ diàn yuán gōng Yǒu de Wǒ men yǒu èr shí sì xiǎo shí sòng cān fú wù Zhè shì fáng kǎ Zhù nín rù zhù yú kuài
酒店员工:有的。我们有二十四小时送餐服务。这是房卡。祝您入住愉快!

Chén Lóng Xiè xie nín
陈龙:谢谢您!

根据课文(二)回答问题
Answer these questions according to the Text B

1. 陈龙在哪里?
2. 陈龙预订了几间商务房?

3. 陈龙和大卫需要哪些酒店服务？

语言点
Language points

1. 带+sb.+去

“带+sb.+去”表示某人带另一个人到一个地方。

“带+sb.+去” is used to express that someone takes another one to a place.

(1)你带我去酒店。

(2)昨天陈龙带我去银行了。

(3)我知道图书馆在哪里。我现在带你去。

2. 是来+purpose+的

“是来+purpose+的”表示某人来这里的目的是什么。疑问形式可以是“是来做什么的？”。

“是来+purpose+的” is used to express the purpose of someone coming to a place. And the interrogative sentence can be “是来做什么的？”.

(1)她是来学习汉语的。

(2)大卫是来开会的。

(3)我是来买面包的。

3. *v*.+的+*n*.

“*v*.+的+*n*.”表示跟某人行为有关的事或物。在此结构中，“*v*.+的”作为名词的修饰语。

“*v*.+的+*n*.” is used to express something which is related to someone’s action. “*v*.+的” is used as a modifier of the noun.

(1)我喜欢你做的菜。

(2)你买的书到了。

(3)这是他住的房间。

4. 看起来

“看起来”表示某人或某物从表面上看怎么样，可以是一种推测。

“看起来” is used to express how someone or something looks. It can be a certain kind of conjecture.

(1)她今天看起来很高兴。

(2)这件衣服看起来质量不错。

(3)这个房间看起来很舒服。

核心句 Key sentences

1. 我已经帮您预订了酒店。
2. 您是来参加商务会议的吗?
3. 我帮您办理手续。
4. 请问您有预订吗?
5. 你们有洗衣服务吗?
6. 你们有送餐服务吗?

综合练习 Comprehensive exercises

(一)熟读短语 Read the following phrases.

(1)帮您预订酒店　帮您买东西　帮您拿东西　帮我买票　帮他开门

(2)带您去酒店　带朋友去超市　带他去图书馆　带我去

(3)看起来很不错　看起来真不错　看起来很好吃　看起来很好

(4)预订酒店　预订房间　预订机票　预订餐厅　预订车票

(5)参加会议　参加活动　参加培训　参加比赛　参加运动会

(6)办理手续　办理入住　办理入学　办理签证(qiānzhèng, visa)　办理银行卡

(二)连词成句 Make correct sentences with the following words

1. 您　机票　我　买　帮

____

2. 吗　可以　去　图书馆　你　我　带

____

3. 大学　真　的　看起来　不错　你

____

4. 帮　吗　餐厅　可以　你　预订　我

____

5. 去　下周　参加　要　我　会议

____

(三)替换练习 Substitution drills

1. 我已经帮您预订了<u>酒店</u>。

房间

机票

门票

2. 我开车带您去酒店。

   超市

   机场(jīchǎng, airport)

   西湖

3. 请给我护照!

   身份证

   学生证

   房卡

4. 我预订了酒店。

   商务房

   餐厅

   门票

5. 请等一下!

   让

   听

   说

6. 您们有洗衣服务吗?

   送餐

   接机(jiējī, pick up)

   充电(chōngdiàn, charge up the battery)

(四)完成对话 Complete the following dialogues

1. A: 我开车带您去_________。您是来参加_________吗?(会议中心、商务)

   B: 是的,谢谢您!

2. A: 大卫,您住的_______________。(到了)

   B: 看起来_____________。(不错)

3. A: 你们有_________吗?(送餐)

   B: 有的,我们有 24 小时_________。这是_________。(电话)

(五)课堂活动 In-class activities

1. 看图说话 Talk about the pictures

   根据每张图片说出简短的句子。Make brief sentences according to each picture.

2. 角色扮演 Role-play

你去商务酒店办理入住时,和一位酒店员工进行交谈。请尽量使用所给的词语或句型。You talk with a hotel staff when you go to the business hotel reserved and check-in. Please try to use the given words or phrases as many as possible.

已经　预订　带　办理　手续　需要　护照　有……服务　房卡

(六)课后作业 After-class exercises

采访3个人,简单记录他们最近入住酒店的基本情况。在下节课介绍给同学们。Please interview three people and write down some basic information about living in hotels recently. Try to introduce the information to your classmates in your next class.

序号	姓名	他/她的职业(profession)	他/她到哪个城市住酒店
例	大卫	商人	他到杭州住商务酒店
1			
2			
3			

课文翻译 Translation of texts

Text A　Arrange accommodation for a friend

Zhang Li: Hello, David! I have already booked a business hotel for you.

David: That's great! Thank you!

Zhang Li: I'll drive you to the hotel. Are you here for business meeting?

David: Yes, sorry to trouble you.

15 minutes later.

Zhang Li: David, we've arrived at the hotel.

David: It looks pretty good.

Zhang Li: May I have your passport please? I'll help you check-in.

David: OK! Thank you!

Text B　Hotel Check-in

Hotel staff :Good evening,Sir! Do you have a reservation?

Chen Long: Good evening! Yes, I do. My name is Chen Long and here is my ID card and David's passport.

Hotel staff: You booked two business rooms, right?

Chen Long: Yes, we would like two quite rooms please.

Hotel staff: OK, please wait a moment!

Chen Long: Do you have laundry service?

Hotel staff: Yes, here is the contact number.

Chen Long: Do you have room service as well?

Hotel staff: Yes, our room service is available 24 hours. Here are your room cards. Enjoy your stay!

Chen Long: Thank you!

12 每天都有好多工作
There is much work to do every day

话题导学 Guidance

1. 你最近忙吗？
   Are you busy recently?
2. 毕业以后你有什么打算？
   What's your plan after graduation?
3. 你做过什么工作？
   What kind of job have you done before?

生词学习(一) New words I

1. 忙 (máng) *adj.* busy　　很忙；太忙了
2. 挺 (tǐng) *adv.* very　　挺好(的)；挺贵的
3. 上班 (shàngbān) *v.* go to work　　9点上班；上班时间
4. 下班 (xiàbān) *v.* get off work　　6点下班；下班时间
5. 休息 (xiūxi) *v.* have a rest　　休息一天；休息日
6. 一定 (yídìng) *adv.* by all means, certainly　　一定去；不一定
7. 累 (lèi) *adj.* tired　　很累；太累了
8. 觉得 (juéde) *v.* think; feel　　觉得很贵；觉得不错
9. 生活 (shēnghuó) *n.* life　　好生活；在中国的生活
10. 有意思 (yǒu yìsi) *adj.* interesting; funny　　有意思；没意思

课文(一) 聚餐
Text A Dine together

马克和大卫是朋友,他们今天约在餐馆见面。

Mark and David are friends. They have an appointment today in a restaurant.

Mǎ kè Dà wèi hǎo jiǔ bú jiàn Zuì jìn máng bu máng
马克:大卫,好久不见!最近忙不忙?

Dà wèi Tǐng máng de Měi tiān dōu yǒu hǎo duō gōng zuò
大卫:挺忙的。每天都有好多工作。

Mǎ kè Tīng shuō nǐ huàn gōng zuò le Nǐ xiàn zài zài nǎ li gōng zuò
马克:听说你换工作了。你现在在哪里工作?

Dà wèi Xiàn zài wǒ zài yì jiā wài mào gōng sī gōng zuò Cóng xīng qī yī dào xīng qī wǔ měi tiān zǎo shang jiǔ diǎn shàng bān wǎn shang liù diǎn xià bān
大卫:现在我在一家外贸公司工作。从星期一到星期五,每天早上九点上班,晚上六点下班。

Mǎ kè Zhōu mò xiū xi ma
马克:周末休息吗?

Dà wèi Bù yí dìng yǒu shí hou zhōu mò hái yào jiā bān
大卫:不一定,有时候周末还要加班。

Mǎ kè Tīng qǐ lai nǐ de gōng zuò tǐng lèi de
马克:听起来你的工作挺累的。

Dà wèi Shì a Bú guò wǒ hěn xǐ huān zhè fèn gōng zuò wǒ jué de zhè yàng de shēng huó hěn yǒu yì si
大卫:是啊。不过我很喜欢这份工作,我觉得这样的生活很有意思。

根据课文(一)回答问题
Answer these questions according to the Text A

1. 大卫最近忙不忙?
2. 大卫现在在哪里工作?他的工作怎么样?
3. 大卫觉得他的生活怎么样?

生词学习(二)
New words II

kuài yào le
1. 快(要)……了 It will... soon 快(要)热死了;快(要)忙死了

zhǎo
2. 找 *v.* look for 找工作;找谁

guǎn lǐ
3. 管 理 *v.* administrate 管理公司;管理专业

fāngmiàn
4. 方 面 *n.* aspect 一方面;这个方面

jīngyàn
5. 经验 *n.* (knowledge of)experience 有经验;工作经验

xué qī
6. 学期 *n.* term; semester 这个学期;一个学期

fēng fù
7. 丰富 *adj.* abundant 经验丰富;丰富的生活

néng
8. 能 *aux.* can; be able to 能说汉语;不能

课文(二) 毕业后的打算
Text B Chat about the plan after graduation

Mǎ kè Ān nà kuàiyào bì yè le nǐ yǒu shén me dǎ suan
马克:安娜,快要毕业了,你有什么打算?

Ān nà Wǒ dǎ suan bì yè yǐ hòu zài Zhōngguó gōngzuò
安娜:我打算毕业以后在中国工作。

Mǎ kè Nǐ xiǎng zhǎo shén me yàng de gōngzuò ne
马克:你想找什么样的工作呢?

Ān nà Wǒ de zhuān yè shì jiǔ diànguǎn lǐ wǒ xiǎng zhǎo zhè fāngmiàn de gōngzuò
安娜:我的专业是酒店管理,我想找这方面的工作。

Mǎ kè Nǐ yǒu zhè fāngmiàn de gōngzuò jīngyàn ma
马克:你有这方面的工作经验吗?

Ān nà Lái Zhōngguó yǐ qián wǒ zài yì jiā jiǔ diàn gōngzuò le liǎngnián Zhè ge xué qī wǒ hái zài xuéxiào fù jìn de jiǔ diàn shí xí le bànnián
安娜:来中国以前,我在一家酒店工作了两年。这个学期我还在学校附近的酒店实习了半年。

Mǎ kè Tīng qǐ lai nǐ de gōngzuò jīngyàn tǐng fēng fù de Xī wàng nǐ néng zhǎo dào yí fèn hǎo gōngzuò
马克:听起来你的工作经验挺丰富的。希望你能找到一份好工作。

Ān nà Xiè xie
安娜:谢谢!

根据课文(二)回答问题
Answer these questions according to the Text B

1. 安娜的专业是什么?
2. 安娜想找什么样的工作?
3. 安娜有哪些工作经验?

语言点
Language points

1. *adj*. + 不 + *adj*.

"*adj*. + 不 + *adj*."是正反问句,意思相当于"*adj*. + 吗"。

In Chinese, "*adj*. + 不 + *adj*." can be used to form interrogative sentences.

(1)那儿的东西贵不贵?(=那儿的东西贵吗?)

(2)北京的冬天冷不冷?(=北京的冬天冷吗?)

注意:正反问句的句尾不用"吗"。When using this form of inquiry, "吗" is excluded.

2. 挺 + *adj*. + 的

表示程度比较高,相当于"很",常跟"的"一起使用。

"挺 + *adj*. + 的" indicates that the adjective is to a rather high degree; this structure is of an equivalence to structure of "很 + *adj*.". It is often used with "的" after the adjective.

(1)学校商店的东西挺贵的。

(2)杭州的冬天挺冷的。

3. 好 + *adj*.

"好 + *adj*."表示程度高,在感叹句中常和"啊"连用,含有感叹语气。

"好 + *adj*." indicates a high degree, often used with "啊" to express exclamatory mood in an exclamatory sentence.

(1)今天的作业好多。

(2)很多留学生觉得汉字好难。

(3)西湖好漂亮啊!

(4)北京的冬天好冷啊!

4. 快(要)……了/要……了

这两个结构都用来表示事件或动作即将发生。区别在于,"要……了"之前可以加表示时间的词或短语修饰。

The two structures all indicate that an incident or an action is about to take place. The difference is that the structure "要……了" can be modified by a phrase which indicates time.

(1)快考试了,我要好好学习了。

(2)要毕业了,你打算做什么?

(3)下星期要放假(fàngjià, have a vacation)了,你打算做什么?

(4)快要到冬天了,我想去商店买衣服。

5. v.+了+时间+(O)

强调已完成动作持续的时间。

This expression is used to emphasize how long an action has lasted.

(1)我学了十年(英语)。

(2)他看了两个小时(电视)。

(3)玛丽在图书馆看了三个小时书。

6. 能愿动词"能"

"能"表示有能力或有可能做某事。

"能" indicates being capable of doing something, or has the possibility to do something.

(1)你能和我一起去吗?

(2)大卫今天不能来上课。

(3)我能说汉语。

核心句 Key sentences

1. 最近忙不忙?
2. 每天都有好多工作。
3. 听起来你的工作挺累的。
4. 快要毕业了。
5. 你有什么打算?
6. 我打算毕业以后在中国工作。
7. 我在一家酒店工作了两年。

综合练习 Comprehensive exercises

(一)熟读短语 Read following phrases

(1)忙不忙　对不对　行不行　好(看)不好看　去不去　喜(欢)不喜欢

(2)挺忙的　挺好的　挺漂亮的　挺贵的　挺便宜的　挺不错的

(3)一定去　一定喜欢　一定很忙　不一定便宜　不一定会去

(4)快毕业了　快上课了　快要考试了　快要迟到了　要回国了

(5)工作了两年　实习了半年　做了两个小时作业　加了一天班　睡了七个小时

(二)替换练习 Substitution drills

1. 每天都有好多工作。

每课　有听写

每周　加班

每年　回家

2. 我　在外贸公司工作。

大卫　图书馆看书

玛丽　超市买东西

王龙　酒店实习

3. A:周末休息吗？　B:不一定,有时候周末还要加班。

每天出去运动　　天气不好就不出去

冬天下雪(xuě, snow)　　不下雪

每天都学习　　和朋友出去玩儿

4. 我　打算毕业以后在中国工作。

玛丽　周末去看电影

我们　下星期去北京旅游

大卫　最近换工作

5. 安娜在一家酒店　工作了两年。

玛丽　工商大学　学习了三年汉语

安娜　图书馆　看了两个小时书

经理　北京　参观(cānguān, visit)了两个星期

(三)改写句子 Rewrite the following sentences with the given words

1. 最近杭州的天气很热。(挺……的)

____

2. 我们打算周末去爬山,你忙吗?一起去吧!(*v.* + 不 + *v.*)

____

3. 工作了一天,真累啊!(好 + *adj.*)

____

(四)完成对话 Complete the following dialogues

1. A:玛丽,好久不见!____________?(*adj.* + 不 + *adj.*)

B:挺忙的。快要考试了,____________。(好好儿)

A:考试以后____________?(打算)

B:我打算____________。

2. A:你在哪里学习/工作?

B:____________。(公司/学校)

A:学习/工作累不累?

B:____________,不过____________。

3. A:你学习什么专业?/你做什么工作?

B:________________________________。

A:你学习/工作了多长时间?

B:________________________________。

(五)课堂活动 In-class activity

1. 看图说话 Talk about the pictures.

看图说出简短的句子。Try to make brief sentences according to each picture.

2. 角色扮演 Role-play

根据下面的问题提示,和同伴进行角色扮演。Role play with your classmates according to the questions below.

(1)你最近忙吗?

(2)你在哪里学习?

(3)你觉得汉语有意思吗?

(4)你已经学习了多长时间汉语?

(5)毕业以后你有什么打算?

(六)课后作业 After-class exercises

联系三位朋友,问问他们的学习或工作情况。Make a contact with your three friends on their study or work.

	在哪里学习/工作	上课/上班时间	周末干什么	其他
朋友1				
朋友2				
朋友3				

课文翻译 Translation of texts

Text A　Dine together

Mark：David, long time no see. Are you busy recently?

David：Very busy. I have a lot of work every day.

Mark：I heard that you changed job. Where are you working now?

David：Now I'm working in a foreign trade company. I work Monday to Friday, from 9 a.m. to 6 p.m.

Mark：Do you have the weekend off?

David：Not always. Sometimes I need work overtime on the weekend.

Mark：It sounds that your job is very tiring.

David：Yes, it is. But I like the job. I think my life (style) is very interesting.

Text B　Chat about plans after graduation

Mark：Anna, graduation is coming soon. What are your plans?

Anna：I plan to work in China after graduation.

Mark：What kind of work do you want to do?

Anna：My major is Hotel Administration. I want to find a job related to this.

Mark：Do you have any work experience about this?

Anna：Before coming to China, I worked in a hotel for two years. Also, this semester I did internship in a hotel near our school for half a year.

Mark：It sounds you have abundant work experience. I hope you can find a good job.

Anna：Thank you!

13 假期安排
Holiday arrangement

话题导学 Guidance

1. 你喜欢暑假吗?
   Do you like summer holiday?
2. 你们学校一般什么时候放暑假?
   When does the summer holiday start in your college generally?
3. 暑假你常常做什么?
   What do you often do in summer holiday?

生词学习(一) New words I

1. 得 (de) *part.* —— 走得快;学得好
2. 又 (yòu) *adv.* again —— 又下雨了;又吃
3. 结束 (jié shù) *v.* finish; come to the end —— 学期结束;结束工作
4. 放假 (fàng jià) *v.* have a holiday —— 下周放假;放假以后
5. 晚 (wǎn) *adj.* late —— 太晚了;很晚
6. 暑假 (shǔ jià) *n.* summer holiday —— 放暑假;暑假结束
7. 长 (cháng) *adj.* long —— 时间很长;路很长
8. 好好儿 (hǎo hāor) *adv.* to one's heart content;all out —— 好好(儿)玩儿
9. 假期 (jià qī) *n.* holiday; vacation —— 假期很长;假期的安排

课文(一) 暑假计划
Text A Talk about summer holiday

玛丽和安娜是不同学校的学生。

Mary and Anna are students from different schools.

Mǎ lì Shí jiān guò de zhēn kuài Yì xué qī yòu yào jié shù le
玛丽：时间过得真快！一学期又要结束了。

Ān nà Shì a Nǐ men xué xiào shén me shí hou fàng jià
安娜：是啊。你们学校什么时候放假？

Mǎ lì Wǒ men xué xiào xià zhōu jiù fàng jià le Nǐ men xué xiào ne
玛丽：我们学校下周就放假了。你们学校呢？

Ān nà Wǒ men xué xiào wǎn yì diǎnr liù yuè èr shí wǔ hào kāi shǐ fàng jià
安娜：我们学校晚一点儿，六月二十五号开始放假。

Mǎ lì Shǔ jià shí jiān hěn cháng wǒ dǎ suan hǎo haor wán wánr Nǐ yǒu shén me ān pái
玛丽：暑假时间很长，我打算好好儿玩玩儿。你有什么安排？

Ān nà Wǒ kuài yào bì yè le Wǒ dǎ suan zhǎo yí fèn gōng zuò
安娜：我快要毕业了。我打算找一份工作。

Mǎ lì Zhù nǐ zhǎo dào yí fèn hǎo gōng zuò
玛丽：祝你找到一份好工作！

Ān nà Xiè xie Zhù nǐ jià qī yú kuài
安娜：谢谢！祝你假期愉快！

根据课文(一)回答问题
Answer these questions according to the Text A

1. 玛丽的学校什么时候放假？
2. 玛丽暑假打算做什么？
3. 安娜暑假有什么安排？

生词学习(二)
New words II

guó qìng
1. 国庆 *n.* National Day 国庆节；国庆假期

zhǔ yi
2. 主意 *n.* idea 好主意；一个主意

lǚ yóu
3. 旅游 *v.* travel 去北京旅游；喜欢旅游

liǎo jiě
4. 了解 *v.* know; understand 了解中国；不了解他

huǒ chē
5. 火车 *n.* train 坐火车;火车票

gāo tiě
6. 高铁 *n.* high-speed railway 坐高铁;高铁站

fēng jǐng
7. 风景 *n.* scenery 风景很好;漂亮的风景

yī jiù
8. 一……就…… as soon as, then... 一放假就去玩儿

chū fā
9. 出发 *v.* start off 几点出发;明天出发

课文(二) 国庆假期安排
Text B Arrangement in the National Day holiday

大卫和陈龙是同事。

David and Chen Long are colleagues.

Dà wèi Chén Lóng guó qìng jià qī kuài dào le nǐ yǒu shén me ān pái ma
大卫:陈龙,国庆假期快到了,你有什么安排吗?

Chén Lóng Wǒ hái méi xiǎng hǎo ne Zuì jìn gōng zuò tài máng le Nǐ yǒu shén me hǎo zhǔ yi ma
陈龙:我还没想好呢。最近工作太忙了。你有什么好主意吗?

Dà wèi Wǒ dǎ suan qù Běi jīng lǚ yóu Wǒ men yì qǐ qù zěn me yàng
大卫:我打算去北京旅游。我们一起去,怎么样?

Chén Lóng Hǎo a Wǒ zhèng xiǎng liǎo jiě yí xià Běi jīng de shì chǎng qù wán wanr kàn kan
陈龙:好啊。我正想了解一下北京的市场,去玩玩儿,看看。

Dà wèi Wǒ men zuò huǒ chē qù hái shi zuò fēi jī qù ne
大卫:我们坐火车去还是坐飞机去呢?

Chén Lóng Zuò gāo tiě qù ba Cóng Háng zhōu dào Běi jīng dà gài liù ge xiǎo shí jiù néng dào hěn fāng biàn hái néng zài chē shang kàn fēng jǐng
陈龙:坐高铁去吧。从杭州到北京大概六个小时就能到,很方便,还能在车上看风景。

Dà wèi Duì Nà wǒ xiàn zài jiù qù wǎng shang mǎi chē piào Wǒ men yí fàng jià jiù chū fā
大卫:对。那我现在就去网上买车票。我们一放假就出发。

根据课文(二)回答问题
Answer these questions according to the Text B

1. 大卫假期有什么安排?
2. 大卫和同事陈龙打算怎么去北京?
3. 大卫在哪里买车票?

语言点
Language points

1. *v*.＋得＋程度补语

一般用形容词短语作动词的补语,表示动作的状态或程度。如果宾语和程度补语同时出现,动词需重复使用。

In this structure, the complement often is an adjective phrase to indicate the state or degree of the verb. If an object and the complement of degree appear together in a sentence, the verb should be used repeatedly.

(1)他写汉字写得非常好。

(2)玛丽(看书)看得很快。

(3)他做得不错。

2. 又

"又"表示重复,一般用于已发生的事情。

"又" indicates repetition, usually of events that have already occurred previously.

(1)大卫今天又迟到了。

(2)今天又下雨了。

(3)他昨天没来,今天又没来。

3. "什么"in"吗"question sentence

"什么"在有"吗"的疑问句中表示"任何,一些",并不是疑问代词。

The pattern is not an interrogative pronoun, but indicates "any, some".

(1)你有什么想吃的吗?

(2)你要买点儿什么吗?

4. 时段＋就＋*v*.

"时段＋就＋*v*."强调动作在很短的时间内完成或发生。

"time segment + 就 + *v*." emphasizes an event which has occurred within a very short time interval.

(1)那儿不太远,一个小时就能到。

(2)今天的作业不多,十几分钟就做完了。

5. 一……就……

"一……就……"表示后一个动作紧接着前一个动作发生。

"一……就……" indicates that the second action occurs immediately after the first action.

(1)他每天一回家就做作业。

(2)我们一到周末就去看电影。

(3)一结束工作我们就去打篮球。

核心句 Key sentences

(1)我们学校下周就放假了。

(2)我打算好好儿玩玩儿。

(3)你有什么安排?

(4)你有什么好主意吗?

(5)我正想了解一下北京的市场。

(6)我们坐火车去还是坐飞机去呢?

(7)我们一放假就出发。

综合练习 Comprehensive exercises

(一)熟读短语 Read following phrases

(1)走得快　篮球打得好　汉字写得漂亮　汉语学得不错　雨下得很大　汉语说得很好

(2)又到周末了　又下雨了　又迟到了　又病了　一学期又结束了

(3)喝一点儿果汁　吃一点儿米饭　晚一点儿　大一点儿　好看一点儿

(4)了解市场　了解问题　了解公司　了解中国文化

(5)汉语书还是英语书　蓝的还是红的　今天去还是明天去　去上海还是去北京　看电影还是听音乐

(二)替换练习 Substitution drills

1. A:你们学校什么时候放假?　B:6月25号放假。

电影	开始	晚上7:30开始
汉语	考试	下周一考试
你们	出发	明天出发

2. 我打算好好玩玩儿。

休息

了解

准备

3. 我想了解一下北京的市场。

试　　这件衣服

去　　卫生间

听　　这首歌

4. 我　去网上买车票。

大卫　图书馆看书

玛丽　超市买东西

我们　北京旅游

5. 我们一放假就　出发。

大卫　回家　　看电视

他们　到周末　出去玩儿

我　　放假　　回家

(三)选词填空 Choose a suitable word for each sentence

了解　就　又　晚　好好　结束　再

(1)小李今天上班________迟到了。

(2)考试终于________了,我们可以________休息了。

(3)大卫明天要去北京出差,今天晚上他很早________睡了。

(4)________了问题以后,我们就要________解决(jiě jué,solve)问题。

(5)我们来________了,商店已经关门了,明天________来吧。

(四)完成对话 Complete the following dialogues

(1) A:____________________________?(什么时候)

B:暑假7月1号开始。

A:____________________________?(安排)

B:暑假我打算找份工作。你呢?

A:____________________________。(打算)

B:祝你假期愉快!

(2)A:大卫,你在中国生活得怎么样?

B:____________________________。(觉得)

A:周末你都干什么?

B:____________________________。($v. + v.$)

(3)A:玛丽,下班以后一起去吃饭,______________?(怎么样)

B:好啊。

A:____________________________________?(还是)

B:我喜欢吃中国菜。

(五)课堂活动 In-class activity

1. 看图说话 Talk about the pictures

根据每张图片说出简短的句子。Make brief sentences according to each picture.

2. 角色扮演 Role-play

根据提示词语，仿照课文说说你的暑假安排。Talk about your arrangement in summer holiday according to following words.

暑假　放假　主意　安排　打算　怎么样

(六)课后作业 After-class exercises

试着规划一下你未来五年的生活。Try to make a plan for your life in the next five years.

课文翻译 Translation of texts

Text A　Plans for summer vacation

Mary：Time goes so fast！A semester is coming to the end again.

Anna：Yeah. When does your school have summer holiday?

Mary：We start from next week. What about yours?

Anna：Our school will be a little late. We start from June 25th.

Mary：Summer holidays are very long. I plan to have a really good time. What's your plan?

Anna：I will graduate soon. I want to find a job.

Mary：Hope you will find a good job.

Anna：Thank you！Have a good holiday！

Text B　Arrangement in the National Day holiday

David：Chen Long，the National Day holiday is coming soon. Do you have any plans?

Chen Long：I have no idea yet. I'm too busy recently. Do you have any (good) ideas?

David：I plan to travel to Beijing. Do you want to go there together?

Chen Long：OK. I want to get to know the market in Beijing and also have some fun.

David：Shall we take a train or plane?

Chen Long：Let's take the high-speed railway. It only takes about 6 hours from Hangzhou to Beijing. It's very convenient and we can also see the scenery on the way.

David：You're right. Then I will buy the tickets online right now. We will set off as soon as the holiday starts.

14 你租的房子怎么样
How is the apartment you rent?

话题导学 Guidance

1. 你住在哪儿?
   Where do you live now?
2. 你租房子住吗?
   Do you rent a house?
3. 你想租一个什么样的房子?
   What kind of house or apartment do you want to rent?

生词学习(一) New words I

1. 租 zū *v.* rent　　租房子;租车子
2. 房子 fáng zi *n.* house　　我的房子;大房子
3. 远 yuǎn *adj.* distant; far　　很远;太远了;真远
4. 比较 bǐ jiào *adv.* relatively　　比较好;比较远;比较贵
5. 间 jiān *mw.* after a numeral word to modify rooms(bedroom, living room, etc.)　　一间卧室;一间教室
6. 房间 fáng jiān *n.* room; apartment　　一个房间;我的房间
7. 客厅 kè tīng *n.* living room　　一个客厅;大客厅
8. 卧室 wò shì *n.* bedroom　　两间卧室;谁的卧室
9. 厨房 chú fáng *n.* kitchen　　大厨房;去厨房;在厨房
10. 卫生间 wèi shēng jiān *n.* bathroom; toilet　　一个卫生间;最大的卫生间

yáng tái
11. 阳台 *n.* balcony　　一个很大的阳台；家里的阳台

fù jìn
12. 附近 *adj.* nearby　　学校附近；超市附近

gōngyuán
13. 公园 *n.* park　　国家公园；西湖公园

课文(一) 谈论公寓的房间
Text A Talk about rooms in the apartment

美玲现在租房子住，玛丽想知道美玲租的房子结构。

Meiling is renting an apartment, and Mary wants to konw the structure of it.

Mǎ lì Měi líng nǐ xiàn zài bú zhù zài xué xiào sù shè le ma
玛丽：美玲，你现在不住在学校宿舍了吗？

Měi Líng Shì de wǒ xiàn zài zì jǐ zū fáng zi zhù Xué xiào sù shè lí wǒ shí xí de gōng sī tài yuǎn le zhù zài wài miàn bǐ jiào fāng biàn
美玲：是的，我现在自己租房子住。学校宿舍离我实习的公司太远了，住在外面比较方便。

Mǎ lì Nǐ zū de fáng zi zěn me yàng Yǒu jǐ jiān fáng jiān
玛丽：你租的房子怎么样？有几间房间？

Měi Líng Zài shì zhōng xīn yǒu yì jiān kè tīng yì jiān wò shì yí gè chú fáng hé yí gè wèi shēng jiān hái yǒu yí gè yáng tái
美玲：在市中心，有一间客厅、一间卧室、一个厨房和一个卫生间，还有一个阳台。

Mǎ lì Mǎi dōng xi fāng biàn ma
玛丽：买东西方便吗？

Měi Líng Fù jìn yǒu gōng yuán hé chāo shì hěn fāng biàn
美玲：附近有公园和超市，很方便。

根据课文(一)回答问题
Answer these questions according to the Text A

1. 美玲现在住哪儿？
2. 美玲为什么租房子住？
3. 美玲租的房子怎么样？有哪些房间？
4. 买东西方便吗？

生词学习(二)
New words II

suǒ yǐ
1. 所以 *conj.* so; therefore　　所以不知道；所以没有来

duōshao
2. 多少 *pron.* how many; how much 多少人;多少钱;多少个

dàn shì
3. 但是 *conj.* but; however 但是没时间;但是不喜欢

lǐ
4. 里 *n.* inside 家里;房间里;超市里

diàn shì jī
5. 电视机 *n.* television 新的电视机;没有电视机

kōng tiáo
6. 空调 *n.* air conditioner 开空调;有空调的公共汽车

bīng xiāng
7. 冰箱 *n.* fridge 冰箱里;我的冰箱;买冰箱

xǐ yī jī
8. 洗衣机 *n.* washing machine 一台洗衣机;买洗衣机

huánjìng
9. 环境 *n.* environment 小区环境;环境很好;环境不好

mǎn yì
10. 满意 *adj.* be satisfied 很满意;不满意;挺满意的

gào sù
11. 告诉 *v.* tell 告诉我;不告诉你

课文(二) 公寓的设施与环境
Text B Talk about house facilities and environment

美玲现在租房子住,安娜明年也要租房子,她想知道美玲租的房子怎么样。

Meiling is renting an apartment, and Anna may need to rent a house next year, so she wants to know how about Meiling's apartment.

Ān nà Měi líng wǒ míng nián yào shí xí le kě néng yě yào zū fáng zi suǒ yǐ xiǎng wèn yi wèn nǐ xiàn zài zū de fáng zi duōshao qián yí ge yuè

安娜:美玲,我明年要实习了,可能也要租房子,所以想问一问,你现在租的房子多少钱一个月?

Měi Líng Sān qiān kuài qián yí ge yuè

美玲:三千块钱一个月。

Ān nà Hěn guì a

安娜:很贵啊。

Měi Líng Shì bù pián yi Dàn shì fáng zi zài shì zhōng xīn fáng jiān li yǒu diàn shì jī kōng tiáo bīng xiāng hé xǐ yī jī xiǎo qū huán jìng yě hěn hǎo suǒ yǐ wǒ hái shì tǐng mǎn yì de

美玲:是不便宜。但是房子在市中心,房间里有电视机、空调、冰箱和洗衣机,小区环境也很好,所以我还是挺满意的。

Ān nà Fù jìn yǒu dì tiě ma

安娜:附近有地铁吗?

Měi Líng Yǒu dì tiě yě yǒu gōng jiāo chē dào xué xiào hé gōng sī
美玲：有地铁，也有公交车到学校和公司。

Ān nà Rú guǒ zhè ge xiǎo qū hái yǒu hǎo de fáng zi nǐ kě yǐ gào sù wǒ ma
安娜：如果这个小区还有好的房子，你可以告诉我吗？

Měi Líng Méi wèn tí Zhè ge zhōu mò lái wǒ jiā wánr ba nǐ kě yǐ kàn yi kàn xiǎo qū de huán jìng
美玲：没问题。这个周末来我家玩儿吧，你可以看一看小区的环境！

Ān nà Hǎo a
安娜：好啊！

根据课文(二)回答问题
Answer these questions according to the Text B

1. 美玲租的房子多少钱一个月？
2. 美玲租的房间里有什么？
3. 小区环境好不好？
4. 小区的附近有地铁吗？

语言点
Language points

1. 比较 + *adj*.

"比较"用于形容词前，表示比较级。

The structure of "比较 + *adj*." is used to express the comparative degree.

(1)这件衣服比较贵，那件便宜一点儿。

(2)学校宿舍没有厨房，住在外面比较方便。

2. ……怎么样

疑问词"怎么样"置于句尾，用于询问某事或某人的情况。

"怎么样" is a question word, which is used at the end of the sentence to ask how something or someone is.

(1)今天天气怎么样？

(2)你租的房子怎么样？

(3)你最近怎么样？

3. 可能

"可能"作为助动词，表示"估计，不确定性"。

"可能"is an auxiliary verb to express the possibility. For example,

(1)我可能也要租房子。

(2)这个周末我可能没有空。

4. v. + 一 + v.

"v. + 一 + v."是动词重叠式的一种,用来表示动作进行的次数少、时间短或尝试。

"v. + 一 + v.", which is a kind of verb reduplication, is used to indicate a small amount of action, a short time, a light degree or try to do something.

(1)我想问一问,你现在租的房子多少钱一个月?

(2)我想看一看你的书。

5. 但是

"但是"是用于连接两个小句的连词,表示转折关系。可用于"虽然……但是……"结构。

"但是" is a conjunction to connect two clauses to express the adversative relation. It could also be used in the conjunction structure of "虽然……但是……".

(1)这个房子很好,但是房租太贵了。

(2)这个周末我想去你的学校玩儿,但是没有时间。

6. 所以

连词"所以"常用在下半句,表示因果关系。

"所以", as a conjunction word, is usually used at the begining of the second half of the sentence to indicate the causal effect.

(1)我明年要实习了,可能也要租房子,所以想问一问,你现在租的房子多少钱一个月?

(2)我没有学过汉语,所以不认识这个汉字。

核心句 Key sentences

1. 我现在自己租房子住。
2. 你租的房子怎么样?
3. 在市中心,有一间客厅、一间卧室、一个厨房和一个卫生间, 还有一个阳台。
4. 附近有公园和超市,很方便。
5. 你现在租的房子多少钱一个月?
6. 这个周末来我家玩儿吧,你可以看一看小区的环境!

综合练习
Comprehensive exercises

(一)熟读短语 Read the following phrases

1. 一间客厅　一间卧室　一个厨房　一个卫生间　一个阳台
2. 附近有公园　附近有超市　附近有餐厅　附近有地铁站
3. 问一问　看一看　学一学　打一打　唱一唱
4. 这个房子怎么样　你的学校怎么样　马克的汉语怎么样
5. 这个房子多少钱一个月　汉语书多少钱一本　咖啡多少钱一杯

(二)根据画线部分提问 Make a question according to the underlined part

1. 美玲租的房子有一间客厅、一间卧室、一个厨房和一个卫生间,还有一个阳台。

____

2. 学校宿舍离我实习的公司太远了。

____

3. 美玲租的房子附近有公园和超市,挺方便的。

____

4. 安娜明年要实习了,所以也要租房子。

____

(三)替换练习 Substitution drills

1. 你现在住的房子怎么样?
   玛丽的汉语
   我们去餐厅吃饭
2. 这个房子多少钱?
   这件大衣
   这个生日蛋糕
   一份西红柿炒鸡蛋
3. 这个房子不便宜,但是在市中心。
   我周末想去打篮球　没有时间
   我想去旅游　没有钱
4. 这个房子在市中心,所以我很满意。
   我在中国学习　会说汉语
   我喜欢游泳　我最喜欢夏天

(四)完成对话 Complete the following dialogues

1. A:你现在住在哪儿?
   B:______________________________。(租房子)

2. A：你打算租房子吗？

B：____。

3. 你租的房子有几个房间？

B：______________________________。(客厅、卧室、厨房、卫生间、阳台)

4. A：你的宿舍怎么样？

B：________________________________。(电视机、空调、冰箱、洗衣机)

5. A：你现在住的房子多少钱一个月？

B：____。

(五)课堂活动 In-class activities

1. 看图说话 Talk about the pictures

根据每张图片说出简单的句子。Make brief sentences according to each picture.

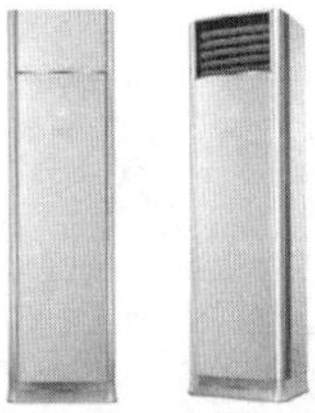

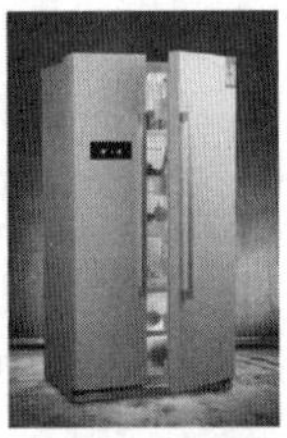

2. 根据图片,分组讨论租房子以及租的房子怎么样。Discuss the topic of renting a house and how the house is by groups.

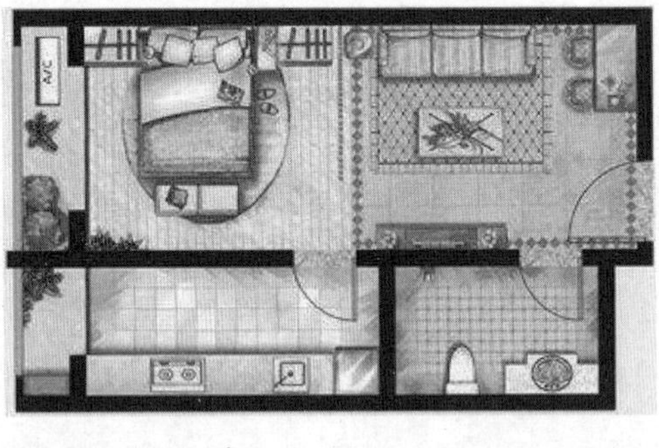

(六)课后练习 After-class exercises

请说一说你想租一个什么样的房子。Please try to describe what kind of house you want to rent.

课文翻译 Translation of the texts

Text A　Talk about rooms in the apartment

Mary: Meiling, Are you living out of school?

Meiling: Yes, I'm renting an apartment. The school dormitory is too far away from my internship company. It's more convenient to live outside.

Mary: How's your apartment you rent? How many rooms does it have?

Meiling: It's in the downtown. There are a living room, a bedroom, a kitchen, a bathroom and a balcony.

Mary: Is it convenient to buy things?

Meiling: There are public parks and supermarkets nearby. It's very convenient.

Text B　Talk about house facilities and environment

Anna: Meiling, I'm going to have an internship next year and will probably rent a house, so I would like to ask you how much you are paying for your current apartment each month.

Meiling: 3,000 *yuan* per month.

Anna: Quite expensive.

Meiling: Yeah, it's not cheap. However, the apartment is in the downtown. There are a television, air-conditioner, a fridge and a washing machine. What's more, the residential environment is also very nice. So I'm quite satisfied.

Anna: Is there a subway line nearby?

Meiling: Yes. There is a subway line and bus route to the school and my company.

Anna: If your community has any other apartments for rent, could you let me know?

Meiling: No problem. Come to my place and hang out this weekend. You can take a look at the environment of the residential area.

Anna: OK!

15 成绩出来了吗
Have the rest results come out?

话题导学 Guidance

1. 如果学习上有问题,你会去学院的办公室吗?
   Will you go to the school office if you've got any questions about your study?
2. 去办公室的时候,应该怎么和老师说比较有礼貌?
   What is a polite way to talk to the teachers in the school office?
3. 你知道你们学校几号放假吗?
   Do you know when this semester ends?

生词学习(一) New words I

1. dǎ rǎo 打扰 *v.* disturb; interrupt 打扰您了;打扰一下
2. xiào lì 校历 *n.* school calendar 新校历;查校历
3. kāi xué 开学 *v.* semester begins 几号开学;开学第一天
4. bào dào 报到 *v.* register 开学报到;来学校报到
5. kè biǎo 课表 *n.* class schedule 新的课表;下学期课表
6. chū lái 出来 *v.* come out; appear 课表出来了;成绩出来了
7. bié 别 *v.* don't; had better not 别担心;别去
8. jí 急 *adj.* anxious; impatient 别急;很急
9. tōng zhī 通知 *v./n.* inform;notice 等通知;通知同学

课文(一)　询问课程安排
Text A　Ask about the course arrangement

Mǎ lì　Mǎ lǎo shī　nín hǎo　dǎ rǎo le
玛丽：马老师，您好，打扰了！
Mǎ lǎo shī　Mǎ lì　nǐ hǎo　yǒu shén me shì ma
马老师：玛丽你好，有什么事吗？
Mǎ lì　Qǐng wèn　wǒ men shén me shí hòu fàng jià
玛丽：请问，我们什么时候放假？
Mǎ lǎo shī　Liù yuè èr shí wǔ hào fàng jià　Nǐ kàn　zhè shì xiào lì
马老师：六月二十五号放假。你看，这是校历。
Mǎ lì　Xiè xie　Nà xīn xué qī　jǐ hào kāi xué
玛丽：谢谢！那新学期几号开学？
Mǎ lǎo shī　Jiǔ yuè bā hào kāi xué　xué shēng bào dào
马老师：九月八号开学，学生报到。
Mǎ lì　Hǎo de lǎo shī　Xīn xué qī　de kè biǎo chū lái le ma
玛丽：好的老师。新学期的课表出来了吗？
Mǎ lǎo shī　Bié jí　kuài chū lái le　qǐng děng tōng zhī
马老师：别急，快出来了，请等通知。
Mǎ lì　Xiè xie nín　Mǎ lǎo shī
玛丽：谢谢您，马老师。
Mǎ lǎo shī　Wǒ gěi nǐ　yì zhāng xīn xué qī　de xiào lì
马老师：我给你一张新学期的校历。

根据课文(一)回答问题
Answer these questions according to the Text A

1. 玛丽想问老师什么问题？
2. 学校几月放假，几月开学？
3. 现在可以看新学期的课表了吗？

生词学习(二)
New words II

1. chéng jì 成绩	*n.* result; mark	学习成绩；成绩出来了
2. dà bù fèn 大部分	*n.* most part	大部分同学；大部分时间
3. mén 门	*mw.* measure word for course	一门课；几门课
4. chá 查	*v.* check	查成绩；查机票

fēn
5. 分 *n.* score; grade　　90分;多少分

xià cì
6. 下次 *n.* next time　　下次去;下次努力

jiā yóu
7. 加油 *v.* cheer sb. on; make more efforts　　学习加油;工作加油

nǔ lì
8. 努力 *v.* make efforts; try hard　　努力学;努力做

课文(二) 去办公室问成绩
Text B Ask about the test results in the school office

Mǎ lì　Nín hǎo　Mǎ lǎo shī　dǎ rǎo yí xià
玛丽:您好,马老师,打扰一下!

Mǎ lǎo shī　Nǐ hǎo ā　Mǎ lì
马老师:你好啊,玛丽。

Mǎ lì　Qǐng wèn yí xià　chéng jì chū lái le ma
玛丽:请问一下,成绩出来了吗?

Mǎ lǎo shī　Dà bù fèn chū lái le　zhǐ yǒu liǎng mén kè de chéng jì hái méi yǒu
马老师:大部分出来了,只有两门课的成绩还没有。

Mǎ lì　Wǒ kě yǐ xiān chá yí xià ma
玛丽:我可以先查一下吗?

Mǎ lǎo shī　Kě yǐ　qǐng nǐ děng yí xià
马老师:可以,请你等一下。

Mǎ lì　Xiè xie　Ā　bā shí fēn　bā shí èr fēn　bú tài hǎo
玛丽:谢谢……啊,八十分,八十二分,不太好。

Mǎ lǎo shī　Yǒu de hái hǎo　yǒu de bú tài hǎo　xià cì　jiā yóu ba
马老师:有的还好,有的不太好,下次加油吧!

Mǎ lì　Xiè xie Mǎ lǎo shī　wǒ yào nǔ lì
玛丽:谢谢马老师,我要努力!

根据课文(二)回答问题
Answer these questions according to the Text B

1. 玛丽去办公室问什么?
2. 玛丽的成绩都出来了吗?
3. 玛丽的成绩好吗?她高兴吗?

语言点
Language points

1. 别 + *v*.

“别”加动词，表示禁止或劝阻，意思同“不要”。另外，“别 + *v*. + 了”则强调劝阻别人停止正在做的事情。

“别” is used before a verb, which means giving commands or advice to other people. The meaning is the same as “不要”. Also, the phrase “别 + *v*. + 了” emphasizes the meaning of dissuading other people from doing something.

(1)晚上别吃太多东西。

(2)考试的时候，别看手机。

(3)别看了，我们出去走走吧。

2. 量词“张”“门”

量词“张”可用于不同的事物，在本课，它用于描述纸、照片等。量词“门”也可用于不同事物，在本课中用于描述功课、技术等。

As a measure word, “张” can be used to describe different items. It means a piece of paper, photo, etc. in this lesson. Measure word “门” also has different meanings, and it is used in the field of study or technical training in the lesson.

(1)一张纸　一张照片

(2)一门课　一门语言　一门技术(jìshu, technology)

核心句
Key sentences

1. 打扰了！/ 打扰一下！
2. 我们什么时候放假？
3. 新学期几号开学？
4. 课表出来了吗？/ 成绩出来了吗？
5. 别急，请等通知。
6. 我可以先查一下吗？
7. 下次加油吧！

综合练习
Comprehensive exercises

(一)熟读短语 Read the following phrases

1. 打扰了　打扰你　打扰他学习　打扰我工作
2. 等通知　等结果　等成绩　等他来　等车子
3. 查成绩　查结果　查生词　查地图　查号码　查一下
4. 不太好　不太冷　不太多　不太喜欢　不太想去
5. 下次加油　下次努力　下次再来　下次再见

(二)词语填空 Choose a suitable word for each sentence

别　打扰　课表　通知　报到

1. 新学期的_________出来了吗?
2. 我们几号放假,老师_________了吗?
3. 请问,我们应该几号到学校_________?
4. 老师,_________一下,我有一个问题。
5. _________急,请等通知。

成绩　门　查　加油　下次

1. 这个学期我有五_________课。
2. 中文课的成绩不太好,我要_________。
3. 我想_________一下什么时候开学。
4. 老师,我的_________怎么样?
5. 今天老师不在,请你_________再来吧。

(三)替换练习 Substitution drills

1. 请问,我们什么时候放假?

　　开学
　　上课
　　开会

2. 新学期的课表出来了吗?

　　考试的成绩
　　面试的时间
　　开会的安排

3. 别急,快出来了。

　　开始
　　下课
　　开门

4. 大部分出来了，只有两门课的成绩还没有。

认识了　　三个字不认识

喜欢　　　辣(là, spicy)的菜不喜欢

同学来了　一个人没来

5. 有的还好，有的不太好。

高兴　　不高兴

懂　　　不懂

贵　　　便宜

(四)完成对话 Complete the following dialogues

1. A:您好，老师，________________！

B:你好，请问有什么事吗？

2. A:请问，我们几号报到？

B:我看一下校历，____________报到。(月、号)

3. A:请问，新的课表______________________吗？

B:还没出来，请等一等。

4. A:老师，我的成绩怎么样？

B:有的_________________，有的_____________________。(不太)

5. A:大卫，我的成绩不太好。

B:别急，_______________________吧！我帮你。(try to encourage others)

(五)课堂活动 In-class exercises

1. 看图说话 Talk about the pictures

根据每张图片说出简单的句子。Make brief sentences according each to picture.

周次	星期						
	一	二	三	四	五	六	日
一	2月20日 上课	21	22	23	24	25	26
二	27	28	3月1日	2	3	4	5
三	6	7	8	9	10	11	12
四	13	14	15	16	17	18	19
五	20	21	22	23	24	25	26
六	27	28	29	30	31	4月1日	2
七	3	4 清明节	5	6	7	8	9
八	10	11	12	13	14	15	16
九	17	18	19	20	21	22	23
十	24	25	26	27	28	29	30
十一	5月1日 劳动节	2	3	4	5	6	7
十二	8	9	10	11	12	13	14
十三	15	16	17	18	19	20	21
十四	22	23	24	25	26	27	28
十五	29	30 端午节	31	6月1日	2	3	4
十六	5	6	7	8	9	10	11
十七	12	13	14	15	16	17	18
十八	19	20	21	22	23	24	25
十九	26	27	28	29	30	7月1日	2
二十	3	4	5	6	7	8 放假	9

2. 角色扮演 Role-play

一位学生去办公室询问上课安排或考试成绩。A student goes to the school office to ask about the course arrangement or the test results.

打扰　开学　校历　通知　门　查　努力

(六)课后练习 After-class exercises

跟办公室或其他同学了解一下学校的安排,并做简单记录。Try to get the information of semester arrangement of other schools and record it.

序号	事项(arrangement)	日期(date)
1	开始考试	月　　日
2	开始放假	月　　日
3	新学期开学	月　　日
4	新学期放假	月　　日

课文翻译 Translation of texts

Text A Ask about the course arrangement

Mary：Hello, Mr. Ma! I'm sorry to interrupt you.

Mr. Ma：Hi, Mary. How can I help you?

Mary：May I ask, when will the holiday start?

Mr. Ma：It starts from June 25th. Look, here is the school calendar.

Mary：Thanks! And when will the new semester begin?

Mr. Ma：It will begin on September 8th. Students need to register on that day.

Mary：OK, Mr. Ma. Has the new class schedule come out already?

Mr. Ma：Don't worry. It will come out soon. Please wait for the notice.

Mary：Thank you, Mr. Ma.

Mr. Ma：Here is a school calendar of the new semester.

Text B Ask about the test results in the school office

Mary：Hello, Mr. Ma! I'm sorry to interrupt you.

Mr. Ma：Hi, Mary!

Mary：May I ask, have the test results come out?

Mr. Ma：Most of them are out already. Only two courses are not yet.

Mary：May I check my scores?

Mr. Ma：Yes. Wait a second, please.

Mary：Thank you ... Oh, 80, 82, not so good.

Mr. Ma：Some are good, some are not. Good luck next time!

Mary：Thank you, Mr. Ma. I need to work harder!

生词表
New words

国际商务 1
跟 1
刮风 3
购物中心 4
果汁 4
给 6
公交车 6
干 8
哥哥 9
工作 9
管理 12
国庆 13
高铁 13
公园 14
告诉 14

H
还是 1
还 3
红酒 4
红色 5
号码 5
会议 6
号 6
换 6
好久不见 7
好吃 7
会 8
孩子 9
或者 9
护照 10
好好儿 13
火车 13
环境 14

I

J
经理 1
见面 1
机票 2
家$_1$ 3
酒 4
健康 4
近 5
寄 5
就 6
鸡蛋 7
加班 8
几$_1$ 8
姐姐 9
几$_2$ 9
酒店 11
觉得 12
经验 12
结束 13
假期 13
间 14
急 15
加油 15

K
可以 1
开会 2
可能 2
空 2
快乐 7
烤 7
口 9
看起来 11
快(要)……了 12
客厅 14
空调 14
开学 15
课表 15

L
绿茶 2
冷 3
零食
楼 5
离 5
路$_1$ 5
了 6
路$_2$ 6
聊天儿 7
篮球 8
练习 8
来 8
留 9
累 12
旅游 13
了解 13
里 14

M
名片 1
门口 4
没(有)7
妈妈 9
妹妹 9
贸易 9
密码 10
美元 10
麻烦 11

编写说明

本教材为带有商务元素的初级汉语口语系列教材,共三册,本册为第一册。本册使用对象为非零起点的汉语学习者,要求学习者已经完成120学时左右的汉语课学习,已通过语音、汉字入门阶段的学习,并对基本词汇和简单句法结构有一定的了解和掌握。

本教材的特点是,将日常口语交流与商务情境相结合,使学生在学习该课程后,能用汉语解决日常学习、生活中的基本问题,也能在商务场合进行简单的口语交流。相较于北京语言大学出版社、北京大学出版社等出版的教材,本教材在内容、情境设置上力求贴合南方院校,尤其是在浙学生的学习环境。在人物背景设置上,相较于以往语言进修生教材中主要人物主要来自欧美、日韩等国,本教材在此基础上增设了亚洲其他国家及非洲国家等人物背景,以符合目前进修生背景多样化的实际情况,使得来自不同国家和地区的学习者更有亲切感。

本册共设15课,在话题上,主要涉及商务情景或包含商务元素,贴近学生实际生活,也有若干篇课文以校园生活为背景,以帮助学生提高在校园生活的语言运用能力。课文主题涉及身份介绍、时间日期、天气、购物、地址介绍、交通方式、用餐、兴趣爱好、职业介绍、人民币兑换、住宿、工作、娱乐等方面。

在结构上,每课都设有"话题导学",每个问题都有英文翻译,以帮助学生更好地了解新课内容,做好学习准备。在生词部分,除了列举词性和英文翻译,还列举了相关常用短语,以帮助学生更好地掌握词汇的用法。为保证教材使用的实用性和有效性,适当照顾各层级学生的水平及课时多寡的需要,每课设有2篇比较简短的课文,在内容上侧重该课话题的不同方面,教师可根据学生学习接受能力和学时安排,使用2篇或选择其中1篇安排教学。每课有5—8个语言点,为便于学习者更好地理解,各语言点后有2—3个例句。核心句部分,要求学生熟练朗读,最好能脱口而出。

本教材的综合练习,以读、说等口语练习的形式为主,另有1—2个部分的书面练习。其中看图说话部分,可根据学生学力水平,要求学生组成简短的句子,或编排简短的小对话。

由于本教材为口语教材,教师可根据实际需要和课程要求,为学生补充适当的汉字书写辅助练习,以帮助初级汉语学习者提高汉字认读、书写能力,便于学生更好地掌握所学词汇等内容,顺利进入更高程度的汉语学习。

在编写安排上,本册第1,2,3,4,5,15课由王晓慧老师编写;第6,7,8,9,14课由吴雅云老师编写;第10,11课由傅翠娟老师编写;第12,13课由吴鸣琴老师编写。编写人员均为一线教师,为编写适合学生实际需要的教材,付出了较多的心血。但因水平和时间所限,恐有疏漏,敬请方家指正。

编者

2019年6月

新视野

初级商务汉语口语(2)

主　　编　王晓华
本册主编　刘　杰
本册编写　刘　杰　楼益龄　孙　蕾

浙江工商大學出版社 ZHEJIANG GONGSHANG UNIVERSITY PRESS | 杭州

图书在版编目(CIP)数据

新视野初级商务汉语口语 / 王晓华主编. — 杭州 :
浙江工商大学出版社，2019.8

ISBN 978-7-5178-3265-2

Ⅰ. ①新… Ⅱ. ①王… Ⅲ. ①商务—汉语—口语—对
外汉语教学—教材 Ⅳ. ①H195.4

中国版本图书馆 CIP 数据核字(2019)第 119196 号

学 习 指 南

Guide to the Use of This Book

课数 Lesson	语法项 Grammar Item	功能项 Functional Items
第 1 课　欢迎来杭州	1. 还＋*adj*. 2. 可＋*v*./*adj*.＋了 3. 不过 4. 对了 5. 挺	1. 介绍自己 2. 表达欢迎和感谢 3. 询问旅游信息
第 2 课　我想换一个双人间	1. *v*.＋一下 2. 给＋object＋*v*. 3. 先……,再…… 4. 可以……吗? 5. 祝	1. 电话应答 2. 申请更换宿舍 3. 询问办理银行卡
第 3 课　我们剧院门口见	1. 虽然……,但是(可是)…… 2. 一＋量词＋(名词)＋也/都不(没)＋*VC* 3. 对……感兴趣 4. A 跟/和 B 差不多 5. 一边……,一边……	1. 跟他人约定见面时间、地点等 2. 参加校园活动 3. 谈论观看演出的感受
第 4 课　在杭州租房	1. A 是 A,就是…… 2. ……的话,…… 3. 动词重叠 *v*.＋*v*. 4. A 比 B…… 5. ……离……	1. 咨询租房信息 2. 介绍中介公司 3. 询问租房手续
第 5 课　去医院看病	1. 要么……,要么…… 2. ……的;(是)……的 3. 除了……,还…… 4. 又要……了	1. 询问就医信息:挂号、问诊、配药 2. 简介中医信息
第 6 课　参加商务宴请	1. 能……吗? 2. ……嘛 3. 真……吗 4. 还是…… 5. ……的话,就……	1. 请求参加宴会 2. 简介餐饮礼仪 3. 介绍当地特色菜

续 表

课数 Lesson	语法项 Grammar Item	功能项 Functional Items
第 7 课　我要订往返机票	1. 打折/打……折 2. 要是……(的话),就…… 3. 看来…… 4. 从……到…… 5. 最好	1. 订飞机票 2. 询问出行交通
第 8 课　我们住的酒店真不错	1. 真＋*adj.* /*v.* 2. 太＋*adj.* /*v.* 3. 就＋*v.* 4. 是……的…… 5. 地点＋有＋sb. /sth. 6. “啊”“吧”“吗”	1. 办理酒店入住 2. 询问酒店信息
第 9 课　我的上海购物经历	1. 被 2. 等(等) 3. 除了……,还…… 4. A 比 B＋*adj.* /*AP* 5. *v.* ＋的 6. A 和 B 一样/不一样	1. 向售货员询问商品信息 2. 买东西的时候和售货员还价 3. 办理会员卡
第 10 课　您的快递到了	1. 你看……行吗? 2. *v.* ＋在＋处所 3. 得＋*v.* 4. 凭	1. 寄送快递 2. 接收快递 3. 与快递员协商取件
第 11 课　请问有包间吗	1. 而且 2. 也就是(说) 3. 对了 4. ……,就是…… 5. ……,尤其是……	1. 预订饭店座位 2. 订外卖、选餐
第 12 课　参观义乌小商品市场	1. ……以内 2. *v.* ＋完 3. 不但……,还…… 4. 数字的读法	1. 查询和购买车票 2. 询问和评价商品 3. 表达对合作的期待

续　表

课数 Lesson	语法项 Grammar Item	功能项 Functional Items
第 13 课　我喜欢广告，喜欢网购	1. 像……一样 2. ……极了 3. 一……就…… 4. 不仅……，而且…… 5. 得 + *v.* 6. 好好 + *v.* 7. ……，此外 8. 把	1. 传递商务信息 2. 陈述简单观点 3. 简单描述事物
第 14 课　快期末考试了	1. 不如$_1$ 2. *v.* + 得…… 3. 忙着…… 4. 又……，又…… 5. 先……，再……	1. 问答学习信息 2. 陈述先后顺序 3. 表述旅游建议
第 15 课　我想找一份兼职	1. 不如$_2$ 2. 对……来说 3. A 是 A，但是…… 4. 贵 + *n.* 5. 最好	1. 进行简单比较 2. 表达强调 3. 敬辞的使用

mù lù

目录

1 欢迎来杭州
Welcome to Hangzhou

话题导学
Guidance

1. 第一次跟别人见面，应该怎样介绍自己？
   How do you introduce yourself for the first time?
2. 怎样表达欢迎和感谢？
   How do you express "welcome" and "thanks"?
3. 去机场接客人时，你应该说些什么？
   What do you say when you pick up at the airport?

生词学习（一）
New words I

1. 接 (jiē) *v.* meet; welcome　　接机；接我
2. 日 (rì) *n.* day　　工作日；休息日
3. 爱上 (ài shàng) *v.* like; love　　爱上你；爱上他
4. 晚点 (wǎn diǎn) *v.* late; behind the schedule　　飞机晚点；火车晚点
5. 行李 (xíng lǐ) *n.* baggage; luggage　　一件行李；没有行李
6. 久等 (jiǔ děng) *v.* wait a long time　　让您久等了
7. 大巴 (dà bā) *n.* bus　　一辆大巴；坐大巴

课文（一）　在机场
Text A　At the airport

马克：你好！我是英国来的马克。
Mǎ kè　Nǐ hǎo　Wǒ shì yīng guó lái de mǎ kè

玛丽：你好，马克。欢迎你！我是工商大学的玛丽。
Mǎ lì　Nǐ hǎo　mǎ kè　Huān yíng nǐ　Wǒ shì gōng shāng dà xué de mǎ lì

马克:玛丽,谢谢你来机场接我。
Mǎ kè Mǎ lì xiè xie nǐ lái jī chǎng jiē wǒ

玛丽:不客气。今天是新生报到日。
Mǎ lì Bú kè qì Jīn tiān shì xīn shēng bào dào rì

马克:哦,谢谢。太好了。我第一次来杭州,谢谢你的帮助。
Mǎ kè Ò xiè xie Tài hǎo le Wǒ dì yī cì lái Háng zhōu xiè xie nǐ de bāng zhù

玛丽:杭州是一个非常美丽的城市,你一定会爱上它的。一路上还好吧?
Mǎ lì Háng zhōu shì yí gè fēi cháng měi lì de chéng shì nǐ yí dìng huì ài shàng tā de Yí lù shang hái hǎo ba

马克:飞机晚点了,不过,其他的还好。让你们久等了。
Mǎ kè Fēi jī wǎn diǎn le bú guò qí tā de hái hǎo Ràng nǐ mén jiǔ děng le

玛丽:没关系。你的行李多不多?
Mǎ lì Méi guān xi Nǐ de xíng lǐ duō bù duō

马克:都在这里了,一共三件。
Mǎ kè Dōu zài zhè lǐ le yí gòng sān jiàn

玛丽:那我们走吧。学校的大巴在那里。
Mǎ lì Nà wǒ mén zǒu ba Xué xiào de dà bā zài nà lǐ

根据课文(一)回答问题
Answer these questions according to the Text A

1. 马克从哪里来?
2. 马克来过杭州吗?
3. 杭州是一个什么样的城市?
4. 马克有几件行李?

生词学习(二)
New words II

1. hǎo wán 好玩 *adj.* interesting　　很好玩;不好玩
2. kě 可 *adv.* so; such　　可好了;可多了
3. duì le 对了 by the way
4. bú cuò 不错 *adj.* pretty good; not bad　　很不错;挺不错
5. lí 离 *v.* be away from　　离学校很近;离家很远
6. fāng biàn 方便 *adj.* convenient　　非常方便;方便的超市

chéng
7. 乘 *v.* by 乘火车;乘飞机

tǐng
8. 挺 *adv.* very; rather 挺好;挺大

dào dá
9. 到达 *v.* arrive at 到达学校;到达中国

huān yíng
10. 欢迎 *v.* welcome 欢迎你;欢迎他们

课文(二) 你好,杭州
Text B Hi, Hangzhou

玛丽:坐了这么长时间的飞机,还好吧?
Mǎ lì Zuò le zhè me cháng shí jiān de fēi jī hái hǎo ba

马克:还好,休息一下就好了。
Mǎ kè Hái hǎo xiū xi yí xià jiù hǎo le

玛丽:从机场到学校,要一个小时的时间。
Mǎ lì Cóng jī chǎng dào xué xiào yào yí gè xiǎo shí de shí jiān

马克:好的。哦,对了,杭州有哪些好玩的地方?我可喜欢旅游了。
Mǎ kè Hǎo de Ò duì le Háng zhōu yǒu nǎ xiē hǎo wán de dì fāng Wǒ kě xǐ huān lǚ yóu le

玛丽:杭州是一个旅游城市,美丽的地方可多了。我觉得西湖就不错。
Mǎ lì Háng zhōu shì yí gè lǚ yóu chéng shì měi lì de dì fāng kě duō le Wǒ jué de xī hú jiù bú cuò

马克:是吗?我想去西湖看看。
Mǎ kè Shì ma Wǒ xiǎng qù xī hú kàn kan

玛丽:从学校去西湖很方便,乘地铁就能到达。西湖是杭州最美的地方,有山有水,非常漂亮。
Mǎ lì Cóng xué xiào qù xī hú hěn fāng biàn chéng dì tiě jiù néng dào dá Xī hú shì Háng zhōu zuì měi de dì fāng yǒu shān yǒu shuǐ fēi cháng piào liàng

马克:太好了!杭州离上海远不远?听说上海挺不错的。
Mǎ kè Tài hǎo le Háng zhōu lí Shàng hǎi yuǎn bù yuǎn Tīng shuō Shàng hǎi tǐng bú cuò de

玛丽:杭州离上海不太远,乘火车一个小时就能到达。
Mǎ lì Háng zhōu lí Shàng hǎi bú tài yuǎn chéng huǒ chē yí gè xiǎo shí jiù néng dào dá

马克:太棒了!在杭州生活这么方便!
Mǎ kè Tài bàng le Zài Háng zhōu shēng huó zhè me fāng biàn

玛丽:快看,前面就是学校。我们快到了。工商大学欢迎你!杭州欢迎你!
Mǎ lì Kuài kàn qián miàn jiù shì xué xiào Wǒ men kuài dào le Gōng shāng dà xué huān yíng nǐ Háng zhōu huān yíng nǐ

马克:工商大学,我来了!杭州,我来了。
Mǎ kè Gōng shāng dà xué wǒ lái le Háng zhōu wǒ lái le

根据课文(二)回答问题
Answer these questions according to the Text B

1. 从机场到学校需要多长时间?
2. 杭州的西湖怎么样?
3. 杭州离上海远不远?
4. 从学校怎么去杭州西湖?

语言点
Language points

1. 还 + *adj*.

一路上还好吧?

Is it OK during the trip?

"还"用在形容词前,表示程度上还过得去,一般是往好的方面说。

When used before an adjective, "还" means "quite" or "just", usually about something positive.

(1)今天的天气还好。

(2)这件衣服还不错。

(3)他的汉语和日语还行。

2. 可 + *v*./*adj*. + 了

我可喜欢旅游了。

I really like traveling.

"可"表示强调,用在动词或者形容词前面。"可 + *v*./*adj*. + 了"经常用于口语表达中。

"可" can be used in front of verbs or adjectives, indicating emphasis. "可 + *v*./*adj*. + 了" is often used in spoken Chinese.

(1)今天的天气可好了。

(2)她可喜欢买东西了。

(3)昨天的考试可难了。

3. 不过

不过,其他的还好。

However, everything else went well.

"不过"是一个连词,有转折的意思。

"不过" is a conjunction. It is the meaning of "but".

(1)今天天气很好。不过,我不想去玩。

(2)他的口语很好。不过,写作不太好。

(3)他很想去旅行。不过,他没有钱。

4. 对了

对了,杭州有哪些好玩的地方?

By the way, where are the interesting places in Hangzhou?

"对了"在口语中常常作为一个插入语,引出另外一个话题。单独使用的"对了"和这个不一样。

"对了" is often used as an parenthesis in spoken language, leading to another topic or sentence. It is different as it is used alone.

(1)今天的天气真好啊。对了,昨天你说假期想去旅行,你想去哪儿?

(2)考试结束了,大家都很开心。对了,你想去旅行吗?

5. 挺

听说上海挺不错的。

I heard that Shanghai is quite nice.

"挺"是一个副词,在口语中常常用于动词和形容词前,表示"很""非常"。

"挺" can be used in front of verbs or adjectives in spoken Chinese, which means "very", "rather", and "quite".

(1)他学习成绩挺好。

(2)这家饭店的菜挺不错。

(3)我挺喜欢旅行的。

核心句
Key sentences

1. 谢谢你来接我。
   Thank you for coming to pick me up.
2. 让你们久等了。
   Sorry to have kept you waiting for a long time.
3. 我可喜欢旅游了。
   I really like travelling.
4. 杭州离上海远不远?
   Is Hangzhou far from Shanghai?
5. 你一定会爱上这个城市的。
   You will love this city.

综合练习
Comprehensive exercises

(一)熟读下列短语 Read the following phrases

1. 一定去　一定买　一定喜欢　一定会唱歌　一定不会打篮球
2. 可好了　可漂亮了　可便宜了　可好玩了　可有意思了　可没意思了
3. 挺好　挺贵　挺多　挺难　挺漂亮　挺不错　挺有意思　挺没意思
4. 乘火车　乘地铁　乘大巴　乘飞机　坐火车　坐地铁　坐大巴
5. 非常方便　方便的交通　方便的地方　乘车很方便　买东西很方便
6. 好玩的地方　好玩的公园　好玩的玩具　游戏很好玩　游泳很好玩
7. 这么方便　这么贵　这么好吃　那么便宜　那么有意思　那么远

(二)替换练习 Substitution drills

1. 今天是新生报到日。

昨天	休息
周一	免费(miǎnfèi,free)
明天	工作

2. 坐了这么长时间的飞机,还好吧?

玩	游戏
跑	步
开	车

3. 杭州离上海远不远?听说上海挺不错的。

北京	天津	天津
学校	西湖	西湖
中国	日本	日本

4. 杭州离上海不太远,坐火车一个小时就能到达。

学校	超市	坐公交车十分钟
宿舍	教室	走路一刻钟
上海	北京	坐飞机一个半小时

5. 我觉得西湖就　　不错。

他	杭州菜	不错
我们	去上海	挺好
她	买一瓶酒	够了
我	多听多说	能学好汉语

6. 我可喜欢　旅游了。
   她　打篮球
   我们　去旅行
   爸爸和妈妈　去爬山
   他　打游戏和玩手机

7. 听说上海挺　不错的。
   法国菜　有名
   苏州园林　漂亮
   他的汉语和韩语　不错

8. 前面就是学校的大门。
   左边　大学的教学楼
   后面　学校的邮局
   南面　图书馆和自习室

(三)完成对话 Complete the following dialogues

1. A:你好,我是英国来的马克。
   B:你好,我是____________________。
   A:谢谢你来机场接我。让你________了。
   B:不客气。欢迎你______________。

2. A:坐了这么长时间的火车,还______吧?
   B:还好,休息休息就好了。从机场到学校________?
   A:从机场到学校不太远,乘______需要_________的时间。
   B:好的。谢谢!哦,对了,杭州___________?我可喜欢旅游了。
   A:杭州是_________________,我觉得__________________。
   B:是吗?我想去看看。

(四)课堂活动 In-class exercises

角色扮演。Role-play.

(1)你去机场接机,遇到了刚下飞机的泰国留学生阿明。你们第一次见面,阿明第一次来杭州。
   参考词语:欢迎　久等　行李　机场

(2)请向新生阿明介绍工商大学和杭州。
   参考词语:下沙　大学城　方便　西湖　代表　旅游城市

(五)课后练习 After-class exercises

采访四位新同学。Interview four new students and record their answers.

	同学 1	同学 2	同学 3	同学 4
1.你叫什么名字?				
2.你从哪里来?				
3.以前你来过中国吗?				
4.你的行李有几件?				
5.你觉得杭州怎么样?				
6.你觉得中国大学怎么样?				

课文翻译 Translation of the texts

Text A At the airport

Mark: Hello! I am Mark, and I come from UK.

Mary: Hello, Mark. Welcome to China. I am Mary,a student in the Gongshang University.

Mark: Hi,Mary. Thank you for picking me up at the airport.

Mary: You are welcome. Today is a registration day.

Mark: Oh, thank you. It is great! It is the first time for me to come to Hangzhou; thank you for your help.

Mary: Hangzhou is a very beautiful city, and you will love it soon. Is it OK in the journey?

Mark: The flight delayed, but everything else is OK. Sorry to have kept you waiting for a long time.

Mary: It doesn't matter. How many luggages do you have?

Mark: There are three pieces here.

Mary: Let's go. The university bus is there.

Text B Hi, Hangzhou

Mary: It took a long time on the journey. Is it OK?

Mark: It is OK. I just need to take a break.

Mary: It takes one hour from the airport to the university.

Mark: OK. Where are the interesting places in Hangzhou? I like travelling.

Mary: Hangzhou is a tourism city, and there are many beautiful places here. I think the West Lake is a nice place.

Mark: Really? I want to go to the West Lake next time.

Mary: It is very convenient to go to the West Lake from the university and you could go there by subway. The West Lake is the most beautiful place in Hangzhou. There are mountains and water there. It is really beautiful.

Mark: Great! And is Hangzhou far from Shanghai? I heard that Shanghai is quite nice.

Mary: Hangzhou is not too far from Shanghai and you can go Shanghai by train in one hour.

Mark: Good! Living in Hangzhou is very convenient!

Mary: Look, there is our universuty. We are coming soon. Welcome to the Gongshang University! Welcome to Hangzhou!

Mark: Gongshang University, I am here! Hangzhou, I am here.

2 我想换一个双人间
I want to change a double room

话题导学 Guidance

1. 给别人打电话的时候应该怎样问候?
   How do you greet in Chinese when you call someone?
2. 怎样表达换宿舍的请求并说明原因?
   How do you request to change dormitory and explain the reasons?
3. 如果你需要办银行卡,应该跟银行咨询哪些事情?
   If you need to apply for a bank card, what should you consult with the bank?

生词学习(一) New words I

1. 刚 (gāng) *adv.* just　　刚来学校;刚知道
2. 宿舍 (sù shè) *n.* dormitory　　学校宿舍;住在宿舍
2. 双人间 (shuāng rén jiān) double room　　住双人间;要双人间
4. 单人间 (dān rén jiān) single room　　有单人间;没有单人间
5. 稍等 (shāo děng) *v.* wait a moment　　请稍等;稍等一会儿
6. 记录 (jì lù) *n./v.* record; to record　　借书记录;记录一下
7. 预约 (yù yuē) *v.* to order　　预约房间;预约饭店
8. 打算 (dǎ suàn) *v.* plan　　打算去爬山;有什么打算
9. 但是 (dàn shì) *conj.* but　　便宜但是质量好
10. 报名 (bào míng) *v.* to apply　　报名参加;报名学习汉语

gānghǎo
11. 刚好 *adv.* happen to be 刚好走了

céng
12. 层 *n.* floor 五层;第一层

bàn
13. 办 *v.* to handle 办事;办手续

shǒu xù
14. 手续 *n.* procedure 入学手续;毕业手续

课文(一) 换宿舍
Text A Change dormitory

英国留学生马克刚到杭州,他给留学生办公室的李老师打电话,问宿舍的事情。

马克:喂,您好! 请问李老师在吗?
Mǎ kè Wéi nín hǎo Qǐng wèn Lǐ lǎo shī zài ma

李老师:你好! 我就是。你是哪位?
Lǐ lǎo shī Nǐ hǎo Wǒ jiù shì Nǐ shì nǎ wèi

马克:我是新来的留学生马克。我想问一下可以换宿舍吗? 我想换一个双人间。
Mǎ kè Wǒ shì xīn lái de liú xué shēng Mǎ kè Wǒ xiǎng wèn yí xià kě yǐ huàn sù shè ma Wǒ xiǎng huàn yí gè shuāng rén jiān

李老师:稍等一下,我看看电脑上的记录。哦,马克,你预约的是一个单人间,为什么要换呢?
Lǐ lǎo shī Shāo děng yí xià wǒ kàn kan diàn nǎo shàng de jì lù Ò Mǎ kè nǐ yù yuē de shì yí gè dān rén jiān wèi shén me yào huàn ne

马克:以前我打算一个人来学习,但是现在我的朋友也报名了,我想跟他一起住。
Mǎ kè Yǐ qián wǒ dǎ suàn yí gè rén lái xué xí dàn shì xiàn zài wǒ de péng yǒu yě bào míng le wǒ xiǎng gēn tā yì qǐ zhù

李老师:好吧。刚好还有一个双人间,在十层,可以吗?
Lǐ lǎo shī Hǎo ba Gāng hǎo hái yǒu yí gè shuāng rén jiān zài shí céng kě yǐ ma

马克:可以的。
Mǎ kè Kě yǐ de

李老师:那你来国际教育学院五〇五办公室办一下换宿舍的手续吧。
Lǐ lǎo shī Nà nǐ lái guó jì jiào yù xué yuàn wǔ líng wǔ bàn gōng shì bàn yí xià huàn sù shè de shǒu xù ba

马克:好的。谢谢您!
Mǎ kè Hǎo de Xiè xie nín

李老师:不客气。
Lǐ lǎo shī Bú kè qi

根据课文(一)回答问题
Answer these questions according to the Text A

1. 马克预约了什么房间？他想换什么房间？
2. 马克为什么要换房间？
3. 李老师说可以换吗？
4. 李老师要求马克做什么？

生词学习(二)
New words II

1.	卡	kǎ	*n.*	card	银行卡;学生卡
2.	客服	kè fú	*n.*	customer service	银行客服;售后客服
3.	带	dài	*v.*	to bring	带书;带钥匙
4.	本人	běn rén	*n.*	oneself	本人参加;本人签名
5.	身份证	shēn fèn zhèng	*n.*	ID card	带身份证;他的身份证
6.	护照	hù zhào	*n.*	passport	办护照;护照照片
7.	填	tián	*v.*	to fill in	填表格
8.	申请	shēn qǐng	*v./n.*	to apply;application	申请奖学金;写申请
9.	表格	biǎo gé	*n.*	form	填申请表格
10.	柜台	guì tái	*n.*	counter	银行柜台;售货柜台
11.	外币	wài bì	*n.*	foreign currency	外币交易;外币还款
12.	多币种	duō bì zhǒng		multi-currency	多币种信用卡
13.	愉快	yú kuài	*adj.*	happy;delightful	生活愉快;工作愉快

课文(二) 办银行卡
Text B Apply for a bank card

银行客服：您好！这里是工商银行，请问您需要什么服务？
Yín háng kè fú Nín hǎo Zhè lǐ shì gōng shāng yín háng qǐng wèn nín xū yào shén me fú wù

美玲：您好！我想咨询一下怎么办银行卡。
Měi líng Nín hǎo Wǒ xiǎng zī xún yí xià zěn me bàn yín háng kǎ

银行客服：好的。那您需要带本人的身份证来银行办理。
Yín háng kè fú Hǎo de Nà nín xū yào dài běn rén de shēn fèn zhèng lái yín háng bàn lǐ

美玲：我是印尼人，没有身份证，护照可以吗？
Měi líng Wǒ shì yìn ní rén méi yǒu shēn fèn zhèng hù zhào kě yǐ ma

银行客服：可以的。那您就带护照来银行，先填一张申请表格，然后到柜台办理就可以了。
Yín háng kè fú Kě yǐ de Nà nín jiù dài hù zhào lái yín háng xiān tián yī zhāng shēn qǐng biǎo gé rán hòu dào guì tái bàn lǐ jiù kě yǐ le

美玲：好的。请问这种银行卡可以存外币吗？
Měi líng Hǎo de Qǐng wèn zhè zhǒng yín háng kǎ kě yǐ cún wài bì ma

银行客服：当然可以。我们的银行卡都是多币种的，可以存取十几种外币。
Yín háng kè fú Dāng rán kě yǐ Wǒ men de yín háng kǎ dōu shì duō bì zhǒng de kě yǐ cún qǔ shí jǐ zhǒng wài bì

美玲：那太好了，明天我就去银行办理。
Měi líng Nà tài hǎo le míng tiān wǒ jiù qù yín háng bàn lǐ

银行客服：女士，您还需要其他服务吗？
Yín háng kè fú Nǚ shì nín hái xū yào qí tā fú wù ma

美玲：不需要了，谢谢！
Měi líng Bù xū yào le xiè xie

银行客服：不客气，女士。祝您生活愉快！再见！
Yín háng kè fú Bù kè qì nǚ shì Zhù nín shēng huó yú kuài Zài jiàn

美玲：再见！
Měi líng Zài jiàn

根据课文(二)回答问题
Answer these questions according to the Text B

1. 美玲给银行客服打电话问什么？
2. 办银行卡需要带什么？
3. 办理银行卡需要先做什么？然后做什么？
4. 美玲要办的银行卡可以存外币吗？

语言点
Language points

1. *v*. +一下

我想问一下可以换宿舍吗？

May I ask if I can change my dormitory?

“一下”加在某些动词后面可以委婉地表达祈使和主观愿望,有缓和语气的作用。

“一下” added to some verbs can be used to euphemistically express the imperative and subjective desire, which has the effect of moderating the tone.

(1)马克,你过来一下。

(2)我想看一下你的书,可以吗?

(3)明天要考试了,你快准备一下吧。

2. 给 + object + *v*.

马克给留学生办公室的李老师打电话。

Mark called Miss Li who was in the overseas students' office.

“给”可以用作介词,引出动作的对象。

“给” can be used as a preposition to elicit the object of the action.

(1)我给王老师写信。

(2)他给我当翻译。

(3)今天我给爸爸做饭。

3. 先……,再……

您先填一张申请表格,再到柜台办理就可以了。

First you can fill out an application form and then go to the counter.

“先……,再……”表示不同动作进行的先后顺序。

“先……,再……” represents the sequence of different actions.

(1)我先去银行取钱,再去超市买东西。

(2)做这个菜应该先放西红柿,再放鸡蛋。

(3)你先给他打个电话,再去他家吧。

4. 可以……吗?

请问这种银行卡可以存外币吗?

Excuse me, can this bank card deposit foreign currency?

“可以……吗?”通常用于询问动作或行为是否被允许或者是否可行。

“可以……吗?” is often used to ask whether actions are permitted or feasible.

(1)我可以进来吗?

(2)在这里可以抽烟吗?

(3)可以用支付宝付钱吗?

5. 祝

祝您生活愉快！

Wish you a happy life!

"祝"常用于句首，表示祝愿。

"祝" is often used at the beginning of the sentences to express good wishes.

(1)祝你生日快乐！

(2)祝你们新年快乐！

(3)祝您早日康复！

核心句
Key sentences

1. 请问李老师在吗？

   May I speak to Miss Li?

2. 我想问一下可以换宿舍吗？我想换一个双人间。

   I want to ask if I can change a dormitory. I want to change a double room.

3. 那你来国际教育学院505办公室办一下换宿舍的手续吧。

   Then please come to Office 505 at College of International Education to do the formalities for changing the dormitory.

4. 我想咨询一下怎么办银行卡。

   I would like to ask how to apply for a bank card.

5. 您需要带本人的身份证来银行办理。

   You need to take your ID card to the bank to handle.

6. 请问这种银行卡可以存外币吗？

   May I ask if this bank card can deposit foreign currency?

7. 祝您生活愉快！

   Wish you happy everyday!

综合练习
Comprehensive exercises

(一)熟读下列短语 Read the following phrases

1. 刚回家　刚吃过饭　刚知道　刚来杭州　刚下飞机　刚写完作业
2. 预约房间　预约座位　预约采访　预约挂号
3. 办事　办手续　办银行卡　办护照　办签证
4. 银行卡　学生卡　会员卡　公园卡　贵宾卡
5. 带书　带手机　带钱包　带照相机　带钥匙

6. 生活愉快　工作愉快　学习愉快　节日愉快

(二)替换练习 Substitution drills

1. 马克给李老师打电话。

　　朋友　发微信

　　弟弟　做饭

　　麦克　买东西

2. 我想咨询一下怎么办银行卡。

　　问　　去工商大学怎么走

　　去　　洗手间

　　了解　这个大学怎么样

3. 先填一张申请表格,然后到柜台办理。

　　去书店买书　　去银行取钱

　　交学费　　去学院办手续

　　插入银行卡　　输入密码

4. 可以换宿舍吗?

　　用支付宝

　　明天再来

　　请假

5. 祝您　生活愉快!

　　妈妈　生日快乐

　　你　　新年快乐

　　老师　教师节快乐

(三)完成对话 Complete the following dialogues

1. A:老师,您好!我想问________我可以换________宿舍吗?

B:为什么呢?

A:因为我想跟朋友一起住。我想换一个________。

B:好吧。现在________有个双人间,但是在十一楼,可以吗?

A:________________。

2. A:您好!我想________一下怎么________银行卡。

B:您好!那您需要________本人的身份证来银行________。

A:我是外国人,没有身份证,________可以吗?

B:当然可以。

A:这种银行卡可以________外币吗?

B:我们的银行卡都是________的,可以存取十几种外币。

(四)课堂活动 In-class exercise

角色扮演。Role-play.

(1)你是新来的留学生,想换一个房间,你给学院办公室的老师打电话。

参考词语:换　刚好　办　手续

(2)你需要办一张银行卡,请给银行客服打电话询问怎么办银行卡。

参考词语:带　本人　身份证　护照　办理　多币种　存取

(五)课后练习 After-class exercises

根据提示,复述课文。Retell the texts.

马克给留学生办公室打电话,问__________。他想换一个__________。以前马克打算一个人来学习,但是现在__________。马克想和他的朋友__________。刚好还有一个__________,在十楼。李老师告诉马克去国际教育学院505办公室______________。

办理银行卡,需要带本人的身份证来银行办理。外国人没有身份证,可以带______________。先填__________,然后到__________。银行卡都是__________,可以存取__________。

课文翻译 Translation of the texts

Text A Change dormitory

(After arriving in Hangzhou, the foreign student Mark called Miss Li who was in the international students' office to ask about the dormitory.)

Mark: Hello! Excuse me, is Miss Li here?

Miss Li: Hello! It's me. Who's calling?

Mark: I'm Mark, a new international student. May I ask if I can change my dormitory? I'd like a double room.

Miss Li: Just a minute. I'll look at the records on the computer. Oh, Mark, you have an appointment for a single room. Why do you want to change it?

Mark: Miss Li, I plan to study by myself, but now my friend has signed up, and I want to live with him.

Miss Li: All right. There's one double room, on the tenth floor, OK?

Mark: All right.

Miss Li: Then you can go to Office 505 in the college of inter national Education to handle procedures.

Mark: All right. Thank you so much!

Miss Li: You're welcome.

Text B Apply for a bank card

(Meliing wants to get a bank card. She calls the customer service.)

Customer service: Hello! This is ICBC. May I help you?

Meiling: Hello! I'd like to apply for a bank card.

Customer service: All right. Then you need to bring your ID card to the bank.

Meiling: I am Indonesian. I have no ID card. Is passport OK?

Customer service: Yes. Then you can bring your passport to the bank and fill out an application form and then go to the counter.

Meiling: All right. Excuse me, can this bank card deposit foreign currency?

Customer service: Sure. Our bank cards are multi-currency cands and can access more than ten kinds of foreign currencies.

Meiling: That's great. I'll go to the bank tomorrow.

Customer service: Do you need any other services, Miss?

Meiling: No, thank you!

Customer service: You're welcome, Miss. Wish you a happy life! Goodbye!

Meiling: Goodbye!

3 我们剧院门口见
Let's meet at the gate of the theatre

话题导学 Guidance

1. 你常跟朋友一起出去吗？
   Do you often go outside with your friends?
2. 你和朋友是怎么约见面的时间和地点的？
   How do you arrange the time and place to meet at?
3. 你参加过学校的什么活动？
   What activities did you take in the university?

生词学习(一) New words I

1. 晚会 (wǎn huì) *n.* gala　　新年晚会;参加晚会
2. 每 (měi) *pron.* every; each　　每天;每年
3. 举办 (jǔ bàn) *v.* to hold　　举办晚会;举办运动会
4. 次 (cì) *mw.* time　　一次;每次;很多次
5. 精彩 (jīng cǎi) *adj.* wonderful　　精彩的表演;比赛很精彩
6. 一定 (yí dìng) *adv.* certainly　　一定去;一定好好学习
7. 活动 (huó dòng) *n.* activity　　交流活动;体育活动
8. 中心 (zhōng xīn) *n.* centre　　购物中心;活动中心
9. 剧院 (jù yuàn) *n.* theatre　　去剧院;在剧院
10. 需要 (xū yào) *v.* need; want　　需要门票;需要帮忙

mén piào
11. 门票 *n.* ticket　　演出门票;公园门票

课文(一) 看演出
Text A Watching the show

英国学生马克和中国学生李明讨论演出的事情。

李明:马克,你知道下周二晚上有一个晚会吗?
Lǐ Míng Mǎ kè nǐ zhī dào xià zhōu èr wǎn shàng yǒu yí gè wǎn huì ma

马克:我听老师说过,是不是叫"出境入镜"中外学生晚会?
Mǎ kè Wǒ tīng lǎo shī shuō guò shì bú shì jiào chū jìng rù jìng zhōng wài xué shēng wǎn huì

李明:对,没错。这个晚会每年举办一次,每次都很精彩,大家很喜欢。
Lǐ Míng Duì méi cuò Zhè ge wǎn huì měi nián jǔ bàn yí cì měi cì dōu hěn jīng cǎi dà jiā hěn xǐ huān

马克:是吗?那我一定要去看看。演出几点开始?在哪里呢?
Mǎ kè Shì ma Nà wǒ yí dìng yào qù kàn kan Yǎn chū jǐ diǎn kāi shǐ Zài nǎ lǐ ne

李明:演出下周二晚上六点半开始,在学生活动中心的剧院。
Lǐ Míng Yǎn chū xià zhōu èr wǎn shàng liù diǎn bàn kāi shǐ zài xué shēng huó dòng zhōng xīn de jù yuàn

马克:看演出需要门票吗?
Mǎ kè Kàn yǎn chū xū yào mén piào ma

李明:是的。我这里有两张门票,我们可以一起去。
Lǐ Míng Shì de Wǒ zhè lǐ yǒu liǎng zhāng mén piào wǒ men kě yǐ yì qǐ qù

马克:那太好了。我们是不是应该早点到?这样可以坐前面。
Mǎ kè Nà tài hǎo le Wǒ men shì bú shì yīng gāi zǎo diǎn dào Zhè yàng kě yǐ zuò qián miàn

李明:你说得没错。那我们六点一刻在剧院门口见,怎么样?
Lǐ Míng Nǐ shuō de méi cuò Nà wǒ men liù diǎn yí kè zài jù yuàn mén kǒu jiàn zěn me yàng

马克:好的,没问题。到时候见!
Mǎ kè Hǎo de méi wèn tí Dào shí hou jiàn

根据课文(一)回答问题
Answer these questions according to the Text A

1. 晚会是谁表演的?
2. 这个晚会每年举办几次?李明觉得这个晚会怎么样?
3. 看晚会需要门票吗?李明有门票吗?
4. 马克和李明几点在哪里见面?

生词学习(二)
New words II

jié shù
1. 结束 *v.* finish; end　　表演结束了;电影结束了

2. 有意思 yǒu yì si	*adj.* interesting	有意思的人；有意思的故事
3. 特别 tè bié	*adv.* especially	特别喜欢；特别有意思
4. 京剧 jīng jù	*n.* Peking Opera	看京剧；唱京剧
5. 的确 dí què	*adv.* indeed	的确不错；的确很难
6. 懂 dǒng	*v.* understand	听懂了；看懂了
7. 化妆 huà zhuāng	*n./v.* make up	化妆舞会；化妆品
8. 脸谱 liǎn pǔ	*n.* facial makeup	京剧脸谱
9. 发音 fā yīn	*v./n.* pronounce; pronunciation	汉语发音；发音练习
10. 主意 zhǔ yi	*n.* idea	好主意；出主意
11. 教 jiāo	*v.* teach	教英语；教唱歌

课文(二) 学唱中国歌
Text B Learn to sing Chinese songs

演出结束了，李明和马克回宿舍。

李明：马克，你觉得今天的表演怎么样？
Lǐ Míng Mǎ kè nǐ jué dé jīn tiān de biǎo yǎn zěn me yàng

马克：我觉得表演太有意思了。我特别喜欢中国学生表演的京剧。
Mǎ kè Wǒ jué dé biǎo yǎn tài yǒu yì si le Wǒ tè bié xǐ huān zhōng guó xué shēng biǎo yǎn de jīng jù

李明：京剧表演的确非常精彩。不过，听懂京剧很不容易。
Lǐ Míng Jīng jù biǎo yǎn dí què fēi cháng jīng cǎi Bú guò tīng dǒng jīng jù hěn bù róng yì

马克：是啊！虽然我一句也没听懂，但是我喜欢他们脸上的化妆，有红色、蓝色、黄色什么的。
Mǎ kè Shì a Suī rán wǒ yí jù yě méi tīng dǒng dàn shì wǒ xǐ huān tā men liǎn shàng de huà zhuāng yǒu hóng sè lán sè huáng sè shén me de

李明：是的，那叫"脸谱"，我也对京剧的脸谱很感兴趣。
Lǐ Míng Shì de nà jiào liǎn pǔ wǒ yě duì jīng jù de liǎn pǔ hěn gǎn xìng qù

马克：李明，你喜欢哪个节目？
Mǎ kè Lǐ Míng nǐ xǐ huān nǎ ge jié mù

李明：我喜欢外国留学生唱中国歌，他们的汉语发音真不错，
Lǐ Míng Wǒ xǐ huān wài guó liú xué shēng chàng zhōng guó gē tā men de hàn yǔ fā yīn zhēn bú cuò

听起来跟中国人唱的差不多。
tīng qǐ lái gēn zhōng guó rén chàng de chà bù duō

马克：是啊，我也喜欢那个节目。我要学唱中国歌，一边学唱歌一边学汉语，多好啊！
Mǎ kè Shì a wǒ yě xǐ huān nà gè jié mù Wǒ yào xué chàng zhōng guó gē yì biān xué chàng gē yì biān xué hàn yǔ duō hǎo a

李明：这真是个好主意。我可以教你。
Lǐ Míng Zhè zhēn shì gè hǎo zhǔ yi Wǒ kě yǐ jiāo nǐ

马克：太好了！我们现在就开始吧。
Mǎ kè Tài hǎo le Wǒ men xiàn zài jiù kāi shǐ ba

根据课文(二)回答问题
Answer these questions according to the Text B

1. 马克觉得今天的表演怎么样？他喜欢哪个节目？
2. 马克能听懂京剧吗？
3. 李明喜欢哪个节目？
4. 马克要学习什么？谁可以教他？

语言点
Language points

1. 虽然……，但是(可是)……

虽然我一句也没听懂，但是我喜欢他们的服装。

Although I don't understand a word, I like their clothes.

表示让步，“虽然”用在前一小句，可在主语前或主语后，“但是”或者“可是”常用在后一小句。

“虽然……，但是(可是)……” expresses concessions. “虽然” is often used in the previous sentence. It can be used before the subject or after the subject,“但是” or“可是” is often used in the back sentence.

(1)虽然今天下雨，但是同学们还是来上课了。

(2)虽然这件衣服很漂亮，可是太贵了。

(3)虽然我见过他好几次，但是我还不知道他叫什么名字。

2. 一 + 量词 + (名词) + 也/都不(没) + *VC*

我一句也没听懂。

I didn't understand a word.

表示完全没有做或完全不做。

It indicates that nothing is done or not done at all.

(1)我刚学汉语的时候,一个汉字也不会写。
(2)他一口茶都不喝。
(3)他在中国一个朋友都不认识。

3. 对……感兴趣
我也对京剧的脸谱很感兴趣。
I'm also interested in Beijing Opera's facial makeup.
表示某人对某事有兴趣,想要了解或者去做。
It indicates someone is interested in something, who want to know or do it.
(1)弟弟对画画很感兴趣。
(2)我对中国文化感兴趣。
(3)你对什么感兴趣?

4. A跟/和B差不多
你唱的听起来跟中国人唱的差不多。
You sing as much as the Chinese do.
表示两种事物之间没有很大差别,几乎一样。
It indicates there is no big difference between the two things, almost the same.
(1)这本书跟那本书差不多。
(2)我的个子和妹妹的个子差不多。
(3)他的汉语水平和你的差不多。

5. 一边……,一边……
一边学唱歌,一边学汉语。
Learn Chinese while singing.
表示同时做两件不同的事情。
It means doing two different things at the same time.
(1)妈妈喜欢一边听音乐,一边做家务。
(2)一边看电视,一边吃饭对身体不好。
(3)一边开车,一边打电话很危险。

核心句
Key sentences

1. 你知道下周二晚上有一个晚会吗?
Do you know there would be a gala next Tuesday evening?

2. 这个晚会学校每年举办一次,是中国学生和外国留学生共同表演的。
   This gala is held once a year. It is performed by Chinese students and foreign students.
3. 那我一定要去看看。
   Then I will surly go there.
4. 我这里有两张门票,我们可以一起去。
   I have two tickets. We can go there together.
5. 我们是不是应该早点到? 这样可以坐前面。
   Should we arrive earlier. Then we can sit in the front.
6. 那我们六点一刻在剧院门口见,怎么样?
   Then we will meet at the gate of the theatre at 6:15. Is it OK?
7. 我特别喜欢中国学生表演的京剧。
   I especially like Peking Opera performed by Chinese students.
8. 我也对京剧的脸谱很感兴趣。
   I am also very interested in Peking Opera.

综合练习 Comprehensive exercises

(一)熟读下列短语 Read the following phrases

1.举办晚会　举办活动　举办比赛　举办运动会　举办一场足球赛
2.演出很精彩　比赛很精彩　他的演讲很精彩　一场精彩的表演
3.一定去　一定买　一定参加　一定告诉她　一定努力学习
4.一句汉语也听不懂　一个汉字也不认识　教室里一个人也没有
5.一边听音乐,一边看书　一边吃饭,一边看电视　一边走路,一边唱歌
6.电影有意思　表演很有意思　有意思的事情　有意思的书
7.教什么　教汉语　教他唱中国歌　教你做中国菜

(二)替换练习 Substitution drills

1. 我对京剧的脸谱很感兴趣。

   玛丽　中国文化
   他　打篮球
   弟弟　运动

2. 虽然我一句也没听懂,但是我喜欢他们的服装。

   今天外边很冷　房间里很暖和
   他只学了一年汉语　他的汉语很不错
   这件衣服不贵　我很喜欢

3. 他的汉语发音跟中国人差不多。

这本书　　那本书

杭州的天气　　上海的天气

他的个子　　我的个子

4. 我们六点一刻在剧院门口见,怎么样?

我们一起吃午饭

你教我说英语

明天我们去爬山

5. 一边学唱歌,一边学汉语。

听音乐　　跑步

吃饭　　看电视

听　　写

6. 我一句也没听懂。

一本　没看

一件　没穿

一个　没吃

(三)完成对话 Complete the following dialogues

1. A:马克,你知道下周二晚上有一个晚会吗?

B:__________,是不是叫"出境入镜"中外学生文艺晚会?

A:对,这个晚会学校每年__________一次,是中国学生和外国留学生__________表演的。

B:这个晚会怎么样?

A:这个晚会很__________,很受__________。

B:那我要去看看。

2. A:马克,你觉得今天的表演__________?

B:我觉得表演太__________了。我喜欢中国学生表演的京剧。

A:京剧表演很精彩。

B:我喜欢他们的__________,还有他们的__________也很特别。

A:那叫"脸谱",我也对京剧的脸谱很__________。

(四)课堂活动 In-class exercises

角色扮演。Role-play.

(1)最近有一个新电影,你想约朋友一起去看,你给朋友打电话。

参考词语:听说　有意思　电影票　见面

(2)电影结束了,你跟朋友谈论电影怎么样。

参考词语:特别　喜欢　内容　感动

(五)课后练习 After-class exercises

根据提示,复述课文。Retell the texts.

下星期二晚上有一个中外学生的晚会,这个晚会________________举办一次,每次晚会很___________,大家都很喜欢。演出________________开始,在_____________的剧院。马克和李明_______________在剧院门口见。

马克觉得今天的表演太_____________了,他___________中国学生表演的京剧。虽然一句也___________,但是马克喜欢他们___________。马克想学唱中国歌,一边_________,一边________。李明觉得这是个好主意。

课文翻译 Translation of the texts

Text A Watching the show

(British student Mark and Chinese student Li Ming talked about the performance.)

Li Ming: Mark, do you know there is an evening party next Tuesday night?

Mark: I have heard it from the teacher. Is it called "出境入镜" Chinese and foreign student art gala?

Li Ming: Yes, that's right. This gala is held once a year. Every time it is wonderful and popular.

Mark: Isn't it? I must go and see it. What time does the performance begin? Where is it?

Li Ming: The show starts at 6:30 p.m. Next Tuesday at the student center theatre.

Mark: Does it need tickets for the show?

Li Ming: Yes. I happen to have two tickets here. We can go together.

Mark: That would be great. Should we arrive early? So we can sit in the for ont a little bit.

Li Ming: You're right. Let's meet at the gate of the theatre at a quarter past six, shall we?

Mark: OK, no problem. See you then!

Text B Learn to sing Chinese songs

(The show is over. Li Ming and Mark are on their way back to the dormitory.)

Li Ming: Mark, what do you think of today's performance?

Mark: I think the acting is very interesting. I especially like Beijing Opera performed by Chinese students.

Li Ming: The Peking Opera is really wonderful. However, Beijing Opera is not easy to understand.

Mark: Yeah! I don't understand a word of it, but I like their makeup on their faces. They have red, blue, yellow and all kinds of colors.

Li Ming: Yes, it's called "facial makeup", and I'm also interested in the Beijing Opera.

Mark: Which program do you like, Li Ming?

Li Ming: I like the Chinese songs sung by foreign students. Their Chinese pronunciation is really good. It sounds similar to the Chinese.

Mark: Yeah, I like that program too. I also want to learn to sing Chinese songs. I can learn to sing while learning Chinese. How good it is!

Li Ming: That's a good idea. I can teach you Chinese songs.

Mark: That's great! Let's start right now.

4 在杭州租房
Renting in Hangzhou

话题导学 Guidance

1. 在杭州怎么租房?
   How do you rent a house in Hangzhou?
2. 想租房怎么找中介公司?
   How do you find an intermediary when you want to rent a house?
3. 怎么办理租房手续?
   How do you go through the rental procedure?

生词学习(一) New words I

1. 外 (wài)	*n.* outside	外面;校外
2. 宿舍 (sù shè)	*n.* dormitory	学生宿舍;我的宿舍
3. 方便 (fāngbiàn)	*adj.* convenient	很方便;方便的交通
4. 租 (zū)	*v.* rent	出租;租房
5. 求 (qiú)	*v.* ask; beg; request	求租; 求人
6. 中介 (zhōng jiè)	*n.* intermediary; medium	一家中介;中介公司
7. 公司 (gōng sī)	*n.* company	中介公司;美国公司
8. 合租 (hé zū)	joint rent	合租房子;我和她合租
9. 双休日 (shuāng xiū rì)	two-day weekend	一个双休日
10. 比较 (bǐ jiào)	*adv.* compare; comparatively	比较好;比较难

kòng
11. 空（儿） *n.* free time; empty　　有空;没空

wǎngshàng
12. 网　上　*n.* on line; on the internet　　网上购物;网上聊天

课文(一)　住校外
Text A　Living outside of the campus

李明、马克、安娜一起讨论租房问题。

安娜:马克,你想住到校外去吗?
Ān nà　Mǎ kè　nǐ xiǎng zhù dào xiào wài qù ma

马克:现在住在学生宿舍不是挺方便的吗?
Mǎ kè　Xiàn zài zhù zài xué shēng sù shè bú shì tǐng fāng biàn de ma

安娜:方便是方便,就是不太自由。周末回来晚的话,进宿舍比较麻烦。
Ān nà　Fāng biàn shì fāng biàn　jiù shì bù tài zì yóu　Zhōu mò huí lái wǎn de huà　jìn sù shè bǐ jiào má fan

马克:这倒是。
Mǎ kè　Zhè dào shì

安娜:所以,我打算下学期住到校外去。
Ān nà　Suǒ yǐ　wǒ dǎ suàn xià xué qī zhù dào xiào wài qù

马克:那我们一起合租吧。可是,怎么租房呢?
Mǎ kè　Nà wǒ men yì qǐ hé zū ba　Kě shì　zěn me zū fáng ne

李明:可以在网上求租,或者直接去中介公司。
Lǐ Míng　Kě yǐ zài wǎng shàng qiú zū　huò zhě zhí jiē qù zhōng jiè gōng sī

安娜:那我们去中介公司问问吧。
Ān nà　Nà wǒ men qù zhōng jiè gōng sī wèn wen ba

李明:双休日有空的话,我带你们去看看。
Lǐ Míng　Shuāng xiū rì yǒu kòng de huà　wǒ dài nǐ men qù kàn kan

安娜:好的。谢谢!
Ān nà　Hǎo de　Xiè xie

马克:好,谢谢!
mǎ kè　hǎo　xiè xiè

根据课文(一)回答问题
Answer these questions according to the Text A

1. 安娜、马克在谈论什么?
2. 他们为什么想住校外?
3. 租房应该找谁?
4. 他们打算什么时候去中介公司?

生词学习(二) New words II

yǒu guān
1. 有关 *v.* concern; relate to 有关学生;有关国家

qíng kuàng
2. 情况 *n.* condition; situation 租房情况;生活情况

fáng yuán
3. 房源 *n.* housing resource 房源情况

jié gòu
4. 结构 *n.* construction; structure 房子结构

yàng shì
5. 样式 *n.* style; type 房子样式

tīng
6. 厅 *n.* drawing room; parlour; hall 客厅;大厅

jià wèi
7. 价位 *n.* price 租房价位;价位很高

lí
8. 离 *v.* leave; part from; be away from 离学校;离市区

shāng liang
9. 商量 *v.* discuss; talk over 商量租房;商量工作

qiān
10. 签 *v.* sign 签合同;签名

shì qū
11. 市区 *n.* downtown area; urban district 在市区;市区的房子

hé tóng
12. 合同 *n.* contract 一份合同;租房合同

课文(二) 去中介公司 Text B Go to an intermediary company

李明陪安娜、马克一起来到中介公司。

李明:您好!这两位想租房,能给我们介绍一下有关情况吗?
Lǐ Míng Nín hǎo Zhè liǎng wèi xiǎng zū fáng néng gěi wǒ men jiè shào yí xià yǒu guān qíng kuàng ma

公司职员甲:你们好!我们的房源很多。结构样式也不少。房子有一室一厅的,也有两室一厅的。
Gōng sī zhí yuán jiǎ Nǐ men hǎo Wǒ men de fáng yuán hěn duō Jié gòu yàng shì yě bù shǎo Fáng zi yǒu yí shì yì tīng de yě yǒu liǎng shì yì tīng de

马克:我们两人合租,要两室一厅的吧。
Mǎ kè Wǒ men liǎng rén hé zū yào liǎng shì yì tīng de ba

公司职员甲:你们要租多长时间?
Gōng sī zhí yuán jiǎ Nǐ men yào zū duō cháng shí jiān

安娜：我们租一年。
Ān nà Wǒ men zū yī nián

马克：价位怎样？
Mǎ kè Jià wèi zěn yàng

公司职员甲：市区的价位比其他地方高。
Gōng sī zhí yuán jiǎ Shì qū de jià wèi bǐ qí tā dì fāng gāo

马克：安娜，咱们在下沙租吧，离学校近。
Mǎ kè Ān nà zán men zài xià shā zū ba lí xué xiào jìn

安娜：好吧。
Ān nà Hǎo ba

公司职员甲：你们商量好，我们就签个合同吧。
Gōng sī zhí yuán jiǎ Nǐ men shāng liàng hǎo wǒ men jiù qiān gè hé tóng ba

马克、安娜：好的，谢谢！
Mǎ kè Ān nà Hǎo de xiè xie

根据课文(二)回答问题
Answer these questions according to the Text B

1. 李明陪安娜和马克去做什么？
2. 他们找了什么样的中介公司？
3. 市区的房租贵吗？
4. 租房的手续怎样？

语言点
Language points

1. A是A，就是……

方便是方便，就是不太自由。

It's convenient, but you have no freedom.

"A是A，就是……"一般表示在肯定的基础上，说明不同的看法，转折程度较轻。

"A is A, which is ..." expresses different views, but based on the tone of offirmation, in which the tone is not very strong.

(1)好看是好看，就是太贵了。
(2)想吃是想吃，就是没带钱。
(3)想租是想租，就是太远了。

2. ……的话，……

双休日有空的话，我带你们去看看。

If you are free, I can take you around?

"……的话,……",这个句式一般表示假设,常用于口语。也可用作"要是(如果)……的话,……"。

This structure is generally assumed to be used in spoken Chinese. It can also be used as "要是(如果)……的话,……"

(1) 便宜的话,我就在市区租房。

(2) 要是你喜欢的话,我们就租这套房子。

(3)如果你去的话,我就去。

3. 动词叠加 *v*. + *v*.

那我们去公司问问吧。

Let's go to the agency and ask.

重复动词,一般表示尝试做某事,也可作"*v*. + 一 + *v*."。

Repeating the verb usually means to try to do something, also can be "*v*. + 一 + *v*.".

(1)我们去中介公司问问吧。

(2)双休日我想去看看朋友。

(3)感冒了,休息休息吧。

4. A比B……

市区的价位比其他地方高。

The rent in downtown is more expensive than anywhere else.

"A比B……"用于比较人或事。

The structure is used for comparison.

(1)这家商店的东西比那家便宜。

(2)他的个子比我高。

(3)我们班女生比男生多。

5. ……离……

咱们在下沙租吧,离学校近。

Let's rent it in Xiasha District. It's close to the university.

"……离……",表示时间或空间的距离。

The structure indicates the interval of time or the distance of space.

(1)杭州离上海很近。

(2)现在离上课时间还早。

(3)我住的地方离学校很近。

核心句
Key sentences

1. 方便是方便，就是不太自由。
   It's convenient, but not free.
2. 我打算去中介公司问问。
   I'm going to the intermediary company to ask.
3. 市区房租比下沙的贵。
   Urban rents are more expensive than Xiasha District.
4. 这儿离学校近。
   It's close to the university.
5. 这倒是。
   That's true.

综合练习
Comprehensive exercises

（一）熟读下列短语 Read the following phrases

1.租房　租一年　租半年　租下沙的房子　租哪里的房子
2.房租　房租贵　房租便宜　交房租　下沙的房租便宜　市区的房租贵
3.合租　一起合租　和他合租　两人一起合租　合租两室两卫一厅的房子
4.问问　看看　听听　想想　休息休息　介绍介绍
5.离学校近　离学校不远　离上课还早　离放假还有一个月

（二）替换练习 Substitution drills

1. <u>方便</u>是<u>方便</u>，就是不太<u>自由</u>。

   便宜　便宜　　好看
   好看　好看　　合适
   好吃　好吃　　便宜

2. 现在住在<u>学生宿舍</u>不是挺<u>方便</u>的吗？

   下沙　　近
   市区　　贵
   学校　　好

3. 双休日<u>有空</u>的话，我带你们去<u>看看</u>。

   方便　　问问
   不忙　　看电影

想吃　　　　　　吃

4. 市区的价位比其他地方高。

房租　　　　贵

房价　　　　高

交通　　　　拥挤

5. 咱们在下沙租房吧,离学校近。

去杭州旅行　　　这儿不远

现在去图书馆　　关门还早

现在去市区　　　交通高峰还早

6. 我们两人合租,要两室一厅的吧。

三人　　　三室一厅

两人　　　一室一厅

四人　　　四室两厅

7. 我打算去中介公司 问问。

西湖　　　看看

马老师家　坐坐

知味观　　尝尝

(三)完成对话 Complete the following dialogues

1. A: 我打算下学期住到校外去。

B: 学校宿舍不是挺__________的吗?

A: __________,就是不太__________。

B: 这__________。

2. A: 听说有的小中介公司不太__________。

B: 那我们去大的__________去问问吧。

A: 听说市区的比较贵。

B: 那我们就在下沙租吧。

A: 你们要租__________?

B: 我们__________一年。

A: 市区的价位__________其他地方高,我们__________在下沙租房吧。

B: 你们商量好,我们就签个__________吧。

(四)课堂活动 In-class exercises

1. 角色扮演。Role-play.

(1)去中介公司租房。

参考词语:租房　房租　签　合同

(2)比较市中心和其他地段的租房情况。

参考词语:离学校　近　远　便宜　贵　高

2. 成段表达。Presentation.

(1)谈谈在校外怎样租房。

中介公司　网上　咨询　求租　签合同

(2)介绍租房情况。

房源　室　厅　卫　结构

(五)课后练习 After-class exercises

采访几位中国人,了解杭州的租房情况。Interview some Chinese people and record their answers。

	租客 1	租客 2	租客 3	租客 4
房屋的结构	室　厅	室　厅	室　厅	室　厅
合租还是整租				
每月租金多少				
月付、季付还是年付				
到附近的地铁站有多远				
到附近的超市有多远				

课后小贴士

如果你要在校外租房,不论是找中介看房,还是直接联系房东,一定要注意安全。不要随便相信大街上随处可见的小广告,要找正规中介或网站;区分房客转租和房东直租,签订合同前一定要索要房产证和房东的身份证件,如果是转租,尽量要求房东到场签约,或提供房东本人亲写的委托书。核对无误,才能签约。

课文翻译 Transletion of the text

Text A　Living outside of the campus

(Li Ming, Mark and Anna are discussing about renting a house.)

Anna: Mark, would you like to live outside of the campus?

Mark: Isn't it convenient to live in a student dormitory?

Anna: It's convenient, but you have no freedom. It's more difficult to get into the dorm when you return home late in the weekend.

Mark: That's true.

Anna: So, I'll plan to live outside of the campus next semester.

Mark: Let's share it together. But what about the rent?

Li Ming: You can rent online or ask the rental agency directly.

Anna: Let's go to the agency and ask.

Li Ming: If I'm free at the weekend, I can take you to the agency.

Anna: OK. Thank you!

Mark: OK, thanks!

Text B　Go to an intermediary company

(Li Ming has arrived to the agency with Anna and Mark.)

Li Ming: Hello! These two want to rent. Can you tell us something about it?

Company employee A: Hello! We have a lot of houses. There are also many structural styles, such as house with one bedroom, one hall and one bathroom, and house with two bedrooms, one hall and two bathrooms.

Mark: Let's share a two-bedroom apartment.

Company employee A: How long will you be renting?

Anna: Let's rent for a year.

Mark: How's the price?

Company employee A: The rent in downtown is more expensive than anywhere else.

Mark: Anna, let's rent it in Xiasha District. It's close to the university.

Anna: OK.

Company employee A: We'll sign the contract after having discussed it.

Make, Anna: OK! thanks!

⑤ 去医院看病
Going to hospital

话题导学
Guidance

1. 去医院看病,怎么挂号?
   How do you register when you go to the hospital?
2. 怎么配合医生问诊?
   How do you cooperate with the doctor?
3. 什么情况下可以去看中医?
   What situations can you go to see a traditional Chinese doctor?

生词学习(一)
New words I

1. 医院 (yī yuàn) *n.* hospital — 一家医院;去医院
2. 看病 (kànbìng) *VO* see a doctor — 去看病;在哪儿看病
3. 挂号 (guàhào) *v.* register — 去挂号;门诊挂号
4. 护照 (hù zhào) *n.* passport — 我的护照;一本护照
5. 带 (dài) *v.* bring — 带东西;带护照
6. 付费 (fù fèi) *v.* pay — 付学费;付餐费
7. 办 (bàn) *v.* do — 办护照;办事情
8. 就诊卡 (jiù zhěn kǎ) patient ID card; medical card — 带就诊卡
9. 病历卡 (bìng lì kǎ) medical record card — 一张病历卡;他的病历卡
10. 自助 (zì zhù) self-service — 自助餐厅

11.	fú wù 服务	*n.* service	自助服务
12.	yì tǐ jī 一体机	all-in-one machine	自助服务一体机
13.	sǎng zi 嗓子	*n.* throat	嗓子疼;嗓子不舒服
14.	ké sou 咳嗽	*v.* cough	感冒咳嗽

课文(一) 挂号
Text A Register in the hospital

李明陪马克去医院看病。

李明:你好。请问在哪儿挂号?我外国朋友病了。
Lǐ Míng Nǐ hǎo Qǐngwèn zài nǎr guàhào Wǒ wàiguó péngyou bìng le

医导:护照带了吗?
Yī dǎo Hù zhào dài le ma

马克:带了。
Mǎ kè Dài le

医导:请先付费,办就诊卡和病历卡。要么在挂号处挂,要么在自助服务一体机上挂号。
Yī dǎo Qǐng xiān fù fèi bàn jiù zhěn kǎ hé bìng lì kǎ Yào me zài guàhào chù guà yào me zài zì zhù fú wù yì tǐ jī shàng guàhào

李明:好的,谢谢!
Lǐ Míng Hǎo de xiè xie

医生:你好!怎么不舒服?
Yī shēng Nǐ hǎo Zěn me bù shū fu

马克:医生,我嗓子疼、咳嗽。
Mǎ kè Yī shēng wǒ sǎng zi téng ké sou

医生:什么时候开始不舒服的?
Yī shēng Shén me shí hou kāi shǐ bù shū fu de

马克:前天开始的。
Mǎ kè Qián tiān kāi shǐ de

医生:张大嘴,我看一下。哦,感冒了。
Yī shēng Zhāng dà zuǐ wǒ kàn yí xià Ò gǎnmào le

李明:医生,严重吗?
Lǐ Míng Yī shēng yán zhòng ma

医生:还好,吃点药,休息休息。这是处方。
Yī shēng Hái hǎo chī diǎn yào xiū xi xiū xi Zhè shì chǔ fāng

马克:谢谢医生。
Mǎ kè Xiè xie yī shēng

李明：马克，我们去付费取药吧。
Lǐ Míng Mǎ kè wǒ men qù fù fèi qǔ yào ba

马克：好的。
Mǎ kè Hǎo de

根据课文(一)回答问题
Answer these questions according to the Text A

1. 李明陪马克去了哪里？
2. 怎么挂号？
3. 马克哪里不舒服？
4. 医生建议马克做什么？

生词学习(二)
New words II

wèikǒu 1. 胃口	*n.* appetite; belly	没胃口；胃口好
shì yìng 2. 适应	*v.* adapt; get with it; fit	适应社会；适应生活
shuì 3. 睡	*v.* sleep	睡觉；睡不好
zhōng yào 4. 中药	*n.* Chinese medicine	服中药；一剂中药
zhōng yī 5. 中医	*n.* traditional Chinese medicine(TCM)	中医养生
guǎn 6. 馆	*n.* a place for cultural activities	中医馆；图书馆
tiáo lǐ 7. 调理	*v.* nurse one's health	调理身体
hǎo xiàng 8. 好像	*adv.* seem; be like	好像没病；好像迟到了
yě xǔ 9. 也许	*adv.* maybe	也许知道；也许生病了
yù jiàn 10. 遇见	*v.* meet; come across	偶然遇见
péi 11. 陪	*v.* accompany	陪同学；陪他

课文(二) 看中医
Text B See a traditional Chinese medicine doctor

在校园，马克遇见他的朋友李明。

马克：李明，你好！最近怎么样？
Mǎ kè Lǐ Míng nǐ hǎo Zuì jìn zěn me yàng

李明：你好，马克！我很好。你呢？
Lǐ Míng Nǐ hǎo Mǎ kè Wǒ hěn hǎo Nǐ ne

马克：最近我总是不舒服。
Mǎ kè Zuì jìn wǒ zǒng shì bù shū fu

李明：怎么啦？
Lǐ Míng Zěn me lā

马克：吃饭没胃口，晚上睡不好。
Mǎ kè Chī fàn méi wèi kǒu wǎn shàng shuì bù hǎo

李明：可能是刚来中国不适应吧？
Lǐ Míng Kě néng shì gāng lái zhōng guó bú shì yìng ba

马克：也许吧。
Mǎ kè Yě xǔ ba

李明：最好去医院看看吧。
Lǐ Míng Zuì hǎo qù yī yuàn kàn kan ba

马克：可是，我好像什么病也没有啊。
Mǎ kè Kě shì wǒ hǎo xiàng shén me bìng yě méi yǒu a

李明：我觉得你可以去看中医。中药可以调理身体。
Lǐ Míng Wǒ jué de nǐ kě yǐ qù kàn zhōng yī Zhōng yào kě yǐ tiáo lǐ shēn tǐ

马克：哦，杭州有有名的中医馆吗？
Mǎ kè Ò háng zhōu yǒu yǒu míng de zhōng yī guǎn ma

李明：有，比如胡庆余堂、方回春堂等。除了中医馆，还有专门的中医院。
Lǐ Míng Yǒu bǐ rú hú qìng yú táng fāng huí chūn táng děng Chú le zhōng yī guǎn hái yǒu zhuān mén de zhōng yī yuàn

马克：那你什么时候有空呢？陪我一起去吧。
Mǎ kè Nà nǐ shén me shí hòu yǒu kòng ne Péi wǒ yì qǐ qù ba

李明：那就后天去吧。
Lǐ Míng Nà jiù hòu tiān qù ba

马克：又要麻烦你了，谢谢啊！
Mǎ kè Yòu yào má fán nǐ le xiè xie a

李明：不客气！
Lǐ Míng Bú kè qi

根据课文(二)回答问题
Answer these questions according to the Text B

1. 马克怎么了？
2. 李明建议马克去哪里看病？
3. 中医可以调理身体吗？

4. 杭州有有名的中医馆吗？

语言点
Language points

1. 要么……,要么……

要么去挂号处挂,要么通过自助服务一体机挂号。

You can go to the registration office or the self-service machine to get a number.

“要么……,要么……”一般表示两个都可以选择。

Generally speaking, the structure means two options are available.

(1)要么看西医,要么看中医。

(2)要么明天去,要么后天去。

(3)要么服西药,要么服中药。

2. ……的;(是)……的

什么时候开始不舒服的？

When did you feel ill?

“是……的”这个格式常用于强调某事。

The structure can be used to emphasize something.

(1)前天开始的。

(2)他是骑车去的。

(3)什么时候开始的？

3. 除了……,还……

除了中医馆,还有专门的中医院。

In addition to famous Chinese medicine museums, there are hospitals of traditional Chinese medicine.

“除了……,还……”表示在前者的基础上,后者有进一步的阐述。

The structure means on the basis of the former, the latter has further elaboration.

(1)除了现金,还可以用支付宝。

(2)除了咳嗽,还头疼。

(3)除了西医,还有中医。

4. 又要……了

又要麻烦你了。

I am about to bother you again.

"又要……了",一般用于说明将要发生某事,常指不喜欢的事将要发生。

The structure is usually used to describe something that you wish it won't happen.

(1)又要考试了。

(2)又要迟到了。

(3)人这么多,又要买不到票了。

核心句 Key sentences

1. 要么去看西医,要么去看中医。

   You can go to see western medicine or go to see traditional Chinese medicine.

2. 请问在哪儿挂号?

   Where can I register, please?

3. 你最好去医院看看。

   You'd better see a doctor.

4. 怎么不舒服?

   What's the matter with you?

5. 什么时候开始不舒服的?

   When did the trouble start?

综合练习 Comprehensive exercises

(一)熟读下列短语 Read the following phrases

1.就诊卡　病历卡　银行卡　信用卡　交通卡　学生卡

2.付费　付钱　付款　刷卡付费　支付宝付费　现金付费

3.中医　西医　中餐　西餐　中药　西药　中式　西式

4.嗓子疼　头疼　眼睛疼　肚子疼　牙疼　脚疼

5.看病　去医院看病　去诊所看病　去中医馆看病　去浙江中医院看病

6.挂号　挂内科　挂外科　挂口腔科　去挂号处挂号　在自助服务一体机上挂号

7.又要麻烦你了　又要考试了　又要去医院了　又要下雨了　又要抢购了　又要涨价了

(二)替换练习 Substitution drills

1. 除了现金,还可以用支付宝。

美金	人民币
网银	微信
电脑	手机

2. 我觉得你可以去看西医,也可以去看中医。

看电影　　看电视

医院　　中医馆

杭州　　苏州

3. 什么时候开始不舒服的?

习惯

喜欢

工作

4. 可能是刚来中国不适应吧?

杭州　习惯

学校　熟悉

浙江　了解

5. 我朋友可能感冒了,挂内科吧?

受伤　　外科

牙疼　　口腔科

发高烧　急诊

6. 要么去看西医,要么去看中医。

在家　　在学校

西安旅行　南京旅行

吃饺子　　吃面条

7. 你最好去医院＿＿＿看看。

在家　　休息休息

去中医院　调理调理

去那家饭店　吃吃

(三)完成对话 Complete the following dialogues

1. A: 你好! 请问在哪儿＿＿＿＿＿?

B: 你要么＿＿＿＿＿挂,要么＿＿＿＿＿挂号。

A: 我没有就诊卡和＿＿＿＿＿。

B: 请先付费,办＿＿＿＿＿和＿＿＿＿＿。

2. A: 你好? 怎么＿＿＿＿＿?

B: 医生,我＿＿＿＿＿。

A: 什么时候开始的?

B: ＿＿＿＿＿开始的。

A: 吃点儿药,休息休息,这是__________。

B: 谢谢医生。

3. A: 我最近总是不舒服。吃饭__________,晚上__________。

B: 去医院看看吧。

A: __________听说不错。

B: 是的,__________能调理身体。明天我陪你去吧。

A: 又要__________你了!

B: 不客气!

(四)课堂活动 In-class exercises

1. 角色扮演。Role-play.

(1)你第一次去医院看病。

参考词语:挂号　配药　付费　就诊卡　病历卡

(2)在中医馆询问老中医。

参考词语:中医　西医　中医馆　慢性病　调理

2. 成段表达。Presentation.

(1)第一次去中医馆看病。

又要……了　是……的　调理身体　最好

(2)去医院看病

挂号　就诊卡　取药　病历卡

(五)课后练习 After-class exercises

采访几个中国学生和国际生,了解他们对中医诊疗的看法。Interview several Chinese students and international students and ask them about their views on TCM treatment.

	中国学生1	中国学生2	国际学生1	国际学生2
你看过中医吗				
中医和西医哪里不一样				
中药和西药哪里不一样				
你觉得中医怎么样				

课后小贴士

中国人有用中医养生的习惯。中医养生,就是指通过各种方法颐养生命、增强体质、预防疾病,从而达到延年益寿的一种医事活动。中医养生重在整体性和系统性,目的是预防疾病,治愈疾病。中医理论的著名代表作品是《黄帝内经》。

课文翻译 Translation of the texts

Text A　Register in the hospital

(Li Ming accompanied Mark to see a doctor.)

Li Ming: Hello! Where can I register? My foreign friend is ill.

Medical guide: Have you got your passport?

Mark: Yes.

Medical guide: Please pay first for the personal office and get a patient ID card and medical record card. You can go to the registration office or the self-service machine to get a number.

Li Ming: OK, thanks!

Doctor: Hello! What's wrong with you?

Mark: Doctor, I have a sore throat and a cough.

Doctor: When did the trouble start?

Mark: It was the day before yesterday.

Doctor: Open your mouth. Let me look at it. Oh, you've got a cold.

Li Ming: Doctor, is it serious?

Doctor: Not so bad. Take some medicine and rest. Here is the prescription.

Mark: Thank you, doctor!

Li Ming: Mark, let's go pay for the medicine.

Mark: OK.

Text B　See a traditional Chinese medicine doctor

(On the campus, Mark met his friend Li Ming.)

Mark: Hi, Li Ming! How are you?

Li Ming: Hi, Mark! I'm fine. What about you?

Mark: I haven't been feeling well recently.

Li Ming: What's wrong with you?

Mark: I have no appetite for dinner. I can't sleep well at night.

Li Ming: Maybe you are not used to Chinese life.

Mark: Maybe.

Li Ming: You'd better see a doctor.

Mark: But, I don't seem to be sick.

Li Ming: I think you can try some traditional Chinese medicine. Chinese medicine can really help people get better.

Mark: Well, is there a famous Chinese medicine clinic in Hangzhou?

Li Ming: Yes, such as Hu Qing Yu Chinese Pharmacy and Fang Huichun Tang, etc. Besides, there are hospitals of traditional Chinese medicine.

Mark: When are you free? Can you go with me?

Li Ming: Let's go the day after tomorrow, OK?

Mark: OK, I'll have to trouble you again. Thank you very much!

Li Ming: You're welcome!

6 参加商务宴请
Attending a business banquet

话题导学 Guidance

1. 参加中国人的商务宴请应该注意什么？
   What would you do when you attend a Chinese business dinner?
2. 你知道中国人的餐饮礼仪吗？
   Do you know the Chinese food etiquette?
3. 杭州的菜有什么特色？
   What's the specialty of Hangzhou cuisine?

生词学习（一） New words I

1. shāng wù 商 务 *n.* business affairs　　商务活动；商务会议
2. yàn huì 宴 会 *n.* banquet　　商务宴会；参加宴会
3. qǐng 请 *v.* invite　　邀请；宴请
4. lǐ jié 礼 节 *n.* etiquette　　西方礼节；传统礼节
5. jiǎng jiu 讲 究 *adj.* dainty　　很讲究；不讲究
6. zhǎng bèi 长 辈 *n.* elder　　他的长辈；尊敬长辈
7. zhòng yào 重 要 *adj.* important　　非常重要；重要的宴会
8. rén wù 人 物 *n.* figures　　重要人物；小说人物
9. wèi zhi 位 置 *n.* seat　　学校的位置；重要位置
10. kào 靠 *v.* rely on　　靠门；靠墙

课文(一) 入乡随俗
Text A As the Romans do

在校园,玛丽、美玲、李明一起谈论商务宴请。

李明:周末我要去参加朋友的商务宴会。
Lǐ Míng Zhōu mò wǒ yào qù cān jiā péngyou de shāng wù yàn huì

玛丽:我对中国人的宴会很感兴趣,能一起去吗?
Mǎ lì Wǒ duì zhōng guó rén de yàn huì hěn gǎn xìng qù néng yì qǐ qù ma

美玲:我也想去,可以吗?
Měi líng Wǒ yě xiǎng qù kě yǐ ma

李明:好的。我朋友想请几位外国朋友一起参加。
Lǐ Míng Hǎo de Wǒ péngyou xiǎng qǐng jǐ wèi wài guó péngyou yì qǐ cān jiā

玛丽:中国人在宴请时,礼节有什么讲究吗?
Mǎ lì Zhōng guó rén zài yàn qǐng shí lǐ jié yǒu shén me jiǎng jiu ma

李明:礼节很多。比如长辈、重要人物要坐重要位置。
Lǐ Míng Lǐ jié hěn duō Bǐ rú zhǎng bèi zhòng yào rén wù yào zuò zhòng yào wèi zhi

美玲:重要的位置在哪里?
Měi líng Zhòng yào de wèi zhi zài nǎ lǐ

李明:一般是椅子靠墙、面对房门的较好。
Lǐ Míng Yì bān shì yǐ zi kào qiáng miàn duì fáng mén de jiào hǎo

美玲:我听说中国有句俗话:酒要满,茶要浅。
Měi líng Wǒ tīng shuō zhōng guó yǒu jù sú huà jiǔ yào mǎn chá yào qiǎn

李明:是的,中国是古老的礼仪之邦嘛!
Lǐ Míng Shì de zhōng guó shì gǔ lǎo de lǐ yí zhī bāng ma

玛丽:那我们周末去参加宴请时得注意啊!
Mǎ lì Nà wǒ men zhōu mò qù cān jiā yàn qǐng shí děi zhù yì a

美玲:是啊,入乡随俗嘛!
Měi líng Shì a rù xiāng suí sú ma

根据课文(一)回答问题
Answer these questions according to the Text A

1. 玛丽他们要去哪里?
2. 中国人宴请时有哪些礼节习俗?
3. 参加中国人的商务宴请要注意什么?
4. 他们打算什么时候去?

生词学习(二)
New words II

cài xì
1. 菜系 *n.* cuisine 八大菜系;南方菜系

fēng shèng 2. 丰 盛	*adj*. abundant	很丰盛;丰盛的饭菜
háng bāng cài 3. 杭 帮 菜	Hangzhou cuisines	吃杭帮菜
tè sè 4. 特色	*n*. feature	杭州特色;很有特色
chuán tǒng 5. 传 统	*adj*. traditional	传统菜;传统音乐
běn dì 6. 本地	*n*. the local	本地菜;本地人
dōng pō ròu 7. 东 坡 肉	Braised Dongpo Pork	
xī hú cù yú 8. 西湖醋鱼	West Lake Fish in Vinegar Gravy	
lóng jǐng xiā rén 9. 龙 井 虾仁	Stir-fried Shrimps with Longjing Tea	
zhèng zōng 10. 正 宗	*adj*. authentic	正宗的菜;不正宗
cháng 11. 尝	*v*. taste	尝尝;品尝
fàn diàn 12. 饭 店	*n*. restaurant	楼外楼饭店;一家饭店
chī huò 13. 吃 货	*n*. foodie; food aficionado	一个吃货;他是吃货
tīng shuō 14. 听 说	*v*. hear of	没有听说;听别人说

专有名词(Proper nouns)

lóu wài lóu
1. 楼外楼 *n*. Louwailou Restaurant

tiān wài tiān
2. 天 外 天 *n*. Tianwaitian Restaurant

zhī wèi guān
3. 知味 观 *n*. Zhiweiguan Restaurant

课文(二) 品尝杭帮菜
Text B Taste Hangzhou cuisine

李明、玛丽、美玲在宴会上。

美玲:菜真丰盛啊!
Měi líng Cài zhēn fēng shèng a

玛丽:听说中国有八大菜系,浙菜是其中的一种,是吗?
Mǎ lì Tīng shuō Zhōng guó yǒu bā dà cài xì zhè cài shì qí zhōng de yì zhǒng shì ma

李明:是的。杭州菜也有自己的特色,叫杭帮菜。
Lǐ Míng Shì de Háng zhōu cài yě yǒu zì jǐ de tè sè jiào Háng bāng cài

美玲:听说杭州本地有很多有名的传统菜。
Měi líng Tīng shuō Háng zhōu běn dì yǒu hěn duō yǒu míng de chuán tǒng cài

李明:是的,比如东坡肉、西湖醋鱼、龙井虾仁等,都是有名的传统菜。
Lǐ Míng Shì de bǐ rú dōng pō ròu xī hú cù yú lóng jǐng xiā rén děng dōu shì yǒu míng de chuán tǒng cài

玛丽:杭州有很多饭店,哪儿能吃到正宗的杭州名菜呢?
Mǎ lì Háng zhōu yǒu hěn duō fàn diàn nǎr néng chī dào zhèng zōng de Háng zhōu míng cài ne

李明:有楼外楼、天外天、知味观等。
Lǐ Míng Yǒu lóu wài lóu tiān wài tiān zhī wèi guān děng

美玲:什么时候我们一起去尝尝吧。
Měi líng Shén me shí hòu wǒ men yì qǐ qù cháng chang ba

玛丽:还是先尝尝这儿的菜吧。
Mǎ lì Hái shì xiān cháng chang zhèr de cài ba

李明:对,多吃点。下个周末有空的话,我们就一起去吧。
Lǐ Míng Duì duō chī diǎn Xià gè zhōu mò yǒu kòng de huà wǒ men jiù yì qǐ qù ba

美玲:好啊,我要尝遍所有的杭帮菜,入乡随俗嘛!
Měi líng Hǎo a wǒ yào cháng biàn suǒ yǒu de Háng bāng cài rù xiāng suí sú ma

玛丽:真是吃货啊,哈哈!
Mǎ lì Zhēn shì chī huò a hā hā

根据课文(二)回答问题
Answer these questions according to the Text B

1. 浙菜是"八大菜系"的一种吗?
2. 杭州有什么有名的传统菜?
3. 吃传统杭州菜,应该去杭州哪些饭店?
4. 什么叫"杭帮菜"?

语言点
Language points

1. 能……吗?

能一起去吗?

Can I go with you?

"能……吗?"表示礼貌地请求。

This structure indicates a polite request.

(1)我能借你的词典吗?

(2)你能和我一起去医院吗?

(3)能帮我一下忙吗?

2. ……嘛

入乡随俗嘛!

when in Rome, do as the Romans do!

"……嘛",说明道理很简单,"嘛"用于句末。

The structure often shows that the statement is obvious. "嘛" is used in the end of sentence.

(1)有不明白的问题,就问嘛!

(2)中国是礼仪之邦嘛!

(3)俗话说:酒要满,茶要浅嘛!

3. 真……啊

真是吃货啊!

What a foodie!

"真……啊",表示感叹,赞叹。

This structure expresses sigh or praise.

(1)菜真丰盛啊!

(2)西湖真美啊!

(3)中国人真多啊!

4. 还是……

还是先尝尝这儿的菜吧。

Let's try some food here first.

"还是……",比较后的选择。一般用于回答"是……,还是……"。

This structure means choosing an option. It is used to answer the structure "是……,还是……".

(1)A:是你去还是我去? B:还是你先去吧。

(2)A:是杭帮菜好吃还是外地菜好吃? B:还是杭帮菜好吃。

(3)A:是动车快还是高铁快? B:还是高铁快。

5. ……的话,就……

下个周末有空的话,我们就一起去吧。

If you are free next weekend, let's go together.

"……的话,就……",表示在假设的条件下,会有一种相应的结果。

The structure means in the case of hypothesis, there is a corresponding result.

(1)你不喜欢吃这个菜的话,就别吃了。

(2)周末有空的话,我们就去西湖玩吧。

(3)不尝的话,就不知道菜的味道。

核心句 Key sentences

1. 我对中国人的宴会感兴趣。

   I'm interested in Chinese banquet.

2. 杭州菜也有自己的特色,叫"杭帮菜"。

   Hangzhou cuisine also has its own characteristics, called "Hang bang cai".

3. 还是先尝尝这儿的菜吧。

   Try the dishes here first.

4. 杭州有很多有名的菜。

   There are many famous dishes in Hangzhou.

5. 入乡随俗嘛!

   When in Rome, do as the Romans do!

综合练习 Comprehensive exercises

(一)熟读下列短语 Read the following phrases

1.讲究礼节　讲究穿　讲究外表　讲究卫生　对穿衣服很讲究　对吃不讲究

2.自己的特色　地方特色　中国特色　杭州特色　特色菜　传统的特色菜

3.靠墙　靠门　靠窗　靠窗的地方　不要靠窗　靠着桌子

4.正宗的中国菜　正宗的杭帮菜　正宗的传统名菜　正宗的绍兴黄酒

5.传统的名菜　传统文化　传统的观念　传统的思想　传统的做法

6.本地人　本地菜　本地饭馆　本地话　本地生活　本地公司

7.对汉语感兴趣　对杭帮菜感兴趣　对传统名菜感兴趣　对中国的商务宴请感兴趣

(二)替换练习 Substitution drills

1. 我<u>周末</u>要去参加一个<u>朋友</u>的<u>商务</u>宴会。

明天	同学	生日
后天	老板	店庆
下周	同事	庆功

2. 我对中国人的宴会很感兴趣。

中国的传统文化

杭州的风味小吃

杭帮菜

3. 我朋友想请几位外国朋友一起参加。

几位同学	参观
几位中国学生	学习
大家	旅游

4. 我要尝遍所有的杭帮菜。

吃	特色菜
玩	旅游景点
看	好电影

5. 下个周末有空的话,我们就一起去吧。

明天下午	一起吃饭
下课以后	去喝咖啡
假期	去旅行

6. 听说杭州本地有很多有名的传统菜。

浙江本地	著名的丝绸产品
下个月	足球比赛
他们学校	国际学生

(三)完成对话 Complete the following dialogues

1. A: 周末我要去参加一个朋友的宴会。
   B: 我对中国人的__________很感兴趣,能一起去吗?
   A: 好的,一起去吧。我朋友想请几位外国朋友一起__________。
   B: 那__________。谢谢!

2. A:听说中国的菜有八大__________,浙菜是其中的一种,是吗?
   B:是的。杭州的菜也有自己的特色,叫__________。
   A:我们一起去尝尝吧。
   B:先尝尝这儿的__________吧。

(四)课堂活动 In-class exercises

1. 角色扮演。Role-play.
   (1)去参加中国朋友的宴会。
   参考词语:礼节　入乡随俗　位置　传统

(2)去饭店吃饭。

参考词语:特色菜　有名　丰盛　吃货

2. 成段表达。Presentation.

(1)介绍杭州或你们国家的名菜。

对……感兴趣　特色　正宗　有名　尝

(2)介绍你们国家的餐饮礼仪。

礼节　礼貌　传统　入乡随俗

(五)课后练习 After-class exercises

采访你的朋友。Interview your friends and record their answers.

	朋友 1	朋友 2	朋友 3	朋友 4
你是哪里人				
你最喜欢的中国菜是什么				
你最喜欢吃的小吃是什么				
你吃过哪些杭州菜				
你喜欢什么味道的菜 (酸、甜、苦、辣、咸)				

课文翻译 Translation of the texts

Text A　As the Romans do

(Mary, Meiling and Li Ming are talking about business dinner in the campus.)

Li Ming: I am going to a friend's business banquet on the weekend.

Mary: I am very interested in Chinese banquets. Can I go with you?

Meiling: Can I go with you?

Li Ming: OK. My friend wants to invite several foreign friends to join us.

Mary: Is there anything to know at the Chinese banquet?

Li Ming: There are many etiquettes. For example, elders, important people should take an important position.

Meiling: Where is the important position?

Li Ming: It is generally better for the chair to face the door against the wall.

Meiling: I heard that there is a saying in China, "The wine is full and the tea is shallow".

Li Ming: Yes, China is an ancient country with many traditional etiquettes.

Mary: Then we have to know something in advance when we go to the banquet on weekends!

Meiling: Yes, do as the Romans do!

Text B　Taste Hangzhou cuisine

(Li Ming, Mary and Meiling are at the banquet.)

Meiling: The dishes are really rich!

Mary: I heard that there are eight major cuisines in China. Zhejiang cuisine is one of them, is it?

Li Ming: Yes. Hangzhou cuisine also has its own characteristics. We called it "Hangbangcai".

Meiling: I heard that there are many famous traditional dishes in Hangzhou.

Li Ming: Yes, for example, Braised Dongpo Pork, West Lake Fish in Vinegar Gravy. Stir-fried Shrimps with Longjing Tea, etc. They are famous traditional dishes.

Mary: There are many restaurants in Hangzhou. Where can I eat authentic Hangzhou famous dishes?

Li Ming: There are Louwailou Restaurant, Tianwaitian Restaurant, Zhiweiguan Restaurant and so on.

Meiling: When are we going to taste it together?

Mary: Still taste the dishes here first.

Li Ming: Yes, enjoy it. If you have time next weekend, let's go together.

Meiling: OK, I have to taste all the Hangbang dishes, and do as the Romans do!

Mary: You are really foodies, haha!

7 我要订往返机票
I want to book a return flight

话题导学 Guidance

1. 预订机票时应该向航空公司询问哪些内容?
   What should you consult with the airline company when you book air tickets?
2. 短距离的旅行,坐汽车方便还是坐火车方便?
   If you go on a short trip, which is more convenient, by train or by bus?
3. 你了解中国火车有哪些种类吗?
   Do you know what kinds of train are there in China?

生词学习(一) New words I

1. 预订 (yù dìng) *v.* book; reserve — 预订机票;预订房间
2. 大概 (dà gài) *adv.* about — 大概五点;大概十个人
3. 出发 (chū fā) *v.* depart — 出发时间;明天出发
4. 以前 (yǐ qián) *n.* before — 吃饭以前;上课以前
5. 到达 (dào dá) *v.* arrive — 到达北京;几点到达
6. 起飞 (qǐ fēi) *v.* take off — 飞机起飞;起飞时间
7. 班 (bān) *mw.* (used for flight or train) — 这班飞机;一班火车
8. 合适 (hé shì) *adj.* proper — 衣服合适;大小不合适
9. 经济舱 (jīng jì cāng) *n.* economy class — 经济舱座位;预订经济舱
10. 单程 (dān chéng) *n.* one way — 单程机票

yuán jià
11. 原价 *n.* original price 原价二百元

dǎ zhé
12. 打折 *v.* discount 裤子打折了；打八折

wǎng fǎn
13. 往返 *v.* round trip 往返机票；往返时间

zǒng é
14. 总额 *n.* total amount 票价总额；总额很高

课文(一) 乘飞机去北京
Text A Fly to Beijing

安娜要去北京看朋友，她给航空公司打电话预订机票。

客服：您好！首都航空公司，请问您需要什么服务？
Kè fú Nín hǎo Shǒu dū háng kōng gōng sī qǐng wèn nín xū yào shén me fú wù

安娜：您好！我想预订杭州到北京的机票。
Ān nà Nín hǎo Wǒ xiǎng yù dìng Háng zhōu dào Běi jīng de jī piào

客服：好的，您要预订哪天的机票？大概什么时间出发？
Kè fú Hǎo de nín yào yù dìng nǎ tiān de jī piào Dà gài shén me shí jiān chū fā

安娜：我想订十二月二十六号的。最好中午以前能到达。
Ān nà Wǒ xiǎng dìng shí èr yuè èr shí liù hào de Zuì hǎo zhōng wǔ yǐ qián néng dào dá

客服：上午九点钟起飞的飞机比较合适，中午十一点到北京。
Kè fú Shàng wǔ jiǔ diǎn zhōng qǐ fēi de fēi jī bǐ jiào hé shì zhōng wǔ shí yī diǎn dào běi jīng

安娜：好的，经济舱的价格是多少钱？
Ān nà Hǎo de jīng jì cāng de jià gé shì duō shǎo qián

客服：女士，单程机票原价是九百元，现在可以打六折，五百四十元。
Kè fú Nǚ shì dān chéng jī piào yuán jià shì jiǔ bǎi yuán xiàn zài kě yǐ dǎ liù zhé wǔ bǎi sì shí yuán

安娜：要是预订往返机票的话，是不是便宜一点儿？
Ān nà Yào shì yù dìng wǎng fǎn jī piào de huà shì bú shì pián yi yì diǎnr

客服：是的，女士。预订往返机票的话，票价总额可以打五折。
Kè fú Shì de nǚ shì Yù dìng wǎng fǎn jī piào de huà piào jià zǒng é kě yǐ dǎ wǔ zhé

安娜：那我预订往返机票吧。北京回杭州的时间是十二月二十九号下午。
Ān nà Nà wǒ yù dìng wǎng fǎn jī piào ba Běi jīng huí Háng zhōu de shí jiān shì shí èr yuè èr shí jiǔ hào xià wǔ

客服：好的。
Kè fú Hǎo de

根据课文(一)回答问题
Answer these questions according to the Text A

1. 安娜要预订哪里到哪里的机票？哪天出发？

2. 经济舱的票价是多少钱?

3. 预订往返机票可以打几折?

4. 安娜什么时候回杭州?

生词学习(二) New words II

1. 离 (lí)	*prep.* be away from	离学校很近;杭州离北京很远
2. 长途 (cháng tú)	*n.* long distance	长途汽车;长途电话
3. 速度 (sù dù)	*n.* speed	速度很快;加快速度
4. 高铁 (gāo tiě)	*n.* G-series high-speed train	坐高铁;买高铁票
5. 麻烦 (má fan)	*adj.* troublesome	很麻烦;不麻烦
6. 一般 (yì bān)	*adv.* usually	一般不吃早饭; 一般走路去
7. 提前 (tí qián)	*adj.* ahead of time	提前买票;提前告诉我
8. 赶 (gǎn)	*v.* catch	赶时间;赶飞机
9. 建议 (jiàn yì)	*n./v.* suggestion; suggest	老师的建议;大家的建议

课文(二) Text B　乘火车去上海 Take the train to Shanghai

玛丽和美玲在谈论怎么去上海。

美玲:玛丽,听说你很喜欢旅行,你去过中国哪些地方?
Měi líng　Mǎ lì　tīng shuō nǐ hěn xǐ huān lǚ xíng　nǐ qù guò Zhōng guó nǎ xiē dì fang

玛丽:我去过北京、上海、广州和苏州。
Mǎ lì　Wǒ qù guò Běi jīng　Shàng hǎi　Guǎng zhōu hé　Sū zhōu

美玲:虽然杭州离上海很近,但是我还没去过呢。
Měi líng　Suī rán Háng zhōu　lí　Shàng hǎi hěn jìn　dàn shì wǒ hái méi qù guò ne

玛丽:从杭州去上海很方便,周末的时候你可以去看看。
Mǎ lì　Cóng Háng zhōu qù Shàng hǎi hěn fāng biàn　zhōu mò de shí hou nǐ kě yǐ qù kàn kan

美玲:从杭州怎么去上海呢?
Měi líng　Cóng Háng zhōu zěn me qù Shàng hǎi ne

玛丽:可以坐长途汽车,但是最方便的是坐火车。中国速度最快
Mǎ lì　Kě yǐ zuò cháng tú qì chē　dàn shì zuì fāng biàn de shì zuò huǒ chē　Zhōng guó sù dù zuì kuài

的火车叫"高铁",从杭州到上海坐高铁一个小时就能到。
de huǒ chē jiào gāo tiě cóng Háng zhōu dào Shàng hǎi zuò gāo tiě yí gè xiǎo shí jiù néng dào

美玲:这么快!看来从杭州去上海一点儿也不麻烦。
Měi líng Zhè me kuài Kàn lái cóng Háng zhōu qù Shàng hǎi yì diǎnr yě bù má fan

玛丽:对,很容易。坐地铁一号线到火车东站下车就可以了。去上海的高铁一般都从火车东站出发。
Mǎ lì Duì hěn róng yì Zuò dì tiě yī hào xiàn dào huǒ chē dōng zhàn xià chē jiù kě yǐ le Qù Shàng hǎi de gāo tiě yì bān dōu cóng huǒ chē dōng zhàn chū fā

美玲:太方便了!需要提前买票吗?
Měi líng Tài fāng biàn le Xū yào tí qián mǎi piào ma

玛丽:要是赶时间,你最好提前买票。要是不赶时间,可以去火车站的时候再买。因为每天从杭州去上海的高铁有很多。
Mǎ lì Yào shì gǎn shí jiān nǐ zuì hǎo tí qián mǎi piào Yào shì bù gǎn shí jiān kě yǐ qù huǒ chē zhàn de shí hòu zài mǎi Yīn wèi měi tiān cóng Háng zhōu qù Shàng hǎi de gāo tiě yǒu hěn duō

美玲:玛丽,谢谢你的建议,现在我知道怎么去上海了。
Měi líng Mǎ lì xiè xie nǐ de jiàn yì xiàn zài wǒ zhī dào zěn me qù Shàng hǎi le

根据课文(二)回答问题
Answer these questions according to the Text B

1. 玛丽去过中国哪些地方?
2. 从杭州怎么去上海?
3. 从杭州到上海坐高铁要多长时间?
4. 坐火车去上海需要提前买票吗?

语言点
Language points

1. 打折/打……折

单程机票原价是九百元,现在可以打六折,就是五百四十元。

The original price for a one-way ticket is 900 yuan. Now you can make a discount of 60 percent, which is 540 yuan.

"打折"可以单独使用,表示得到折扣。也可以中间加入数字一至九,或保留小数点后一位数字。例如:"打九折"就是原价的90%,"打八五折"就是原价的85%。

"打折" can be used alone, indicating a discount. You can also add the number one to nine in the middle, or one digit after the decimal point. For example, "打九折" is 90% of the original price. "打八五折" is 85% of the original price.

(1)这里的衣服不打折。

(2)这本书原价100块,现在打八折,80块。

(3)这条裤子原价500块,现在打六八折,340块可以买到。

2. 要是……(的话),就……

要是预订往返机票的话,是不是价格能便宜一点儿?

Is it cheaper if I book a round trip ticket?

表示假设发生某种情况,会有什么结果。"要是"和"的话"可以单独使用,也可以一起使用。

It means that if something happens, there is something would be led to. "要是" and "的话" can be used separately or together.

(1)要是明天下雨,我们就不去爬山了。

(2)你来杭州的话,给我打电话。

(3)要是明天你有时间的话,就跟我们一起去吧。

3. 看来……

看来从杭州去上海一点儿也不麻烦。

It seems that it is not troublesome to go to Shanghai from Hangzhou.

表示根据某个情况或者事实对某事做出判断。

The structure means that one can make a judgment about something according to a situation or fact.

(1)已经这么晚了,看来今天他不会来了。

(2)看来要下雨了。

(3)看来你比我更了解他。

4. 从……到……

从杭州到上海坐高铁一个小时就能到。

It takes an hour to from Hangzhou to Shanghai.

表示处所、时间等之间间隔的距离或时间。

The distance or interval between two places or time, etc.

(1)从北京到上海坐飞机要多长时间?

(2)他的上班时间是从早上8点到下午5点。

(3)从2015年到2017年,他一直在中国学习。

5. 最好

要是赶时间,你最好提前买票。

If you're in a hurry, you'd better buy a ticket in advance.

"最好"常用于动词前,表示建议某人做某事。

"最好" is often used before verbs to suggest someone to do something.

(1)明天你最好早点儿起床。

(2)你最好走这条路,近一些。

(3)你最好现在就买机票,太晚了就买不到了。

核心句
Key sentences

1. 我想预订杭州到北京的机票。

   I'd like to book a flight to Beijing, please.

2. 单程机票原价是九百元,现在可以打六折,五百四十元。

   The original price for a one-way ticket is 900 yuan. Now you can make a 60 percent discount, which is 540 yuan.

3. 预订往返机票的话,票价总额可以打五折。

   For a round trip ticket, the total fare can be 50% off.

4. 虽然杭州离上海很近,但是我还没去过呢。

   Although Hangzhou is very close to Shanghai, I haven't been there yet.

5. 从杭州到上海坐高铁一个小时就能到。

   It takes an hour to from Hangzhou to Shanghai.

6. 要是赶时间,你最好提前买票。

   If you're in a hurry, you'd better buy a ticket in advance.

7. 谢谢你的建议,现在我知道怎么去上海了。

   Thanks for your advice. Now I know how to get to Shanghai.

综合练习
Comprehensive exercises

(一)熟读下列短语 Read the following phrases

1.什么时候出发　八点出发　明天出发　从杭州出发

2.到达北京　到达上海　几点到达　到达时间

3.十点以前　上课以前　晚饭以前　睡觉以前

4.打几折　打九折　打八五折　打不打折

5.长途汽车　长途电话　长途旅行

6.一般不吃早饭　一般很晚睡觉　一般去食堂吃饭

7.提前下课　提前预订房间　提前准备考试　提前告诉她

8.赶时间　赶火车　赶飞机　赶不上

(二)替换练习 Substitution drills

1. <u>单程机票</u>原价是<u>九百元</u>,现在可以打<u>六</u>折,<u>五百四十元</u>。

   这件衣服　　1000 元　　　　八　　800 元

这本书	100元	八五	85元
这个书包	300元	七	210元

2. 要是预订往返机票的话,是不是便宜一点儿?

明天天气好	我们一起去公园吧。
你参加	我就参加。
你不好好准备	可能不能通过考试。

3. 看来从杭州去上海一点儿也不麻烦。

他生气了

你不太喜欢这个菜

今天我们不能出去玩儿了

4. 你最好提前买票。

早点儿去

买往返票

跟王老师说一下

5. 从杭州到上海坐高铁一个小时就能到。

杭州	北京	五
杭州	南京	一个半
杭州	义乌	半小时

6. 虽然杭州离上海很近,但是我还没去过呢。

今天天气不太好	我们还是想去踢足球
这件衣服有点贵	妈妈还是想买给我
明天有考试	他们现在还是想去酒吧

(三)完成对话 Complete the following dialogues

1. A: 您好! 请问您需要________?

B: 您好! 我想预订________。

A: 好的,您要预订哪天的机票? 大概________出发的?

B: 我想订十二月二十六号的。最好中午以前能________。

A: 那您坐上午九点钟起飞的飞机比较________,中午十一点到北京。

B: 要是预订往返机票的话,是不是价格能便宜一点儿?

A: 是的,女士。预订________机票的话,票价可以打五折。

B: 那我预订往返机票吧。北京回杭州的时间是十二月二十九号下午。

A: 好的。

2. A: 从杭州怎么去上海呢?

B：可以坐＿＿＿＿＿＿，但是最方便的是坐火车。现在中国速度最快的火车叫“高铁”，＿＿＿＿＿杭州＿＿＿＿＿上海坐高铁一个小时就能到。

A：这么快！从杭州去上海一点儿也不麻烦。＿＿＿＿＿提前买票吗？

B：要是＿＿＿＿＿，你最好提前买票。要是不赶时间，就可以去火车站的时候再买。

A：谢谢你的＿＿＿＿＿，现在我知道怎么去上海了。

（四）课堂活动 In-class exercises

角色扮演。Role-play.

(1)你要去香港看朋友，请给航空公司打电话预订机票。

参考词语：往返票　经济舱　原价　打折　接机

(2)你打算去南京旅行，跟中国朋友问问怎么去南京。

参考词语：长途汽车　高铁　提前　赶时间　从……到……　建议

（五）课后练习 After-class exercises

复述课文。Retell the texts.

安娜想预订十二月＿＿＿＿＿号杭州到＿＿＿＿＿的机票。单程票价是＿＿＿＿＿，现在可以打＿＿＿＿＿。预订＿＿＿＿＿机票可以打五折。北京回杭州的时间是十二月＿＿＿＿＿号。

玛丽很喜欢旅行，她去过＿＿＿＿＿＿＿＿。美玲想去上海。玛丽告诉她，可以坐＿＿＿＿，但是最方便的是＿＿＿＿。中国最快的火车是＿＿＿＿，从杭州到上海坐高铁＿＿＿＿就能到。

课文翻译 Translation of the text

Text A　Flying to Beijing

(Anna is going to visit her friend in Beijing. She calls the airline to book a flight.)

Customer service: Hello! Capital airlines, may I help you?

Anna: Hello! I'd like to book a flight to Beijing, please.

Customer service: OK, which day would you like to book? What time does it start?

Anna: I'd like to make a reservation for December 26th. It's best to arrive before noon.

Customer service: That's a good flight for you to take off at nine o'clock in the morning. Eleven o'clock to Beijing.

Anna: OK, what's the fare for economy class?

Customer service: The original price for a one-way ticket is 900 yuan, Miss. Now you can make a 60 percent discount, which is 540 yuan.

Anna: Is it cheaper to book a round trip ticket?

Customer service: Yes, Miss. For a round trip ticket, the total fare can be 50% off.

Anna: Then I'd like to book a round trip ticket. I will return to Hangzhou on the afternoon of December 29th.

Customer service: OK.

Text B　Take the train to Shanghai

(Mary and Meiling are talking about how to get to Shanghai.)

Meiling: Mary, I heard you love to travel. Where have you been in China?

Mary: I have been to Beijing, Shanghai, Guangzhou and Suzhou.

Meiling: Although Hangzhou is very close to Shanghai, I haven't been there yet.

Mary: It's very convenient to go to Shanghai from Hangzhou. You can go there at the weekend.

Meiling: How do I get to Shanghai from Hangzhou?

Mary: You can take a coach, but the most convenient way is by train. Now the fastest train in China is called "high-speed train", and it takes no more than an hour to from Hangzhou to Shanghai.

Meiling: So fast! It seems that it is not troublesome to go to Shanghai from Hangzhou.

Mary: Yeah, it's easy. Come out of our dorm, take the subway line 1 and get off at the Hangzhou East Railway Station. The high-speed trains to Shanghai are usually set off from the East Railway Station.

Meiling: Too convenient! Do I need to buy tickets in advance?

Mary: If you're in a hurry, you'd better buy a ticket in advance. If you're not in a hurry, you can buy it at the train station. Because there are a lot of high-speed trains from Hangzhou to Shanghai every day.

Meiling: Mary, thanks for your advice. Now I know how to get to Shanghai.

8 我们住的酒店真不错
The hotel we live is very nice

话题导学 Guidance

1. 在杭州和上海怎么乘地铁?
   How do you take the metro in Hangzhou and Shanghai?
2. 怎么查找和预定酒店?
   How do you find and book a hotel?
3. 入住酒店时,要办理哪些手续?
   Which procedures do you need to apply when you check in at the hotel?

生词学习(一) New words I

1. 交通 jiāo tōng	*n.* traffic;transportation	交通工具
2. 站 zhàn	*n.* station	火车站;汽车站;巴士站
3. 准备 zhǔn bèi	*v.* prepare;plan	准备考试;准备去旅行
4. 办理 bàn lǐ	*v.* handle;deal with	办理签证;办理银行卡
5. 手续 shǒu xù	*n.* procedure;formality	手续很多;办理登机手续
6. 转 zhuǎn	*v.* transfer	转公交;转地铁
7. 公交卡 gōng jiāo kǎ	*NP* traffic card	一张公交卡;公交卡充值
8. 直接 zhí jiē	*adv.* directly	直接去学校;直接回家
9. 刷卡 shuā kǎ	*VP* swipe	刷卡机;刷银行卡
10. 出口 chū kǒu	*n.* exit	地铁出口;公园的出口

课文(一) 上海虹桥站到了
Text A Shanghai Hongqiao Station is here

安娜和美玲乘高铁到东方财经大学参加“中国商务论坛”，刚下火车。

安娜：看，上海虹桥站到了。从杭州到上海，五十多分钟就到了。真快啊！
Ān nà Kàn Shàng hǎi Hóng qiáo zhàn dào le Cóng Háng zhōu dào Shàng hǎi wǔ shí duō fēn zhōng jiù dào le Zhēn kuài a

美玲：中国的交通真是太方便了。准备下车吧。
Měi líng Zhōng guó de jiāo tōng zhēn shì tài fāng biàn le Zhǔn bèi xià chē ba

安娜：现在已经十二点了。我们的酒店离火车站有一点儿远。
Ān nà Xiàn zài yǐ jīng shí èr diǎn le Wǒ men de jiǔ diàn lí huǒ chē zhàn yǒu yī diǎnr yuǎn

美玲：没关系，下了火车就乘地铁过去。酒店一点以后办理入住手续。
Měi líng Méi guān xì xià le huǒ chē jiù chéng dì tiě guò qù Jiǔ diàn yì diǎn yǐ hòu bàn lǐ rù zhù shǒu xù

安娜：那不用着急。
Ān nà Nà bù yòng zháo jí

美玲：十号线转八号线，一个小时就能到。我们乘地铁去吧。
Měi líng Shí hào xiàn zhuǎn bā hào xiàn yí gè xiǎo shí jiù néng dào Wǒ men chéng dì tiě qù ba

安娜：好的。我有两张上海公交卡。我们可以直接刷卡进站。
Ān nà Hǎo de Wǒ yǒu liǎng zhāng Shǎng hǎi gōng jiāo kǎ Wǒ men kě yǐ zhí jiē shuā kǎ jìn zhàn

美玲：太好了。我们走吧。
Měi líng Tài hǎo le Wǒ men zǒu ba

安娜和美玲出站了。

安娜：酒店是在那里吗？就在地铁站一号出口旁边。
Ān nà Jiǔ diàn shì zài nà lǐ ma Jiù zài dì tiě zhàn yī hào chū kǒu páng biān

美玲：我看到了，就是那个黄色的楼。酒店真不错，旁边就是购物中心和地铁站。
Měi líng Wǒ kàn dào le jiù shì nà gè huáng sè de lóu Jiǔ diàn zhēn bú cuò páng biān jiù shì gòu wù zhōng xīn hé dì tiě zhàn

根据课文(一)回答问题
Answer these questions according to the Text A

1. 十号线转八号线，多长时间能到？
2. 安娜和美玲预定的酒店在哪儿？
3. 酒店几点办理入住手续？
4. 安娜和美玲住的酒店怎么样？

生词学习(二) New words II

1. 商务 shāng wù *n.* business　　中国商务;商务汉语
2. 论坛 lùn tán *n.* forum　　一个论坛;财经论坛
3. 购物 gòu wù *n.* shopping　　购物商场;购物时间
4. 公共 gōng gòng *adj.* public　　公共汽车;公共卫生间
5. 步行 bù xíng *v.* walk　　步行去学校;喜欢步行
6. 参加 cān jiā *v.* attend; participate　　参加活动;参加比赛
7. 逛 guàng *v.* stroll; visit　　逛街;逛商场
8. 押金 yā jīn *n.* deposit　　租房押金;没有押金
9. 单 dān *n.* bill　　账单;押金单
10. 房卡 fáng kǎ *n.* room card　　一张房卡;酒店房卡
11. 结算 jié suàn *v.* settle accounts　　账户结算;年终结算
12. 指南 zhǐ nán *n.* guidebook　　旅游指南;住宿指南

课文(二) 酒店在市中心 Text B The hotel is in the city center

在酒店前台。

安娜:你好,我们是来参加"中国商务"论坛的,预定了酒店。
Ān nà　Nǐ hǎo　wǒ men shì lái cān jiā　zhōng guó shāng wù　lùn tán de　yù dìng le jiǔ diàn

前台:你们好!欢迎入住商务中心。请出示你们的护照。
Qián tái　Nǐ men hǎo　Huān yíng rù zhù shāng wù zhōng xīn　Qǐng chū shì nǐ men de hù zhào

美玲:这是我们的护照。她叫安娜,我叫美玲。我们是从杭州来的。
Měi líng　Zhè shì wǒ men de hù zhào　Tā jiào Ān nà　wǒ jiào Měi líng　Wǒ men shì cóng Háng zhōu lái de

前台:谢谢!欢迎你们。
Qián tái　Xiè xie　Huān yíng nǐ men

安娜：你们酒店真不错，旁边就是购物中心和地铁站。
Ān nà Nǐ men jiǔ diàn zhēn bù cuò páng biān jiù shì gòu wù zhōng xīn hé dì tiě zhàn

前台：我们酒店在市中心，离大学很近，可以步行过去。这是你们的护照，请收好！
Qián tái Wǒ men jiǔ diàn zài shì zhōng xīn lí dà xué hěn jìn kě yǐ bù xíng guò qù Zhè shì nǐ men de hù zhào qǐng shōu hǎo

美玲：谢谢！我第一次来上海，有时间的话想到处逛逛。
Měi líng Xiè xie Wǒ dì yī cì lái Shàng hǎi yǒu shí jiān de huà xiǎng dào chù guàng guang

前台：酒店出门左转就是地铁站。对了，请付一百块押金。
Qián tái Jiǔ diàn chū mén zuǒ zhuǎn jiù shì dì tiě zhàn Duì le qǐng fù yī bǎi kuài yā jīn

美玲：好的。谢谢！给你押金。
Měi líng Hǎo de Xiè xie Gěi nǐ yā jīn

前台：这是你们的押金单，请收好。这是房卡，四〇六房间。
Qián tái Zhè shì nǐ men de yā jīn dān qǐng shōu hǎo Zhè shì fáng kǎ sì líng liù fáng jiān

安娜：好的，谢谢！
Ān nà Hǎo de xiè xie

前台：餐费和住宿费一起结算，可以吗？
Qián tái Cān fèi hé zhù sù fèi yī qǐ jié suàn kě yǐ ma

美玲：可以，没问题。请问怎么去四〇六房间？
Měi líng Kě yǐ méi wèn tí Qǐng wèn zěn me qù sì líng liù fáng jiān

前台：右转直走就是电梯。房间里有服务指南。你们有什么要求，可以随时跟我们联系。非常乐意为您服务！
Qián tái Yòu zhuǎn zhí zǒu jiù shì diàn tī Fáng jiān lǐ yǒu fú wù zhǐ nán Nǐ men yǒu shén me yāo qiú kě yǐ suí shí gēn wǒ men lián xì fēi cháng lè yì wèi nín fú wù

安娜、美玲：好的，非常感谢！酒店的服务真不错啊。
Ān nà Měi líng Hǎo de fēi cháng gǎn xiè Jiǔ diàn de fú wù zhēn bú cuò a

根据课文(二)回答问题
Answer these questions according to the Text B

1. 安娜和美玲是从哪里来的？
2. 酒店要求付多少钱的押金？
3. 安娜和美玲的房间号是多少？
4. 酒店有服务指南吗？在哪里？

语言点
Language points

1. 真 + *adj.*/*v.*

真快啊！/酒店真不错。

It is really fast! / The hotel is really good.

“真”放在形容词或者动词前面,表示的确、实在怎么样。

“真” is a adverb here. It means “really”, “indeed” before a verb or an adjective.

(1)我真喜欢杭州的西湖,有山有水。

(2)他的汉字写得真漂亮!

(3)这家饭店的菜真好吃,下次我还来。

2. 太 + *adj.* /*v.*

中国的交通真是太方便了。

The public transportation in China is really convenient.

“太”是一个副词,用在动词或者形容词前,表示程度很高,常常和“了”一起使用。

“太” is a adverb here, means “very”, “super”. It is often used with “了”。

(1)这件衣服太贵了,要三千多块钱。

(2)今天的天气实在太热了,有三十五度。

(3)他学习汉语太努力了,周五晚上还在图书馆学习。

3. 就 + *v.*

我看到了,就是那个黄色的楼。

“就”是一个副词,用在动词前,表示事实就是这样。

“就” is a adverb here, means “exacting” or “precisely”.

(1)这个人就是他哥哥。

(2)工商大学就在超市前面。

(3)他就是喜欢晚睡晚起,这是他的习惯。

4. 是……的……

我们是从杭州来的。

We come from Hangzhou.

“是……的……”强调已经发生或者完成的动作或者行为的时间、地点、方式和目的等。

“是……的……”emphasizes the time, place, manner or purpose, etc. of a movement or action that already happened or been completed.

(1)他们是昨天来杭州的。

(2)你是坐飞机去北京的吗?

(3)她是来工商大学学习汉语的。

5. 地点 + 有 + sb. /sth.

房间里有服务指南。

There is a service guide in the room.

这是一个存在句结构。

This is a structure existential sentence in Chinese.

(1)工商大学门口有一个地铁站。

(2)她衣服上有一朵蓝色的花。

(3)留学生楼左边有一家西餐厅。

6. “啊”“吧”“吗”

真快啊!

It is so fast!

准备下车吧。

Let's get ready to get off.

酒店是在那里吗?

Is the hotel there?

“啊”“吧”“吗”是汉语口语中常见的语气词。语气词“啊”可用在句尾,表赞叹或者肯定。例如“今天的天气真好啊”“多美丽的大学啊”。语气词“吧”用在句末,常常可以表示商量、提议、请求和命令。例如“我们去吃饭吧”,“明天我们去超市买东西吧”。语气词“吗”用在句末,表示疑问,是是非疑问句的标志。

“啊”“吧”“吗” are common modal particles in spoken Chinese. “啊” can be used at the end of the sentence to indicate the admiration or affirmation. “吧” can be used at the end of a sentence, implying soliciting sb's advice, suggestion, request or mild command. “吗” used at the end of a sentence to indicate a yes-no question.

核心句
Key sentences

1. 中国的交通真是太方便了。

   The public transportation is really convenient in China.

2. 我们是从杭州来的。

   We come from Hangzhou.

3. 酒店真不错,旁边就是购物中心和地铁站。

   The hotel is really good, surrounded by shopping malls and metro stations.

4. 你们有什么要求,可以随时跟前台联系。

   Please contact the reception at any time if you need.

5. 我们非常乐意为您服务!

   We are willing to provide you with excellent service.

综合练习
Comprehensive exercises

(一)熟读下列短语 Read the following phrases

1. 高铁站　火车站　汽车站　公交车站　几个站
2. 准备下车　准备工作　准备学习　准备吃饭　准备下班
3. 10号线转8号线　10路转20路　地铁转公交　火车转地铁
4. 公交卡　银行卡　学生卡　借书卡　信用卡　暂住卡
5. 参加论坛　参加会议　参加活动　参加比赛　参加考试
6. 押金单　付款单　收款单　成绩单　酒水单　礼品单
7. 服务指南　学习指南　生活指南　入学指南　旅行指南
8. 乘火车　乘地铁　乘飞机　乘坐汽车　乘坐飞机

(二)替换练习 Substitution drills

1. 从杭州到上海，五十多分钟就到了。

　　学校　超市　二十多分钟
　　我家　他家　半小时
　　这里　他们学校　一刻钟

2. 中国的交通真是太方便了。

　　哈尔滨的冬天　冷
　　这家饭店的菜　好吃
　　这次考试　难

3. 我们的酒店离火车站有一点儿远。

　　北京　南京
　　工商大学　外国语大学
　　我的家　她的家

4. 十号线转八号线，一个小时就能到。

　　地铁　公交　半小时
　　飞机　火车　五个小时
　　15路　33路　一刻钟

5. 我看到了，就是那个黄色的楼。

　　知道　这个学校
　　听到　她的歌声
　　看到　那个美丽的地方

6. 酒店一点以后办理入住手续。
   学校九月一号　入学
   他们四月十号　结婚
   图书馆下午两点　借书

7. 我们非常乐意为您服务!
   老师和同学　帮助你
   我的朋友　为我请假
   公司　为员工提供帮助

8. 房间里有　服务指南。
   图书馆旁边　一个花园
   留学生楼下面　一个停车场
   桌子上　一个杯子和三支笔

(三)完成对话 Complete the following dialogues

1. A: 从杭州到上海,乘火车五十多分钟__________到了。
   B: 中国的交通真是__________。
   A: 你们住的酒店在哪儿?
   B: 下了火车就乘地铁__________,酒店____________________。
   A: 酒店怎么样?
   B: 酒店真不错,____________________。

2. A: 你好,我们是来参加“中国商务”论坛的,__________了你们酒店。
   B: 欢迎入住,请__________你们的护照。我们酒店在市中心,____________很近。
   A: 我第一次来上海,__________的话我还想到处__________。
   B: 酒店出门左转就是地铁站,很方便。你们有什么要求,可以随时____________联系。
   A: 好的,非常感谢! 酒店的服务__________。
   B: 不客气。我们非常乐意__________!

(四)课堂活动 In-class exercises

角色扮演。Role-play.

(1)你和你的朋友一起去北京或者上海旅行,需要入住一家酒店。根据课文所学内容,模拟办理酒店入住的过程。
参考词语:护照　押金　房卡　地铁站　飞机场

(2)作为老生,请向新生介绍一下从杭州去上海或者从杭州去周边城市的交通工具和出行方式。

(五)课后练习 After-class exercises

复述课文。Retell the texts.

安娜和美玲从杭州去上海，________多分钟就到了。她们下了火车就乘________过去。酒店一点以后办理____________。安娜有两张上海____________，她们可以直接____________。

在酒店前台，安娜和美玲出示了她们的__________，付了一百块____________。安娜说酒店的____________，旁边就是__________________。美玲第一次来上海，有时间的话，她还想____________。服务员说，房间里有___________，有什么要求，可以随时跟_________。

课文翻译 Translation of the texts

Text A Shanghai Hongqiao station is here

(Anna and Meiling took the high-speed rail to Oriental University of Finance and Economics to participate in China Business Forum, just off the train.)

Anna: Look, there is Shanghai Hongqiao Railway Station. It's about 50 minutes from Hangzhou to Shanghai. How fast it is!

Meiling: The transportation in China is really convenient. Let us get off now.

Anna: It's already twelve o'clock. Our hotel is a little far from the railway station.

Meiling: It doesn't matter. We will take the subway when we get off the train. We will check in after one o'clock.

Anna: Don't worry about it.

Meiling: Take line ten and then transfer to line eight. We will be there in an hour. Let's take the subway right now.

Anna: All right. I have two Shanghai subuay cards. We can directly enter the station with subuay cards.

Meiling: Great! Let's go.

(Anna and Meiling left the station.)

Anna: Is the hotel there? It's close to exit one of the metro station.

Meiling: I see it. It is the yellow building. The hotel is surrounded by shopping centers and subway stations. It is very good.

Text B The hotel is in the city center

(At the hotel reception.)

Anna: Hello, we come to attend the Chinese Business Forum and have booked your hotel before.

Reception: Hello! Welcome to the business center. Your passports please.

Meiling: This is our passports. Her name is Anna. My name is Meiling. We are from Hangzhou.

Reception: Thank you! Welcome to Shanghai.

Anna: The environment of your hotel is very good. There are shopping centers and subway stations around it.

Reception: Our hotel is in the center of Shanghai and is close to the University. You can go to the university on foot. Here are your passports.

Meiling: Thank you! It is the first time for me to come to Shanghai, so I want to go around, if I have time.

Reception：There is a subway station on the left of the hotel. By the way, please pay 100 yuan deposit.

Anna：OK. Thank you! Here's the deposit.

Reception：Here is your deposit reception. Please keep it well. And this is room card, 406.

Meiling：OK, thank you!

Reception：Can we settle the meals and the accommodation fee together?

Anna：It is OK, no problem. How can I get to room 406, please?

Reception：Please turn right and go straight and you will see the elevator there. There is a service guide in your room. Any requirements you have, please contact us at any time. It is a great pleasure to serve you.

Anna, Meiling：OK, thank you very much! The service is very nice here.

9 我的上海购物经历
My shopping experience in Shanghai

话题导学
Guidance

1. 怎么向售货员询问商品信息？
   How do you ask the salesperson for product information?
2. 买东西的时候，怎么跟售货员讨价还价？
   How do you bargain with the salesperson?
3. 作为顾客，怎样办理会员卡？
   As a customer, how do you apply for a membership card?

生词学习（一）
New words I

1.	bèi 被 *prep.* by	被打；被吃了
2.	zhōnghuá 中华 *n.* China	中华人民共和国
3.	dì yī 第一 *num.* the first	第一个；第一人
4.	zhùmíng 著名 *adj.* famous	著名的大学；著名的老师
5.	bǎihuò 百货 *n.* general merchandise	百货商店；百货商场
6.	shípǐn 食品 *n.* food	买食品；食品店
7.	shízhuāng 时装 *n.* fashionable dress	时装店；卖时装
8.	chú le 除了 *conj.* except; besides	除了星期一；除了他们
9.	pǐncháng 品尝 *v.* taste	品尝中国菜；品尝好酒
10.	měishí 美食 *n.* delicious food	很多美食；喜欢美食

11. 一样 yí yàng *adj.* the same; alike 一样的学校;不一样的国家

12. 点心 diǎn xīn *n.* dessert;light refreshments 一些点心;吃点心

课文(一) 南京路
Text A Nanjing Road

会议结束后,安娜和美玲一起去购物。

安娜:中国人都说,去上海,一定要去南京路。这是为什么?
Ān nà Zhōngguó rén dōushuō qù Shànghǎi yí dìngyào qù Nánjīng lù Zhè shì wèi shén me

美玲:因为南京路被称为"中华第一街",是一条商业街。那里有很多著名的购物中心和商店。
Měi líng Yīn wèi Nánjīng lù bèi chēngwéi Zhōnghuá dì yī jiē shì yī tiáo shāng yè jiē Nà lǐ yǒu hěn duō zhù míng de gòu wù zhōng xīn hé shāngdiàn

安娜:有哪些著名的商店呢?
Ān nà Yǒu nǎ xiē zhù míng de shāngdiàn ne

美玲:永安百货、第一食品商店、上海时装公司等。
Měi líng Yǒng ān bǎi huò Dì yī shí pǐn shāngdiàn Shànghǎi shí zhuānggōng sī děng

安娜:在南京路,除了购物还可以做什么?
Ān nà Zài Nánjīng lù chú le gòu wù hái kě yǐ zuò shén me

美玲:在南京路,除了购物还可以品尝上海的美食。
Měi líng Zài Nánjīng lù chú le gòu wù hái kě yǐ pǐn cháng Shànghǎi de měi shí

安娜:太好了。上海的食物和杭州的食物一样吗?
Ān nà Tài hǎo le Shànghǎi de shí wù hé Hángzhōu de shí wù yí yàng ma

美玲:有的一样,有的不一样。我们去"沈大成"看看吧,那是南京路很有名的点心店。
Měi líng Yǒu de yí yàng yǒu de bù yí yàng Wǒ men qù Shěn Dà Chéng kàn kan ba nà shì Nánjīng lù hěn yǒumíng de diǎn xīn diàn

安娜:我想给朋友带一些上海的点心。
Ān nà Wǒ xiǎng gěi péngyou dài yì xiē shànghǎi de diǎn xīn

美玲:我想去南京路买一些吃的和穿的。我们一起走吧。
Měi líng Wǒ xiǎng qù Nánjīng lù mǎi yì xiē chī de hé chuān de Wǒ men yì qǐ zǒu ba

根据课文(一)回答问题
Answer these questions according to the Text A

1. 为什么去上海一定要去南京路?
2. 南京路有哪些著名的商店?
3. 上海的食物和杭州的食物一样吗?
4. "沈大成"是什么商店?

生词学习(二)
New words II

guàng
1. 逛 *v.* stroll; ramble; wander about 逛街;逛商场

jué dìng
2. 决定 *v.* decide; make up one's mind 决定去;决定买

zhōng shì
3. 中式 *n.* Chinese style 中式饭馆;中式食物

nǚ zhuāng
4. 女装 *n.* women's dress 一套女装;女装店

yán sè
5. 颜色 *n.* colour 颜色深;颜色很好

hào
6. 号 *n.* size 大号;中号

hé shì
7. 合适 *adj.* suitable; appropriate 不合适;合适的鞋子

sī chóu
8. 丝绸 *n.* silk 丝绸店;丝绸衣服

dǎ zhé
9. 打折 *v.* sell at a discount 不打折;经常打折

huì yuán
10. 会员 *n.* member 会员卡;不是会员

zhèng jiàn
11. 证件 *n.* certificate 他的证件;什么证件

dìng zhì
12. 订制 *v.* custom-made 订制鞋子;订制汽车

lè yì
13. 乐意 *adj.* be pleased; be willing to 不乐意;乐意帮助他

课文(二) 办会员卡
Text B Apply for a member card

安娜和美玲一起在南京路购物。

安娜:逛了两个小时了,你决定买什么了吗?
Ān nà Guàng le liǎng gè xiǎo shí le nǐ jué dìng mǎi shén me le ma

美玲:除了买鞋子,我还想买一件中式的衣服。
Měi líng Chú le mǎi xié zi wǒ hái xiǎng mǎi yī jiàn zhōng shì de yī fú

安娜:我觉得你穿旗袍就不错。
Ān nà Wǒ jué dé nǐ chuān qí páo jiù bù cuò

美玲:我喜欢上海旗袍,想多看看。你觉得这件蓝的怎么样?
Měi líng Wǒ xǐ huān Shàng hǎi qí páo xiǎng duō kàn kan Nǐ jué dé zhè jiàn lán de zěn me yàng

安娜：这件漂亮极了。颜色、样子都比刚才那件好看。
Ān nà Zhè jiàn piào liàng jí le Yán sè yàng zi dōu bǐ gāng cái nà jiàn hǎo kàn

售货员：这件比那件大一号。你个子高，穿这件合适。
Shòu huò yuán Zhè jiàn bǐ nà jiàn dà yí hào Nǐ gè zi gāo chuān zhè jiàn hé shì

美玲：这件的价格和那件一样吗？
Měi líng Zhè jiàn de jià gé hé nà jiàn yí yàng ma

售货员：这件是丝绸的，价格比那件贵。我们店是上海老字号。
Shòu huò yuán Zhè jiàn shì sī chóu de jià gé bǐ nà jiàn guì Wǒ men diàn shì Shàng hǎi lǎo zì hào

美玲：能打折吗？
Měi líng Néng dǎ zhé ma

售货员：如果是会员，有打折和贵宾服务。
Shòu huò yuán Rú guǒ shì huì yuán yǒu dǎ zhé hé guì bīn fú wù

安娜：请问怎么办理会员卡？
Ān nà Qǐng wèn zěn me bàn lǐ huì yuán kǎ

售货员：请提供证件、电话和邮箱，很快就能办好。
Shòu huò yuán Qǐng tí gōng zhèng jiàn diàn huà hé yóu xiāng hěn kuài jiù néng bàn hǎo

美玲：那我就买这件吧。谢谢！这是我的护照、电话和邮箱。
Měi líng Nà wǒ jiù mǎi zhè jiàn ba Xiè xie Zhè shì wǒ de hù zhào diàn huà hé yóu xiāng

安娜：请问可以定制旗袍吗？我想给我妈妈定制一件。
Ān nà Qǐng wèn kě yǐ dìng zhì qí páo ma Wǒ xiǎng gěi wǒ mā mā dìng zhì yī jiàn

售货员：当然可以。我们非常乐意提供定制服务。
Shòu huò yuán Dāng rán kě yǐ Wǒ men fēi cháng lè yì tí gōng dìng zhì fú wù

根据课文(二)回答问题
Answer these questions according to the Text B

1. 美玲决定买旗袍吗？
2. 丝绸旗袍价格贵不贵？
3. 怎么办理会员卡？
4. 商店可以定制旗袍吗？

语言点
Language points

1. 被

南京路被称为“中华第一街”。

Nanjing Road is known as China's First Street.

“被”是一个介词，用在句子中表示主语是受事，施事放在“被”字后，常常省略。

“被” used in a passive sentence to indicate that the subject is the object of the action. The agent follows the “被”, and is often omitted.

(1)杭州被称为人间天堂。

(2)电脑被弄坏了。

(3)那本词典被借走了。

2. 等(等)

永安百货、第一食品商店、上海时装公司等。

There are Yong'an Department Store, The First Food Store, Shanghai Fashion Company and so on.

"等(等)",用于句末表示列举未尽。

"等(等)" used at the end of the sentence and indicate there are more examples.

(1)我去过北京、上海、天津、南京等。

(2)他吃了米饭、面条、饺子、馒头等。

(3)她想去超市买吃的、喝的、穿的、用的等。

3. 除了……,还……

除了买鞋子,我还想买一件中式的衣服。

In addition to shirts, I also want to buy a Chinese-style dress.

"除了……,还……"表示排除已知,补充其他的。

"除了……,还……" similar to"in addition to"or "other than",is used to exclude the items already known and add further information.

(1)除了亚洲学生,他们班还有非洲学生。

(2)除了汉语,马丁还学习法语和日语。

(3)除了打篮球,我们还喜欢游泳和踢足球。

4. A比B+*adj.*/*AP*

这件比那件大一号。

This one is bigger than that one.

"A比B+*adj.*/*AP*",用于比较程度和性状的差别。

"A比B+*adj.*/*AP*", is used to compare differences in properties and degrees.

(1)她比他高。

(2)今天比昨天冷一点儿。

(3)这双鞋比那双贵五十块。

5. *v.*+的

我想去南京路买一些吃的和穿的。

I want to buy some food and clothes in Nanjing Road.

动词、名词、形容词等后面可以加“的”构成“的”字短语。“的”字短语的功能相当于名词。

A verb, noun or an adjective become a phrase with “的” when the word “的” is attached to it. A phrase with “的” functions as a noun.

(1)v. + 的　买的　卖的　做点心的　骑自行车的

(2)n. + 的　中国的　南美的　学校的　丝绸的

(3)adj. + 的　白色的　长的　新的　年轻的

6. A 和 B 一样/不一样

这件的价格和那件一样吗?

Is the price of this one the same as that one?

“A 和 B 一样”表示两种事物没有差别。“A 和 B 不一样”表示两种事物不同。

“A 和 B 一样” means A and B are the same. “A 和 B 不一样” means A is different from B.

(1)他的手机和我的手机一样。

(2)我的习惯和哥哥的习惯不一样。

(3)杭州的天气和北京的不一样。

核心句 Key sentences

1. 去上海,一定要去南京路。
   You should visit Nanjing Rood if you go to Shanghai.
2. 在南京路,除了购物还可以做什么?
   What else do you do besides shopping in Nanjing Road?
3. 上海的食物和杭州的食物一样吗?
   Is the food in Shanghai the same as the food in Hangzhou?
4. 我想去南京路买一些吃的和穿的。
   I want to go to Nanjing Road to buy some food and clothes.
5. 这件比那件大一号。
   This one is bigger than that one.
6. 我们非常乐意提供定制服务。
   We are very happy to provide customized services.

综合练习
Comprehensive exercises

(一)熟读下列短语 Read the following phrases

1.被打　被骂　被吃了　被喝了　被骗了　被打碎了　被洗了　被卖了

2.决定喝茶　决定去学校　决定去医院　决定先睡觉　决定不回家　决定不买

3.中式　西式　男式　女式　美国式　新式　老式　旧式

4.大一号　小一号　号不对　大号　中号　小号　这个号

5.一样　不一样　一样的地方　一样的食物　不一样的老师　和她不一样

6.第一　第二　第一个　第一年　第一个老师　第一个城市　没有第一

7.蓝的　男的　多的　新的　去年的　买的　卖的　吃的　喝的　穿的　用的

8.订制旗袍　订制鞋子　订制蛋糕　订制汽车　订制衣服　订制手机

(二)替换练习 Substitution drills

1. 南京路有　永安百货、第一食品商店、上海时装公司等。

工商大学　教学楼、运动场、图书馆

杭州　西湖、千岛湖、灵隐寺

学生食堂　饺子、米饭、面条

2. 南京路被称为“中华第一街”。

杭州和苏州　人间天堂

那个城市　中国最美丽的地方

医生　白衣天使

3. 除了衬衫,我还想买一件中式的衣服。

笔　买一本笔记本

游泳　会打网球

上海　去北京和西安

4. 这件衣服比那件衣服 大一号。

今天　昨天　冷一点儿

这个手机　那个　贵两百块

我的书　他的　多十本

5. 这件的价格和那件一样吗?

今天的天气　昨天

你的自行车　他的

南方的粽子　北方的

6. 我觉得你穿旗袍就不错。
   妈妈　我做饭
   他　　买这件衣服
   我　　去上海和杭州留学

7. 请问可以订制旗袍吗？我想给我妈妈订制一件。
   鞋子　　一双
   裙子　　一条
   手提包　一个

8. 你觉得这件 蓝的怎么样？
   那个 大的
   这条 长的
   那双 打折的

(三)完成对话 Complete the following dialogues

1. A：去上海，一定要去南京路。这是__________？
   B：因为南京路____________________。那里有很多著名的购物中心和商店。
   A：在南京路，____________购物还可以做什么？
   B：在南京路，除了购物还可以____________________。
   A：我想给朋友________________。
   B：我想去南京路买一些________和________。我们一起走吧。

2. A：________了两个小时了，你决定买什么了吗？我觉得你穿旗袍就________。
   B：我想多________。你觉得这件蓝的________？
   A：这件漂亮________。颜色、样子都________刚才那件________。
   B：我想买一件________的，贵一点儿没关系。这家店是上海________。

(四)课堂活动 In-class exercises

1. 角色扮演。Role-play.
   根据课文内容，双人对话。

2. 成段表达。Presentation.
   我的一次购物经历
   参考词语和句式：逛　购物　等等　打折　品尝　除了……，还……　A 比 B + adj. /AP　A 和 B 一样/不一样

(五)课后练习 After-class exercises

采访你的同学。Interview your classmates and record their answers.

	同学 1	同学 2	同学 3	同学 4
你经常去哪里购物				
你经常买什么				
你经常去哪里买衣服				
你知道杭州有哪些购物中心				
你知道杭州有哪些商品品牌(famous brand)				

课文翻译 Translation of the texts

Text A Nanjing Road

(After the meeting, Anna and Meiling go shopping together.)

Anna: Chinese people say that when you visit Shanghai, you should go to Nanjing Road. Why are they saying this?

Meiling: Because Nanjing Road is called First Street in China. It is a commercial street. There are many famous shopping centers and shops there.

Anna: What famous shops are there?

Meiling: Yong'an Department Store, First Food Store, Shanghai Fashion Company, etc.

Anna: What can I do in addition to shopping at Nanjing Road?

Meiling: You can taste Shanghai cuisine at Nanjing Rood.

Anna: That's great. Is the food in Shanghai the same as the food in Hangzhou?

Meiling: Some are same, some are different. Let's take a look at Shen Da Cheng, which is a famous snack shop in Nanjing Road.

Anna: I want to bring some Shanghai snacks to my friends.

Meiling: I want to go to Nanjing Road to buy some food and clothes. Let's go together.

Text B Apply for a member card

(Anna and Meiling are shopping together in Nanjing Road.)

Anna: We have been shopping for two hours. Have you decided to buy anything?

Meiling: In addition to shoes, I want to buy a Chinese-style dress.

Ana: I think cheangsam is suitable for you.

Meiling: I like Shanghai cheongsam and want to see more. What do you think of this blue one?

Anna: This is very beautiful. The color and appearance are better than the one just we saw.

Salesperson: This one is bigger than that one. You are tall and it is more suitable to wear this one.

Meiling: Is the price of this piece the same as that one?

Salesperson: This piece is silk, and the price is more expensive. Our shop is time-honored brand in Shanghai.

Meiling: Can I have a discount?

Salesperson: If you are a member, you have discounts and VIP services.

Anna: How do I apply for a membership card?

Salesperson: Please show your ID, phone number and e-mail. You will be our member soon.

Meiling: OK. I want to buy this one. Thank you! This is my passport, phone number and e-mail.

Anna: Can you provide customized services? I want to customize for my mother.

Salesperson: Of course. We are very happy to provide customized services.

10 您的快递到了
Your express package has arrived

话题导学 Guidance

1. 你经常寄快递吗?
   Do you often post express package?
2. 寄快递时需要做什么?
   What do you need to do when you post a express package?
3. 你觉得中国的快递和你们国家的快递有什么不同?
   What are the differences between the express in China and your country?

生词学习(一) New words I

1. 寄 (jì) *v.* post; mail　寄书;寄东西
2. 礼物 (lǐ wù) *n.* gift; present　生日礼物;新年礼物
3. 快递 (kuài dì) *n.* express package　寄快递;快递公司
4. 容易 (róng yì) *adj./adv.* easy; easily　容易学;容易读
5. 碎 (suì) *adj.* fragmentary; fragile　杯子碎了;眼镜碎了
6. 特殊 (tè shū) *adj.* special　特殊的日子;特殊情况
7. 包装 (bāo zhuāng) *n./v.* pack　食品包装;礼物包装
8. 填 (tián) *v.* fill in　填单子
9. 单 (dān) *n.* list　名单;菜单
10. 详细 (xiáng xì) *adj.* detailed　详细地址;详细情况

dì zhǐ
11. 地址 *n.* address 家的地址；学校地址

lián xì
12. 联系 *v./n.* contact 联系电话；跟朋友联系

课文(一) 在快递公司
Text A At the express company

马克要给朋友寄礼物，他来到了快递公司。

马克：你好！我想寄两瓶酒到上海。
Mǎ kè Nǐ hǎo wǒ xiǎng jì liǎng píng jiǔ dào Shàng hǎi

快递员：酒是容易碎的东西。您有特殊的包装吗？
Kuài dì yuán Jiǔ shì róng yì suì de dōng xī Nín yǒu tè shū de bāo zhuāng ma

马克：你看这个盒子可以吗？
Mǎ kè Nǐ kàn zhè ge hé zǐ kě yǐ ma

快递员：可以的。那请您填一下这张快递单，写好收件人的详细地址和联系电话。
Kuài dì yuán Kě yǐ de Nà qǐng nín tián yí xià zhè zhāng kuài dì dān xiě hǎo shōu jiàn rén de xiáng xì dì zhǐ hé lián xì diàn huà

马克：写好了，你看这样行吗？
Mǎ kè Xiě hǎo le nǐ kàn zhè yàng xíng ma

快递员：可以了。快递费是十五块。
Kuài dì yuán Kě yǐ le Kuài dì fèi shì shí wǔ kuài

马克：好的，给你钱。从杭州寄到上海几天能到？
Mǎ kè Hǎo de gěi nǐ qián Cóng Háng zhōu jì dào Shàng hǎi jǐ tiān néng dào

快递员：快的话明天就能到，最晚两天能到。
Kuài dì yuán Kuài de huà míng tiān jiù néng dào zuì wǎn liǎng tiān néng dào

马克：好的，谢谢！
Mǎ kè Hǎo de xiè xie

根据课文(一)回答问题
Answer these questions according to the Text A

1. 马克要寄什么东西？寄到哪里？
2. 马克寄的东西为什么需要特殊包装？
3. 从杭州寄东西到上海几天能到？

生词学习(二)
New words II

lóu xià
1. 楼下 *n.* downstairs 在楼下；楼下的房间

2. 同屋 (tóng wū) *n.* roommate　我的同屋;你的同屋

3. 代收 (dài shōu) *v.* collecting for another agency　代收快递;代收业务

4. 超市 (chāo shì) *n.* supermarket　在超市;去超市

5. 业务 (yè wù) *n.* bussiness　银行业务; 业务员

6. 付 (fù) *v.* pay　付钱;付学费

7. 取 (qǔ) *v.* get　取钱;取快递

8. 得 (děi) *v.* have to　我得走了;我得早点去

9. 带 (dài) *v.* take; bring　带钱;带照相机

10. 证件 (zhèng jiàn) *n.* credentials　学生证;身份证

11. 货 (huò) *v.* goods　取货;进货;卖货

12. 号码 (hào mǎ) *v.* number　手机号码;银行卡号码

13. 凭 (píng) *prep.* base on　凭学生证;凭身份证

课文(二)　取快递
Text B　Take express package

美玲接到快递员打来的电话。

快递员:喂,您好!您的快递到了,能到楼下来拿一下吗?
Kuài dì yuán Wèi nín hǎo Nín de kuài dì dào le néng dào lóu xià lái ná yí xià ma

美玲:哎呀!我现在不在宿舍,我在外边呢。
Měi líng Āi ya Wǒ xiàn zài bú zài sù shè wǒ zài wài biān ne

快递员:您有同屋或者朋友可以帮您代收一下吗?
Kuài dì yuán Nín yǒu tóng wū huò zhě péng you kě yǐ bāng nín dài shōu yí xià ma

美玲:她们也都不在宿舍,怎么办呢?
Měi líng Tā men yě dōu bú zài sù shè zěn me bàn ne

快递员:那您看这样行吗?我给您放在宿舍楼下的超市里,他们有代收快递的业务,但是您去取东西时,得付给超市一块钱。
Kuài dì yuán Nà nín kàn zhè yàng xíng ma Wǒ gěi nín fàng zài sù shě lóu xià de chāo shì lǐ tā men yǒu dài shōu kuài dì de yè wù dàn shì nín qù qǔ dōng xī shí děi fù gěi chāo shì yí kuài qián

美玲:好吧,只好这样了。但是我怎么取快递呢?需要带证件吗?
Měi líng Hǎo ba zhǐ hǎo zhè yàng le Dàn shì wǒ zěn me qǔ kuài dì ne Xū yào dài zhèng jiàn ma

快递员：我会给您的手机发送一个取货号码，您凭这个号码就可以取快递了。
Kuài dì yuán Wǒ huì gěi nín de shǒu jī fā sòng yí gè qǔ huò hào mǎ nín píng zhè gè hào mǎ jiù kě yǐ qǔ kuài dì le

美玲：好的，我知道了，谢谢！
Měi líng Hǎo de wǒ zhī dào le xiè xie

快递员：不客气。
Kuài dì yuán Bú kè qi

根据课文(二)回答问题
Answer these questions according to the Text B

1. 美玲为什么不能到楼下拿快递?
2. 同屋可以帮她拿吗?
3. 快递员是怎么说的?
4. 美玲怎么去超市取快递?

语言点
Language points

1. 你看……行吗?

你看这样行吗?

Is that OK with you?

"看"在这里的意思是"觉得""认为"。"你看……行吗?"用于征求听话人的意见。

"看" here means "feel" or "think". "你看……行吗?" is used to ask for the advice of the listener.

(1)你看我明天去找你行吗?
(2)你看我这样写行吗?
(3)你看咱们两个人一起去行吗?

2. *v*. + 在 + 处所

我给您放在宿舍楼下的超市里。

I'll put it in the supermarket under the dormitory building.

这个结构表示通过动作使事物到某处，宾语为表示处所的词语。

It indicates things are put by actions and the indirect object is formed with prepositional phrases of places.

(1)箱子放在这里就可以了。
(2)垃圾要扔在垃圾桶里。
(3)他的手机掉在地上了。

3. 得 + *v*.

您去取东西时,得付给超市一块钱。

When you go to fetch something, you have to pay one *yuan* to the supermarket.

"得"读作"děi",助动词,意思为"应该""必须",表示情理上、事实上或意志上的需要;不能单独回答问题。表示否定用"不用",不能用"不得",用于口语。

"得" is read as "děi", auxiliary verb, means "should be" or "must be", to indicate the necessity in the sense of reason, fact and will. It can't be used to answer the question alone.

(1)太晚了,我得走了。

(2)明天有考试,我得早点儿起床。

(3)你的感冒越来越厉害,你得去医院看看。

4. 凭

您凭这个号码就可以取快递了。

You can take the express by this number.

"凭"在这里用作介词,表示凭借、依靠、根据,一般跟名词组合。

"凭" is used as a preposition, which means "by virtue of","depend on"and"on the basis of". It usually combine with a noun.

(1)凭学生证买火车票可以打八折。

(2)看演出要凭票入场。

(3)他凭自己的能力找到了一个好工作。

核心句 Key sentences

1. 我想寄两瓶酒到上海。

   I'd like to send two bottles of wine to Shanghai.

2. 酒是容易碎的东西。

   Wine is a fragile thing.

3. 请写好收件人的详细地址和联系电话。

   Please write down the address and contacting number of the recipient.

4. 您的快递到了,能到楼下来拿一下吗?

   Your delivery is here. Can you come downstairs and get it?

5. 您有同屋或者朋友可以帮您代收一下吗?

   Do you have a roommate or a friend to collect?

6. 您凭这个号码就可以取快递了。

   You can take delivery by this number.

综合练习
Comprehensive exercises

(一)熟读下列短语 Read the following phrases

1.寄快递　寄信　寄礼物　寄书
2.容易说　容易写　容易做　容易看懂
3.提供服务　提供帮助　提供食宿　提供留学机会
4.得回家　得复习　得休息一下　得去学校上课
5.取钱　取快递　取东西　取包裹
6.付钱　付电费　付学费　付车费
7.凭学生证借书　凭交通卡乘车　凭医生证明休息　凭票进场
8.放在地上　挂在墙上　带在身边　扔在那里

(二)替换练习 Substitution drills

1. 能到楼下来拿一下吗?
   早一点儿来学校
   帮我买一瓶可乐
   告诉我马克的手机号码

2. 您得付给超市一块钱。
   我　好好准备考试
   你　跟王老师请假
   我　早点儿起床

3. 放在宿舍楼下的超市里。
   书包里
   教室里
   办公室的桌子上

4. 凭这个号码就可以取快递了。
   学生证　买半价火车票
   会员卡　打折
   图书证　在图书馆借书

5. 我想寄两瓶酒到　上海。
   三本书　北京
   一份礼物　巴黎
   一台电脑　西安

(三)完成对话 Complete the following dialogues

1. A：你好！我想寄两瓶酒到上海。

B：酒是__________的东西。您自己有__________吗？

A：你看这个盒子可以吗？

B：这个盒子不行。我们可以给您__________包装，能__________酒瓶不会碎。

A：好的。杭州__________上海几天能到？

B：快的话明天就能到，__________两天能到。

A：好的，谢谢！

2. A：您好！您的__________到了，能到__________来拿一下吗？

B：我在外边呢，怎么办？

A：您有同屋或者朋友可以帮您__________一下吗？

B：他们也都不在宿舍。

A：那您看这样行吗？我给您__________在宿舍楼下的超市里，他们有代收快递的，但是您取东西时，__________付给超市一元钱。

B：好吧。

A：我会给您的手机__________一个取货号码，您__________这个号码就可以取快递了。

B：好的，谢谢！

(四)课堂活动 In-class exercises

角色扮演。Role-play.

(1)你要给朋友寄礼物，来到快递公司寄快递。

参考词语：快递　特殊　包装　费用　时间

(2)你的快递到了，但是你不在宿舍，你请朋友代收快递。

参考词语：楼下　代收　告诉　手机号码　签名

(五)课后练习 After-class exercises

采访中国学生和国际学生。Interview Chinese students and international students and record their answers.

	中国学生1	中国学生2	国际学生1	国际学生2
你经常寄快递或者收快递吗				
你一个月收几个快递				
你常常在哪里收快递				
你常常在哪里寄快递				
你常常在网上买什么				

课文翻译 Translation of the texts

Text A　At the express company

(Mark has to send a gift to his friend and he come to the express company.)

Anna: Hello! I'd like to send two bottles of wine to Shanghai.

Courier: Hello! Wine is a fragile thing. Do you have your own special packing?

Mark: How about this box?

Courier: All right. Would you please fill out this express form? Please write down the address and contacting number of the recipient.

Mark: All right, do you think that's OK?

Courier: OK. The express fee is 15 yuan.

Mark: All right, here's the money. How many days will it cost from Hangzhou to Shanghai?

Courier: If it is fast, it will arrive tomorrow. Two days at the latest.

Mark: OK, thank you!

Text B　Take express package

(Meiling got a call from the delivery man.)

Courier: Hello! Your delivery is here. Can you come downstairs and get it?

Meiling: Oh, dear! I am not in the dormitory now, I am outside.

Courier: Do you have a roommate or a friend to collect?

Meiling: They are not in the dormitory. What do I do?

Courier: Is that OK with you? I will put it in the supermarket under the dormitory building, because they have the business of collecting express delivery, but when you go to fetch it, you have to pay one yuan to the supermarket.

Meiling: All right. But how do I pick up the express? Do I need some identification?

Courier: I will send a pickup number to your mobile phone, and you can take delivery by this number.

Meiling: OK, I see. Thank you!

11 请问有包间吗？
Is there a private room?

话题导学 Guidance

1. 在中国你预订过饭店吗？应该怎么预订？
   Have you booked a restaurant in China? How do you book it?
2. 你觉得在中国叫外卖方便吗？叫外卖的时候你常点什么菜？
   Do you think is it convenient to order take-out in China? What dishes do you often order?
3. 你喜欢中国菜吗？你不习惯吃哪些中国菜？
   Do you like Chinese dishes? What Chinese dishes are you not used to?

生词学习(一) New words I

1. 聚会 (jù huì) *n.* get-together　　生日聚会；家庭聚会
2. 座位 (zuò wèi) *n.* seat　　预订座位；一个座位
3. 下 (xià) *n.* next　　下星期；下个月
4. 包间 (bāo jiān) *n.* private room　　要一个包间
5. 找 (zhǎo) *v.* to look for　　找手机；找钱包
6. 安静 (ān jìng) *adj.* quiet　　很安静；安静的地方
7. 内 (nèi) *n.* within; inner　　教室内；一个月内
8. 低 (dī) *adj.* low　　低价；低收入
9. 消费 (xiāo fèi) *v.* expense　　消费者；消费水平
10. 酒水 (jiǔ shuǐ) *n.* drinks　　自带酒水

bāo kuò
11. 包括 *v.* include 包括酒水；不包括

chāo guò
12. 超过 *v.* exceed 超过二十人

课文(一) 定包间
Text A Booking a private room

周末，同学们有一个聚会，马克来到一家饭店预订座位。

马克：你好！请问下星期三晚上八个人的座位，还有吗？
Mǎ kè Nǐ hǎo Qǐng wèn xià xīng qī sān wǎn shàng bā gè rén de zuò wèi hái yǒu ma

服务员：还有的，先生。您可以预订。
Fú wù yuán Hái yǒu de xiān shēng Nín kě yǐ yù dìng

马克：那太好了。对了，有包间吗？我们想找个安静点儿的地方。
Mǎ kè Nà tài hǎo le Duì le yǒu bāo jiān ma Wǒ men xiǎng zhǎo gè ān jìng diǎnr de dì fāng

服务员：还有包间。不过包间里是大圆桌，可以坐十个人，而且包间的最低消费是五百块。
Fú wù yuán Hái yǒu bāo jiān Bú guò bāo jiān lǐ shì dà yuán zhuō kě yǐ zuò shí gè rén ér qiě bāo jiān de zuì dī xiāo fèi shì wǔ bǎi kuài

马克：也就是说我们必须点五百块以上的菜才可以，是吧？
Mǎ kè Yě jiù shì shuō wǒ men bì xū diǎn wǔ bǎi kuài yǐ shàng de cài cái kě yǐ shì ba

服务员：是的。酒水也包括在内。
Fú wù yuán Shì de Jiǔ shuǐ yě bāo kuò zài nèi

马克：好吧。我们人多，消费应该会超过五百块的。
Mǎ kè Hǎo ba Wǒ men rén duō xiāo fèi yīng gāi huì chāo guò wǔ bǎi kuài de

服务员：请您写一下联系人的名字和手机号码。
Fú wù yuán Qǐng nín xiě yí xià lián xì rén de míng zì hé shǒu jī hào mǎ

马克：好的。
Mǎ kè Hǎo de

根据课文(一)回答问题
Answer these questions according to the Text A

1. 马克为什么要到饭店预订座位？
2. 马克要预订什么时候的座位？他们一共几个人？
3. 马克为什么想要包间？
4. 预订包间有什么要求？

生词学习(二)
New words II

wài mài
1. 外卖 *n.* take-out 叫外卖；买外卖

2. 主食 (zhǔ shí)	*n.* staple diet	今天的主食是米饭
3. 尤其 (yóu qí)	*adv.* especially	尤其喜欢杭州菜;尤其喜欢足球
4. 辣 (là)	*adj.* spicy	很辣;辣的菜
5. 换 (huàn)	*v.* change	换钱;换成别的菜
6. 直接 (zhí jiē)	*adv.* directly	直接告诉我;直接说
7. 支付宝 (zhī fù bǎo)	*n.* Alipay	用支付宝很方便
8. 当然 (dāng rán)	*adv.* of course	当然可以;当然好
9. 光临 (guāng lín)	*n.* presence (of a guest, etc.)	欢迎光临
10. 西红柿炒鸡蛋 (xī hóng shì chǎo jī dàn)	*n.* Stir-fried Eggs with Tomato	
11. 麻婆豆腐 (má pó dòu fǔ)	*n.* Mapo Tofu	
12. 蔬菜汤 (shū cài tāng)	*n.* vegetable soup	
13. 豆腐 (dòu fu)	*n.* Tofu; bean curd	

课文(二) 叫外卖
Text B Call for a take-out

玛丽今天不想做饭,她给饭店打电话叫外卖。

玛丽:你好! 我想要一份外卖。
Mǎ lì Nǐ hǎo Wǒ xiǎng yào yí fèn wài mài

服务员:您好! 请问您要点什么? 米饭套餐还是面条套餐?
Fú wù yuán Nín hǎo Qǐng wèn nín yào diǎn shén me Mǐ fàn tào cān hái shì miàn tiáo tào cān

玛丽:主食我想要米饭,米饭套餐里都有什么菜呢?
Mǎ lì Zhǔ shí wǒ xiǎng yào mǐ fàn mǐ fàn tào cān lǐ dōu yǒu shén me cài ne

服务员:今天的菜是东坡肉、西红柿炒鸡蛋、麻婆豆腐,还有蔬菜汤。
Fú wù yuán Jīn tiān de cài shì dōng pō ròu xī hóng shì chǎo jī dàn má pó dòu fu hái yǒu shū cài tāng

玛丽:别的菜都挺好的,就是我不爱吃豆腐,尤其是辣豆腐。麻婆豆腐可以换成别的菜吗?
Mǎ lì Bié de cài dōu tǐng hǎo de jiù shì wǒ bú ài chī dòu fu yóu qí shì là dòu fu Má pó dòu fu kě yǐ huàn chéng bié de cài ma

服务员：可以的。给您换成炒土豆丝，怎么样？
Fú wù yuán Kě yǐ de Gěi nín huàn chéng chǎo tǔ dòu sī zěn me yàng

玛丽：好的，我喜欢土豆丝。
Mǎ lì Hǎo de wǒ xǐ huān tǔ dòu sī

服务员：那请您说一下地址和手机号码吧。
Fú wù yuán Nà qǐng nín shuō yí xià dì zhǐ hé shǒu jī hào mǎ ba

玛丽：地址是工商大学宿舍区五号楼一〇一房间。手机号码是15859593678。
Mǎ lì Dì zhǐ shì gōng shāng dà xué sù shè qū wǔ hào lóu yī líng yī fáng jiān shǒu jī hào mǎ shì yāo wǔ bā wǔ jiǔ wǔ jiǔ sān liú qī bā

服务员：好的。您的外卖一个小时内送达，一共是二十五块，您直接付给送餐员就可以了。
Fú wù yuán Hǎo de Nín de wài mài yī gè xiǎo shí nèi sòng dá yí gòng shì èr shí wǔ kuài nín zhí jiē fù gěi sòng cān yuán jiù kě yǐ le

玛丽：好的，可以用支付宝付钱吗？
Mǎ lì Hǎo de kě yǐ yòng zhī fù bǎo fù qián ma

服务员：当然可以。谢谢光临！再见！
Fú wù yuán Dāng rán kě yǐ Xiè xie guāng lín Zài jiàn

玛丽：再见！
Mǎ lì Zài jiàn

根据课文(二)回答问题
Answer these questions according to the Text B

1. 玛丽要了什么套餐？
2. 玛丽不喜欢吃什么菜？可以换成别的菜吗？
3. 外卖多长时间可以送到？
4. 可以用支付宝付钱吗？

语言点
Language points

1. 而且

包间里是大圆桌，可以坐十个人，而且包间内的最低消费是五百块。

The private room is a large round table with 10 people, and the minimum charge is 500 yuan.

"而且"做连词，连接并列的形容词、动词、副词等表示意思更进一层。

"而且"is a conjunction which connecting the adjective, verb, adverb, etc., to make the meanning of the sentence go further.

(1)这个房间很干净，而且价格也不贵。

(2)最近我很忙，而且也没有那么多钱，所以不能去旅行。

(3)他很聪明,而且学习也很努力。

2. 也就是(说)

也就是说我们必须点五百块以上的菜才可以,是吧?

That means we have to order more than 500 yuan, right?

"也就是说"常用来进一步解释前面提到的内容。"说"有时可以省略。

"也就是说" is often used to explain what was previously mentioned further. "说" sometimes can be omitted.

(1)后天,也就是下星期一,我们有一个会议。

(2)今天苹果买一斤送一斤,也就是说买一斤可以得到两斤。

(3)对不起,你已经被辞退了,也就是说明天开始你不用来上班了。

3. 对了

对了,请问有包间吗?我们想找个安静点儿的地方。

By the way, is there a private room? We want to find a quieter place.

"对了"用在句首,表示说话人突然想起了什么事。

"对了" used at the beginning of the sentence, to indicate the speaker suddenly thinks of something.

(1)对了,你给妈妈买生日礼物了吗?

(2)对了,你买回家的机票了吗?

(3)对了,你的 HSK 考试通过了吗?

4. ……,就是……

别的菜都挺好的,就是我不爱吃豆腐。

All the other dishes are good, but I don't like tofu.

"就是"在这里有"只是"的意思,表示其他情况都令人满意,只有某个情况不尽如人意。

"就是" means "but" here, indicating that everything else is satisfactory, except that one situation is not satisfactory.

(1)坐公共汽车很便宜,就是人太多了。

(2)这个菜挺好吃的,就是有点儿咸。

(3)这个房子很大,也很新,就是楼层太高了。

5. ……,尤其是……

我不爱吃豆腐,尤其是辣豆腐。

I don't like tofu, especially spicy tofu.

“……,尤其是……”指出最为突出的情况,一般用在句子的后一部分。

“……,尤其是……” points out the most prominent case, usually used in the latter part of the sentence.

(1)他很喜欢运动,尤其是踢足球。

(2)我爱吃中国菜,尤其是川菜。

(3)他很爱家人,尤其是他的妈妈。

核心句 Key sentences

1. 有包间吗？我们想找个安静点儿的地方。

   Is there a private room? We want to find a quieter place.

2. 也就是说我们必须点五百块以上的菜才可以,是吧？

   That means we have to order more than 500 *yuan*, right?

3. 你好！我想要一份外卖。

   Hello! I want a take-one.

4. 别的菜都挺好的,就是我不爱吃豆腐,尤其是辣豆腐。

   All the other dishes are good, but I don't like tofu, especially spicy tofu.

5. 麻婆豆腐可以换成别的菜吗？

   Can Mapo Tofu be exchanged for other dishes?

6. 您的外卖一小时内送达,一共是二十五块。

   Your delivery will be delivered within one hour. The total cost is 25 yuan.

7. 可以用支付宝付钱吗？

   Can I pay with Alipay?

综合练习 Comprehensive exercises

(一)熟读下列短语 Read the following phrases

1.生日聚会　一个聚会　聚会时间　聚会地点

2.下个学期　下个月　下个星期　下一个人

3.找书　找手机　找钱包　找钥匙

4.很安静　安静的房间　安静地学习　安静地工作

5.尤其喜欢四川菜　尤其喜欢踢足球　尤其不习惯这里的天气

6.直接去　直接付给快递员　直接告诉妈妈　直接去办公室办理

7.当然知道　当然可以　当然漂亮　当然没去过

8.换衣服　换房子　换教室　换了一个老师

(二)替换练习 Substitution drills

1. 包间里是大圆桌,可以坐十个人,而且包间内的最低消费是五百块。

这家商店的东西好	价格也不贵
这里的风景很美	人也不多
这件衣服的样式很新	颜色也很好看

2. 包间内的最低消费五百块,也就是说我们必须点五百块以上的菜才可以,是吧?

大家一起吃饭AA制	我们每个人付自己的钱
他每个月只休息四天	每周只休息一天
医生说这种药一天吃三次	每八个小时吃一次

3. 别的菜都挺好的,就是我不爱吃豆腐。

西湖的风景美极了	今天人太多了
这个超市里什么都有	东西有点儿贵
他这个人什么都好	有时候脾气不太好

4. 麻婆豆腐可以换成别的菜吗?

套餐里的可乐	果汁
这件S号的大衣	M号的
黑色的皮鞋	咖啡色的

5. 我不爱吃豆腐,尤其是辣豆腐。

喜欢运动	跑步
想看电影	喜剧影片
穿裙子	长裙

(三)完成对话 Complete the following dialogues

1. A:你好!请问这里可以__________座位吗?

B:可以的,先生。您想预订哪天的,有几位客人?

A:我想订下星期三晚上的,一共8个人。对了,请问有包间吗?我们想找个__________点儿的环境。

B:下周三晚上还有包间。不过包间内的最低__________是500块。

A:我们必须点500块以上的菜才可以,是吧?

B:是的。酒水也__________在内。

A:好吧。我们人多,消费应该会__________500块的。

2. A:你好!我想要一份__________。

B:您好!请问您要__________什么?米饭套餐__________面条套餐?

A:我想要米饭,米饭套餐里都有什么菜呢?

B:今天的是东坡肉、西红柿炒鸡蛋、麻婆豆腐还有蔬菜汤

A:别的菜都________,就是我不爱吃豆腐,________辣豆腐。麻婆豆腐可以换成别的菜吗?

B:可以的。给您__________清炒土豆丝,怎么样?

A:好的,我__________喜欢土豆丝。

(四)课堂活动 In-class exercises

角色扮演。Role-play.

(1)生日的时候,你要请朋友吃饭,你来到饭店预订座位。

参考词语:预订　大厅　包间　最低消费　圆桌　套餐

(2)今天你不去食堂吃饭了,你给一家饭店打电话叫外卖。

参考词语:套餐　配菜　餐费　送餐费　付钱

(五)课后练习 After-class exercises

采访中国学生和国际学生。Interview Chinese students and international student, then record their answers.

	中国学生 1	中国学生 2	国际学生 1	国际学生 2
你经常叫外卖吗				
你一周叫几次外卖				
你为什么叫外卖				
你经常叫什么外卖				
叫一次外卖一般多少钱				

课文翻译 Translation of the texts

Text A Booking a private room

(The students had a party at the weekend and Mark went to a hotel to reserve a seat.)

Mark: Hello! I'd like to book a total of eight people for Wednesday evening.

Waiter: Yes, Sir. You can book it.

Mark: That would be great. By the way, is there a private room? We want to find a quieter place.

Waiter: Yes, there is. But it's a big round table for 10 people, and the minimum charge is 500 *yuan*.

Mark: That means we have to spend more than 500 *yuan* to order food, right?

Waiter: Yes. drinks are also included.

Mark: All right. We have many people, so we would spend more than 500 yuan.

Waiter: All right. Please write down your contacting name and mobile number.

Mark: Okey.

Text B Call for a take-out

(Mary didn't feel like cooking today. She called the restaurant to order take-out.)

Mary: Hello! I want a take-out.

Waiter: Hello! What do you want, rice or noodles?

Mary: I'd like to have rice. What's in the rice set?

Waiter: There are Braised DongPo Pork, Scrambled Eggs with Tomatoes, Mapo Tofu and vegetable soup.

Mary: All the other dishes are good, but I don't like tofu, especially spicy tofu. Can mapo tofu be exchanged for other dishes?

Waiter: You can. How about replacing it with Fried Potatoes?

Mary: OK, I like potatoes.

Waiter: Then please tell me the address and the phone number of the consignee.

Mary: The address is room 101, building 5, dormitory area, Gongshang university. The mobile number is 15859593687.

Waiter: All right. Your delivery will be delivered within one hour. The total cost is 25 yuan. You can pay to the courier directly.

Mary: OK, can I pay with Alipay?

Waiter: Sure. Thanks for your calling! Good bye!

Mary: Good bye!

12 参观义乌小商品市场
Visiting the Yiwu Small Commodity Market

话题导学 Guidance

1. 如何查询和购买火车票？
   How do you check and buy a train ticket?
2. 如何询问和评价商品？
   How do you inquire about the commodity and bargain with a salesperson?
3. 怎样表达对合作的期待？
   How do you express your expectations for cooperation?

生词学习(一) New words I

1. xiǎo shāng pǐn 小商品 *n.* small commodity　小商品市场；卖小商品
2. pī fā 批发 *v./n.* wholesale　服装批发；批发商品
3. shì chǎng 市场 *n.* market　服装市场；人才市场
4. quán qiú 全球 *n.* global　全球市场；全球经济
5. huà zhuāng pǐn 化妆品 *n.* cosmetic　一盒化妆品；买化妆品
6. ér tóng 儿童 *n.* child　儿童服装；儿童用品
7. wán jù 玩具 *n.* toy　一个玩具；玩具市场
8. pǔ tōng 普通 *adj.* ordinary　很普通；普通人
9. dà bā 大巴 *n.* bus　一辆大巴；大巴司机
10. liáo tiān 聊天 *v.* to chat　一起聊天；和她聊天

fēngjǐng
11. 风景 *n.* landscape 自然风景;景色优美

课文(一) 义乌在哪里
Text A Where is Yiwu?

王老师和同学们打算去义乌小商品市场参观,同学们在讨论。

王老师:下个星期我们有一次旅行,参观义乌小商品市场。
Wáng lǎo shī Xià ge xīng qī wǒ men yǒu yí cì lǚ xíng cān guān Yì wū xiǎo shāng pǐn shì chǎng

玛丽:太好了!我听说过义乌,但是不知道义乌在哪儿。
Mǎ lì Tài hǎo le Wǒ tīng shuō guò Yì wū dàn shì bù zhī dào Yì wū zài nǎr

王老师:义乌在浙江省中部。它是全球最大的小商品批发市场。
Wáng lǎo shī Yì wū zài zhè jiāng shěng zhōng bù Tā shì quán qiú zuì dà de xiǎo shāng pǐn pī fā shì chǎng

马克:王老师,什么是小商品?什么是批发?
Mǎ kè Wáng lǎo shī shén me shì xiǎo shāng pǐn Shén me shì pī fā

王老师:小商品是我们的日用品。批发就是一次买很多,价格很便宜。
Wáng lǎo shī Xiǎo shāng pǐn shì wǒ men de rì yòng pǐn Pī fā jiù shì yī cì mǎi hěn duō jià gé hěn pián yi

安娜:我对化妆品感兴趣。
Ān nà Wǒ duì huà zhuāng pǐn gǎn xìng qù

美玲:我对儿童玩具感兴趣。从杭州怎么去义乌呢?
Měi líng Wǒ duì ér tóng wán jù gǎn xìng qù Cóng Háng zhōu zěn me qù Yì wū ne

王老师:坐火车、坐大巴、坐高铁都可以,两小时以内可以到达。
Wáng lǎo shī Zuò huǒ chē zuò dà bā zuò gāo tiě dōu kě yǐ liǎng xiǎo shí yǐ nèi kě yǐ dào dá

马克:中国朋友告诉我,普通火车二十一块五元,一个半小时到。高铁五十元,四十分钟到。大巴五十元,一个半小时到。
Mǎ kè Zhōng guó péng yǒu gào sù wǒ pǔ tōng huǒ chē èr shí yī kuài wǔ yuán yí gè bàn xiǎo shí dào Gāo tiě wǔ shí yuán sì shí fēn zhōng dào Dà bā wǔ shí yuán yí gè bàn xiǎo shí dào

美玲:我们乘坐普通火车吧,价钱很便宜。我们可以一边聊天,一边看风景。
Měi líng Wǒ men chéng zuò pǔ tōng huǒ chē ba jià qián hěn pián yi Wǒ men kě yǐ yì biān liáo tiān yì biān kàn fēng jǐng

根据课文(一)回答问题
Answer these questions according to the Text A

1. 义乌在哪里?
2. 什么是批发?
3. 从杭州到义乌,怎么去最快?怎么去最便宜?

4. 什么是小商品批发市场？

生词学习(二)
New words II

1. 商贸 shāngmào *v.* trade　　商贸活动；商贸公司
2. 海洋 hǎiyáng *n.* ocean　　海洋动物；海洋贸易
3. 天堂 tiāntáng *n.* heaven　　人间天堂；去天堂
4. 毛绒 máoróng *n.* plush　　毛绒玩具
5. 电动 diàndòng *adj.* electric　　电动自行车；电动玩具
6. 生产 shēngchǎn *v.* produce　　生产产品；生产玩具
7. 代理 dàilǐ *n.* agent　　代理商；代理人
8. 样子 yàngzi *n.* appearance　　样子不错；样子很好

课文(二)　义乌商贸城
Text B　International Trade City of Yiwu

美玲：听说义乌商贸城非常大。有多大呢？
Měi Líng　Tīngshuō Yìwū shāngmàochéng fēicháng dà　Yǒu duō dà ne

王老师：商贸城是全球最大的批发市场。如果想全部逛完，可能一个星期都不够。
Wáng lǎoshī　Shāngmàochéng shì quánqiú zuì dà de pīfā shìchǎng　Rúguǒ xiǎng quánbù guàng wán　kěnéng yí gè xīngqī dōu bú gòu

美玲：我的天哪，我们一天可逛不完。那得有多少商店啊？
Měi Líng　Wǒ de tiān na　wǒmen yì tiān kě guàng bù wán　Nà děi yǒu duōshǎo shāngdiàn a

王老师：商贸城有二十万个商人，有五万多家商店。
Wáng lǎoshī　Shāngmàochéng yǒu èrshí wàn gè shāngrén　yǒu wǔ wàn duō jiā shāngdiàn

美玲：在商贸城，我能买到哪些小商品呢？
Měi Líng　Zài shāngmàochéng　wǒ néng mǎidào nǎxiē xiǎoshāngpǐn ne

王老师：义乌是“小商品的海洋，购物者的天堂”。你能想到的小商品，这里都能找到。
Wáng lǎoshī　Yìwū shì　xiǎoshāngpǐn de hǎiyáng　gòuwùzhě de tiāntáng　Nǐ néng xiǎngdào de xiǎoshāngpǐn　zhèlǐ dōu néng zhǎodào

在义乌商贸城。

售货员：欢迎光临，有什么可以帮忙的吗？
Shòuhuòyuán Huānyíng guānglín yǒu shénme kěyǐ bāngmáng de ma

美玲：你好，请问有三到七岁儿童的玩具吗？
Měilíng Nǐ hǎo qǐngwèn yǒu sān dào qī suì értóng de wánjù ma

售货员：当然有。我们有毛绒玩具、电动玩具、普通玩具等。
Shòuhuòyuán Dāngrán yǒu Wǒmen yǒu máoróng wánjù diàndòng wánjù pǔtōng wánjù děng

美玲：这种毛绒玩具多少钱一个？
Měilíng Zhè zhǒng máoróng wánjù duōshǎo qián yī gè

售货员：零售一百二十块，批发价格可以再谈。
Shòuhuòyuán Língshòu yī bǎi èr shí kuài pīfā jiàgé kěyǐ zài tán

美玲：你们公司出口玩具吗？
Měilíng Nǐmen gōngsī chūkǒu wánjù ma

售货员：我们公司的玩具品种很多，出口到世界五十多个国家。
Shòuhuòyuán Wǒmen gōngsī de wánjù pǐnzhǒng hěn duō chūkǒu dào shìjiè wǔ shí duō gè guójiā

美玲：我是印尼留学生。你们在印尼有代理吗？
Měilíng Wǒ shì yìnní liúxuéshēng Nǐmen zài yìnní yǒu dàilǐ ma

售货员：我们公司在泰国有，在印尼还没有。
Shòuhuòyuán Wǒmen gōngsī zài Tàiguó yǒu zài yìnní hái méiyǒu

美玲：你们的玩具不但价格便宜，样子还不错。也许我们可以合作。
Měilíng Nǐmen de wánjù bùdàn jiàgé piányi yàngzi hái bùcuò Yěxǔ wǒmen kěyǐ hézuò

售货员：太好了，非常感谢。这是公司的资料和联系方式。
Shòuhuòyuán Tài hǎo le fēicháng gǎnxiè Zhè shì gōngsī de zīliào hé liánxì fāngshì

根据课文(二)回答问题
Answer these questions according to the Text B

1. 义乌商贸城有多少商人和商店？
2. 毛绒玩具的零售价和批发价一样吗？
3. 公司的玩具出口到世界多少个国家？
4. 那家商店的玩具怎么样？

语言点
Language points

1. ……以内

两小时以内可以到达。

“以内”表示在一定的时间、范围、数量、处所的界限内。

“以内” meas within a certain the time, scope, number, position, etc.

(1)三天以内　一小时以内　十分钟以内

(2)一百块以内　五百米以内　三十人以内

(3)杭州以内　学校以内　长城以内

2. *v.*＋完

如果想全部逛完，可能一个星期都不够。

“完”用在动词后，表示动作已经完成。否定形式是“没(有)＋*v.*＋完”。动词或者形容词，用在动词后表示动作的结果。

“完” is used after verb, indicating the action is completed. The negative form is “没(有)＋*v.*＋完”. In Chinese, a verb coming after verb or an adjective after a verb indicates the results of an action.

(1)*v.*＋完：吃完　看完　写完　运动完　没喝完

(2)*v.*＋好：买好　做好　修好　准备好　没休息好

(3)*v.*＋满：坐满　站满　写满　装满　没排满

(4)*v.*＋到：送到　吃到　听到　买到　没看到

(5)*v.*＋上：穿上　带上　戴上　关上　没写上

3. 不但……，还……

你们的玩具不但价格便宜，样子还不错。

“不但……，还……”连接两个分句，表示递进关系。“还”，有时候也可以用“而且”。

“不但……，还……” means “not only…but also…”, which joins two clauses to show a progressive relationship. “还” is equialent to “而且” and sometimes.

(1)这家饭店的菜不但好吃，还很便宜。

(2)妈妈不但会做饭，而且会弹钢琴。

(3)马克不但是我的哥哥，还是我的同学。

4. 数字的读法

208：二百零八　　1,102：一千一百零二

666：六百六十六　　5,000 五千

9,009 九千零九　　30,000 三万

80,430 八万零四百三十　　246,489 二十四万六千四百八十九

1,200,461 一百二十万零四百六四一

90,170,389 九千零十七万零三百八十九

核心句
Key sentences

1. 我对化妆品感兴趣。
   I am interested in cosmetics.
2. 两小时以内可以到达。
   It can be reached within two hours.
3. 听说义乌商贸城非常大。
   I heard that Yiwu International Trade City is very large.
4. 欢迎光临,有什么可以帮忙的吗?
   Welcome, can I help you?
5. 不但价格便宜,样子还不错。
   Not only is it cheap, but the appearance is nice.
6. 我们可以一边聊天,一边看风景。
   We can chat together while watching the scenery.

综合练习
Comprehensive exercises

(一)熟读下列词和短语 Read the following phrases

1.参观市场　参观学校　参观这家公司　参观一家有名的工厂　欢迎参观
2.中部　西部　东部　南部　北部　上部　下部
3.日用品　商品　食品　物品　产品　礼品　药品　化妆品
4.两小时以内　一周以内　两年以内　十块钱以内　一百人以内
5.普通火车　普通人　普通学校　普通衣服　普通公司　普通家庭
6.全球　全国　全校　全班　全亚洲　全宿舍　全浙江　全公司
7.购物者　学习者　领导者　旅游者　记者　长者　老者　弱者
8.逛完　卖完　买完　吃完　喝完　写完作业　做完工作　洗完衣服
9.出口玩具　出口商品　出口产品　进口玩具　进口商品　进口产品

(二)替换练习 Substitution drills

1. 我听说过<u>义乌</u>,但是<u>不知道义乌在哪儿</u>。
   西安　没有去过西安
   他的故事　没有见过他
   这种水果　没有吃过
2. 我对<u>化妆品</u>感兴趣,对<u>手机</u>不感兴趣。
   踢足球　跑步

看书　　看电影

电子产品　　运动

3. 你们的玩具不但价格便宜，样子还不错。

这种水果　　好看　　味道

这家超市　　价格便宜　东西

他女朋友　　聪明　　长相

4. 我们可以一边聊天，一边看风景。

喝咖啡　　聊天

跑步　　听音乐

做饭　　看电视

5. 酒我没有喝完，你喝完了吗？

作业　　做好　　做好

苹果　　买到　　买到

门　　关上　　关上

6. 从杭州怎么去义乌？

上海　　北京

纽约　　伦敦

下沙　　西湖

7. 两小时以内可以到达。

十分钟　　完成

一星期　　写好

三年　　毕业

8. 这种毛绒玩具多少钱一个？

衣服　　一件

青苹果　　斤

黑裤子　　条

(三) 完成对话 Complete the following dialogues

1. A：我________过义乌，但是不知道义乌在哪儿。

B：义乌在浙江省________。它是全球最大的____________________市场。

A：什么是小商品？什么是批发？

B：小商品是我们的________________，批发是____________________，价格很便宜。

A：从杭州怎么去义乌呢？

B：坐__________________都可以。

2. A:________义乌商贸城非常大。有多大呢?

B:商贸城是________最大的批发市场。如果想全部________,可能一个星期都不够。

A:在商贸城,我能买到哪些小商品呢?

B:义乌是"小商品的________,购物者的________"。你能想到的小商品,这里都能找到。

(四)课堂活动 In-class exercises

1. 角色扮演。Role-play.

根据课文内容,多人对话。

2. 成段表达。Presentation.

(1)询问商品信息。

(2)如何买汽车票和火车票。

(五)课后练习 After-class exercises

复述课文。Retell the texts.

义乌在________________,它是全球最大的小商品________________。小商品就是________________,批发就是________________,价格很便宜。从杭州去义乌,坐________________都可以,________________可以到达。

商贸城是全球最大的__________。如果想全部逛完,可能__________都不够。商贸城有二十多万个________,有五万多家________。义乌是"小商品的________,购物者的________"。你能想到的________,这里都能找到。

课文翻译 Translation of the texts

Text A　Where is Yiwu?

(Teacher Wang and his students plan to visit the Yiwu Small Commodity Maket, and the students are dicussing.)

Teacher Wang: We will have a trip to visit the Yiwu Small Commodity Market next week.

Mary: Great! I have heard of Yiwu, but I don't know where Yiwu is.

Teacher Wang: Yiwu is in the middle of Zhejiang Province. It is the world's largest wholesale market for small commodities.

Mark: Teacher Wang, what is a small commodity? What is wholesale?

Teacher Wang: Small commodities are our daily necessities. Wholesale is to buy a lot one time, and the price is very cheap.

Anna: I am interested in cosmetics.

Meiling: I am interested in children's toys. How can we get to Yiwu from Hangzhou?

Teacher Wang: You can take the train, bus, or the high-speed train. you can arrive there within two hours.

Mark: Chinese friends told me that 21.5 yuan and 1.5 hours for the ordinary train, 50 yuan, and 40 minutes for high-speed train. 50 yuan, and 1.5 hours for the the bus.

Meiling: It is very cheap to take a regular train. We can chat while watching the scenery.

Text B　International trade city of Yiwu

Meiling: I heard that International Trade City of Yiwu is very large. How big is it?

Teacher Wang: International Trade City is the largest wholesale market in the world. If you want to go to all stores, it may not be enough for a week.

Meiling: My God. How many stores do they have?

Teacher: There are more than 200,000 merchants in the International Trade City and more than 50,000 stores there.

Meiling: What small commodities can we buy in the City?

Teacher: Yiwu is "the ocean of small commodities, the paradise of shoppers". Every small commodities you need can be bought there.

(In the Yiwu International Trade City.)

Salesperson: Welcome, can I help you?

Meiling: Hello, may I have a toy for children from 3 to 7 years old?

Salesperson: Of course. We have plush toys, electric toys, ordinary toys and so on.

Meiling: How much is the kind of plush toy?

Salesperson: 120 yuan per one, but wholesale can be discounted.

Meiling: Does your company export toys?

Salesperson: There are many varieties of toys in our company and we exports to more than 50 countries in the world every year.

Meiling: I am an Indonesian student. Do you have an agent in Indonesia?

Salesperson: There is an agent in Thailand but not in Indonesia.

Meiling: Your toys are not only cheap, but also good design. We can cooperate later.

Salesperson: Great, thank you very much! This is the company's introduction and contact information.

13 我喜欢广告，喜欢网购
I like advertisements and shopping online

话题导学 Guidance

1. 你喜欢商业广告吗？

   Do you like commercial advertisements?

2. 中文广告词有什么特点？

   What are the characteristics of Chinese advertisements?

3. 你喜欢网购吗？

   Do you like shopping online?

生词学习(一) New words I

1. 文章 wén zhāng	*n.* article ;essay	写文章；一篇文章
2. 诗歌 shī gē	*n.* poetry; poem	写诗；一首诗
3. 传递 chuán dì	*v.* transmit; delivery	传递信息；传递资料
4. 信息 xìn xī	*n.* message; information	市场信息；求职信息
5. 刺激 cì jī	*v.* stimulate	刺激需求；刺激很大
6. 需求 xū qiú	*n.* needs; need; demand; requirement	市场需求
7. 传播 chuán bō	*v.* spread	传播消息
8. 易 yì	*adj.* easy	易懂；易写
9. 懂 dǒng	*v.* understand	不懂；懂不懂
10. 记 jì	*v.* bear in mind; remember	记得；记住

11. 传 chuán *v.* spread 传消息;传资料

12. 刚才 gāngcái *adv.* just now; a short while ago 刚才听见

13. 广告 guǎnggào *n.* advertisement 商业广告;一则广告

14. 网购 wǎnggòu *v.* online shopping 网购东西;喜欢网购

课文(一) 中文广告
Text A Chinese advertisment

安娜、马克和王老师一起谈论广告。

王老师:你们喜欢中文广告吗?
Wáng lǎoshī Nǐmen xǐhuan zhōngwén guǎnggào ma

马克:我觉得中文的广告很有意思。比如"喝孔府宴酒,做天下文章",像诗歌一样,很好听。
Mǎkè Wǒ juéde zhōngwén de guǎnggào hěn yǒu yìsi Bǐrú hē kǒng fǔ yàn jiǔ zuò tiānxià wénzhāng xiàng shīgē yíyàng hěn hǎotīng

安娜:我觉得中文的广告不难懂,比如"味道好极了"。
Ān nà Wǒ juéde zhōngwén de guǎnggào bù nándǒng bǐrú wèidào hǎo jí le

马克:那是雀巢咖啡的广告词,一听就明白。
Mǎkè Nà shì quècháo kāfēi de guǎnggào cí yì tīng jiù míngbai

王老师:说得对。广告语言是一种艺术,最重要是传递信息、刺激需求。
Wáng lǎoshī Shuō de duì Guǎnggào yǔyán shì yì zhǒng yìshù zuì zhòngyào shì chuándì xìnxī cìjī xūqiú

安娜:那为什么刚才说的广告词这么简单呢?
Ān nà Nà wèishénme gāngcái shuō de guǎnggào cí zhème jiǎndān ne

马克:广告首先要让人明白,我说得对吗,老师?
Mǎkè Guǎnggào shǒuxiān yào ràng rén míngbai wǒ shuō dé duì ma lǎoshī

王老师:对,广告要传播,广告词就得易懂、易记、易传。
Wáng lǎoshī Duì guǎnggào yào chuánbō guǎnggào cí jiù děi yì dǒng yì jì yì chuán

安娜:我以后要多注意中文的广告词。
Ān nà Wǒ yǐhòu yào duō zhùyì zhōngwén de guǎnggào cí

马克:我们得好好学学广告的语言艺术。
Mǎkè Wǒmen děi hǎohao xuéxue guǎnggào de yǔyán yìshù

根据课文(一)回答问题
Answer these questions according to the Text A

1. 广告是什么?

2. 商业广告的目的是什么？

3. 中文广告词有什么特点？

4. 马克有什么建议？

生词学习(二) New words II

1. gòu wù 购物 *vo.* shoping　网上购物；超市购物
2. kuài dì 快递 *n.* express delivery; fast mail　快递公司；快递员
3. sòng huò 送货 deliver goods　送货上门；送货时间
4. shàng mén 上门 come or go to see sb.　送货上门；上门服务
5. cǐ wài 此外 *conj.* in addition; besides
6. gòu wù chē 购物车 *n.* shopping trolley　我的购物车
7. xià dān 下单 *v.* place an order　马上下单
8. qiǎng gòu 抢购 *v.* rush to purchase　抢购东西；抢购商品
9. guàng 逛 *v.* stroll; saunter　逛街；逛商场
10. tiāo 挑 *v.* choose; pick　挑选；挑时间
11. táo bǎo 淘宝 *n.* Taobao　淘宝网
12. shuāng shí yī 双十一 Double Eleven
13. tí qián 提前 *ad.* in advance; ahead of time　提前准备；提前下课
14. dǎ zhé 打折 *v.* discount; on sale　购物打折；不打折

课文(二) 淘宝购物 Text B Shopping in Taobao

安娜、美玲在讨论网购。

美玲：在杭州买东西真方便。
Měi líng　Zài Háng zhōu mǎi dōng xī zhēn fāng biàn

安娜：听说不带现金，手机支付就可以跑遍杭城。
Ān nà Tīngshuō bù dài xiàn jīn shǒu jī zhī fù jiù kě yǐ pǎo biàn háng chéng

美玲：我更喜欢在淘宝购物。
Měi líng Wǒ gèng xǐ huān zài táo bǎo gòu wù

安娜：是啊，淘宝买东西不仅便宜，而且会送货上门。
Ān nà Shì a táo bǎo mǎi dōng xī bù jǐn pián yí ér qiě huì sòng huò shàng mén

美玲：此外，买了不满意的话，还可以免费退货呢。
Měi líng Cǐ wài mǎi le bù mǎn yì de huà hái kě yǐ miǎn fèi tuì huò ne

安娜：哎，"双十一"快到了，打折会很多。
Ān nà Āi shuāng shí yī kuài dào le dǎ zhé huì hěn duō

美玲：是啊，我有很多东西要买。
Měi líng Shì a wǒ yǒu hěn duō dōng xī yào mǎi

安娜：我也要买很多东西。
Ān nà Wǒ yě yào mǎi hěn duō dōng xī

美玲：那我们得提前把东西挑好，放在购物车里。"双十一"一到就可以下单。
Měi líng Nà wǒ men děi tí qián bǎ dōng xī tiāo hǎo fàng zài gòu wù chē lǐ Shuāng shí yī yí dào jiù kě yǐ xià dān

安娜：好的东西得抢购啊。
Ān nà Hǎo de dōng xī děi qiǎng gòu a

美玲：有空赶紧逛逛淘宝网。
Měi líng Yǒu kòng gǎn jǐn guàng guang táo bǎo wǎng

根据课文(二)回答问题
Answer these questions according to the Text B

1. 为什么在杭州买东西很方便？
2. 淘宝购物和逛街购物有什么不同？
3. "双十一"是什么意思？
4. 为什么要在"双十一"购物？

语言点
Language points

1. 像……一样

像诗歌一样。

It reads like a poem.

"像……一样"，用于比喻，让意思更明白。

"像……一样" is used for metaphor, to make the meaning clearer.

(1) 她美得像花一样。

(2) 广告词像诗一样。

(3) 他的汉语说得像中国人一样。

2. ………极了

味道好极了。

It tastes great.

"……极了"，一般用在形容词后，表示程度深，有"非常"的意思。

It is usually used after adjectives with deep meaning.

(1)我今天累极了。

(2)西湖美极了。

(3)这个广告好极了。

3. 一……就……

"双十一"一到就可以下单。

You can place the order when the Double Eleven is coming.

"一……就……"表示做完一件事马上做另一件事。

This structure means to do one thing and do another thing at once.

(1)他一吃完早饭就去教室。

(2)他一下班就回家。

(3)他一放假就回国。

4. 不仅……，而且……

在淘宝买东西不仅便宜，而且快递会送货上门。

Shopping on Taobao is not only cheap, but also convenient for delivering to your home.

在"不仅……，而且……"这一结构中，"而且……"表示进一步的意思。

In the structure, "而且……" indicates further meaning.

(1)不仅可以用现金，而且可以用支付宝。

(2)不仅咳嗽，而且头疼。

(3)不仅可以看西医，而且可以看中医。

5. 得 + *v*.

那我们得提前把东西挑好。

Well, we have to pick our stuff up ahead of time.

"得"在动词前表示"必须"的意思。

when "得" is precede the verb, it means "must".

(1)我们得努力学好汉语。

(2)我们得提前准备。

(3)我们得好好写汉字。

6. 好好 + *v*.

好好逛逛。

let's have a nice look.

"好好 + *v*.","好好"用在动词前,表示一定要做某事。

"好好" is used before the verb, which means one is supposed to do something.

(1)让我们好好学习。

(2)这个广告不错,我们好好欣赏。

(3)好好休息吧。

7. ……,此外

此外,买了不满意的话,还可以免费退货呢。

Besides, if you don't like it, you can return it for free.

"此外",表示"除了某事,还有……"。

The structure means "in addition to", "besides", "furthermore".

(1)感冒要好好吃药,此外,还得好好休息。

(2)此外,你还要认真做作业。

(3)此外,我还要请你帮忙呢。

8. 把

那我们得提前把东西挑好,放在购物车里。

Well, we have to pick our stuff up ahead of time and put it in our shopping cart.

"把"在这里作介词,*v*. + 把 + *n*.,构成"把"字句,有强调宾语的意思。

"把",in is a preposition, in, which forms a sentence pattern of "把". it is used to emphasize the object.

(1)把书翻到第13课。

(2)把生词抄写几遍。

(3)请你把手机放好。

核心句 Key sentences

1. 味道好极了。

It tastes great.

2. 一听就明白。

You'll see at once.

3. 我们得好好学学广告的语言艺术。

We must learn the language art of advertising well.

4. 我更喜欢在淘宝购物。

I prefer to be on Taobao shopping.

6. 我有很多东西要买。

I have a lot to buy.

综合练习 Comprehensive exercises

(一)熟读下列短语 Read the following phrases

1. 传递信息　传递东西　传递纸条　传递资料
2. 提前上课　提前报名　提前去机场　提前买教材　提前挑好东西
3. 网上购物　淘宝购物　超市购物　商店购物　一起去购物
4. 刺激需求　生活需求　市场需求　基本需求　顾客需求
5. 挑东西　挑衣服　挑时间　挑地点　挑选礼物
6. 易懂　易看　易写　易读　易做　易改
7. 逛商场　逛书店　逛校园　逛街　逛上海　逛河坊街

(二)替换练习 Substitution drills

1. 我觉得中文的广告词很有意思，有的像诗歌一样。

汉字	图画
汉语的发音	唱歌
电影	生活

2. 那是雀巢咖啡的广告词，一听就明白。

上课讲过	课文	看	懂
老师讲过	生词	学	会
杭州传统	名菜	吃	喜欢

3. 淘宝买东西不仅便宜，而且快递会送货上门。

好的广告	能传递信息	能刺激需求
网上购物	方便	便宜
中医	能治病	能养生

4. 我们得提前把东西挑好，放在购物车里。

准备　　包
选　　书包
做　　教室

5. 我们得好好学学广告的语言艺术。

学习学习电影
了解了解诗歌
欣赏欣赏小说

(三)完成对话 Complete the following dialogues

1. A：广告语言是一种________艺术，最重要是传递________刺激________。
   B：那为什么刚才说的________词这么简单呢？
   A：广告要________，广告词就得易懂、易记、易传。
   B：我们得好好学学广告的语言艺术。

2. A：淘宝买东西便宜，而且快递会送货上门。
   B：________，买了不满意的话，还可以免费退货呢。
   A：“双十一”快到了，________力度会很大。
   B：那我们得________把东西挑好，放在购物车里。“双十一”一到就可以下单。

(四)课堂活动 In-class exercises

1. 角色扮演。Role-play.
   (1)讨论广告的作用。
   参考词语：广告词　传播　信息　需求　刺激
   (2)讨论网上购物的好处。
   参考词语：购物车　挑　网购　下单　快递

2. 成段表达。Presentation.
   (1)自选一则广告，说说广告的语言艺术。
   参考词语：传播　易懂　易记　形象　生动
   (2)说说网购的好处。
   参考词语：网上购物　购物车　快递　方便

(五)课后练习 After-class exercises

采访中国人并记录他们的答案。Interview some Chinese people and record their answers.

	中国人 1	中国人 2	中国人 3	中国人 4
你喜欢网上购物还是实体店购物				

续　表

	中国人 1	中国人 2	中国人 3	中国人 4
你经常在网上购买哪些东西				
网上购物的好处是什么				
你多长时间网购一次				
每次网购大概花费多少钱				

课后小贴士

快节奏的生活让不少在职消费群体不愿再为购物走街串巷。随着互联网的广泛运用，方便、快捷的网络购物方式反倒备受青睐。基本上只要是节日都会有大的优惠活动。春节、元旦、元宵、五一、六一、中秋、十一、双十一、双十二等，节日网购的热度都会持续一段时间。每年的十一月十一号，以天猫为代表的大型电子商务网站一般会利用这一天进行一些大规模的打折促销活动，以提高销售额度，“双十一”由此成为中国互联网最大规模的商业活动。

课文翻译

Text A Chinese advertisement

(Anna, Mark and Teacher Wang talk about the AD.)

Teacher Wang: Do you like Chinese advertisements?

Mark: I think Chinese advertisements are very interesting. For example, "drinking Confucian banquet wine, writing the world articles", like poem, very nice.

Anna: I don't think Chinese advertisements are difficult to understand, such as "It tastes great".

Mark: That's the word of Nestle coffee advertise. It's clear.

Teacher Wang: That's right. Advertising language is an art, and the most important thing is to convey information and stimulate demand.

Anna: So why is the slogan so simple?

Mark: The first thing you want to do is to make sure you understand. Right, teacher?

Teacher Wang: Yes, advertising is about to spread and the words should be easy to read, easy to remember and easy to spread.

Anna: I will pay more attention to the advertisements in Chinese.

Mark: We have to learn the language art of advertising well.

Text B Shopping in Taobao

(Anna and Meiling are discussing online shopping.)

Meiling: It's really convenient to buy things in Hangzhou.

Anna: I've heard that without cash, mobile payment can be used all over the city.

Meiling: I prefer to go shopping on Taobao.

Anna: You are right. It's not only cheap, but also convenieat for delivering to your home.

Meiling: Besides, if you don't like it, you can return it for free.

Anna: Well, the Double Eleven is coming and the discount will be great.

Meiling: Yes, I have a lot to buy.

Anna: I want to buy a lot of things, too.

Meiling: Well, we have to pick our stuff up ahead of time and put it in our shopping trolley. You can place the order when the Double Eleven is coming.

Anna: Well, you have to snap up the good stuff.

Meiling: If you're free, hang out on Taobao.

14 快放假了
Approach the final exam

话题导学
Guidance

1. 怎么准备期末考试?

   How do you prepare for the final exam?

2. 去哪里复习比较好?

   Where do you go for review?

3. 假期打算去哪里旅游?

   Where do you plan to travel on vacation?

生词学习(一)
New words I

1.	shí jiān 时间	*n.* time	没有时间;上课时间
2.	kǎo shì 考试	*n.* examination	一个考试;期末考试
3.	fù xí 复习	*v.* review	复习生词;复习汉语
4.	zhǔn bèi 准备	*v.* prepare	准备考试;准备早饭
5.	chǎo 吵	*v.* make a noise	不要吵;太吵了
6.	xiǎng 响	*adj.* loud	声音响;闹钟响
7.	dà shēng 大声	in a loud voice	大声说话;说话很大声
8.	yǐng xiǎng 影响	*v.* affect	影响别人;影响他们
9.	tú shū guǎn 图书馆	*n.* library	学校图书馆;两个图书馆
10.	ān jìng 安静	*adj.* quiet	很安静;安静的校园

fàng
11. 放 *v.* play 放音乐

yīn yuè
12. 音乐 *n.* music 中国音乐;喜欢音乐

bié rén
13. 别人 *n.* other people 别人的书;帮助别人

课文(一) 快期末考试了
Text A Approach the final exam

美玲、安娜在讨论期末考试。

美玲:时间过得真快啊!
Měi líng Shí jiān guò dé zhēn kuài a

安娜:是啊,快要期末考试了。
Ān nà Shì a kuài yào qī mò kǎo shì le

美玲:我们得好好准备,好好复习。
Měi líng Wǒ men děi hǎo hao zhǔn bèi hǎo hao fù xí

安娜:我觉得宿舍里太吵,不如去图书馆复习吧。
Ān nà Wǒ jué de sù shè lǐ tài chǎo bù rú qù tú shū guǎn fù xí ba

美玲:是啊,经常有同学把音乐放得很响,影响别人学习。
Měi líng Shì a jīng cháng yǒu tóng xué bǎ yīn yuè fàng dé hěn xiǎng yǐng xiǎng bié rén xué xí

安娜:有的还睡得很晚,还大声说话。
Ān nà Yǒu de hái shuì de hěn wǎn hái dà shēng shuō huà

美玲:那我们一起去图书馆复习吧。
Měi líng Nà wǒ men yì qǐ qù tú shū guǎn fù xí ba

安娜:好的,图书馆又安静又方便。
Ān nà Hǎo de tú shū guǎn yòu ān jìng yòu fāng biàn

美玲:那我们今天晚上就去图书馆吧。
Měi líng Nà wǒ men jīn tiān wǎn shàng jiù qù tú shū guǎn ba

安娜:好的。
Ān nà Hǎo de

根据课文(一)回答问题
Answer these questions according to the Text A

1. 美玲为什么建议去图书馆?
2. 宿舍里晚上安静吗?
3. 在图书馆复习怎么样?

生词学习(二)
New words II

jià qī
1. 假期 *n.* vacation; holiday 一个假期;假期短

lǚ yóu
2. 旅游 *v.* travel 去旅游;旅游的地方

gǔ dū
3. 古都 *n.* ancient capital 一个古都;西安古都

míng shèng
4. 名胜 *n.* scenic spots 风景名胜

gǔ jì
5. 古迹 *n.* historical sites 名胜古迹

gù shi
6. 故事 *n.* story 动人的故事;好故事

chuán shuō
7. 传说 *n.* legend 许多传说;古代传说

专有名词(Preper nouns)

nán sòng
1. 南宋 *n.* the Southern Song Dynasty (1127—1279)

xī líng yìn shè
2. 西泠印社 *n.* Xiling Society of Seal Arts

xī xī shī dì
3. 西溪湿地 *n.* Xixi Wetland

yuè wáng miào
4. 岳王庙 *n.* Yue Fei Temple

líng yǐn sì
5. 灵隐寺 *n.* Ling yin Temple

duàn qiáo
6. 断桥 *n.* Broken Bridge

bái dī
7. 白堤 *n.* Bai Causeway

wàn sōng shū yuàn
8. 万松书院 *n.* Wansong Academy

liáng zhù
9. 梁祝 *n.* The Butterfly Lovers

bái shé zhuàn
10. 白蛇传 *n.* Legend of White Snake

课文(二) 在杭州玩儿吧
Text B To travel in Hangzhou

安娜、美玲、李明在讨论假期旅游。

美玲:安娜,假期里,你打算去哪儿旅游?
Měi líng Ān nà jiǎ qī lǐ nǐ dǎ suàn qù nǎr lǚ yóu

安娜:我想去的地方很多,比如北京、上海、重庆、西安、桂林等,
Ān nà Wǒ xiǎng qù de dì fāng hěn duō bǐ rú Běi jīng Shàng hǎi Chóng qìng Xī'ān Guì lín děng

特别想去看看古都。
tè bié xiǎng qù kànkan gǔ dū

李明：杭州就是南宋古都。你们玩过了吗？
Lǐ Míng Hángzhōu jiù shì nánsòng gǔ dū Nǐ men wánguò le ma

安娜：忙着学习，还没怎么玩呢。
Ān nà Mángzhě xué xí hái méi zěn me wán ne

美玲：我也是。杭州有哪些名胜古迹呢？
Měi líng Wǒ yě shì Hángzhōu yǒu nǎ xiē míngshèng gǔ jì ne

李明：有西湖十景、西泠印社、西溪湿地、岳王庙、灵隐寺等。
Lǐ Míng Yǒu Xī hú shí jǐng Xī líng yìn shè Xī xī shī dì Yuèwángmiào Líng yǐn sì děng

美玲：听说《白蛇传》里的断桥就在西湖？
Měi líng Tīngshuō Bái shé zhuàn lǐ de Duànqiáo jiù zài Xī hú

李明：是的，断桥在西湖的白堤。传说故事就发生在那里。
Lǐ Míng Shì de Duànqiáo zài Xī hú de Bái dī Chuánshuō gù shì jiù fā shēng zài nà lǐ

安娜：我想起来了，《梁祝》故事，也发生在杭州，是吗？
Ān nà wǒ xiǎng qǐ lái le Liángzhù gù shì yě fā shēng zài hángzhōu shì ma

李明：是的，在万松书院。
Lǐ Míng Shì de zài Wànsōng shū yuàn

安娜：那太好了！我们先在杭州好好玩玩儿吧。
Ān nà Nà tài hǎo le Wǒ men xiān zài Hángzhōu hǎo hǎo wán wánr ba

美玲：对，以后再去别的古都玩。
Měi líng Duì yǐ hòu zài qù bié de gǔ dū wán

李明：假期里我给你们当导游吧。
Lǐ Míng Jià qī lǐ wǒ gěi nǐ men dāng dǎo yóu ba

安娜、美玲：好的，谢谢！
Ān nà Měi líng Hǎo de xiè xie

根据课文(二)回答问题
Answer these questions according to the Text B

1. 安娜、美玲喜欢去哪里旅游？
2. 杭州有什么名胜古迹？
3. 你知道《白蛇传》和《梁祝》的故事吗？
4. 你喜欢杭州哪些地方？

语言点
Language points

1. ……不如……

不如去图书馆复习吧。

Why don't you go to the library and go over it?

"……不如……"用于比较,意思是"比不上"。有选择后者的意思。

This expression is used for comparison, meaning the latter is preferable.

(1)去外地旅游不如先在杭州旅游。

(2)在宿舍复习不如去图书馆。

(3)北方的冬天不如南方温暖。

2. *v*. + 得……

时间过得真快啊!

How time flies!

"*v*. + 得……"动词后面是补语,"得"后常加形容词,表示程度的不同。

When the verb is followed by the degree complement, the word "得" is often added before the adjective that is used to describe the degree.

(1)有的人睡得很晚。

(2)他每天起得很早。

(3)我们学得很快。

3. 忙着……

我忙着学习。

I'm busy with my studies.

"忙着……",表示在某方面很忙。

This expression is used to say someone is very busy doing something.

(1)马克一直忙着学习。

(2)他们最近忙着工作。

(3)他最近忙着玩游戏。

4. 又……,又……

图书馆又安静又方便。

The library is quiet and convenient.

"又……,又……",表示具备两方面的特点或同时做两件事。

This expression can be used to indicate one object is equipped with two attribute or two actions are carried out at the same time.

(1)这儿的校园又大又漂亮。

(2)他汉字写得又清楚又好看。

(3)他又工作又学习。

5．先……，再……

先玩杭州，再玩别的古都。

Let's enjoy Hangzhou first and go to the other ancient capitals later.

"先……，再……"表示先后做某事。

This expression can be used to say when someone carries out two actions successively, "先……" is the fivst action while "再" is the latter one.

(1)我们先做作业，再看电影。

(2)我们先锻炼，再去吃饭。

(3)我们先预习，再复习。

核心句 Key sentences

1．时间过得真快啊！

How time flies!

2．图书馆又安静又方便。

The library is both quiet and convenient.

3．不如去图书馆复习。

It's better to go to the library to review.

4．他忙着学习。

He is busy with his studies.

5．你打算去哪儿旅游呢？

Where are you going to travel?

综合练习 Comprehensive exercises

（一）熟读下列短语 Read the following phrases

(1)准备考试　准备复习　准备旅游　准备去别的城市旅游　准备做饭

(2)影响学习　影响休息　影响睡觉　影响别人上课　影响室友看书

(3)声音很响　说话很响　音乐放得很响　电视放得太响　上课说得太响

(4)打算去旅游　打算去学习　打算去参加宴会　打算去图书馆复习　打算早点起床

(5)宿舍里太吵　教室里太吵　窗外太吵　酒吧太吵　饭店里太吵

（二）替换练习 Substitution drills

1．快要期末考试了。我们得好好复习。

放假	收拾东西
开学	预习课文

毕业　　　　　　　　准备论文

2. 我觉得宿舍里太吵,不如去图书馆复习吧。

教室里人太多　　寝室学习

这家店东西太少　　超市买

北方太冷　　南方生活

3. 图书馆又安静又方便。

寝室里　温暖　舒适

校园　宁静　漂亮

杭州　美丽　安全

4. 忙着学习,还没怎么玩呢。

复习　　休息

看书　　看电影

学汉语　　去旅游

5. 我们先在杭州好好玩玩,以后再去别的古都玩。

学校好好学习　　出去好好玩

教室里看书　　去图书馆学习

网上购物　　去市中心购物

(三)完成对话 Complete the following dialogues

1. A: 快要期末________了。

B: 我们得好好准备,好好________。

A: 图书馆又________又________。

B: 那我们一起去复习吧。

2. A: 杭州就是________古都。你们玩过了吗?

B: 这学期忙着学习,还没怎么玩呢。

A: 假期里,你打算去哪儿玩?

B: 先在杭州________玩,以后再去________。

(四)课堂活动 In-class exercises

1. 角色扮演。Role-play.

(1)在哪儿复习比较好。

参考词语:安静　吵　方便　图书馆

(2)假期去哪儿旅行。

参考词语:先……,再……　名胜古迹　古都

2. 成段表达。Presentation.

(1)说说杭州的名胜古迹。

参考词语:西湖十景　传说　故事

(2)说说假期打算去哪儿旅游。

参考词语:古都　先　再　然后　旅行

(五)课后练习 After-class exercises

1. 走访杭州老街,了解西湖文化。Visit Hangzhou old street to learn about Hangzhou's culture.

杭州著名的旅游景点有哪些	
杭州有哪些著名的历史人物	
关于西湖,有哪些故事和传说	
杭州有哪些著名的老街	
杭州有哪些有名的特产	

2. 选一个关于西湖的故事或者传说,向全班同学讲述。Pick a story or legend about the West Lake and tell the class.

课后小贴士

"中国古都"是指由中国古都学会通过并经国内史学家承认的古代都城。中国八大古都包括洛阳、西安、南京、北京、开封、杭州、安阳、郑州八个城市,其中西安、洛阳、南京和北京并称为中国四大古都。

杭州在五代十国时期为吴越之首都(907年—978年)。南宋建炎三年(1129年),赵构南渡至杭州,升杭州为临安府。绍兴八年(1138年),南宋正式定都临安,历时140余年。因此,杭州曾是两朝古都。

课文翻译

Test A　Approach the final exam

(Meiling, Anna are talking about the final exam.)

Meiling: How time flies!

Anna: Yes, the final exam is coming.

Meiling: We have to get prepared for it and review the lessons.

Anna: I think the dorm is too noisy. Why don't you go to the library and go over it?

Meiling: Yes, there are some students who often play music loud and influence others' study.

Anna: Some of them were sleeping very late and talking loudly.

Meiling: Let's go to the library together.

Anna: Yes, the library is quiet and convenient.

Meiling: Well, let's go to the library tonight.

Anna: All right.

Text B　To travel in Hangzhou

(Anna, Meiling, Li Ming are talking about their holiday travel.)

Meiling: Anna, where are you going to travel during the holidays?

Anna: I want to go to a lot of places, such as Beijing, Shanghai, Chongqing, Xi'an, Guilin, etc., and I especially want to go to the ancient capital.

Li Ming: Hangzhou is the ancient capital of the Southern Song Dynasty. Have you ever spent some days in Hangzhou?

Anna: I'm busy with my studies. I haven't had a lot of free-time.

Meiling: Same here. What places of interest are here in Hangzhou?

Li Ming: The West Lake, Xixi National Wetland Park, YueFei tomb, LinYin Temple, etc.

Meiling: I've heard the Broken Bridge in the Legend of the White Snake is in West lake, isn't it?

Li Ming: Yes, the bridge is in Bai Causeway on the West Lake. That legend has happened over there.

Anna: I remember that the story of The Butterfly Louers, happened at thc West Lake, right?

Li Ming: Yes, at Wansong Academy.

Anna: That's great! Let's enjoy Hangzhou first.

Meiling: Yes. I'll go to the other ancient capitals later.

Li Ming: I'll be your guide during these holidays.

Anna, Meiling: OK, thanks!

15 我想找一份兼职 I want to find a part-time job

话题导学 Guidance

1. 假期你想做兼职吗?
   Do you want to do a part-time jod during the holidays?
2. 大学生怎么找兼职?
   How do university students find part-time jobs?
3. 怎样准备简历和面试?
   How do you prepare your resume and interview?

生词学习(一) New words I

1. 放假 (fàng jià) *VP.* have a vacation　什么时候放假;没有放假
2. 不如 (bù rú) *v.* be inferior to　晚起晚睡不如早起早睡
3. 兼职 (jiān zhí) *n.* part-time job　一份兼职;兼职工作
4. 相关 (xiāng guān) *adj.* related　与他相关;和你们相关
5. 翻译 (fān yì) *n.* translator;interpreter　当翻译;一个翻译
6. 外贸 (wài mào) *n.* foreign trade　外贸工作;做外贸
7. 外企 (wài qǐ) *n.* foreign company　一家外企;在外企
8. 国际 (guó jì) *adj.* international　国际学生;国际学校
9. 人才 (rén cái) *n.* talent;staff　优秀人才;人才信息

课文(一) 讨论兼职
Text A Discussing part-time jobs

马克、玛丽和李明在一起讨论兼职。

马克：放假了，我觉得天天休息不如去工作。我想找一份兼职。
Mǎ kè Fàng jià le wǒ jué de tiān tiān xiū xī bù rú qù gōng zuò Wǒ xiǎng zhǎo yí fèn jiān zhí

李明：假期里做兼职，可以一边休息一边工作。那你想做什么工作呢？
Lǐ Míng Jià qī lǐ zuò jiān zhí kě yǐ yì biān xiū xī yì biān gōng zuò nà nǐ xiǎng zuò shén me gōng zuò ne

马克：我想做和英语相关的工作，因为我的英语非常好。
Mǎ kè Wǒ xiǎng zuò hé yīng yǔ xiāng guān de gōng zuò yīn wéi wǒ de yīng yǔ fēi cháng hǎo

李明：对你来说，做英语老师或者翻译都不错。现在有很多英语老师和翻译的工作。
Lǐ Míng Duì nǐ lái shuō zuò yīng yǔ lǎo shī huò zhě fān yì dōu bú cuò Xiàn zài yǒu hěn duō yīng yǔ lǎo shī hé fān yì de gōng zuò

玛丽：我想去外贸公司工作。忙是忙，但是能学到很多东西。
Mǎ lì Wǒ xiǎng qù wài mào gōng sī gōng zuò Máng shì máng dàn shì néng xué dào hěn duō dōng xi

李明：对你来说，去外贸公司做兼职挺合适的。杭州有很多外企，需要懂汉语的国际人才。
Lǐ Míng Duì nǐ lái shuō qù wài mào gōng sī zuò jiān zhí tǐng hé shì de Háng zhōu yǒu hěn duō wài qǐ xū yào dǒng hàn yǔ de guó jì rén cái

马克：上哪里可以找到合适的兼职信息呢？
Mǎ kè Shàng nǎ lǐ kě yǐ zhǎo dào hé shì de jiān zhí xìn xī ne

李明：学校勤工助学中心和网上都有。不如先去学校看看吧。
Lǐ Míng Xué xiào qín gōng zhù xué zhōng xīn hé wǎng shàng dōu yǒu Bù rú xiān qù xué xiào kàn kan ba

根据课文(一)回答问题
Answer these questions according to the Text A

1. 马克想找什么工作？
2. 玛丽想找什么工作？
3. 在哪里可以找到兼职信息？
4. 马克做翻译合适吗？

生词学习(二)
New words II

1. 出口 (chū kǒu) *v.* export　　商品出口；出口一批货物

zhāo pìn
2. 招聘 v./n. recruitment　　招聘员工;招聘广告

mào yì
3. 贸易 n. trading　　贸易公司;出口贸易

wǎng zhàn
4. 网站 n. website　　学校网站;一个网站

xiáng xì
5. 详细 adj. detailed　　非常详细;详细的信息

běn tǔ
6. 本土 n. native　　本土企业;本土市场

xiān
7. 先 adv. in advance　　先吃饭;先回家

jiǎn lì
8. 简历 n. resume;curriculum vitae　　我的简历;一份简历

rén shì
9. 人事 n. human affairs　　人事部;人事处

miàn shì
10. 面试 v. interview　　参加面试;面试他们

jǐn zhāng
11. 紧张 adj. nervous　　非常紧张;紧张的心情

课文(二) 准备简历和面试
Text B Prepare resume and interview

玛丽给诚成公司李小姐打电话。

玛丽:李小姐你好,我是工商大学的玛丽,看到了你们的招聘信息。我可以问一下贵公司的情况吗?
Mǎ lì　Lǐ xiǎo jiě nǐ hǎo wǒ shì gōng shāng dà xué de Mǎ lì kàn dào le nǐ men de zhāo pìn xìn xī　wǒ kě yǐ wèn yī xià guì gōng sī de qíng kuàng ma

李小姐:玛丽,你好!当然可以。我们诚成公司主要面向非洲出口服装。公司网站有详细的信息。
Lǐ xiǎo jiě　Mǎ lì nǐ hǎo　Dāng rán kě yǐ　Wǒ men chéng chéng gōng sī zhǔ yào miàn xiàng fēi zhōu chū kǒu fú zhuāng　Gōng sī wǎng zhàn yǒu xiáng xì de xìn xī

玛丽:我想应聘贵公司市场部的工作。请问可以兼职吗?
Mǎ lì　Wǒ xiǎng yìng pìn guì gōng sī shì chǎng bù de gōng zuò　Qǐng wèn kě yǐ jiān zhí ma

李小姐:当然可以。请问你的专业是什么?是哪国人?
Lǐ xiǎo jiě　Dāng rán kě yǐ　Qǐng wèn nǐ de zhuān yè shì shén me　Shì nǎ guó rén

玛丽:我的专业是商务汉语,南非人。除了英语,我还会说法语和汉语。
Mǎ lì　wǒ de zhuān yè shì shāng wù hàn yǔ nán fēi rén　chú le yīng yǔ wǒ hái huì shuō fǎ yǔ hé hàn yǔ

李小姐:太好了,我们非常欢迎本土员工。请先把简历给我们
Lǐ xiǎo jiě　Tài hǎo liǎo　wǒ men fēi cháng huān yíng běn tǔ yuán gōng　Qǐng xiān bǎ jiǎn lì gěi wǒ men

看看吧。
kànkan ba

玛丽：好的。我非常喜欢非中贸易工作。请问简历用英文还是中文？
Mǎ lì Hǎo de Wǒ fēi cháng xǐ huān fēi zhōng mào yì gōng zuò Qǐng wèn jiǎn lì yòng yīng wén hái shì zhōng wén

李小姐：最好中英文都有。请用电子邮件发送。收到简历一周内，如果合适，人事部会通知面试。
Lǐ xiǎo jiě Zuì hǎo zhōng yīng wén dōu yǒu Qǐng yòng diàn zǐ yóu jiàn fā sòng Shōu dào jiǎn lì yī zhōu nèi rú guǒ hé shì rén shì bù huì tōng zhī miàn shì

玛丽：面试需要做什么准备吗？这是我第一次在中国找工作。
Mǎ lì Miàn shì xū yào zuò shén me zhǔn bèi ma Zhè shì wǒ dì yī cì zài zhōng guó zhǎo gōng zuò

李小姐：不用紧张，面试就是到公司聊一聊，相互了解一下。
Lǐ xiǎo jiě Bù yòng jǐn zhāng miàn shì jiù shì dào gōng sī liáo yī liáo xiāng hù liǎo jiě yī xià

玛丽：非常感谢！
Mǎ lì Fēi cháng gǎn xiè

根据课文(二)回答问题
Answer these questions according to the Text B

1. 诚成公司主要出口什么？
2. 玛丽想应聘什么工作？
3. 玛丽是哪国人？会说什么语？
4. 玛丽的简历应该用英文还是用中文？

语言点
Language points

1. 不如

我觉得天天休息不如去工作。

I think going to work is better than sleeping at home every day.

“A不如B”表示A和B相比，B更好。A和B，可以是名词、代词或者是动词短语。

“A不如B” is used to indicate that A cannot be compared to B. A and B can be acted by nouns, pronouns, verbs or verb phrases.

(1)说运动，他不如我；说唱歌，我不如他。
(2)想减肥的话，不吃饭不如多运动。
(3)想了解中国传统文化，上海不如西安。

2. 对……来说

对你来说，做英语老师或者翻译都不错。

It is quite appropriate for you to do an English teacher or a translator.

"对……来说"强调对象的特指性,常用于句子的开头。"来说"也可以是"而言"。

"对……来说" emphasize the specific object. It is often used at the beginning of with a sentence."来说" could be replaced by "而言".

(1)对她来说,学好法语非常重要。

(2)对你们公司而言,最重要的是提高服务质量。

(3)对学习汉语来说,听说读写都很重要。

3. A是A,但是……

忙是忙,但是能学到很多东西。

Although the work is very busy, I can learn a lot.

"A是A,但是……"是一个口语句式,有强调A的意味。在这里,"A"是一个形容词。

"A是A,但是……" is a spoken expression with the emphasis on "A". "A" is an adjective here.

(1)北方的冬天冷是冷,但是雪景很漂亮。

(2)这道菜辣是辣,但是特别好吃。

(3)这件衣服漂亮是漂亮,但是太贵了。

4. 贵

我可以问一下贵公司的情况吗?

Can I ask some information about the company?

"贵"是汉语敬辞,常用于正式场合,表示尊重对方。

"贵" is a Chinese term for showing respect to other side, often used in formal occasions.

(1)请问您贵姓?

(2)我想到贵校工作。

(3)请问贵公司有多少员工?

5. 最好

最好中英文都有。

It is best to have both Chinese and English.

"最好"是一个口语结构,常置于动词前,表示提出合理建议。

"最好" is a spoken expression, placed before a verb. It indicates a reasonable suggestion.

(1)你最好不要迟到。

(2)你们公司最好和我们合作。

(3)明天最好不要出门,有大雨。

核心句 Key sentences

1. 天天休息不如去工作。
   Going to work is better than sleeping at home every day.
2. 对你来说,做英语老师或者翻译都不错。
   Being an English teacher or a translator is nice for you.
3. 我可以了解一下贵公司的情况吗?
   Can I ask some information about the company?
4. 除了英语,我还会说法语和汉语。
   In addition to English, I can speak French and Chinese.
5. 请问简历用英文还是中文?
   Is the resume in English or Chinese?
6. 面试就是到公司聊一聊,相互了解一下。
   The interview is to communicate and get to know each other.

综合练习 Comprehensive exercises

(一)熟读下列短语 Read the following phrases

(1)放假　放三天假　放一个月假　不放假　放很长时间的假
(2)和英语相关　和工作相关　跟你们相关　跟你们的工作不相关
(3)市民中心　商业中心　贸易中心　交易中心　学生活动中心
(4)聊天　聊天气　聊工作　聊学习　聊聊家庭　聊一聊生意
(5)先去学校　先去和经理问好　先回家再吃饭　先洗澡再睡觉
(6)对她来说　对公司来说　对你们学校来说　对他们国家来说
(7)本土公司　本土老师　本土企业　本土语言　本土文化
(8)一周内　一年内　十公里内　两周以内　十人以内　一百块以内

(二)替换练习 Substitution drills

(1)我觉得<u>天天休息</u>不如<u>去工作</u>。

去北京	去上海
早上跑步	晚上跑步
叫外卖	自己做饭

(2)我想<u>做</u>和<u>英语</u>相关的<u>工作</u>。

学	商务	专业
看	贸易	书

买　汉语学习　词典

(3)忙是忙,但是能学到很多东西。

累　累　我很快乐

便宜　便宜　不好用

好吃　好吃　太贵了

(4)我想应聘贵公司的市场部专员的工作。

贵校　法语老师

贵院　图书管理员

贵公司　商务秘书

(5)除了英语,我还会说法语和汉语。

打篮球　会踢足球　打排球

听音乐　喜欢旅行　运动

北京　去过南京　武汉

(6)如果合适,人事部会通知面试。

公司　告诉我们

他们　到那里工作

我们　去上海学习

(7)最好中英文都有。

衣服裤子　买

今天明天　去

汉语日语　学

(三)完成对话 Complete the following dialogues

1. A: 放假了,我觉得天天休息________去工作。我想找________兼职。

B: 你想做什么工作呢?

A: 我想做和__________相关的工作,因为__________非常好。

B: 对你来说,做____________________都不错。

2. A: 我想应聘贵公司的______________的工作。请问可以________吗?

B: 当然可以。请问你的________是什么?是哪______人?

A: 我的专业是________,________人。

B: 请先把________给我们看看吧。

A: 请问简历用英文还是中文?

B: 最好______________。

(四)课堂活动 In-class exercises

角色扮演。Role-play.

(1)玛丽和诚成公司李小姐的对话。

(2)大家说一说,如果有时间,你会做什么兼职,为什么。

(五)课后练习 After-class exercises

根据提示,复述课文。Retell the texts.

放假了,马克觉得天天休息不如__________,他想找一份________。对马克来说,做_____________都不错。玛丽想去__________工作。虽然_________,但是____________。学校勤工助学中心和___________有兼职信息。

玛丽给李小姐打电话。她想了解诚成公司的_________。诚成公司主要面向非洲_________。玛丽告诉李小姐,她想应聘公司的__________。玛丽的专业是_________,______人。除了英语,她还会说__________。李小姐说,简历最好__________。面试就是到公司________,相互了解一下。

课文翻译

Text A Discussing part-time jobs

(Mark, Mary and Li Ming are discussing part-time jobs together.)

Mark: I think going to work is better than sleeping at home every day during the holidays. I want to look for a part-time job.

Li Ming: If you do part-time job during the holidays, you don't have to work every day and you have a lot of rest time. So what do you want to do?

Mark: I want to do English-related job because my English is very good.

Li Ming: It is quite appropriate for you to be an English teacher or a translator. There are many jobs now in English teaching and translation.

Mary: I want to work for a foreign trade company. Although the work is very busy, I can learn a lot.

Li Ming: It is quite appropriate for you to go to a foreign trade company to work. There are many foreign companies in Hangzhou. They need international talents who understand Chinese.

Mark: Where can I find the work information?

Li Ming: There is some information in the student center. It is better to go to university first.

Text B Prepare the resume and interview

(Mary is calling Miss Li of Chengcheng Company.)

Mary: Hello, Miss Li, I am Mary of the Gongshang University. I saw your recruitment information. Can I ask some information about the company?

Miss Li: Hello, Mary! Of course you can. Our company mainly exports garments to Africa. There is detailed information on the company website.

Mary: I want to apply for the job of the marketing department. Can I work in my spare time?

Miss Li: Of course. What is your major? Where are you from?

Mary: My major is business Chinese. I am from South Africa. In addition to English, I can speak French and Chinese.

Miss Li: Great! We welcome local staff. Please send us your resume first.

Mary: OK. I really like the work of Africa-Chinese trade. Is the resume in English or Chinese?

Miss Li: It is best to have both Chinese and English. Please send me your resume by e-mail. Within one week of receiving the resume, the Personnel Department will tell you the result.

Mary: What preparations do I need to do for the interview? This is the first time for me to look for a job in China.

Miss Li: Don't be nervous. The interview is to communicate and get to know each other.

Mary: Thank you very much!

生词表
New words

饭店 6
房卡 8
付 10
风景 12
复习 15
放 15
翻译 15

G
刚 2
刚好 2
柜台 2
公司 4
挂号 5
馆 5
高铁 7
赶 7
公交卡 8
购物 8
公共 8
逛 8
光临 11
刚才 13
广告 13
逛 13
购物车 13
古都 14
古迹 14
故事 14
国际 15

H
好玩 1
欢迎 1
护照 2
活动 3
化装 3
合同 4
好像 5
杭帮菜 6
合适 7
号 9
会员 9
货 10
号码 10
环境 11
换 11
化妆品 12
海洋 12

I

J
接 1
久等 1
记录 2
举办 3
精彩 3
剧院 3
结束 3
教 3
结构 4
价位 4
就诊卡 5
讲究 6
经济舱 7
建议 7
交通 8
结算 8
决定 9
寄 10
聚会 11
酒水 11
记 13
假期 15
兼职 15
简历 15
紧张 15

K
可 1
卡 2
客服 2
京剧 3
看病 5
咳嗽 5
靠 6
快递 10
快递 13
考试 14

L
离 1
脸谱 3
离 4
礼节 6
龙井虾仁 6
楼外楼 6
离 7
论坛 8
乐意 9
礼物 10
联系 10
楼下 10
辣 11

编写说明

本教材是为商务汉语口语学习者编写的口语教材,是“商务汉语口语”系列教材中的第二册。第二册与第一册相衔接,也可以单独使用。本教材适合已经学习了不少于150小时基础汉语的学习者使用。教材的编写,采用“结构、功能、语法”相结合的理念,注重商务元素与基础汉语语法相结合,实际生活场景与地域文化相结合,注重词语扩展、关键句型和小型对话的操练。通过师生的共同努力,教材能较好地满足来华留学生日常口语交际的实际需要。

从教材课文的编选上,遵循第二语言教材编写的针对性、实用性、趣味性等原则,课文内容来源于来华留学生的实际生活、真实场景和实际表达的需要。本册教材的课文内容,涉及新生报到、校内换宿舍、看中医、参加商务宴请、购买机票等生活场景。课文(一)是主课文,平均五到六个话轮,加注拼音,适当降低初级阶段学生汉字识读的难度。课文(二)是副课文,是提高性学习,平均六到八个话轮,标注拼音、声调。教师在实际教学中,针对学生的实际水平和需要,可做灵活安排和处理。

从教材的结构编排上,落实贯彻汉语作为第二语言教学的学习规律和认知规律,积极吸收优秀教材的编排特点。内容设置从生词、课文、语言点到练习,注重语言结构与生词扩展、句型操练密切配合,交际任务与语言功能紧密结合,文化因素和商务元素有机融入。本册教材设置了初级阶段的七十余个常用语法点,四十余个交际功能项。作为口语教材,练习的设置偏重于常用句型的表达训练,通过角色扮演、复述等环节的训练,提升学习者句子和段落的表达能力。

从编写规范上,本教材参考了《汉语水平等级标准与语法大纲》《汉语水平词汇与汉字等级大纲》《国际汉语教学通用课程大纲》《新汉语水平考试大纲》《商务汉语考试大纲》等大纲和标准,积极吸收国内已经出版的优秀汉语教材的体例和范式。关于词汇的选取问题,在商务汉语和基础汉语词汇之间进行了平衡,对词汇难度进行了有效控制,词汇量尽量控制在词汇大纲甲级词的范畴内。对于生活中的常用词、高频新词则没有完全摈弃。商务汉语口语课教学主要侧重于听说,词汇的学习能运用于口语交际的实际需要即可,不要求难字难词的书写、再认。在实际教学中,教师可根据学生的实际情况,对学生提出合适的要求。

“商务汉语”属专门用途汉语,隶属于汉语作为第二语言教学的范畴。与基础汉语相比,“商务汉语”具有商务元素和特色。如何理解商务元素和特色,国内对外汉语教学界一直以来有不少的讨论和争议。在汉语作为第二语言学习的初级阶段,“商务汉语”不是商务知识和汉语作为第二语言教学的简单组合,而是在汉语作为第二语言教学的范畴内,教学内容的场景,词汇、句型的选取和使用具有商务沟通交际的特色。初中级阶段的商务汉语口语教材,商务汉语词汇、商务文化知识与基础汉语的词汇语法点的恰当融合,难度的把控,词汇的筛选和控制是公认的难题。因此市面上虽有商务汉语口语教材的需求,但合适的教材一直比较稀缺。需要说明的是,本教材的“商务”是以校园生活为中心的广义的商务和社会交往,并不完全局限于狭义的商务环境。

本教材将基础汉语语法和商务元素适度融合,是具有浙江地域文化特色的汉语口语教材的积极尝试。教材由有多年教龄的一线对外汉语教师集体编写,编写的具体分工是,楼益龄老师负责第4,5,6,13,14课的编写,孙蕾老师负责第2,3,7,10,11课的编写,刘杰老师负责第1,8,9,12,15课的编写,同时承担前期样课的设计和后期的修改统稿,王晓华主任负责全书的审读统筹。

众所周知,汉语作为第二语言的教材难编,商务汉语教材更难编。我们迎难而上,愿意接受方家的批评。同时,我们也希望得到一线教师和学生的宝贵意见,不断修改和完善教材,帮助更多的国际生学好汉语,切实提高其商务汉语听说水平。

编者

2018年秋

新视野

初级商务汉语口语(3)

主　　编　王晓华
本册主编　孙鹏飞
本册编写　孙鹏飞　赵　军　许飞燕

浙江工商大学出版社 | 杭州
ZHEJIANG GONGSHANG UNIVERSITY PRESS

图书在版编目(CIP)数据

新视野初级商务汉语口语 / 王晓华主编. — 杭州 ：浙江工商大学出版社，2019.8

ISBN 978-7-5178-3265-2

Ⅰ. ①新… Ⅱ. ①王… Ⅲ. ①商务—汉语—口语—对外汉语教学—教材 Ⅳ. ①H195.4

中国版本图书馆 CIP 数据核字(2019)第 119196 号

学 习 指 南

Guide to the Use of This Book

课数 Lesson	语法项 Grammar Item	功能项 Functional Items
第 1 课　欢迎来到我的国家	1. ……等。 2. 不但……，而且…… 3. 到时候…… 4. 除了……，也……	1. 赞扬 2. 安慰
第 2 课　我们一起去参加中国人的婚礼吧	1. 看情况，…… 2. A 跟 B 关系非常好 3. 越来越……	1. 领悟、明白 2. 邀请
第 3 课　梅雨季节	1. 都…… 2. *num.* ＋*mw.* ＋左右 3. 陪＋人＋*v.* ＋…… 4. ……转……	1. 失望 2. 惊讶
第 4 课　网上购物真方便	1. 首先……，然后……，最后…… 2. 够……的 3. 虽然……，但是…… 4. 如果……，……	1. 请求 2. 同意
第 5 课　美丽的西湖	1. *v.* ＋过 2. *num.* ＋多＋*mw.* 3. 得…… 4. 快(要)……了	1. 感叹
第 6 课　共享时代	1. 除了……，还…… 2. 这么＋*adj.* 3. 对了，…… 4. 地方＋有＋人/物 5. 要不……	1. 开启新话题 2. 建议
第 7 课　吃在中国	1. 就 2. 又……又…… 3. 入乡随俗 4. 动词重叠	1. 感谢 2. 询问别人的观点

续　表

课数 Lesson	语法项 Grammar Item	功能项 Functional Items
第 8 课　运动健身	1. ……以后/……以前 2. 还是$_1$ 3. 存现句 4. 对……有好处	1. 时间与频次 2. 表示称赞
第 9 课　我的微信好友	1. 对……来说 2. "把"字句$_1$ 3. 祝…… 4. 抱歉	1. 祝福 2. 拒绝
第 10 课　移动支付	1. *v.* ＋好 2. "把"字句$_2$ 3. 最好…… 4. 才	1. 同意 2. 顺序
第 11 课　租房与买房	1. A 还是 B? 2. 一方面……,另一方面…… 3. 也就是说 4. 喝西北风	
第 12 课　在中国实习	1. 是……的 2. 首先,……其次,……再次……,最后…… 3. 挺……的	
第 13 课　请喝茶	1. ……极了 2. ……的话 3. 倒 4. 呢	
第 14 课　报名参加 HSK	1. 还是$_2$ 2. 正反问句(知不知道) 3. 情态补语	
第 15 课　G20 峰会	1. 最……不过 2. 进行 3. 可	

mù lù

目录

1 欢迎来到我的国家
Welcome to my country

话题导学
Guidance

你知道图片中是哪个国家的国旗吗？你们国家的国旗是什么样的？

Do you know which country's national flag is in the picture?

What's the national flag of your country? Can you draw it?

生词学习(一)
New words I

1. 等 (děng) *part.* etc.; and so on　　中国、美国等；书、笔等
2. 羡慕 (xiàn mù) *v.* admire　　羡慕别人；羡慕朋友
3. 东南 (dōng nán) *n.* southeast　　中国东南；杭州东南
4. 海鲜 (hǎi xiān) *n.* seafood　　吃海鲜；买海鲜
5. 热情 (rè qíng) *adj.* enthusiastic　　很热情；热情的朋友
6. 好玩儿 (hǎo wánr) *adj.* interesting　　真好玩儿；好玩儿的地方

dà xiàng
7. 大 象　*n.* elephant　大象表演;一头大象

biǎo yǎn
8. 表 演　*v.* perform　表演节目;大象表演

yǒu míng
9. 有 名　*adj.* famous　有名的人;很有名

tài shì àn mó
10. 泰式按摩　*NP* Thai massage　做泰式按摩

dān xīn
11. 担心　*v.* to worry　别担心;担心父母

gēn
12. 跟　*v.* to follow　跟旅行团;跟朋友

lǚ xíng tuán
13. 旅 行 团　*NP* tour group　跟旅行团

chūn jié
14. 春 节　*n.* Spring Festival　过春节;春节的时候

dǎo yóu
15. 导 游　*n.* tour guide　找导游;跟导游

专有名词 (Proper nouns)

Yà zhōu
1. 亚 洲　*n.*　Asia

Měi guó
2. 美 国　*n.*　the United States of America

Tài guó
3. 泰 国　*n.*　Thailand

课文(一)　美丽的泰国
Text A　Beautiful Thailand

艾琳和马克在宿舍聊天。

艾琳:我听说你很喜欢旅行,你去过多少个国家?

马克:十多个,比如中国、美国、韩国等。

艾琳:真羡慕你,你去过我的国家吗?

马克:我还没去过泰国,你给我介绍一下吧?

艾琳:好的,泰国在亚洲的东南边,有漂亮的大海,那儿的海鲜不但好吃,而且便宜,泰国人也非常热情。

马克:我最喜欢大海了,还有别的好玩儿的事情吗?

艾琳:很多,泰国的大象表演很有名,如果累了,做一个泰式按摩也不错。

马克:听起来很有意思,但是我不会说泰语,怎么办?

艾琳：别担心，泰国是一个旅游国家，很多人都能说一点儿英语。

马克：太好了，那我就不需要跟旅行团一起了。对了，春节的时候你回国吗？

艾琳：回国啊，到时候我给你当导游。

马克：你真好，谢谢你。

Ài lín hé Mǎ kè zài sù shè liáo tiān。(**Ailin is talking with Mark in the dormitory.**)

Ài lín：Wǒ tīng shuō nǐ hěn xǐ huān lǚ xíng，nǐ qù guo duō shǎo gè guó jiā？

Mǎ kè：Shí duō gè，bǐ rú Zhōng guó、Měi guó、Hán guó děng。

Ài lín：Zhēn xiàn mù nǐ，nǐ qù guo wǒ de guó jiā ma？

Mǎ kè：Wǒ hái méi qù guò tài guó，nǐ gěi wǒ jiè shào yí xià ba？

Ài lín：Hǎo de，tài guó zài yà zhōu de dōng nán biān，yǒu piào liàng de dà hǎi，nàr de hǎi xiān bú dàn hǎo chī，ér qiě pián yi，tài guó rén yě fēi cháng rè qíng。

Mǎ kè：Wǒ zuì xǐ huān dà hǎi le，hái yǒu bié de hǎo wánr de shì qing ma？

Ài lín：Hěn duō，tài guó de dà xiàng biǎo yǎn hěn yǒu míng，rú guǒ lèi le，zuò yí gè tài shì àn mó yě bú cuò。

Mǎ kè：Tīng qǐ lái hěn yǒu yì si，dàn shì wǒ bú huì shuō tài yǔ，zěn me bàn？

Ài lín：Bié dān xīn，tài guó shì yí gè lǚ yóu guó jiā，hěn duō rén dōu néng shuō yì diǎnr yīng yǔ。

Mǎ kè：Tài hǎo le，nà wǒ jiù bù xū yào gēn lǚ xíng tuán yì qǐ le。Duì le，chūn jié de shí hou nǐ huí guó ma？

Ài lín：Huí guó a，dào shí hòu wǒ gěi nǐ dāng dǎo yóu。

Mǎ kè：Nǐ zhēn hǎo，xiè xie nǐ。

根据课文(一)回答问题
Answer these questions according to the Text A

1. 马克去了哪些国家？
2. 艾琳是哪国人？
3. 泰国怎么样？
4. 春节的时候，艾琳回国吗？

生词学习(二)
New words II

jiā xiāng
1. 家 乡　*n.* hometown　　介绍家乡；我的家乡

shǒu dū
2. 首都 *n.* capital 中国的首都;哪国的首都

kǎo ròu
3. 烤肉 *n.* roast meat 吃烤肉;做烤肉

qǐng kè
4. 请客 *VO* treat;invite sb. to dinner 谁请客;我请客

é luó sī wá wa
5. 俄罗斯娃娃 *NP* Russian Dolls 买俄罗斯娃娃

chéng shì
6. 城市 *n.* city 最大的城市;小城市

chú le
7. 除了 *prep.* besides 除了你,我也去

huǒ guō
8. 火锅 *n.* hot pot 吃火锅;火锅店

专有名词(Proper nouns)

Hán guó
1. 韩国 *n.* South Korea

Shǒu ěr
2. 首尔 *n.* Seoul

É luó sī
3. 俄罗斯 *n.* Russia

Mò sī kē
4. 莫斯科 *n.* Moscow

Bā xī
5. 巴西 *n.* Brazil

Shèng bǎo luó
6. 圣保罗 *n.* St. Paul

Sì chuān
7. 四川 *n.* Sichuan Provincel(A province of China)

Chéng dū
8. 成都 *n.* Chengdu(the capital of Sichuan Province)

Fú tè jiā
9. 伏特加 *n.* Vodka

课文(二) 介绍家乡
Text B Introduce hometown

在教室里。

马老师:同学们好,今天大家谈谈自己的家乡吧?

金明学:好啊,我先说吧。我是韩国人,我的家乡在首尔,首尔是韩国的首都,那儿的烤肉很有名,以后大家来,我请客。

安娜：我的国家是俄罗斯，我的家乡在莫斯科，也是俄罗斯的首都，欢迎大家来玩儿。我们的俄罗斯娃娃非常有名，如果你喜欢喝酒，也可以买一瓶伏特加带回家。

马老师：你俩说得非常好，卡卡，你也介绍一下你的家乡吧。

卡卡：我是巴西人，我的家乡是圣保罗市。虽然它不是首都，但是是巴西最大的城市。你们知道我们家乡什么最有名吗？

同学们：足球。

卡卡：对，除了足球，巴西的舞蹈也很有名，大家以后来看看吧。

同学们：老师，您的家乡在哪儿啊？

马老师：我的家乡在成都，成都人都喜欢吃辣的，大家都吃过火锅吧？四川的火锅又辣又好吃。下课以后，我请你们吃火锅。

同学们：太好了，谢谢老师！

Zài jiào shì lǐ。(in the classroom.)

Mǎ lǎoshī: Tóng xué men hǎo,jīn tiān dà jiā tán tan zì jǐ de jiā xiāng ba。

Jīn míng xué:Hǎo a,wǒ xiān shuō ba。wǒ shì Hán guó rén,wǒ de jiā xiāng zài Shǒu ěr, Shǒu ěr shì Hán guó de shǒu dū,nàr de kǎo ròu hěn yǒu míng,yǐ hòu dà jiā lái,wǒ qǐng kè。

Ān nà:Wǒ de guó jiā shì É luó sī,wǒ de jiā xiāng zài Mò sī kē,yě shì É luó sī de shǒu dū,huān yíng dà jiā lái wánr。Wǒ men de É luó sī wá wa fēi cháng yǒu míng,rú guǒ nǐ xǐ huān hē jiǔ,yě kě yǐ mǎi yì píng Fú tè jiā dài huí jiā。

Mǎ lǎo shī:Nǐ liǎ shuō de fēi cháng hǎo,Kǎ kǎ,nǐ yě jiè shào yí xià nǐ de jiā xiāng ba。

Kǎ kǎ:Wǒ shì bā xī rén, wǒ de jiā xiāng shì Shèng bǎo luó shì。Suī rán tā bú shì shǒu dū,dàn shì shì Bā xī zuì dà de chéng shì。Nǐ men zhī dào wǒ men jiā xiāng shén me zuì yǒu míng ma?

Tóng xué men:Zú qiú。

Kǎ kǎ:Duì,chú le zú qiú,Bā xī de wǔ dǎo yě hěn yǒu míng,dà jiā yǐ hòu lái kàn kan ba。

Tóng xué men:Lǎo shī,nín de jiā xiāng zài nǎr a?

Mǎ lǎo shī:Wǒ de jiā xiāng zài Chéng dū,Chéng dū rén dōu xǐ huān chī là de,dà jiā dōu chī guò huǒ guō ba? Sì chuān de huǒ guō yòu là yòu hǎo chī。Xià kè yǐ hòu,wǒ qǐng nǐ men chī huǒ guō。

Tóng xué men:Tài hǎo le,xiè xie lǎo shī!

根据课文(二)回答问题
Answer these questions according to the Text B

1. 韩国的首都是哪里?

2. 安娜是哪国人？

3. 圣保罗是巴西的首都吗？

4. 成都人喜欢吃什么？

语言点 Language points

1. ……等。

比如美国、泰国、韩国等。

"等"表示列举未尽，常用于句子的结尾。

"等" means "etc." or "and so on", expressing the list is unfinished. it is often used in the end of a sentence.

(1)A：你今天去超市买了什么水果？

B：苹果、香蕉、西瓜等。

(2)A：这学期你有哪些课？

B：口语、听力等。

2. 不但……，而且……

那儿的海鲜不但好吃，而且便宜。

"不但……，而且……"表示递进关系，相当于英语中的"not only..., but also..."。

The structure "不但……，而且……" indicates progressive relation, which is equivalent to "not only..., but also..." in English.

3. 到时候……

到时候我给你当导游。

"到时候"意思是"到那个时候"，这里的"时候"是指上一句中提到的时间。

The phrase "到时候" means "at that time". "时候" refer to the time in the previous sentence.

(1)下个星期我的朋友来中国，到时候我教他学习汉语。

(2)明天下午我去找你，到时候我给你打电话。

4. 除了……，也……

除了足球，巴西的美女也很有名。

"除了……，也……"意思是"除此之外，还有别的"，是对前一句的补充。

The structure "除了……，也……" means "in addition, ..." "也……" expresses a supplement to the previous sentence.

(1)今天除了有口语课,也有听力课。

(2)他除了会说汉语,也会说英语。

功能会话
Functional expression

1. 赞扬(Praise)

   (1)你考了100分,真羡慕你。

   (2)你的女朋友很漂亮,真羡慕你。

2. 安慰(Comfort)

   (1)别担心,我帮你。

   (2)别担心,汉语不太难。

综合练习
Comprehensive exercises

(一)熟读短语 Read the following phrases

1. 羡慕朋友　羡慕同学　羡慕大家
2. 有名的城市　有名的菜　有名的人
3. 担心身体　担心父母　担心考试

(二)完成句子 Complete the following sentences

1. 我的早饭有____________________等。
2. 我的好朋友有____________________等。
3. 中国的______________很有名。
4. 我们国家的____________________非常有名。
5. 他除了喜欢打篮球,也________________。
6. 除了__________,他也是留学生。

(三)课堂练习 In-class exercises

1. 比一比。Make a comparison.

   全班分为两组,看哪一组说出下列国旗的国家多,哪组胜利。

   The class is divided into two groups. The group which can tell more national flags in the picture will win the game.

2. 头脑风暴。Brainstorm.

介绍一个你家乡最有名的人、地方或东西，看看同学们有没有听说过？

Introduce one of the most famous people, places, or things in your hometown. Then ask if the students have ever heard of?

(四)课后练习 After-class exercises

调查三个同学，写出他们的洲、国家和首都的名字。Please survey three students in the class, then write the names of their continents, countries and capitals.

	洲	国家	首都
同学 1			
同学 2			
同学 3			

课文翻译 Translation of the texts

Text A　Beautiful Thailand

Ailin：I heard that you like traveling very much. How many countries have you gone to?

Mark：More than ten, such as China, the United States, South Korea and so on.

Ailin：I really envy you. Have you ever been to my country?

Mark：I haven't been to Thailand yet. Can you give me a brief introduction?

Ailin：OK, Thailand is on the southeastern side of Asia, it has beautiful sea. The seafood there is not only delicious, but also cheap, and the Thais are also very enthusiastic.

Mark：I like the sea best. Is there anything else interesting?

Ailin：Quite a lot. The elephant performance in Thailand is very famous. If you are tired, it is also good to do a Thai massage.

Mark：It sounds interesting, but I can't speak Thai. What do I do?

Ailin：Don't worry. Thailand is a tourist country, and many people can speak a little English.

Mark：That's great. I don't need to be with the tour group. By the way, are you going back to Thailand during the Spring Festival?

Ailin：Yes, I can be your tour guide at the time.

Mark：You are so kind. Thank you.

Text B　Introduce hometown

Teacher Ma：Hello, everybody. Let's talk about your hometown today.

Jin Mingxue：Well, let me say it first. I am a Korean; my hometown is Seoul; Seoul is the capital of Korea, and the roast meat is famous there. If you come in the future, I will treat you.

Anna：My country is Russia; my hometown is Moscow, and it is also the capital of Russia. Welcome to my hometown. Our Russian dolls are very famous. If you like drinking, you can buy a bottle of vodka and take it home.

Teacher Ma：You two talk very well. Kaka, could you introduce your hometown too?

Kaka：I'm a Brazilian, and my hometown is St. Paul. Although it is not the capital, it is the largest city in Brazil. Do you know what is most famous in our hometown?

Students：Soccer.

Kaka：Yes, besides soccer, the beauty of Brazil is also famous. You can come to see in the future.

Students：Where is your hometown, teacher?

Teacher Ma: My hometown is Chengdu. People in Chengdu like spicy food. Have you ever eaten hot pot? The hot pot in Sichuan is spicty and tasty. After class, I'll invite you to eat hot pot.

Students: Great, thank you, teacher!

② 我们一起去参加中国人的婚礼吧
Let's go to attend Chinese wedding

话题导学
Guidance

你参加过中国人的婚礼吗？你知道下图什么意思吗？

Have you ever attended a Chinese wedding? Do you know what is the meaning of the following pictures?

生词学习(一)
New words I

1. 婚礼 (hūn lǐ) *n.* wedding　　参加婚礼；中国人的婚礼
2. 结婚 (jié hūn) *v.* marry　　跟谁结婚；跟他结婚
3. 参加 (cān jiā) *v.* join; take part in　　参加婚礼；参加活动
4. 农历 (nóng lì) *n.* Lunar Calendar　　农历八月十五
5. 挑 (tiāo) *v.* pick; choose　　挑礼物；挑日子

jí lì
6. 吉利 *adj.* lucky　　吉利的日子；吉利的数字

rì zi
7. 日子 *n.* days　　好日子；吉利的日子

ò
8. 哦 *int.* Oh　　哦，知道了；哦，好的

shù zì
9. 数字 *n.* number　　喜欢什么数字；奇怪的数字

biǎo shì
10. 表示 *v.* mean; indicate　　表示同意；表示反对

shùn lì
11. 顺利 *adj.* smoothly　　顺利通过；一路顺利

hóng bāo
12. 红包 *n.* red packet　　给红包；送红包

hé shì
13. 合适 *adj.* suitable; appropriate　　合适的价格；合适的时间

kàn qíng kuàng
14. 看情况 *VO* it depends　　看情况吧

xīn láng
15. 新郎 *n.* groom　　谁是新郎；新郎来了

xīn niáng
16. 新娘 *n.* bride　　谁是新娘；漂亮的新娘

guān xì
17. 关系 *n.* relationship　　关系好；关系不好

zhǔ yì
18. 主意 *n.* idea　　好主意；坏主意

chū fā
19. 出发 *v.* set out; start off　　几点出发；快出发吧

课文(一)　老师结婚了
Text A　Teacher got married

安娜和美玲在教室聊天。

安娜：咱们的口语老师明天结婚，我们一起去参加她的婚礼吧？

美玲：明天是星期一，老师为什么不在周末结婚呢？

安娜：因为明天是中国的农历六月六日，中国人喜欢挑一个吉利的日子结婚。

美玲：哦，我明白了，中国人非常喜欢数字“6”和“8”。

安娜：是的，“6”表示“顺利”，“8”表示“有钱”。

美玲：我们去参加婚礼需要带礼物吗？

安娜：当然啦，在中国，去参加婚礼需要送红包。

美玲：红包里放多少钱合适呢？

安娜：看情况，如果你跟新郎、新娘关系非常好，你就多放一点儿；如果关系一般，就少放一点儿。

美玲：我很喜欢我们的口语老师，我放666元吧。

安娜：哈哈，好主意，老师一定很高兴。

美玲：明天我们什么时候出发？

安娜：明天早上八点半，我们一起坐出租车去，怎么样？

美玲：好的，明天见。

Ān nà hé Měi líng zài jiào shì liáo tiān。(Anna is talking with Meiling in the classroom.)

Ān nà：Zán men de kǒu yǔ lǎo shī míng tiān jié hūn，wǒ men yì qǐ qù cān jiā tā de hūn lǐ ba？

Měi líng：Míng tiān shì xīng qī yī，lǎo shī wèi shén me bú zài zhōu mò jié hūn ne？

Ān nà：Yīn wèi míng tiān shì zhōng guó de nóng lì liù yuè liù rì，zhōng guó rén xǐ huān tiāo yí gè jí lì de rì zi jié hūn。

Měi líng：Ò，wǒ míng bái le，zhōng guó rén fēi cháng xǐ huān shù zì "liù" hé "bā"。

Ān nà：Shì de，"liù" biǎo shì "shùn lì"，"bā" biǎo shì "yǒu qián"。

Měi líng：Wǒ men qù cān jiā hūn lǐ xū yào dài lǐ wù ma？

Ānnà：Dāng rán la，zài zhōng guó，qù cān jiā hūn lǐ xū yào sòng hóng bāo。

Měi líng：Hóng bāo lǐ fàng duō shǎo qián hé shì ne？

Ānnà：Kàn qíng kuàng，rú guǒ nǐ gēn xīn láng、xīn niáng guān xì fēi cháng hǎo，nǐ jiù duō fàng yì diǎnr，rú guǒ guān xì yì bān，jiù shǎo fàng yì diǎnr。

Měi líng：Wǒ hěn xǐ huān wǒ men de kǒu yǔ lǎo shī，wǒ fàng liù bǎi liù shí liù yuán ba。

Ānnà：Hā hā，hǎo zhǔyì，lǎo shī yí dìng hěn gāo xìng。

Měi líng：Míng tiān wǒ men shén me shí hou chū fā？

Ānnà：Míng tiān zǎo shàng bā diǎn bàn，wǒ men yì qǐ zuò chū zū chē qù，zěn me yàng？

Měi líng：Hǎo de，míng tiān jiàn。

根据课文(一)回答问题
Answer these questions according to the Text A

1. 老师为什么不在周末结婚？
2. 在中国，参加婚礼需要带礼物吗？
3. 美玲在红包里放了多少钱？
4. 她们怎么去参加婚礼？

生词学习(二) New words II

1. tōng zhī 通知	*v.*/*n.* notice	通知同学;一个通知
2. yuè lái yuè 越来越	more and more	越来越冷;越来越胖
3. nuǎnhuo 暖和	*adj.* warm	很暖和;不暖和
4. fēngjǐng 风景	*n.* scenery; landscape	漂亮的风景
5. kōng qì 空气	*n.* air	空气很好;空气不好
6. xīn xiān 新鲜	*adj.* fresh	新鲜的空气;新鲜的水果
7. wán yóu xì 玩游戏	*VO* play game	一起玩游戏
8. yě cān 野餐	*n.* picnic	一起野餐;吃野餐
9. lián xì 联系	*v.* contact	联系我;联系朋友

专有名词(Proper noun)

Tài zǐ wān gōng yuán
太子湾公园　Taiziwan Park

课文(二) 通知 Text B Notice

通　知

春天到了,天气越来越暖和了,这个周末我们班打算去太子湾公园,那里风景非常漂亮,空气也很新鲜。我们可以爬山、玩游戏,还可以野餐。如果你愿意参加这次活动,请和我们联系。

出发时间:周六早上6点

出发地点:1号宿舍楼门口

联系人:安娜

手机:13888888888

Tōng zhī

Chūn tiān dào le, tiān qì yuè lái yuè nuǎn huo le, zhè ge zhōu mò wǒ men bān dǎ suàn qù

Tài zǐ wān gōng yuán,nà lǐ fēng jǐng fēi cháng piào liang,kōng qì yě hěn xīn xiān。Wǒ men kě yǐ pá shān、wán yóu xì,hái kě yǐ yě cān。Rú guǒ nǐ yuàn yì cān jiā zhè cì huó dòng,qǐng hé wǒ men lián xì。

Chū fā shí jiān:Zhōu liù zǎo shàng liù diǎn

Chū fā dì diǎn:Yī hào sù shè lóu mén kǒu

Lián xì rén:Ān nà

Shǒu jī:Yī sān bā bā bā bā bā bā bā bā bā

根据课文(二)回答问题
Answer these questions according to the Text B

1. 这个周末我们班去哪儿?

2. 什么时候出发?

3. 如果想参加这次活动,应该跟谁联系?

语言点
Language points

1. 看情况,……

看情况,如果你跟新郎、新娘关系非常好,你就多放一点儿。

"看情况"意思是"根据实际的情况而定",常常单独成句。

"看情况" means depending on the actual situation. It is often used as a single sentence.

(1)A:你明天跟我一起去爬山吗?

B:看情况。如果我的感冒好了,我就去。

(2)A:你放假回国吗?

B:看情况吧。

2. A 跟 B 关系非常好

如果你跟新郎、新娘关系非常好。

"A 跟 B 关系非常好"意思是"A 和 B 有非常好的关系","A""B"常常是"人""国家"等。

The structure "A 跟 B 关系非常好" means "A have a very good relationship with B". "A" "B" often refers to people, country and so on.

(1)他跟老师关系非常好。

(2)他跟他的同屋关系非常好。

3. 越来越……

天气越来越暖和了。

"越来越"是指人或事物的数量或程度随着时间的推移而不断发展或变化。常用在形容词或动词前。

"越来越……" means the number or degree of person or things continue to develop or change as time goes on. It is often used before an adjective or verb.

(1)她越来越漂亮了。

(2)汉语越来越难了。

(3)我越来越喜欢杭州了。

功能会话 Functional expression

1. 领悟、明白(Comprehension or understanding)

(1)A:老师,马丁生病了,今天不来上课。

B:哦。

(2)A:明天考试,别忘了。

B:哦。

2. 邀请(Invitation)

(1)请和我们联系。

(2)如果你想参加,请和我联系。

综合练习 Comprehensive exercises

(一)熟读短语 Read the following phrases

1. 参加比赛　参加婚礼　参加活动
2. 挑日子　挑水果　挑衣服
3. 吉利的数字　吉利的号码　吉利的日子
4. 联系人　联系老师　联系学校

(二)替换练习 Substitution

1. 你跟新郎、新娘关系非常好。

我	爸爸	很好
她	同学	很好
他	男朋友	不好

2. 请和我们联系。

老师

办公室

我的朋友

3. 天气越来越暖和了。

啤酒　　贵

留学生　多

杭州　　热

(三)课堂活动 In-class Activities

1. 比一比。Make a comparison.

说一说,你们国家的结婚习俗和中国有什么不同?Tell us, what are the differences of marriage custom between China and your country?

	中国	你们的国家
结婚习俗		

2. 头脑风暴。Brainstorm.

说一说,你梦想的婚礼是什么样的?Tell us, What's your dream wedding like?

(四)课后练习 After-class exercises

模仿课文(二),写一则关于邀请同学参加生日晚会的通知,然后跟同学们说一说。Imitate the Text B, write a note about inviting students to participate in the birthday party, then tell the classmates.

通　知

请同学参加你的生日晚会。

时间:

地点:

联系人:

手机:

课文翻译 Translation of the texts

Text A　Teacher got married

Anna: Our oral teacher will get married tomorrow. Shall we go to her wedding?

Meiling: Tomorrow is Monday. Why doesn't the teacher get married on the weekend?

Anna: Because tomorrow is the Chinese Lunar Calendar June 6th, Chinese people like to pick a lucky day to marry.

Meiling: Oh, I see, Chinese people like the number "6" and "8" very much.

Anna: Yes, "6" means "smooth" and "8" means "rich".

Meiling: Do we need to bring a gift to the wedding?

Anna: Of course. In China, you need to send a red packet while attending a wedding.

Meiling: How much money is appropriate in the red packet?

Anna: It depends. If you have a very good relationship with the bride and groom, you can put a little more; if the relationship is general, just a little less.

Meiling: I like our oral teacher very much. Let me put 666 *yuan*.

Anna: Haha, good idea. The teacher must be very happy.

Meiling: When are we going to leave tomorrow?

Anna: Let's go by taxi together at half past eight tomorrow morning, OK?

Meiling: OK, see you tomorrow.

Text B　Notice

Notice

Spring is coming, and the weather is getting warmer and warmer. Our class plans to go to Taiziwan Park this weekend. The scenery is very beautiful and the air is very fresh there. We can climb mountains, play games, and have a picnic. If you are willing to take part in the event, please contact us.

Departure time: 6 a.m. on Saturday morning

Departure place: gate of No. 1 dormitory building

Contact: Anna

Cell phone: 13888888888

3 梅雨季节
Plum rain season

话题导学
Guidance

你知道下图分别是什么季节吗?

Do you know what season is in the following picture?

生词学习(一)
New words I

1. tiān qì 天气 *n.* weather　　好天气;天气很热
2. yù bào 预报 *n.* forecast　　天气预报;节目预报
3. wēn dù 温度 *n.* temperature　　温度很高;温度很低
4. dù 度 *mw.* centigrade　　多少度;二十八度
5. fēng 风 *n.* wind　　大风;台风
6. jí 级 *n.* level;grade　　三级风;五级风

ài
7. 唉 *int.* alas(express disappointment or hopelessness)

dōu
8. 都 *adv.* already 都十点了;都冬天了

zhèng cháng
9. 正常 *adj.* normal 很正常;不正常

méi yǔ
10. 梅雨 *n.* plum rain 不喜欢梅雨

jì jié
11. 季节 *n.* season 梅雨季节;什么季节

duàn
12. 段 *mw.* period;section 一段时间;一段课文

méi zi
13. 梅子 *n.* plum 吃梅子;洗梅子

chéng shú
14. 成熟 *adj.* ripe;mature 梅子成熟了

tǎo yàn
15. 讨厌 *v.* disgust 讨厌梅雨;讨厌啤酒

gān
16. 干 *adj.* dry 衣服干了;头发干了

dà gài
17. 大概 *adv.* probably 大概多长时间;大概什么时候

yì bān
18. 一般 *adv.* generally 一般几点起床;一般不吃

zuǒ yòu
19. 左右 *n.* or so;about 八点左右;十八岁左右

péi
20. 陪 *v.* accompany 陪我去学校;陪她去医院

课文(一) 买把雨伞吧
Text A Accompany me to buy an umbrella

玛丽和美玲在食堂聊天。

玛丽:你看明天的天气预报了吗?天气怎么样?

美玲:看了。明天有雨,温度20℃,南风3级。唉,雨都下了一个星期了。

玛丽:很正常,杭州现在是梅雨季节。

美玲:什么是梅雨季节?我第一次听说。

玛丽:每年6月到7月的时候,中国的南方会经常下雨,因为这段时间是梅子成熟的时候,所以叫“梅雨季节”。

美玲:我讨厌梅雨季节。洗了衣服以后总是不能干。

玛丽：是啊，刚来的时候，我也不习惯，现在习惯了。

美玲："梅雨季节"大概有多长时间？

玛丽：一般三个星期左右，有时候一个月。

美玲：天哪，还有三个星期。

玛丽：别担心，也不是每天都下雨。

美玲：走，你陪我去买一把雨伞吧？

玛丽：没问题。

Mǎ lì hé Měi líng zài shí táng liáo tian。(**Mary is talking with Mei Ling in the canteen.**)

Mǎ lì:Nǐ kàn míng tiān de tiān qì yù bào le ma? Tiān qì zěn me yàng?

Měi líng:Kàn le。Míng tiān yǒu yǔ,wēn dù èr shí dù,nán fēng sān jí。Ài,yǔ dōu xià le yí gè xīng qī le。

Mǎ lì:Hěn zhèng cháng,Háng zhōu xiàn zài shì méi yǔ jìjié。

Měi líng:Shén me shì méi yǔ jì jié? Wǒ dì yí cì tīng shuō。

Mǎ lì:Měi nián liù yuè dào qī yuè de shí hou,zhōng guó de nán fāng huì jīng cháng xià yǔ,yīn wèi zhè duàn shí jiān shì méi zi chéng shú de shí hou,suǒ yǐ jiào"méi yǔ jì jié"。

Měi líng:Wǒ tǎo yàn méi yǔ jì jié。Xǐ le yī fu yǐ hòu zǒng shì bù néng gān。

Mǎ lì:Shì a,gāng lái de shí hou,wǒ yě bù xí guàn,xiàn zài xí guàn le。

Měi líng:"Méi yǔ jì jié" dà gài yǒu duō cháng shí jiān?

Mǎ lì:Yì bān sān gè xīng qī zuǒ yòu,yǒu shí hou yí ge yuè。

Měi líng:Tiān na,hái yǒu sān gè xīng qī。

Mǎ lì:Bié dān xīn,yě bú shì měi tiān dōu xià yǔ。

Měi líng:Zǒu,nǐ péi wǒ qù mǎi yì bǎ yǔ sǎn ba?

Mǎ lì:Méi wèn tí。

根据课文(一)回答问题
Answer these questions according to the Text A

1. 明天天气怎么样？
2. 什么是"梅雨季节"？
3. "梅雨季节"大概多长时间？

生词学习(二)
New words II

1. 市 (shì) *n.* city　　　杭州市；北京市

bái tiān
2. 白天 *n.* daytime　　白天很热;白天睡觉

duō yún
3. 多云 *adj.* cloudy　　今天多云;白天多云

zhuǎn
4. 转 *v.* change　　多云转晴

qíng
5. 晴 *adj.* sunny　　晴转多云;晴天

zuì
6. 最 *adv.* most　　最高;最冷

yè jiān
7. 夜间 *n.* nighttime　　夜间很冷;夜间多云

líng xià
8. 零下 *n.* below zero;sub-zero　　零下十度;零下三度

zhù yì
9. 注意 *v.* pay attention to;be careful　　注意安全

bǎo nuǎn
10. 保暖 *VP* keep warm　　注意保暖

yīn
11. 阴 *adj.* overcast　　阴天;多云转阴

yōu
12. 优 *adj.* excellent　　空气优

课文(二) 杭州市区天气预报
Text B Weather forecast of Hangzhou city

12月5日

白天多云转晴,最高气温16℃,最低气温7℃,南风2—3级。夜间有小雨,请大家注意保暖。

12月6日

白天阴转小雨,最高气温10℃,最低气温-1℃,北风4级。空气优,夜间小雨转晴。

shí èr yuè wǔ rì

Bái tiān duō yún zhuǎn qíng,zuì gāo qì wēn shí liù dù,zuì dī qì wēn qī dù,nán fēng èr dào sān jí。Yè jiān yǒu xiǎo yǔ,qǐng dà jiā zhù yì bǎo nuǎn。

shí èr yuè liù rì

Bái tiān yīn zhuǎn xiǎo yǔ,zuì gāo qì wēn shí dù,zuì dī qì wēn líng xià yī dù,běi fēng sì jí。Kōng qì yōu,yè jiān xiǎo yǔ zhuǎn qíng。

根据课文(二)回答问题
Answer these questions according to the Text B

1. 12 月 5 日的最高温度是多少?
2. 12 月 6 日白天天气怎么样?
3. 12 月 6 日的空气怎么样?

语言点
Language points

1. 都……

雨都下了一个星期了。

在这个句子中,"都"的意思是"已经",经常用在动词的前面。

In this sentence,"都" means "already"; it is often used before a verb.

(1)都下课了,他才来。

(2)他都来中国一年了。

2. *num*. + *mw*. + 左右

一般三个星期左右。

"数词+量词+左右"意思为"接近某个数字"。

"*num*. + *mw*. + 左右" means "a little more than or less than the amount".

(1)这件衣服五百块左右。

(2)我十二点左右睡觉。

3. 陪+人+*v*. +……

你陪我去买一把雨伞吧?

在此中,"陪+人+*v*. +……"结构意思是"陪某人去做某事"。

In this sentence,the structure "陪+人+*v*. +……" means "accompany sb. to do sth."

(1)我陪同学去办公室。

(2)他陪朋友买东西。

4. ……转……

白天多云转晴。

"转"意思是"改变形势、情况",常用于天气预报。

"转" means "change the situation", it is often used in weather forecast.

(1)明天晴转小雪。

(2)今天晚上多云转小雨。

功能会话 Functional expression

1. 失望(Disappointment)

(1)唉！这次考试成绩又不好。

(2)唉！我又感冒了。

2. 惊讶(Surprise)

(1)天哪！太贵了！

(2)天哪！我忘了拿我的手机。

综合练习 Comprehensive exercises

(一)熟读短语 Read the following phrases

1. 一段时间　一段故事　一段课文
2. 讨厌学习　讨厌感冒　讨厌下雨
3. 三岁左右　五点左右　一个月左右
4. 最好　最冷　最漂亮
5. 注意身体　注意汽车　注意保暖

(二)替换练习 Substitution drills

1. 雨都　下了一个星期了。

他　看了一个小时电视了

爸爸　喝了五瓶啤酒了

朋友　写了三个小时汉字了

2. 一般三个星期左右。

五天

三百块

两个小时

3. 你陪　我去买一把雨伞吧？

爸爸　我来中国。

朋友　我去超市。

老师　他去医院。

(三)课堂练习 In-class exercises

1. 说一说。Have a talk.

你的国家有几个季节？你最喜欢哪一个季节？为什么？How many seasons do you have

in your country? Which season do you like best? Why?

2. 头脑风暴。Brainstorm.

猜猜下面的图片分别表示什么天气？你还知道别的天气吗？Guess what weather is the following pictures mean? Do you know anything else?

(四)课后练习(After-class exercises)

模仿课文，自己准备一个天气预报，在班上说一说。Imitating the text, prepare a weather forecast by yourself and talk about it in the class.

天气预报	
天气	
温度	
风	
空气	

课文翻译 Translation of the texts

Text A　Accompany me to buy an umbrella

Mary: Did you watch the weather forecast for tomorrow? What's the weather like ?

Meiling: Yes. It will rain tomorrow, the temperature is 20 degrees centigrade, and the south wind is grade 3. alas, it's been raining for a week.

Mary: It's very normal, Hangzhou is now the plum rain season.

Meiling: What is the plum rain season? It's first time I'm hearing about this.

Mary: Every year from June to July, it often rains in the south of China, because plum is mature during this period, so it is called "plum rain season".

Meiling: I disgust the plum rain season. The clothes always cannot dry after you washed them.

Mary: Yes, I was not used to it before, but I'm used to it now.

Meiling: How long is the "plum rain season"?

Mary: It usually lasts three weeks. Sometimes one month.

Meiling: My God! There are still three weeks left.

Mary: Don't worry; it doesn't rain every day.

Meiling: Let's go. Will you accompany me to buy an umbrella?

Mary: No problem!

Text B　Weather forecast of Hangzhou city

December 5th

Cloudy day changes into sunny during the daytime. The highest temperature is 16 degrees centigrade, and the lowest temperature is 7 centigrade; the south wind is about grade 2 or 3. There is light rain at night. Please pay attention to keep warm.

December 6th

Overcast day changes into light rain during the daytime. The highest temperature is 10 centigrade, and the lowest temperature is negative 1 degree centigrade; the north wind is grade 4. The air is excellent. Light rain will change into sunny at night.

4 网上购物真方便
Shopping online is really convenient

话题导学
Guidance

买东西的时候，你用过图片中的方式吗？在你的国家有没有？

Did you use the following ways to buy things? Is it the same way in your country?

生词学习(一)
New words I

gòu wù
1. 购物 *v.* go shopping　　去购物；喜欢购物

guàng jiē
2. 逛街 *VO* stroll along the street　　去逛街

dà yī
3. 大衣 *n.* overcoat　　穿大衣；买大衣

shǒuxiān
4. 首先 *adv.* firstly　　首先……，然后……

ránhòu
5. 然后 *conj.* then　　首先……，然后……

wǎng zhàn
6. 网 站 *n.* website 购物网站;一个网站

sōu suǒ
7. 搜 索 *v.* search 搜索网站;搜索信息

tí jiāo
8. 提 交 *v.* submit 提交订单;提交申请

dìng dān
9. 订 单 *n.* order for goods 提交订单;取消订单

fù qián
10. 付 钱 *VO* pay 没付钱;朋友付钱

kuài dì
11. 快 递 *n.* express delivery 拿快递;取快递

kàn lái
12. 看 来 *adv.* seems 看来要下雨;看来不错

suí shí
13. 随 时 *adv.* at any time 随时来;随时出发

专有名词 (Proper nouns)

Táo bǎo wǎng
1. 淘 宝 网 *n.* Taobao(one of Chinese e-commerce company)

Zhī fù bǎo
2. 支付宝 *n.* Alipay

课文(一) 教我在网上购物吧
Text A Please teach me to go shopping online

玛丽和美玲在宿舍聊天。

玛丽:美玲,你周末打算干什么?

美玲:我想去逛街,天气冷了,我需要买一件大衣。

玛丽:你为什么不在网上买呢?网上买东西又便宜又方便。

美玲:我没买过,麻烦你教我一下吧?

玛丽:好的,首先你要打开淘宝网的网站,搜索你想买的东西,然后提交订单,最后付钱就可以了。

美玲:听起来很容易,可是,我应该怎么付钱呢?

玛丽:你有支付宝或者微信吗?

美玲:当然有了,我觉得在杭州每个留学生都有支付宝。

玛丽:你用支付宝付钱以后,他们会给你发快递,一般一两天就到了。

美玲:这么快啊,看来以后我都不用去逛街啦。

玛丽:是啊,而且随时都可以买。

美玲：玛丽，谢谢你教我在网上买东西。

玛丽：不客气。

Mǎ lì hé Měi líng zài sù shè liáo tiān。(**Mary is talking with Meiling in the dormitory.**)

Mǎ lì：Měi líng，nǐ zhōu mò dǎ suan gàn shén me?

Měi líng：Wǒ xiǎng qù guàng jiē，tiān qì lěng le，wǒ xū yào mǎi yí jiàn dà yī。

Mǎ lì：Nǐ wèi shén me bù zài wǎng shàng mǎi ne? Wǎng shàng mǎi dōng xi yòu pián yí yòu fāng biàn。

Měi líng：Wǒ méi mǎi guò，má fan nǐ jiāo wǒ yí xià ba?

Mǎ lì：Hǎo de，shǒu xiān nǐ yào dǎ kāi Táo bǎo wǎng，sōu suǒ nǐ xiǎng mǎi de dōng xi，rán hòu tí jiāo dìng dān，zuì hòu fù qián jiù kě yǐ le。

Měi líng：Tīng qǐ lái hěn róng yì，kě shì，wǒ yīng gāi zěn me fù qián ne?

Mǎ lì：Nǐ yǒu Zhī fù bǎo huò zhě Wēi xìn ma?

Měi líng：Dāng rán yǒu le，wǒ jué de zài háng zhōu měi gè liú xué shēng dōu yǒu zhī fù bǎo。

Mǎ lì：Nǐ yòng Zhī fù bǎo fù qián yǐ hòu，tā men huì gěi nǐ fā kuài dì，yì bān yì liǎng tiān jiù dào le。

Měi líng：Zhè me kuài a，kàn lái yǐ hòu wǒ dōu bú yòng qù guàng jiē la。

Mǎ lì：Shì a，ér qiě suí shí dōu kě yǐ mǎi。

Měi líng：Mǎ lì，xièxie nǐ jiāo wǒ zài wǎng shàng mǎi dōng xi。

Mǎ lì：Bú kè qì。

根据课文(一)回答问题
Answer these questions according to the Text A

1. 美玲想买什么?
2. 玛丽在网上买过衣服吗?
3. 在网上买衣服应该怎么做?
4. 美玲有没有支付宝?

生词学习(二)
New words II

1. 稍微 (shāo wēi) *adv.* slightly　　稍微有点大;稍微有点贵

2. 质量 (zhì liàng) *n.* quality　　质量很好;质量不好

3. 虽然 (suī rán) *conj.* although　　虽然……,但是……

4. 但是 (dàn shì) *conj.* but　　虽然……,但是……

5. 缺点 (quē diǎn) *n.* shortcoming　　有缺点;很多缺点

6. 如果 (rú guǒ) *conj.* if　　如果……,就……

7. 保留 (bǎo liú) *v.* keep　　保留宿舍;保留座位

8. 发票 (fā piào) *n.* receipt　　要发票;保留发票

9. 商品 (shāng pǐn) *n.* goods　　很多商品;买商品

10. 半价 (bàn jià) *NP* half-price　　半价商品;半价衣服

课文(二) 双十一
Text B Double Eleven

第二天。

美玲:看,我的新大衣已经到了。

玛丽:真够快的。新大衣合适吗?

美玲:稍微有点儿大,不过质量不错,我非常喜欢。

玛丽:嗯,虽然网上购物很方便,但是也有缺点,就是你不能试衣服。

美玲:对啊,如果我想换衣服,怎么办呢?

玛丽:你一定要保留好发票,换衣服的时候,把衣服和发票一起寄给他们就可以了。

美玲:明白了,这次我忘了要发票,下次一定要记住。

玛丽:对了,你听说过"双十一"吗?

美玲:没有,"双十一"是什么意思?

玛丽:就是在11月11日这天,网上很多商品都是半价。

美玲:太好了,明年"双十一",我们一起网上购物吧。

玛丽:没问题。

Dì èr tiān。(the next day.)

Měi líng:Kàn,wǒ de xīn dà yī yǐ jīng dào le。

Mǎ lì:Zhēn gòu kuài de。Xīn dà yī hé shì ma?

Měi líng:Shāo wēi yǒu diǎnr dà,bú guò zhì liàng bú cuò,wǒ fēi cháng xǐ huān。

Mǎ lì:Ēn,suī rán wǎng shàng gòu wù hěn fāng biàn,dàn shì yě yǒu quē diǎn,jiù shì nǐ bù néng shì yī fu。

Měi líng:Duì a,rú guǒ wǒ xiǎng huàn yī fu,zěn me bàn ne?

Mǎ lì:Nǐ yí dìng yào bǎo liú hǎo fā piào,huàn yī fu de shí hòu,bǎ yī fu hé fā piào yì qǐ jì gěi tā men jiù kě yǐ le。

Měi líng:Míng bái le,zhè cì wǒ wàng le yào fā piào,xià cì yí dìng yào jì zhù。

Mǎ lì:Duì le,nǐ tīng shuō guò "shuāng shí yī" ma?

Měi líng:Méi yǒu,"shuāng shí yī" shì shén me yì si?

Mǎ lì:Jiù shì zài shí yī yuè shí yī rì zhè tiān,wǎng shàng hěn duō shāng pǐn dōu shì bàn jià。

Měi líng:Tài hǎo le,míng nián "shuāng shí yī",wǒ men yì qǐ wǎng shàng gòu wù ba。

Mǎ lì:Méi wèn tí。

根据课文(二)回答问题
Answer these questions according to the Text B

1. 美玲买的大衣怎么样?

2. 如果换衣服,需要怎么做?

3. "双十一"是什么意思?

语言点
Language points

1. 首先……,然后……,最后……

首先你要打开淘宝网的网站,搜索你想买的东西,然后提交订单,最后付钱就可以了。

"首先……,然后……,最后……"常用于表达做某事或说明原因的先后顺序。

The structure "首先……,然后……,最后……" means "first…, then…, finally…", which is often used to express the order of doing something or explanation.

(1)下课以后,首先去食堂吃饭,然后去图书馆。

(2)上课的时候,我们首先学习生词,然后学习课文。

2. 够……的

真够快的。

"够……的"结构表示程度深,与"很"的意思相当,中间一般为形容词。

In this sentence, the structure "够……的" means the degree is high, similar to the meaning of "so" or "very". Generally, there is an adjective in the middle.

(1)今天够冷的。

(2)这件衣服够贵的。

3. 虽然……,但是……

虽然网上购物很方便,但是也有缺点。

"虽然……,但是……"表示转折关系。

In this sentence, the structure "虽然……,但是……" means "although...", which indicates adversative relation.

(1)虽然他病了,但是他还是来上课。

(2)虽然汉语很难,但是我也喜欢。

4. 如果……,……

如果我想换衣服,怎么办呢?

在"如果……,……"结构中,"如果"是一个表达假设的连词,后一分句常常为前一分句假设后的结果。

In the structure of "如果……,……","如果" is a hypothetical conjunction, which means "if". The latter clause often assumes the result of the previous clause.

(1)老师,如果明天我不去上课,可以吗?

(2)如果你们累了,我们就休息一下。

功能会话 Functional expression

1. 请求(Request)

(1)麻烦您教我一下吧。

(2)麻烦你帮我一下吧。

2. 同意(Agreement)

(1)A:可以看看你的书吗?

B:没问题!

(2)A:你能借我一百块钱吗?

B:没问题!

综合练习 Comprehensive exercises

(一)熟读短语 Read the following phrases

1. 搜索商品　搜索文件　搜索

2. 提交订单　提交作业
3. 发快递　寄快递　取快递
4. 保留发票　保留照片　保留意见

(二)替换练习 Substitution drills

1. 首先你要打开淘宝网，搜索你想买的东西，然后提交订单。

打电话　　去老师家
去超市　　回宿舍
洗澡　　睡觉

2. 够快的。

辣
贵
热

3. 虽然网上购物很方便，但是也有缺点。

很冷　　也去跑步
下雨了　　也去爬山
很累　　去图书馆

(三)课堂练习 In-class exercises

1. 团队合作。Teamwork.

全班分为两组，一组找网上购物的优点，另一组找缺点，找得多的组胜利。The class was divided into two groups. One group look for the advantages of online shopping, and the other look for disadvantages. The team which find more win the game.

	网上购物
优点(advantages)	
缺点(disadvantages)	

2. 头脑风暴。Brainstorm.

你在网上买过飞机票或者火车票吗？说说你买票的经历。Have you ever bought an airplane ticket or a train ticket on the internet? Tell us about your experience of buying tickets.

(四)课后练习 After-class exercises

比较以下几种商品在网上与超市的价格。Compare the prices of the following items on the internet and supermarkets.

	网上价格	超市价格

课文翻译 Translation of the texts

Text A　Please teach me to go shopping online

Mary: Meiling, what are you going to do this weekend?

Meiling: I want to go shopping. It's cold. I need to buy a coat.

Mary: Why don't you buy it on the internet? It's cheap and convenient to buy things on the internet.

Meiling: I haven't bought things on the internet. Would you please teach me?

Mary: Well, first of all, you should open the website of Taobao, and search the things that you want to buy, then submit the order, and finally pay the money.

Meiling: It sounds easy, but how should I pay for it?

Mary: Do you have Alipay or WeChat Pay?

Meiling: Yes, of course. I think every oversea students in Hangzhou has Alipay.

Mary: After you pay with Alipay, they will send you the express delivery. It's usually needs one or two days.

Meiling: So fast! It seems that I don't need go shopping in the future.

Mary: Yes, and you can buy it anytime.

Meiling: Mary, thank you for teaching me to buy things on the internet.

Mary: You're welcome.

Text B　Double Eleven

Meiling: Look, my new coat has arrived.

Mary: It's very fast. Does the new coat fit?

Meiling: It's a little big, but the quality is good. I like it very much.

Mary: Well, although shopping online is very convenient, there are also shortcomings, that is, you can not try clothes.

Meiling: Yes, If I want to exchange clothes, how can I do?

Mary: You must keep the invoice, and post the clothes and the invoice to them when you change clothes.

Meiling: I see. I forgot to ask for the invoice this time. I must remember it next time.

Mary: By the way, have you ever heard of "Double Eleven"?

Meiling: No, what does "Double Eleven" mean?

Mary: It is on November 11th that a lot of goods on the internet are half price.

Meiling: That's great. Let's go shopping together on the internet next "Double Eleven".

Mary: No problem.

5 美丽的西湖
The beauties of the West Lake

话题导学 Guidance

你知道这些景点吗？你去过吗？

Do you know these local sights? Have you ever been there ?

生词学习(一) New words I

1. yóu kè 游客 *n.* tourist　　很多游客；游客朋友
2. yóu lǎn 游览 *v.* go sightseeing　　游览西湖；游览长城
3. piào jià 票价 *n.* ticket price　　景点票价；飞机票价
4. fāng biàn 方便 *adj.* convenient　　非常方便；不太方便
5. jīng guò 经过 *v.* pass　　经过那儿；经过学校
6. jǐng diǎn 景点 *n.* view spot　　著名景点；景点地图

guo
7. 过　*part.* used after a verb to indicate a past action or state　去过;学过

qí tā
8. 其他　*pron.* other ;else　其他地方;其他人

bù fen
9. 部分　*n.* part; section　大部分;小部分

bǐ rú shuō
10. 比如说　for instance; such as　比如说这样;比如说我

děi
11. 得　*v.* need, must, have to　得学习;得买票

gǎn kuài
12. 赶快　*adv.* hurry up　赶快回去;赶快上车

专有名词(Proper nouns)

Qū yuàn fēng hé
1. 曲院风荷　*n.*　Breeze-ruffled Lotus Beside the Winery

Sān tán yìn yuè
2. 三潭印月　*n.*　Three Pools Mirroring the Moon

课文(一)　乘坐游览车
Text A　Taking a sightseeing bus

马克和阿布来在西湖边聊天。

"尊敬的游客请注意,车子来了。"

马克:看,那是什么车?

阿布来:那是游览车。咱们走了半个小时了,你累不累?

马克:我有点儿累了,咱们去坐那个游览车怎么样?

阿布来:好啊! 票价四十元,我们可以坐车游览一个多小时,很方便。

马克:你知道它会经过哪些景点吗?

阿布来:我坐过这辆车,一共有四站,最后一站是岳王庙。

马克:我们可以在其他地方上车和下车吗?

阿布来:不可以。别担心,大部分有名的景点我们都能在车上看见。比如说断桥、白堤、曲院风荷等等。

马克:对了,我想去看看一块钱人民币上的那个景点。

阿布来:你说的是三潭印月吧。我们得坐船去。

"尊敬的游客请注意,车子来了。"

马克:又一辆游览车来了,咱们赶快上车吧。

阿布来:咱们得先买票,再上车。

Mǎ kè hé Ā bù lái zài Xī Hú bian liáo tiān。(Mark is talking with Abylai nearby the West Lake.)

"Zūn jìng de yóu kè qǐng zhù yì, chē zi lái le。"

Mǎ kè: Kàn, nà shì shén me chē?

Ā bù lái: Nà shì yóu lǎn chē。Zán me zǒu le bàn ge xiǎo shí le, nǐ lèi bu lèi?

Mǎ kè: Wǒ yǒu diǎnr lèi le, zán men qù zuò nà ge yóu lǎn chē zěn me yàng?

Ā bù lái: Hǎo a! Piào jià sì shí yuán, kě yǐ zuò chē yóu lǎn yí ge duō xiǎo shí, hěn fāng biàn。

Mǎ kè: Nǐ zhī dào tā huì jīng guò nǎ xiē jǐng diǎn ma?

Ā bù lái: Wǒ zuò guò zhè liàng chē, yí gòng yǒu sì zhàn, zuì hòu yí zhàn shì yuè wáng miào。

Mǎ kè: Wǒ men kě yǐ zài qí tā dì fang shàng chē hé xià chē ma?

Ā bù lái: Bù kě yǐ。Bié dān xīn, dà bù fèn yǒu míng de jǐng diǎn wǒ men dōu néng zài chē shang kàn jian。Bǐ rú shuō Duàn qiáo、Bái dī、Qǔ yuàn fēng hé děng děng。

Mǎ kè: Duì le, wǒ xiǎng qù kàn kan yí kuài qián rén mín bì shàng de nà ge jǐng diǎn。

Ā bù lái: Nǐ shuō de shì Sān tán yìn yuè ba。Wǒ men děi zuò chuán qu。

"Zūn jìng de yóu kè qǐng zhù yì, chē zi lái le。"

Mǎ kè: Yòu yí liàng yóu lǎn chē lái le, zán men gǎn kuài shàng chē ba。

Ā bù lái: Zán men děi xiān mǎi piào, zài shàng chē。

根据课文(一)回答问题
Answer these questions according to the Text A

1. 游览车的票价是多少?
2. 他们坐车会经过哪些景点?
3. 一块钱人民币上的景点是什么?

生词学习(二)
New words II

1. 浪漫 (làng màn) *adj.* romantic　　浪漫的晚餐;浪漫的音乐
2. 发生 (fā shēng) *v.* take place　　发生火灾;发生时间
3. 爱情 (ài qíng) *n.* love　　爱情故事;美好的爱情
4. 故事 (gù shi) *n.* story　　讲故事;历史故事

pēn quán
5. 喷 泉 *n.* fountain 音乐喷泉；观看喷泉

nǔ lì
6. 努力 *v.* make great efforts 努力学习；不努力

jiāng lái
7. 将 来 *n.* in the future 将来的事情；预测将来

dāng
8. 当 *v.* become 当总统；当妈妈

专有名词 (Proper nouns)

Léi fēng tǎ
1. 雷 峰 塔 *n.* Leifeng Tower

zài jiā kào fù mǔ chū mén kào péng you
2. 在家靠父母，出 门 靠 朋 友 *idm.* Relying on parents at home, relying on friends abroad.

课文(二) 一个浪漫的城市
Text B A romantic city

下午，马克和阿布来在游览车上聊天。

马克：杭州真是一个浪漫的城市！

阿布来：为什么这么说？

马克：因为在这儿发生过很多爱情故事。

阿布来：你说说，我听听。

马克：你知道《白蛇传》吗？

阿布来：当然知道！看，快到断桥了。

马克：咱们要在这儿下车吗？

阿布来：对，这儿是雷峰塔，咱们可以去塔上看三潭印月。

马克：不坐船了吗？

阿布来：坐船太慢了。晚上，我还想带你去看看附近的音乐喷泉。

马克：太棒了！在家靠父母，出门靠朋友。你就是我的西湖导游。

阿布来：我会努力学习汉语。将来当一名导游，给中国游客介绍我们国家的景点。

Xià wǔ, Mǎ kè hé ā bù lái zài yóu lǎn chē shang liáo tiān。(Mark is talking with Abylai on the tourist bus.)

Mǎ kè：Háng zhōu zhēn shì yí ge làng màn de chéng shì!

Ā bù lái: Wèi shén me zhè me shuō?

Mǎ kè: Yīn wèi zài zhèr fā shēng guo hěn duō ài qíng gù shi。

Ā bù lái: Nǐ shuō shuo, wǒ tīng ting。

Mǎ kè: Nǐ zhī dao《Bái shé zhuàn》ma?

Ā bù lái: Dāng rán zhī dao! Kàn, kuài dào Duàn qiáo le。

Mǎ kè: Zán men yào zài zhèr xià chē ma?

Ā bù lái: Duì, zhèr shì Léi fēng tǎ, zán men kě yǐ qù tǎ shang kàn Sān tán yìn yuè。

Mǎ kè: Bú zuò chuán le ma?

Ā bù lái: Zuò chuán tài màn le。Wǎn shang, wǒ hái xiǎng dài nǐ qù kàn kan fù jìn de yīn yuè pēn quán。

Mǎ kè: Tài bàng le! Zài jiā kào fù mǔ, chū mén kào péng you。Nǐ jiù shì wǒ de Xī hú dǎo yóu。

Ā bù lái: Wǒ huì nǔ lì xué xí hàn yǔ。Jiāng lái dāng yì míng dǎo yóu, gěi Zhōng guó yóu kè jiè shào wǒ men guó jiā de jǐng diǎn。

根据课文(二)回答问题
Answer these questions according to the Text B

1. 为什么说杭州是个浪漫的城市?
2. 他们准备在哪儿下车?
3. 晚上,阿布来打算带马克去哪儿?

语言点
Language points

1. *v.* + 过

我坐过这辆车。

"*v.* + 过"表示过去的某种经历。否定形式为"sb. + 没(有) + 过 + O"。

The structure "*v.* + 过" indicates the past experience. The negative form is "sb. + 没(有) + 过 + O".

(1) A:我去过北京,你呢?

B:我没去过。

(2) A:我吃过饺子,你吃过吗?

B:我也吃过。

2. *num.* + 多 + *mw.*

我们可以坐车游览一个多小时。

这个结构表示概数

The structure "*num*. + 多 + *mw*." is used to express approximate number.

(1)他买了二十多瓶啤酒。

(2)这件衣服要一千多块钱。

3. 得(děi)

那儿得坐船过去。

"得(děi)"用在动词前,表示不得已。

Used before verbs, "得" indicates that there is no other alternative.

(1)明天早上八点上课,我得早一点儿起床。

(2)我的手机坏了,我得买一个新手机。

4. 快(要)……了

快到断桥了。

"快……了",表示事件或动作即将发生。

This pattern indicate that an incident or action is about to take place, or will happen soon.

(1)快考试了,我们得复习复习。

(2)快回国了,我想给朋友们准备一些礼物。

(3)新年快到了,商场里到处都在打折。

功能会话 Functional expression

1. 感叹 (Exclamation)

(1)杭州真是一个浪漫的城市!

(2)太棒了!

综合练习 Comprehensive exercises

(一)熟读短语 Read the following phrases

1. 去过　学过　看过　……过
2. 大部分　小部分　几个部分　……部分
3. 赶快来　赶快去　赶快吃　赶快……
4. 讲故事　听故事　爱情故事　……故事
5. 当导游　当老师　当医生　当……

(二)替换练习 Substitution drills

1. 来中国以前,你v.过……吗?

吃	饺子	对,我v.过。
看	中国电影	
听	中国音乐	不,我没v.过。
用	筷子	

2. 我有二十多个朋友。(20—30)

   我有________块钱。(100—200)。

   我画了________个小时。(30—40)

   今天________度。(20—30)

3. 我的手机坏了,得买一个新的。

   明天早上有课　早点儿起床。

   我的自行车丢了　走路去教室。

   天气太冷了　多穿一件衣服。

(三)课堂练习 In-class exercises

1. 比一比。Make a comparison.

   请圈出"西湖十景",查一查它们的名字叫什么,比一比谁知道的多。Please circle Ten Scenes of the West Lake, and search their names on the internet; who can tell more will win the game.

2. 头脑风暴。Brainstorm.

   设计一个"西湖一日游"的路线方案。Please design a route of West Lake one-day tour.

   Eg: 上午8:00—10:00,从断桥残雪到曲院风荷,骑自行车。

   线路1:____

   线路2:____

   线路3:____

(四)课后练习 After-class exercises

角色表演:我在西湖迷路了。Role play: I'm lost nearby the West Lake.

一个人扮演导游,一个人扮演迷路的游客,编写对话并表演。One student acts as a guide, and one student acts as a tourist; please make a dialogue according to this situation.

课文翻译 Translation of the texts

Text A Taking a sightseeing bus

"Dear tourists, here comes the bus."

Mark: Look, what is that?

Abylai: That is the tourist bus. We have walked for half an hour, are you tired?

Mark: Kind of, what about going over there to take that bus?

Abylai: Great! The price is 40 yuan for each person, and we can go sightseeing on the bus for over an hour. It's pretty convenient.

Mark: What view spots will it pass, do you know it ?

Abylai: I've taken this bus, there are four stops, the last stop is Yue Fei Temple.

Mark: Can we get on or get off at other places?

Abylai: No, we can't. Don't worry, we can see most of the famous view spots on the bus, such as the Broken Bridge, Bai Causeway, Breeze-ruffled Lotus Beside the Winery and so on.

Mark: By the way, I'd like to visit the view spot on the note of one *yuan*.

Abylai: You mean Three Pools Mirroring the Moon, right? We have to take a boat there.

"Dear tourists, here comes the bus."

Mark: Here comes another tourist bus; let's get on it immediately.

Abylai: We have to pay for the ticket before getting on.

Text B A romantic city

Mark: Hangzhou is such a romantic city !

Abylai: Why do you think so?

Mark: Because many love stories were set around here.

Abylai: Yes, I'm listening what do you know.

Mark: For example, the Legend of the White Snake is one of them , don't you know it?

Abylai: Of course I know it. Look, there is just the Broken Bridge.

Mark: Shall we get it off here?

Abylai: Yes, this stop is Leifeng Tower. I'll take you to look around Three Pools Mirroring the Moon on the tower.

Mark: Don't we take the boat there?

Abylai: It is too slow by boat. I plan to take you to go sightseeing at the music fountain tonight.

Mark: Fantastic! There is an old saying: Relying on parents at home, relying on friends abroad. You are exactly my West Lake guide.

Abylai: I will learn Chinese well so that I can be as a real guide after I going back to my country in the future. At that time I am able to introduce the view spots of my own country to Chinese tourists.

6 共享时代
Sharing era

话题导学
Guidance

你知道图片中是什么吗？在你的国家有没有？

Do you know what are in the pictures? Do you have the same things in your country?

生词学习(一)
New words I

1. 共享 (gòngxiǎng) *v.* share　　共享汽车；共享单车
2. 单车 (dānchē) *n.* bike　　共享单车；骑单车
3. 当然 (dāngrán) *adv.* certainly; of course　　当然可以；当然去
4. 骑 (qí) *v.* ride　　骑自行车；骑马
5. 下载 (xiàzài) *v.* download　　下载文件；下载音乐
6. App *n.* Application　　下载 App；用 App
7. 除了 (chú le) *prep.* except; besides　　除了……，也……

8. 扫 (sǎo) *v.* scan 扫二维码

9. 二维码 (èr wéi mǎ) *n.* Two-Dimensional Code 扫二维码

10. 出现 (chū xiàn) *v.* appear 出现错误;出现密码

11. 密码 (mì mǎ) *n.* password 手机密码;银行密码

12. 输入 (shū rù) *v.* input 输入密码;输入汉字

13. 这么 (zhè me) *adv.* so 这么快;这么贵

14. 有时候 (yǒu shí hou) *VO* sometimes 有时候用

15. 免费 (miǎn fèi) *adj.* free 免费电影;免费食品

16. 本来 (běn lái) *adj.* originally 本来想;本来喜欢

17. 到处 (dào chù) *adv.* everywhere 到处有;到处看

课文(一) Text A 你知道共享单车吗? Do you know shared bike?

马克和卡卡在食堂聊天。

马克:你知道共享单车吗?

卡卡:当然知道啦,昨天我还骑共享单车去教室呢。

马克:你能告诉我怎么用吗? 我也想骑。

卡卡:好的,第一次用的时候,你需要下载一个共享单车的App。

马克:嗯,除了下载App,还需要做什么呢?

卡卡:下载以后,扫一下共享单车上的二维码,手机上就会出现一个密码,输入密码就可以了。

马克:这么方便啊,我现在就下载App,对了,共享单车贵不贵啊?

卡卡:半个小时一块钱,如果是学生,只需要五毛钱,有时候还免费呢。

马克:太好了! 我本来想买一辆自行车呢。

卡卡:现在不用买啦,到处都是共享单车。

马克:是啊,我下午就试试。

卡卡:好,如果有问题,就给我打电话。

Mǎ kè hé Kǎ kǎ zài shí táng liáo tiān。(Mark is talking with Kaka in the canteen.)

Mǎ kè:Nǐ zhī dào gòng xiǎng dān chē ma?

Kǎ kǎ:Dāng rán zhī dào la,zuó tiān wǒ hái qí gòng xiǎng dān chē qù jiào shì ne。

Mǎ kè:Nǐ néng gào sù wǒ zěn me yòng ma? Wǒ yě xiǎng qí。

Kǎ kǎ:Hǎo de,dì yí cì yòng de shí hou,nǐ xū yào xià zǎi yí gè gòng xiǎng dān chē de App。

Mǎ kè:Ēn,chú le xià zǎi App,hái xū yào zuò shén me ne?

Kǎ kǎ:Xià zǎi yǐ hòu,sǎo yí xià gòng xiǎng dān chē shàng de èr wéi mǎ,shǒu jī shàng jiù huì chū xiàn yí gè mì mǎ,shū rù mì mǎ jiù kě yǐ le。

Mǎ kè:Zhè me fāng biàn a,wǒ xiàn zài jiù xià zǎi App,duì le,gòng xiǎng dān chē guì bú guì a?

Kǎ kǎ:Bàn gè xiǎo shí yí kuài qián,rú guǒ shì xué shēng,zhǐ xū yào wǔ máo qián,yǒu shí hòu hái miǎn fèi ne。

Mǎ kè:Tài hǎo le! Wǒ běn lái xiǎng mǎi yí liàng zì xíng chē ne。

Kǎ kǎ:Xiàn zài bú yòng mǎi le,dào chù dōu shì gòng xiǎng dān chē。

Mǎ kè:Shì a,wǒ xià wǔ jiù shì shi。

Kǎ kǎ:Hǎo,rú guǒ yǒu wèn tí,jiù gěi wǒ dǎ diàn huà。

根据课文(一)回答问题
Answer these questions according to the Text A

1. 卡卡骑过共享单车吗?
2. 第一次骑共享单车需要怎么做?
3. 共享单车有密码吗?
4. 骑一次共享单车需要多少钱?

生词学习(二)
New words II

1. 流行 (liú xíng) *adj.* popular　　很流行;流行歌曲
2. 要不 (yào bù) *conj.* (indicate suggestion)
3. 经常 (jīngcháng) *adv.* often　　经常回家;经常去
4. 偶尔 (ǒu ěr) *adv.* occasionally　　偶尔看书;偶尔打电话
5. 希望 (xī wàng) *v.* hope;wish　　希望快乐;希望通过

diàn dòng chē
6. 电 动 车　*NP* electric bike　　骑电动车

xīn wén
7. 新 闻　*n.* news　　看新闻;听新闻

shí dài
8. 时代　*n.* era　　共享时代;网络时代

专有名词 (Proper nouns)

1. ofo　a brand of a shared bike company

Mó bài
2. 摩拜　a brand of a shared bike company

课文(二)　共享时代来了
Text B　Sharing era is coming

马克:看,那儿有很多黄色的共享单车。

卡卡:这种黄色的单车叫 ofo,现在 ofo 和摩拜单车很流行。

马克:嗯,要不我们一起骑车去教室吧?

卡卡:好啊,我也不想走路了,宿舍离教室太远了。

马克:是的,每次走路需要半个小时。对了,你经常骑共享单车吗?

卡卡:不是,我也是偶尔骑一次。

马克:共享单车真的很方便,你的国家有共享单车吗?

卡卡:还没有,你的国家呢?

马克:也没有,我希望以后会有吧。

卡卡:嗯,如果有共享电动车就更方便了。

马克:听说已经有了。我今天看新闻,共享汽车也出现了。

卡卡:啊! 这么快啊! 共享时代真的来啦。

Mǎ kè:Kàn,nàr yǒu hěn duō huáng sè de gòng xiǎng dān chē。

Kǎ kǎ:Zhè zhǒng huáng sè de dān chē jiào ofo,xiàn zài ofo hé Mó bài dān chē hěn liú xíng。

Mǎ kè:Ēn,yào bu wǒ men yì qǐ qí chē qù jiào shì ba?

Kǎ kǎ:Hǎo a,wǒ yě bù xiǎng zǒu lù le,sù shè lí jiào shì tài yuǎn le。

Mǎ kè:Shì de, měi cì zǒu lù xū yào bàn ge xiǎo shí。Duì le,nǐ jīng cháng qí gòng xiǎng dān chē ma?

Kǎ kǎ:Bú shì,wǒ yě shì ǒu ěr qí yí cì。

Mǎ kè: Gòng xiǎng dān chē zhēn de hěn fāng biàn, nǐ de guó jiā yǒu gòng xiǎng dān chē ma?

Kǎ kǎ: Hái méi yǒu, nǐ de guó jiā ne?

Mǎ kè: Yě méi yǒu, wǒ xī wàng yǐ hòu huì yǒu ba。

Kǎkǎ: Ēn, rú guǒ yǒu gòng xiǎng diàn dòng chē jiù gèng fāng biàn le。

Mǎ kè: Tīng shuō yǐ jīng yǒu le。Wǒ jīn tiān kàn xīn wén, gòng xiǎng qì chē yě chū xiàn le。

Kǎ kǎ: Ā! Zhè me kuài a! Gòng xiǎng shí dài zhēn de lái la。

根据课文(二)回答问题
Answer these questions according to the Text B

1. 摩拜单车是黄色的。 (   )
2. 他们的宿舍离教室很远。 (   )
3. 卡卡经常骑共享单车。 (   )
4. 卡卡的国家也有共享单车。 (   )

语言点
Language points

1. 除了……,还……

除了下载 App,还需要做什么呢?

"除了"表示"排除已知",后面常跟"还"搭配,对前一句进行补充说明。

"除了" indicates "exclude the known things", which often matches with "还", adding a supplement to the previous sentence.

(1)今天除了有口语课,还有听力课。

(2)他除了会说汉语,还会说英语。

2. 这么 + *adj*.

这么方便啊!

"这么"的意思是"很""非常",常用在动词或形容词的前面,表示感叹的语气。

In this sentence, "这么" means "so" or "very", which is often used before an adjective or verb, expressing exclamatory mood.

(1)今天这么热。

(2)你的汉语这么好。

3. 对了,……

对了,共享单车贵不贵啊?

“对了”表示“突然想起某事”,常用于句首,开启一个新话题。

“对了” indicates “thinking of something suddenly”, similar to “by the way”. It is often used at the beginning of a sentence for starting a new topic.

A:我们一起回宿舍吧?

B:好的。对了,你下午去图书馆吗?

4. 地方 + 有 + 人/物

那儿有很多黄色的共享单车。

这是一个存在句,这类存在句的句型为“地方 + 有 + 人/物”,意思是“某个地方存在某人或某物”。

This sentence is an existential sentence. The sentence pattern is “地方(place) + 有 + 人/物(people/things)”, which means “there is/are people/things in some place”.

(1)教室里有很多留学生。

(2)桌子上有一台电脑。

5. 要不……

要不我们一起骑车去教室吧?

“要不”常常用在句首,表示提出某种建议。

“要不” Leads to an option or advice. It is often used at the beginning of a sentence.

(1)中国菜太辣了,要不我们吃韩国菜吧。

(2)太累了,要不我们休息一下吧。

功能会话 Functional expression

1. 开启新话题(Starting a new topic)

(1)对了,你知道什么时候放假吗?

(2)对了,你明天有没有时间?

2. 建议(Suggestion)

(1)走路太慢了,要不我们打的去吧。

(2)食堂的菜不好吃,要不我们做饭吧。

综合练习 Comprehensive exercises

(一)熟读短语 Read the following phrases

1. 共享单车　共享汽车　共享时代

2. 骑自行车　骑摩托车　骑马
3. 下载电影　下载游戏　下载歌曲
4. 输入密码　输入汉字　输入姓名
5. 免费学习　免费吃饭　免费电影

(二)替换练习 Substitution drills

1. 除了买书，　还买了笔、书包。
   吃面包　吃苹果和西瓜
   会说汉语　会说英语、法语
   有美国学生　有津巴布韦学生
2. 这么方便啊。
   漂亮
   贵
   有意思
3. 那儿有　很多黄色的共享单车。
   超市里　很多啤酒和面包
   书包里　书和笔
   桌子上　电脑、钱包

(三)课堂练习 In-class exercises

1. 团队合作。Teamwork.

全班分为两组，一组找共享单车/汽车的优点，另一组找缺点，找得多的组胜利。The class was divided into two groups. One group look for the advantages of shared bike or car, and the other look for disadvantages. The team which find more will win the game.

	共享单车/汽车
优点(advantages)	
缺点(disadvantages)	

2. 头脑风暴。Brainstorm.

说一说，你觉得在共享时代，还有什么可以共享?

Let's say, is there anything else to share in the era of sharing?

(四)课后练习 After-class exercises

完成一次骑共享单车的任务，然后告诉同学们。包括：从什么地方到什么地方，怎么使用，多少钱，感觉怎么样，等等。Finish the task of riding a shared bike. And then answer these questions: From where to where? How to use it? How much is it? How did you feel? Etc.

课文翻译 Translation of the texts

Text A　Have you heard about "shared bicycle"?

Mark: Do you know "shared bicycle"?

Kaka: Of course, I went to the classroom by a shared bicycle yesterday.

Mark: Can you tell me how to use it? I want to ride too.

Kaka: OK, when you use it for the first time, you need to download an App for a shared bike.

Mark: Well, what do I need to do besides downloading App?

Kaka: After downloading, you should scan the two-dimensional code on the shared bike, then a password will appear on the phone, it will be OK after entering the password.

Mark: So convenient, I'm downloading APP now. By the way, is it expensive to use a shared bike?

Kaka: One yuan for half an hour. If you are a student, it only needs half a *yuan*, and sometimes it is free.

Mark: That's great! I wanted to buy a bike originally.

Kaka: You needn't to buy it now. There are shared bikes everywhere.

Mark: Yes, I'll try it in the afternoon.

Kaka: OK, if you have a problem, just call me.

Text B　Sharing era is coming

Mark: Look, there are a lot of yellow shared bicycles there.

Kaka: The yellow bike named ofo, ofo and Mobike are very popular now.

Mark: Well, shall we ride to the classroom together?

Kaka: OK, I don't want to walk too. The dorm is too far away from the classroom.

Mark: Yes, it takes half an hour to walk every time. By the way, do you often ride shared bike?

Kaka: No, I also ride occasionally.

Mark: Shared bike is very convenient. Do you have shared bike in your country?

Kaka: Not yet. What about your country?

Mark: No, I hope we'll have it in the future.

Kaka: Well, it will be more convenient if there's a shared electric bike.

Mark: I heard it appeared already. I read the news today, and the shared car has also appeared.

Kaka: Ah! So fast! The era of sharing is really coming.

7 吃在中国 Dining in China

话题导学 Guidance

你知道哪些有名的中国菜?

Do you know any famous Chinese cuisine?

生词学习(一) New words I

1. 外卖 (wài mài) *n.* Food Delivered; take-out　　点外卖;送外卖
2. 汉堡 (hàn bǎo) *n.* hamburger　　鸡肉汉堡;牛肉汉堡
3. 对 (duì) *mw.* pair　　一对鸡翅;一对夫妻
4. 鸡翅 (jī chì) *n.* chicken wings　　一个鸡翅;薯条和鸡翅
5. 加 (jiā) *v.* add　　加辣;加冰
6. 地址 (dì zhǐ) *v.* address　　学校地址;公司地址
7. 麻烦 (má fan) *adj.* troublesome　　比较麻烦;麻烦你
8. 注意 (zhù yì) *v.* pay attention　　注意安全;注意身体
9. 取 (qǔ) *v.* take　　取钱;取餐
10. 辛苦 (xīn kǔ) *adj.* show one's thanks to others hard work　　特别辛苦;辛苦你了

课文(一) 点外卖
Text A Ordering delivery

下雨天，金明学在宿舍点外卖。

金明学：喂，你好。我要点外卖。

店员：请问你要吃什么呢？

金明学：我要一个牛肉汉堡、一对鸡翅和一杯可乐。

店员：可乐要加冰吗？

金明学：对，我要冰可乐。

店员：好的，请问送到哪里？你订单上的地址对吗？

金明学：对的。麻烦你送到工商大学留学生宿舍。地址是学林街401号。多长时间能送到？

店员：二十分钟就能送到。请注意你的手机，外卖员会打电话给你。

金明学：好的。谢谢！

四十分钟以后。

外卖员：你好，请问是金明学吗？你的外卖到了，请下楼取一下。

金明学：好，我马上下来。请稍等。

五分钟以后。

金明学：下雨天，您送外卖辛苦了。非常感谢！再见！

外卖员：不客气。再见！

Xià yǔ tiān, Jīn Míng xué zài sù shè diǎn wài mài。(It is raining outside, Jin Mingxue is ordering delivery at dorm.)

Jīn Míng xué: Wéi, nǐ hǎo。Wǒ yào diǎn wài mài。

Diàn yuán: Qǐng wèn, nǐ yào chī shén me ne?

Jīn Míng xué: Wǒ yào yí ge niú ròu hàn bǎo、yí duì jī chì hé yì bēi kě lè。

Diàn yuán: Kě lè yào jiā bīng ma?

Jīn Míng xué: Duì, wǒ yào bīng kě lè。

Diàn yuán: Hǎo de, qǐng wèn sòng dào nǎ lǐ? Nǐ dìng dān shàng de dì zhǐ duì ma?

Jīn Míng xué: Duì de。Má fan nǐ sòng dào Gōng shāng dà xué liú xué shēng sù shè。Dì zhǐ shì xué lín jiē sì bǎi líng yī hào。Duō cháng shí jiān néng sòng dào?

Diàn yuán: Èr shí fèn zhōng jiù néng sòng dào。Qǐng zhù yì nǐ de shǒu jī, wài mài yuán huì dǎ diàn huà gěi nǐ。

Jīn Míng xué：Hǎo de，Xiè xie！

Sì shí fèn zhōng yǐ hòu。(40 minutes later)

Wài mài yuán：Nǐ hǎo，qǐng wèn shì Jīn Míng xué ma？ Nǐ de wài mài dào le，qǐng xià lóu qǔ yí xià。

Jīn Míng xué：Hǎo，wǒ mǎ shang xià lai，qǐng shāo děng。

Wǔ fèn zhōng yǐ hòu (5 minutes later)

Jīn Míng xué：Xià yǔ tiān，nín sòng wài mài xīn kǔ le，fēi cháng gǎn xiè！ Zài jiàn！

Wài mài yuán：Bú kè qi，zài jiàn！

根据课文(一)回答问题
Answer these questions according to the Text A

1. 金明学要吃什么？
2. 外卖送到哪儿？
3. 金明学为什么感谢外卖员？

生词学习(二)
New words II

1. 附近 (fù jìn) *n.* nearby　　学校附近；机场附近
2. 又……又…… (yòu … yòu …) both… and…　　又快又好；又白又胖
3. 入乡随俗 (rù xiāng suí sú) *idm* Do in Rome as Rome does
4. 油 (yóu) *adj.* oily　　黄油；加油
5. 辣 (là) *adj.* spicy　　辣椒；麻辣
6. 咸 (xián) *adj.* salty　　咸味；咸肉
7. 其实 (qí shí) *adv.* in fact; actually
8. 清淡 (qīng dàn) *adj.* mild flavor　　口味清淡；比较清淡
9. 非常 (fēi cháng) *adv.* very; extremely　　非常喜欢；非常好吃

chá
10. 查　*v.* check　　查成绩;查地图

xiǎo lóng bāo
11. 小笼包　*n.* small steamed bun　　一笼小笼包

专有名词(Proper noun)

Bǎi dù dì tú
百度地图　*n.*　Baidu Map

课文(二)　咱们去吃小笼包吧
Text B　Let's get some steamed buns

下午,金明学和马克在教室里讨论晚饭吃什么。

金明学:我中午叫了外卖,晚饭咱们出去吃,好不好?

马克:好啊,我也想去外面吃。

金明学:学校附近新开了一家西餐馆,咱们去尝尝吧。

马克:我觉得中国菜又好吃又便宜,入乡随俗嘛,咱们应该多吃中国菜,你说呢?

金明学:但是有些中国菜太油了,我也不喜欢吃太辣太咸的菜。

马克:你说的那些菜是川菜吧?其实,中国菜也有清淡的菜,比如杭州菜。

金明学:对!我非常喜欢杭州菜。要不咱们去吃小笼包吧?

马克:好的,我先打开百度地图,查查哪儿有小笼包店。

金明学:找到了,最近的一家小笼包店在这儿,离我们有八百米。

马克:我们骑共享单车去,怎么样?

金明学:好主意!

Xià wǔ, Jīn Míng xué hé Mǎ kè zài jiào shì li tǎo lùn wǎn fàn chī shén me。(**Afternoon, Jin Mingxue is talking to Mark about the dinner in the classroom.**)

Jīn Míng xué: Wǒ zhōng wǔ jiào le wài mài, wǎn fàn zán men chū qu chī, hǎo bu hǎo?

Mǎ kè: Hǎo a, wǒ yě xiǎng qù wài mian chī。

Jīn Míng xué: Xué xiào fù jìn xīn kāi le yì jiā xī cān guǎn, zán men qù cháng chang ba。

Mǎ kè: Wǒ jué de Zhōng guó cài yòu hǎo chī yòu pián yi, rù xiāng suí sú ma, zán men yīng gāi duō chī Zhōng guó cài, nǐ shuō ne?

Jīn Míng xué: Dàn shi yǒu xiē Zhōng guó cài tài yóu le, wǒ yě bù xǐ huan chī tài là tài xián de cài。

Mǎ kè:Nǐ shuō de nà xiē cài shì Chuān cài ba? Qí shí,Zhōng guó cài yě yǒu qīng dàn de cài,bǐ rú Háng zhōu cài。

Jīn Míng xué:Duì! Wǒ fēi cháng xǐ huān Háng zhōu cài。Yào bu zán men qù chī xiǎo lóng bāo ba?

Mǎ kè:Hǎo de,wǒ xiān dǎ kāi Bǎi dù dì tú,chá cha nǎr yǒu xiǎo lóng bāo diàn。

Jīn Míng xué:Zhǎo dào le,zuì jìn de yì jiā xiǎo lóng bāo diàn zài zhèr,lí wo men yǒu bā bǎi mǐ。

Mǎ kè:Wǒ men qí gòng xiǎng dān chē qù,zěn me yàng?

Jīn Míng xué:Hǎo zhǔ yì!

根据课文(二)回答问题
Answer these questions according to the Text B

1. 马克觉得中国菜怎么样?
2. 金明学觉得中国菜怎么样?
3. 他们打算吃什么晚饭?

语言点
Language points

1. 就

二十分钟就能送到。

"就"强调动作行为发生得早或快。

"就" emphasis that an action happen either very early or quickly.

(1) 他身体不好,晚上九点就睡觉了。

(2) 我学了半年汉语,就通过 HSK4 了。

(3) 走路五分钟就到了。

2. 又……又……

我觉得中国菜又好吃又便宜。

"又……又……"表示两种状态或两个动作同时存在,形容词同为褒义或同为贬义。

The structure "又……又……" indicates two states or actions exit at the same time,similar to "both...and...".

(1) 这个房间又大又漂亮。

(2) 他的男朋友又高又帅。

(3) 那个地方又脏又乱。

3. 入乡随俗

入乡随俗嘛,咱们应该多吃中国菜。

“入乡随俗”是一个成语,建议外乡人到当地,应该善于观察,尊重当地风俗,尽量和当地人保持一致的风俗和习惯。

It is a Chinese idiom, which means that you'd better be observant when you are abroad. Do in Rome as Rome does.

(1) 中国人吃饭的时候喜欢劝酒,你会入乡随俗吗?

(2) 不是每一个外国人都愿意入乡随俗的。

4. 动词重叠

尝尝、查查

动词重叠,表示短时、轻松和随便的意味。一般表示一种习惯性的行为和动作。

Verbal reduplication indicates an informal, casual tone of voice; this form can express a regular action at usual time.

(1)周末的时候我喜欢看看书,听听音乐,放松放松。

(2)和朋友们在一起吃吃饭,聊聊天儿,我觉得很高兴。

功能会话 Functional expression

1. 感谢(Gratitude)

(1)谢谢你!

(2)非常感谢!

(3)辛苦了!

2. 询问别人的观点(Ask for other's opinions)

(1)好不好?

(2)你说呢?

(3)怎么样?

综合练习 Comprehensive exercises

(一)熟读短语 Read the following phrases

1. 叫外卖　点外卖　送外卖

2. 一对鸡翅　一对儿女　一对夫妻

3. 注意安全　注意一下　请注意

4. 取快递　取外卖　取出来

5. 查成绩　查身体　安全检查

(二)选词填空 Fill in the blanks

外卖　地址　取　其实　辛苦

(1)我想给朋友寄一张贺卡,但是我不知道他的________。

(2)下课的时候,同学们常常说:"老师,您________了!"。

(3)我的银行卡丢了,不能________钱了。

(4)星期六,很多同学不去食堂吃饭,他们一般会叫________。

(5)大家都觉得汉语很难,________,汉语的听和说不太难。

(三)课堂练习 In-class exercises

1. 看图说话。Express the pictures with the given words.

又……又……

2. 小组讨论。Discussion.

四个人一组讨论:你觉得怎么样的饮食结构(diet)比较健康? Discuss with your partners about the healthy diet and fill in this form according to your eating habits in daily life.

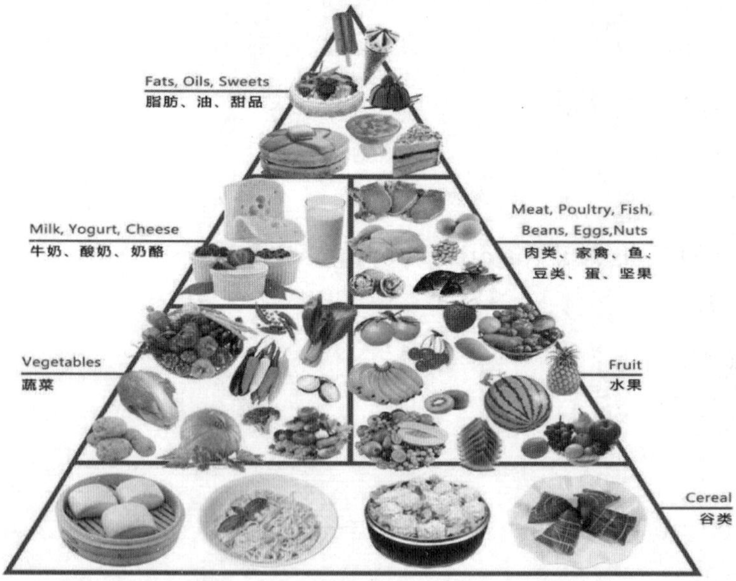

食物种类 food	谷类 cereal	蔬菜 vegetable	水 果 fruit	牛奶 milk	肉类 meat	油/甜品 oils/sweets
比例(%)						

3. 头脑风暴。Brainstorm.

说一说,外卖会带来哪些问题?

Please discuss with your partner: What are the problems of take-out?

(四)课后练习 After-class exercises

介绍一道你们国家的传统菜。说一说它的做法和味道。如果可以,带一些你们国家的食物给同学们尝一尝。Please introduce a traditional food of your country and please explain the way to cook. If it possible, share some snacks which are made in your country to your classmates.

课文翻译 Translation of the text

Text A Ordering delivery

Jin Mingxue: Hello, I'd like to order delivery.

Staff: What do you want?

Jin Mingxue: I'd like a beef hamburger, a pair of chicken wings and a cup of cola.

Staff: Would you like to add some ice to your coke?

Jin Mingxue: Yes, coke with ice.

Staff: Got it ,where are you? Is it correct the address on your order list?

Jin Mingxue: It is correct. Please deliver to international students dorm of Gongshang University. The complete address is No.401 Xuelin Street. How long will it take?

Staff: Probably in 20 minutes. Please keep an eye on your phone, because the delivery man will call you soon.

Jin Mingxue: All right. Thanks.

40 minutes later.

delivery man: Hello, is that Jin Mingxue? This is the delivery man. I've arrived, and please go downstairs to take your food.

Jin Mingxue: OK, I am coming. Waite a minute.

5 minutes later.

Jin Mingxue: Thanks for delivering food in such a rainy day. Goodbye.

delivery man: You are welcome. Goodbye.

Text B Let's get some steamed buns

Jin Mingxue: I ordered the delivery at noon. Let's go to a restaurant for dinner, do you agree?

Mark: All right. I'd like to go outside for dinner.

Jin Mingxue: There is a new opened west food restaurant; we can have a taste.

Mark: I think Chinese food is both delicious and cheap. When in Rome, do as the Romans do. We should eat more Chinese food, how do you think?

Jin Mingxue: Yeah, but Chinese food is too oily, I don't like too much spice or salt in dishes.

Mark: You mean those Sichuan cuisine right? Actually,Chinese food do have mild flavor dishes. Such as Hangzhou cuisine.

Jin Mingxue: You are right! I like Hangzhou cuisine so much. Let's go to eat small steamed bun, shall we?

Mark: Great. Let me open Baidu Map to check where those small steamed bun resturuant located in.

Jin Mingxue: I find one. The nearest one is here, 800 meters away to us.

Mark: We can ride the sharing bike there, do you agree?

Jin Mingxue: Good idea!

8 运动健身
Physical exercise

话题导学
Guidance

你喜欢运动吗？你常常在哪里运动？

Do you like sport? Where do you sport usually?

生词学习(一)
New words I

1. ān pái 安排	*v./n.*	arrange; arrangement	安排时间；具体安排
2. jiàn shēn fáng 健身房	*n.*	gym	去健身房；一家健身房
3. duàn liàn 锻炼	*v.*	physical exercise	锻炼身体；加强锻炼
4. cì 次	*mw.*	time	一次；几次
5. dài 带	*v.*	take	带着；带你去
6. dà tīng 大厅	*n.*	hall; lobby	一楼大厅；银行大厅
7. bàn 办	*v.*	do	办卡；办事
8. nián kǎ 年卡	*n.*	year card	一张年卡；办年卡
9. tǐ yàn 体验	*v./n.*	experience	体验一下儿；真实体验

míng bai
10. 明 白 *v.* understand 不太明白;明白了

jué dìng
11. 决 定 *v.* decide 最后的决定;还没决定

课文(一) 去健身房
Text A Go to the gym

马克和卡卡课间在教室聊天。

马克:下课以后你有什么安排?

卡卡:我打算去学校对面的健身房锻炼身体。

马克:你每天都去健身房吗?

卡卡:不,我一周去三次,每次大概运动两个小时。

马克:我也想锻炼身体,今天你可以带我一起去吗?

卡卡:当然可以啊,我们四点半从学校出发,怎么样?

马克:我得先回宿舍换一下衣服和鞋子,你先过去吧。

卡卡:行,那我在健身房一楼大厅等你。

马克:对了,价格怎么样?每小时多少钱?

卡卡:我办了一张年卡,一共一千五百块钱,每天都可以去。你可以先去体验一下,每小时三十块钱。

马克:明白了。我还是先试一试再决定要不要办卡。

Mǎ kè hé Kǎ kǎ kè jiān zài jiào shì liáo tiān。(Mark is talking with Kaka in the classroom during the rest time.)

Mǎ kè:Xià kè yǐ hòu nǐ yǒu shén me ān pái?

Kǎ kǎ:Wǒ dǎ suàn qù xué xiào duì miàn de jiàn shēn fáng duàn liàn shēn tǐ。

Mǎ kè:Nǐ měi tiān dōu qù jiàn shēn fáng ma?

Kǎ kǎ:Bù,wǒ yì zhōu qù sān cì,měi cì dà gài yùn dòng liǎng ge xiǎo shí。

Mǎ kè:Wǒ yě xiǎng duàn liàn shēn tǐ,jīn tiān nǐ kě yǐ dài wǒ yì qǐ qù ma?

Kǎ kǎ:Dāng rán kě yǐ a,wǒ men sì diǎn bàn cóng xué xiào chū fā,zěn me yàng?

Mǎ kè:Wǒ děi xiān huí sù shè huàn yí xià yī fu hé xié zi,nǐ xiān guò qu ba。

Kǎ kǎ:Xíng,nà wǒ zài jiàn shēn fáng yī lóu dà tīng děng nǐ。

Mǎ kè:Duì le,jià gé zěn me yàng? Měi xiǎo shí duō shao qián?

Kǎ kǎ:Wǒ bàn le yì zhāng nián kǎ,yí gòng yì qiān wǔ bǎi kuài qián,měi tiān dōu kě yǐ qù。Nǐ kě yǐ xiān qù tǐ yàn yí xià,měi xiǎo shí sān shí kuài qián。

Mǎ kè:Míng bai le。Wǒ hái shì xiān shì yi shì zài jué dìng yào bú yào bàn kǎ。

根据课文(一)回答问题
Answer these questions according to the Text A

1. 卡卡每周大概运动几个小时？
2. 下课以后谁先去健身房？
3. 那个健身房的价格怎么样？

生词学习(二)
New words II

1. 速度 (sù dù)	*n.*	speed	跑步速度；加快速度
2. 习惯 (xí guàn)	*v.*	be used to	学习习惯；不太习惯
3. 放 (fàng)	*v.*	put; set	放着；放下
4. 跑步机 (pǎo bù jī)	*n.*	treadmill	一台跑步机；在跑步机上
5. 坚持 (jiān chí)	*v.*	hold on; insist on	坚持一下儿；坚持锻炼
6. 继续 (jì xù)	*v.*	continue; keep on	继续努力；继续学习
7. 特别 (tè bié)	*adj./adv.*	special; especially	非常特别；特别喜欢
8. 室内 (shì nèi)	*n.*	indoor	室内运动；室内活动
9. 户外 (hù wài)	*n.*	outdoor	户外运动；户外活动
10. 达人 (dá rén)	*n.*	talent; expert	运动达人；音乐达人

课文(二) 运动达人
Text B Sports enthusiast

下午马克和卡卡在健身房运动。

马克：你跑步的速度真快啊！好厉害！你不累吗？

卡卡：我以前跟你一样，只能慢慢跑，跑一会儿就累死了。

马克：我不习惯在跑步机上跑步，我想休息一下。

卡卡：这儿一共放了五十多台跑步机呢。看，大家都在坚持。

马克：但是我真的不能继续跑步了。我肚子特别饿，我觉得我现在可以吃完三个汉堡。

卡卡：运动对身体有好处。我的身体越来越好了。

马克：除了跑步，你还喜欢什么运动？

卡卡：游泳啊，骑车啊，打球啊……室内运动和户外运动我都喜欢。

马克：你真是一个运动达人！

Xià wǔ Mǎ kè hé Kǎ kǎ zài jiàn shēn fáng yùn dòng。(**Mark and KaKa take exercises at the gym in the afternoon.**)

Mǎ kè：Nǐ pǎo bù de sù dù zhēn kuài a！ Hǎo lì hài！ Nǐ bú lè i ma?

Kǎ kǎ：Wǒ yǐ qián gēn nǐ yí yàng，zhǐ néng màn man pǎo，pǎo yí huìr jiù lèi sǐ le。

Mǎ kè：Wǒ bù xí guàn zài pǎo bù jī shang pǎo bù，wǒ xiǎng xiū xi yī xià。

Kǎ kǎ：Zhèr yí gòng fàng le wǔ shí duō tái pǎo bù jī ne。Kàn，dà jiā dōu zài jiān chí。

Mǎ kè：Dàn shì wǒ zhēn de bù néng jì xù pǎo bù le。Wǒ dù zi tè bié è，wǒ jué de wǒ xiàn zài kě yǐ chī wán sān ge hàn bǎo。

Kǎ kǎ：Yùn dòng duì shēn tǐ yǒu hǎo chù。Wǒ de shēn tǐ yuè lái yuè hǎo le。

Mǎ kè：Chú le pǎo bù，nǐ hái xǐ huān shén me yùn dòng?

Kǎ kǎ：Yóu yǒng a，qí chē a，dǎ qiú a……Shì nèi yùn dòng hé hù wài yùn dòng wǒ dōu xǐ huān。

Mǎ kè：Nǐ zhēn shì yí ge yùn dòng dá rén！

根据课文(二)回答问题
Answer these questions according to the Text B

1. 卡卡以前跑步快不快？
2. 马克为什么不能继续跑步了？
3. 卡卡喜欢哪些运动？

语言点
Language points

1. ……以后/……以前　after/before

我以前跟你一样，只能慢慢跑，跑一会儿就累死了。

(1) 下课以后，我想去游泳。

(2) 来中国以前，我不会说汉语。

(3) 以前，我没有很多朋友。以后，我希望我能交更多朋友。

2. 还是1

我觉得我还是先试一试,再决定要不要办卡。

"还是"在这里表示坚持自己原来的打算,不被别人所劝服。

In this sentence,"还是" means you still insist on your owe plan.

(1) 我们还是坐高铁去北京吧,坐飞机太麻烦了。

(2) 他还是决定取消明天的会议,因为他必须去医院检查身体了。

3. 存现句

这儿一共放了五十几台跑步机呢。(地点 + *v.* + 了 + *num.* + *n.*)

表示某处存在某人或某物。

This pattern is used to indicate that there is something or somebody in someplace.

(1) 地铁站贴了很多广告。

(2) 学校门口停了几辆共享单车。

4. 对……有好处

运动对身体有好处。

"对……有好处"表示某物或做某事给某个对象带来正面影响。

This pattern means there is some benefit to someone or something, the opposite structure is "对……有坏处".

(1) 多吃水果对身体有好处。

(2) 这次合作对我们公司有好处。

功能会话 Functional expression

1. 时间和频次(Time and frequency)
   (1)一天两次
   (2)一周三次
   (3)一个月一次
2. 表示称赞(Praise)
   (1)好厉害!
   (2)你真是一个……达人!

综合练习 Comprehensive exercises

(一)熟读短语 Read the following phrases

1. 体验一下　体验生活　学习体验
2. 加快速度　减慢速度　平均速度
3. 坚持一下　坚持锻炼　坚持学习
4. 越来越好　越来越胖　越来越瘦
5. 运动达人　音乐达人　时尚达人

(二)完成句子 Complete the following sentences

1. 五年以前,我________________________。
2. 十年以后,我________________________。
3. 这件衣服太大了,你还是________________。
4. 我的桌子上放着________________________。
5. ____________________对身体有好处。

(三)课堂练习 In-class exercises

1. 辩论。Debate.

户外运动比室内运动好 vs 室内运动比户外运动好

	原因(reasons)
户外运动比室内运动好	
室内运动比户外运动好	

2. 头脑风暴。Brainstorm.

请你为这家健身房设计两句广告。Please design two advertisement slogans for this gym.

广告 1 slogan 1

____

广告 2 slogan 2

____

(四)课后练习 After-class exercises

和同伴讨论,给自己制定一个健身减肥的计划。包括体重目标(target weight)、运动时间、运动项目、饮食结构等。Discuss with your partners about your sports plan. If you want to lose weight, please make a detailed plan including the target weight, sporting time, programs and diet.

课文翻译 Translation of the text

Text A　Go to the gym

Mark: What's your plan after class?

KaKa: I plan to go to the gym across from our school.

Mark: Do you go there everyday?

Kaka: No, I go to the gym three times a week, for each time I exercise about two hours.

Mark: I also want to exercise my body; would you take me go to the gym today?

Kaka: It's my pleasure. How about setting out at 4:30 p.m. from school?

Mark: I have to go back to the dorm to change my clothes, you can go first.

Kaka: OK, I'll wait for you at the lobby on the first floor.

Mark: By the way, what is the price for each hour?

Kaka: I bought a year card. There is 1,500 yuan in the card, and I can go to the gym everyday. I suggest you to go there for try, and it charges you 30 yuan per hour.

Mark: I got it. I will try it first then consider to buy a year card or not.

Text B　Sports enthusiast

Mark: You run so fast! Amazing! Aren't you tired?

KaKa: I was the same as you before. I run very slowly, and got very tired for running a while.

Mark: I'm not used to running on the treadmill. I'd like to have a rest.

KaKa: More than fifty treadmills are set here. Look, everyone holds on it.

Mark: But I can't keep on running anymore. I'm so hungry to death. Now I could eat up three hamburgers.

Kaka: Sports is good for our health. I am getting more and more healthy.

Mark: Besides of running, which kind of sports do you like?

Kaka: Such as swim ,cycle, balls... No matter of indoors or outdoors, I like both.

Mark: You are such a sport expert.

9 我的微信好友
My WeChat friends

话题导学 Guidance

你知道这些社交网络吗？你用过哪些？

Do you know these social media? Which one do you have used?

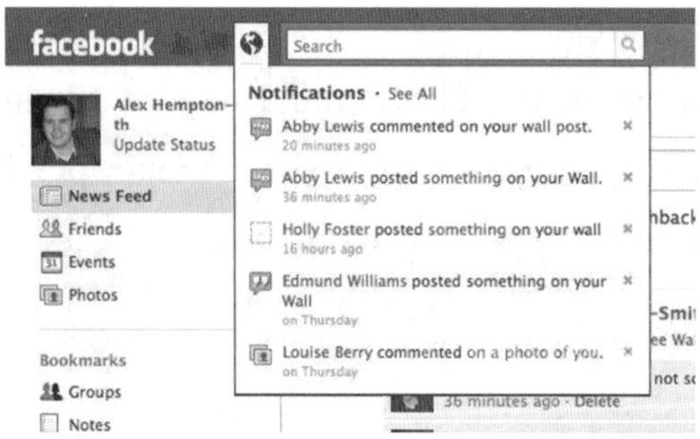

生词学习(一) New words I

1. 方法	fāng fǎ	*n.* method	学习方法；好方法
2. 好友	hǎo yǒu	*n.* friend	微信好友；加好友
3. 愿意	yuàn yì	*v.* be willing to	愿意去；愿意嫁给他
4. 成为	chéng wéi	*v.* become	成为朋友；成为明星
5. 语伴	yǔ bàn	*n.* language partner	介绍语伴；需要语伴
6. 见面	jiàn miàn	*v.* meet	和他见面；常常见面
7. 花	huā	*v.* spend	花钱；花时间
8. 水平	shuǐ píng	*n.* level	汉语水平；水平高
9. 提高	tí gāo	*v.* improve	提高水平；提高成绩

yǔ yīn
10. 语音 *n.* voice call　　微信语音;语音电话

shì pín
11. 视频 *n.* visual call　　视频通话;看视频

jié yuē
12. 节约 *v.* save; economize　　节约时间;节约用水

zhù
13. 祝 *v.* wish; bless　　祝你好运;祝你幸福

yú kuài
14. 愉快 *adj.* happy; joyful　　愉快的生活;心情愉快

专有名词(Proper nouns)

Wēixìn
1. 微信 *n.* WeChat
2. Kakaotalk *n.* a Korea social software

课文(一) 你有微信吗
Text A Do you have WeChat?

金明学和马老师课间聊天。

金明学:老师,您好,我可以和您聊聊吗?

马老师:当然可以,聊什么呢?

金明学:是这样,我觉得我的汉语不太好,您有什么好的学习方法吗?

马老师:你是韩国人,阅读和写作都很不错,口语和听力还需要练习。

金明学:您说得太对了。对我来说,读和写比较容易,听和说比较难。

马老师:你有微信吗?

金明学:我有,不过我不常常用微信,我喜欢用 Kakaotalk。

马老师:你有中国朋友吗?

金明学:还没有。我的微信好友大部分都是韩国人。

马老师:如果你愿意,我把我的中国学生介绍给你。

金明学:我非常愿意认识一些中国朋友,请老师帮我介绍介绍。

马老师:有一位中国女生非常想学习外语,我把她的微信号发给你,你们可以成为语伴。你教她说韩语,她教你说汉语,怎么样?

金明学:好主意,可是我上汉语课太忙了,我们没有时间见面。

马老师:你们可以在微信上聊天啊,每天花十五分钟和中国人说汉语,你的口语水平一定会提高。

金明学:明白了,我们还可以用微信语音和微信视频。不但能多练习汉语,而且还可以节约时间。

马老师:祝你们聊天愉快!

Jīn Míng xué hé Mǎ lǎo shī kè jiān liáo tiān。(Jin Mingxue is talking with teacher Ma during their break time.)

Jīn Míng xué:Lǎo shī,nín hǎo,wǒ kě yǐ hé nín liáo liao ma?

Mǎ lǎo shī:Dāng rán kě yǐ,liáo shén me ne?

Jīn Míng xué:Shì zhè yàng,wǒ jué de wǒ de hàn yǔ bú tài hǎo,nín yǒu shén me hǎo de xué xí fāng fǎ ma?

Mǎ lǎo shī:Nǐ shì Hán guó rén,yuè dú hé xiě zuò dōu hěn bú cuò,kǒu yǔ hé tīng lì hái xū yào liàn xí。

Jīn Míng xué:Nín shuō de tài duì le,duì wǒ lái shuō,dú hé xiě bǐ jiào róng yì,tīng hé shuō bǐ jiào nán。

Mǎ lǎo shī:Nǐ yǒu Wēi xìn ma?

Jīn Míng xué: Wǒ yǒu, bú guò wǒ bù cháng chang yòng Wēi xìn, wǒ xǐ huān yòng Kakaotalk。

Mǎ lǎo shī:Nǐ yǒu Zhōng guó péng you ma?

Jīn Míng xué:Hái méi yǒu。Wǒ de Wēi xìn hǎo yǒu dà bù fèn dōu shì Hán guó rén。

Mǎ lǎo shī:Rú guǒ nǐ yuàn yì,wǒ bǎ wǒ de Zhōng guó xué shēng jiè shào gěi nǐ。

Jīn Míng xué:Wǒ fēi cháng yuàn yì rèn shi yì xiē Zhōng guó péng you,qǐng lǎo shī bāng wǒ jiè shao jiè shao。

Mǎ lǎo shī:Yǒu yí wèi Zhōng guó nǚ shēng fēi cháng xiǎng xué xí wài yǔ,wǒ bǎ tā de Wēi xìn hào fā gěi nǐ,nǐ men kě yǐ chéng wéi yǔ bàn。Nǐ jiāo tā shuō hán yǔ,tā jiāo nǐ shuō hàn yǔ,zěn me yàng?

Jīn Míng xué:Hǎo zhǔ yì,kě shì wǒ shàng hàn yǔ kè tài máng le,wǒ men méi yǒu shí jiān jiàn miàn。

Mǎ lǎo shī:Nǐ men kě yǐ zài Wēi xìn shang liáo tiān a,měi tiān huā shí wǔ fēn zhōng hé Zhōng guó rén shuō hàn yǔ,nǐ de kǒu yǔ shuǐ píng yí dìng huì tí gāo。

Jīn Míng xué:Míng bái le,wǒ men hái kě yǐ yòng Wēi xìn yǔ yīn hé Wēi xìn shì pín。Bú dàn néng duō liàn xí hàn yǔ,ér qiě hái kě yǐ jié yuē shí jiān。

Mǎ lǎo shī:Zhù nǐ men liáo tiān yú kuài!

根据课文(一)回答问题
Answer these questions according to the Text A

1. 金明学的汉语怎么样?

2. 金明学常常用微信吗？
3. 你觉得什么是语伴？你有语伴吗？
4. 马老师建议(suggest)金明学怎么学习汉语？

生词学习(二)
New words II

1.	bàoqiàn 抱歉	*adj.* be sorry	很抱歉；真抱歉
2.	diànyǐng 电影	*n.* movie	看电影；中国电影
3.	xìng gé 性格	*n.* character; personality	性格外向；性格内向
4.	lǐ mào 礼貌	*n.* polite	有礼貌；没礼貌
5.	bāngzhù 帮助	*v.* help	帮助别人；接受帮助
6.	cōngming 聪明	*adj.* smart	特别聪明；聪明的孩子
7.	lì hai 厉害	*adj.* excellent	很厉害；厉害的人
8.	kǎo lǜ 考虑	*v.* consider	考虑一下；考虑了很久

课文(二) 我的中国语伴
Text B My Chinese language partner

一个星期以后，卡卡和金明学在宿舍聊天。

卡卡：最近你在忙什么呢？周末要不要和我们一起去踢足球？

金明学：抱歉，这个周末我有事。我要和几个中国朋友一起去看电影。

卡卡：你认识中国朋友了？他们的性格怎么样？我也想认识认识。

金明学：他们都很有礼貌，也很喜欢帮助别人。

卡卡：我听说中国女生比较安静，不爱说话，对吗？

金明学：不一定。我认识的一个中国女生非常爱说话，她每天都会和我微信语音一个多小时。

卡卡：这么长时间，你们都聊什么呢？

金明学：聊得最多的是爱好吧。她对学习外语很感兴趣。她不但会说自己的语言，而且还会说韩语和西班牙语，是个又聪明又努力的女生。

卡卡：她会说西班牙语？她是个天才。你把她的微信号发给我吧，我也想和她成为语伴。

金明学:这个,我得考虑考虑。

Yí ge xīng qī yǐ hòu, Kǎ kǎ hé Jīn Míng xué zài sù shè liáo tiān。(One week later,Kaka is talking with Jin Mingxue at the dorm.)

Kǎ kǎ:Zuì jìn nǐ zài máng shén me ne? Zhōu mò yào bú yào hé wǒ men yì qǐ qù tī zú qiú?

Jīn Míng xué:Bào qiàn,zhè ge zhōu mò wǒ yǒu shì。Wǒ yào hé jǐ ge Zhōng guó péng you yì qǐ qù kàn diàn yǐng。

Kǎ kǎ:Nǐ rèn shi Zhōng guó péng you le? Tā men de xìng gé zěn me yàng? Wǒ yě xiǎng rèn shi rèn shi。

Jīn Míng xué:Tā men dōu hěn yǒu lǐ mào,yě hěn xǐ huān bāng zhù bié rén。

Kǎ kǎ:Wǒ tīng shuō Zhōng guó nǚ shēng bǐ jiào ān jìng,bú ài shuō huà,duì ma?

Jīn Míng xué:Bù yí dìng。Wǒ rèn shi de yí ge Zhōng guó nǚ shēng fēi cháng ài shuō huà,tā měi tiān dōu huì hé wǒ wēi xìn yǔ yīn yí ge duō xiǎo shí。

Kǎ kǎ:Zhè me cháng shí jiān,nǐ men dōu liáo shén me ne?

Jīn Míng xué:Liáo de zuì duō de shì ài hào ba。Tā duì xué xí wài yǔ hěn gǎn xìng qù。Tā bú dàn huì shuō zì jǐ de yǔ yán,ér qiě hái huì shuō hán yǔ hé xī bān yá yǔ,shì ge yòu cōng ming yòu nǔ lì de nǚ shēng。

Kǎ kǎ:Tā huì shuō xī bān yá yǔ? Tā shì ge tiān cái。Nǐ bǎ tā de wēi xìn hào fā gěi wǒ ba。Wǒ yě xiǎng hé tā chéng wéi yǔ bàn。

Jīn Míng xué:Zhè ge,wǒ děi kǎo lü kǎo lü。

根据课文(二)回答问题
Answer these questions according to the Text B

1. 金明学和卡卡这个周末打算做什么?
2. 金明学觉得中国朋友怎么样?
3. 你觉得金明学会不会把那个中国女生的微信号给卡卡?

语言点
Language points

1. 对……来说

对我来说,读和写比较容易,听和说比较难。

“对……来说”,引出对象。

The structure “对 sb.来说” indicates the object.

(1) 对日本人来说,学习汉字比较容易,但是对欧美人来说,学习汉字特别难。

(2) 对你来说,什么是最重要的事情?

2. "把"字句[1]

我把我的中国学生介绍给你。

"把"字句[1]:sb. + 把 + *n*.1 + *v*. + 给(在/到/进/成……) + *n*.2

表示sb.通过 *v*.使 *n*.1 变成 *n*.2 表示的位置或状态。

This pattern is used to express that the position or the status of *n*.1 is changed into *n*.2 through the action.

(1) 你把她的微信号发给我吧。

(2) 我把手机放在包里了。

(3) 老师把我们的作业拿到办公室里了。

3. 祝……

祝你们聊天儿愉快!

"祝……"表达祝福和祝愿。

"祝……" can be expressed good wishes.

(1)祝你生日快乐!

(2)祝你成功! 祝你好运!

4. 抱歉

抱歉,这个周末我有事。

用"抱歉"来委婉和礼貌地表示拒绝。

You can use "抱歉" to refuse someone's requirement or show your shame.

(1)抱歉,我明天不能参加这个会议,因为我家里有事儿。

(2)大家久等了,真抱歉!

功能会话
Functional expression

1. 祝福(Good wishes)

 (1)祝你们聊天儿愉快!

 (2)祝你工作顺利!

 (3)祝你学习进步!

2. 拒绝 (Refusal)

 (1)抱歉!

(2)我得考虑考虑。

综合练习 Comprehensive exercises

(一)熟读短语 Read the following phrases

1. 和他见面　在门口见面　天天见面
2. 成为朋友　成为语伴　成为老师
3. 汉语水平　英语水平　提高水平
4. 节约时间　节约钱　节约水
5. 努力学习　努力工作　非常努力

(二)改写句子 Rewrite the sentences with the given words

1. 我觉得汉语不太难。(对我来说……)

____

2. 他觉得用微信很方便。(对他来说……)

____

3. 我给他我的名片。(sb. + 把 + *n*.1 + *v*. + 给(在/到/进/成……) + *n*.2)

____

4. 妈妈送妹妹去学校。(sb. + 把 + *n*.1 + *v*. + 给(在/到/进/成……) + *n*.2)

____

(三)课堂练习 In-class exercises

1. 小组讨论。Make a discussion.

请讨论社交网络的优点和缺点。Please discuss the advantages and disadvantages of the social media.

	微信/Facebook/GaGa
优点(advantages)	
缺点(disadvantages)	

2. 头脑风暴。Brainstorm.

根据课文内容,说一说韩国学生金明学、西班牙学生和那个中国女生的性格。Please choice the proper words for each person according to their personalities.

幽默　好学　努力　小气　大方　善良

金明学:

卡卡:

中国女生:

后来,金明学把那个中国女生的微信号给卡卡了,请写一个关于卡卡和那个中国女生的对话。两个人一组,表演对话。Jin Mingxue shares that Chinese girl's WeChat ID to Kaka finally. Please make a new dialogue between Kaka and that Chinese girl. If it possible, play the roles with your partner.

(四)课后练习 After-class exercises

通过各种办法,加五个中国微信好友,介绍一下他们每一个人的名字、职业、爱好、性格。讨论并概括中国人的主要性格特点。Please add five Chinese contacts by WeChat, and please introduce their names, jobs, hobbies and personalities. Try to sum up the main characters of the Chinese.

课文翻译 Translation of the texts

Text A　Do you have WeChat?

Jin Mingxue: Hello, Mr. Ma, May I have a talk with you?

Teacher Ma: Of course, what do you want to chat with me?

Jin Mingxue: Well, I think my Chinese is not so good; can you suggest me any good learning methods?

Teacher Ma: You are Korean, and you guys are very good at reading and writing; just the speaking and listening are still need to be practice more.

Jin Mingxue: I can't agree with you more. For me, reading and writing are quietly easy, but listening and speaking are still very difficult.

Teacher Ma: Do you have WeChat?

Jin Mingxue: I have, but I don't use WeChat so often. I like Kakaotalk.

Teacher Ma: Do you have some Chinese friends?

Jin Mingxue: I don't have one. Most of my WeChat friends are Korean.

Teacher Ma: If you are willing to know more Chinese friends, I can introduce some students to you.

Jin Mingxue: I'm very pleasure to know more Chinese friends, please introduce someone to me.

Teacher Ma: There is a Chinese girl, she was my student and she is very interested in learning foreign language. I am going to give you her WeChat ID, and you can be language partners of each other. You teach her Korea while she teaches you Chinese. How do you think?

Jin Mingxue: Great idea! But I am busy on learning Chinese classes, I don't have enough time to practice with them face to face.

Teacher Ma: You can chat on WeChat by speaking Chinese with her around fifteen minutes everyday. Your Chinese level will definitely be improved.

Jin Mingxue: I got your point. What's more, we can also use voice call and video call. In this way, I will not only practice more Chinese but also save my time.

Teacher Ma: Wish you guys can have a happy talk.

Text B　My Chinese language partner

KaKa: Hey, What's going on? Would you join us to paly football this weekend?

Jin Mingxue: Sorry, I have my plan this weekend. I am going to watch a movie with some Chinese guys.

Kaka: You've got some Chinese friends? How are their personalities like? I really want to know them.

Jin Mingxue: They are all very polite and they are willing to help others.

Kaka: I heard that Chinese girls are all very quiet; they are not so talkative, right?

Jin Mingxue: Not every girl. I know a Chinese girl who is very like to talk with people; we talk on voice call for over an hour everyday.

KaKa: During such a long time call, what do you talk about?

Jin Mingxue: Hobby is our main topic. She is interested in leaning foreign languages. She can not only speak her own language but also can speak Korea and Spanish. She is smart and diligent.

KaKa: She can even speak Spanish? She is a genius! Please share her WeChat ID with me, can you? I also want to become her language partner.

Jin Mingxue: Well, let me think about it.

10 移动支付 Mobile payment

话题导学 Guidance

你觉得哪种支付方式更方便?

Which payment is more convenient in your opinion ?

生词学习(一) New words I

1. 支付 (zhī fù)	*v.* pay	支付方式;现金支付
2. 现金 (xiàn jīn)	*n.* cash	用现金;带现金
3. 刷卡 (shuā kǎ)	*v.* swing card	刷卡支付;刷卡机
4. 账户 (zhàng hù)	*n.* account	银行账户;支付宝账户
5. 注册 (zhù cè)	*v.* register; enroll	注册账户;免费注册
6. 风险 (fēng xiǎn)	*n.* risk	有风险;冒风险
7. 扣 (kòu)	*v.* deduct money	扣钱;扣分
8. 设置 (shè zhì)	*v.* set up	设置密码;设置表格
9. 感谢 (gǎn xiè)	*v.* thanks ;be grateful	非常感谢;感谢父母

课文(一) 支付宝付款
Text A Alipay payment

李明和马克在商场购物，李明和营业员对话。

李明：请问，这里一共多少钱？

营业员：一共一百二十块，您用支付宝、现金还是刷卡？

李明：我用支付宝，扫哪里？

营业员：支付宝付款请扫描这个二维码。

李明：好的，我付好了。

营业员：谢谢，欢迎下次再来。

马克：我也想用支付宝，可是我还没有支付宝账户？

李明：你去网上注册一个支付宝账户吧，用支付宝很方便。

马克：你觉得用支付宝安全吗？有没有风险？别人把你的钱扣错了，怎么办？

李明：大部分中国人都在用支付宝或者微信付款，如果你担心有风险，就设置一个支付密码。

马克：好主意！下午你有空吗？能不能帮我注册一个支付宝账户？

李明：可以啊，我下午一点钟以后来你的宿舍吧，咱们可以在电脑上注册。

马克：行！太感谢你了！下午见！

李明：再见！

Lǐ Míng hé Mǎ kè zài shāng chǎng gòu wù, Lǐ Míng hé yíng yè yuán duì huà。(Li Ming and Mark are at a shopping mall, Li Ming is talking with the salesgirl.)

Lǐ Míng: Qǐng wèn, zhè li yí gòng duō shao qián?

Yíng yè yuán: Yí gòng yì bǎi èr shí kuài, nín yòng Zhī fù bǎo、xiàn jīn hái shì shuā kǎ?

Lǐ Míng: Wǒ yòng Zhī fù bǎo, sǎo nǎ lǐ?

Yíng yè yuán: Zhī fù bǎo fù kuǎn qǐng sǎo miáo zhè ge èr wéi mǎ。

Lǐ Míng: Hǎo de, wǒ fù hǎo le。

Yíng yè yuán: Xiè xie, huān yíng xià cì zài lái。

Mǎ kè: Wǒ yě xiǎng yòng Zhī fù bǎo, kě shì wǒ hái méi yǒu Zhī fù bǎo zhàng hù?

Lǐ Míng: Nǐ qù wǎng shàng zhù cè yí ge Zhī fù bǎo zhàng hù ba, yòng Zhī fù bǎo hěn fāng biàn。

Mǎ kè: Nǐ jué de yòng Zhī fù bǎo ān quán ma? Yǒu méi yǒu fēng xiǎn? Bié rén bǎ nǐ de qián kòu cuò le, zěn me bàn?

Lǐ Míng: Dà bù fèn Zhōng guó rén dōu zài yòng Zhī fù bǎo huò zhě Wēi xìn fù kuǎn, rú guǒ nǐ dān xīn yǒu fēng xiǎn,jiù shè zhì yí ge zhī fù mì mǎ。

Mǎ kè:Hǎo zhǔ yi! Xià wǔ nǐ yǒu kòng ma? Néng bù néng bāng wǒ zhù cè yí ge Zhī fù bǎo zhàng hù?

Lǐ Míng:Kě yǐ a,wǒ xià wǔ yī diǎn zhōng yǐ hòu lái nǐ de sù shè ba,zán men kě yǐ zài diàn nǎo shang zhù cè。

Mǎ kè:Xíng! Tài gǎn xiè nǐ le! Xià wǔ jiàn!

Lǐ Míng:Zài jiàn!

根据课文(一)回答问题
Answer these questions according to the Text A

1. 李明怎么付钱?
2. 马克有支付宝账户吗?
3. 李明下午一点钟以后去马克宿舍做什么?

生词学习(二)
New words II

1. 登录 (dēng lù) *v.* log in; enter　　登录网站;登录微信
2. 网站 (wǎng zhàn) *n.* website　　学校网站;公司网站
3. 选择 (xuǎn zé) *v.* choose　　正确选择;选择放弃
4. 个人 (gè rén) *adj.* individual; personal　　个人原因;个人账户
5. 国籍 (guó jí) *n.* nationality　　中国国籍;双国籍
6. 上传 (shàng chuán) *v.* upload　　上传照片;上传资料
7. 护照 (hù zhào) *n.* passport　　护照号码;办护照
8. 邮箱 (yóu xiāng) *n.* mailbox　　邮箱地址;公共邮箱
9. 步 (bù) *n.* step　　进步;下一步
10. 等待 (děng dài) *v.* wait for　　耐心等待;等待通知
11. 审核 (shěn hé) *v.* examine and verify　　等待审核;审核通过
12. 结果 (jié guǒ) *n.* result　　好结果;等待结果

课文(二) 注册账户
Text B Sign up for an account

下午李明来给马克注册支付宝账户。

马克:下午好!

李明:下午好!

马克:你帮我注册一个支付宝账户吧。

李明:好的,我先打开电脑,登录支付宝的网站 www.alipay.com。然后我们选择个人账户,你来自英国对吗?

马克:是的。这里的国籍和手机号码,我自己来输入吧。

李明:还需要上传你的护照,你有护照的照片吗?

马克:没问题,我的邮箱里有护照的照片,我先下载一下。

李明:对了,你还需要输入一个银行卡账号。

马克:什么银行的卡都可以吗?

李明:最好是中国的银行卡。

马克:都输入好了,下一步做什么?

李明:让我看看。哦,下一步就是等待审核了。一般需要24个小时,咱们明天才能知道审核结果。

马克:没关系,我的钱包里还有一百块现金。只是中国人现在不太喜欢找零钱。

李明:大家都习惯用支付宝了。

Xià wǔ Lǐ Míng lái gěi Mǎ kè zhù cè zhī fù bǎo zhàng hù。(Li Ming is coming to visits Mark for applying for an Alipay account.)

Mǎ kè:Xià wǔ hǎo!

Lǐ Míng:Xià wǔ hǎo!

Mǎ kè:Nǐ bāng wǒ zhù cè yí ge Zhī fù bǎo zhàng hù ba。

Lǐ Míng:Hǎo de,wǒ xiān dǎ kāi diàn nǎo,dēng lù Zhī fù bǎo de wǎng zhàn www.alipay.com,rán hòu wǒ men xuǎn zé gè rén zhàng hù,nǐ lái zì Yīng guó,duì ma?

Mǎ Kè:Shì de。Zhè lǐ de guó jí hé shǒu jī hào mǎ,wǒ zì jǐ lái shū rù ba。

Lǐ Míng:Hái xū yào shàng chuán nǐ de hù zhào,nǐ yǒu hù zhào de zhào piàn ma?

Mǎ kè:Méi wèn tí,wǒ de yóu xiāng lǐ yǒu hù zhào de zhào piàn,wǒ xiān xià zài yí xià。

Lǐ Míng:Duì le,nǐ hái xū yào shū rù yí ge yín háng kǎ zhàng hào。

Mǎ kè: Shén me yín háng de kǎ dōu kě yǐ ma?

Lǐ Míng: Zuì hǎo shì Zhōng guó de yín háng kǎ。

Mǎ kè: Dōu shū rù hǎo le, xià yí bù zuò shén me?

Lǐ Míng: Ràng wǒ kàn kan。Ò, xià yí bù jiù shì děng dài shěn hé le。Yì bān xū yào èr shí sì ge xiǎo shí, zán men míng tiān cái néng zhī dao shěn hé jié guǒ。

Mǎ kè: Méi guān xi, wǒ de qián bāo li hái yǒu yì bǎi kuài xiàn jīn。Zhǐ shì Zhōng guó rén xiàn zài bú tài xǐ huan zhǎo líng qián。

Lǐ Míng: Dà jiā dōu xí guàn yòng Zhī fù bǎo le。

根据课文(二)回答问题
Answer these questions according to the Text B

1. 注册一个支付宝账户需要输入什么?
2. 等待审核一般需要多长时间?
3. 你觉得中国人现在习惯用支付宝还是现金?

语言点
Language points

1. *v.* + 好

我付好了。

"*v.* + 好"表示完成某事,是一个结果补语。

"*v.* + 好" means finish doing something, which is a result complement.

(1) 我们吃好了。

(2) 你作业做好了吗?

(3) 他终于写好那个商业计划书了。

2. "把"字句$_2$

别人把你的钱扣错了。

"把"字句$_2$:sb. + 把 + *n*. + *v*. + 结果补语(complements)

表示 sb.通过动作 *v*.使 *n*.产生变化,达到某种目的或目标。

This pattern is used to indicate that target is achieved after this action.

(1)我把那瓶红酒喝完了。

(2)妈妈把我的衣服洗干净了。

3. 最好……

最好是中国的银行卡。

"最好……"表示提出比较好的建议。

"最好……" means you'd better to do something.

(1)明天上午我们经理很忙,你最好下午过来。

(2)你们的报告有一些错误,最好重新写一份。

4. 才

咱们明天才能知道审核结果。

"才"强调事情或动作对于说话人来说发生得晚或者慢。

"才" emphasizes that an action happens late or slow for the speaker.

(1)他今天上午十点半才起床。

(2)我三岁以后才开始说话。

(3)我们花了五年时间才设计出这个机器。

功能会话 Functional expression

1. 同意(Agreement)

(1)好主意!

(2)没问题!

(3)行!

(4)可以啊!

2. 顺序(Order)

(1)先……然后……

(2)再……

(3)下一步……

综合练习 Comprehensive exercises

(一)熟读短语 Read the following phrases

1. 现金支付　刷卡支付　微信支付

2. 银行账户　个人账户　学校账户

3. 手机密码　电脑密码　登录密码

4. 上传照片　上传资料　上传文件

5. 第一步　第二步　上一步

(二)替换练习 Substitution drills

1. 如果<u>下雨</u>,我就<u>不去爬山</u>。

没有现金 用支付宝

想学汉语 来中国

身体不好 不去上课

2. 我付好了。

吃

写

做

3. 他早上十点半才 起床。

晚上十二点半 睡觉

学了三年汉语 会说一点儿

写了两个小时 写好

(三)课堂练习 In-class exercises

1. 小组调查。Group survey.

哪些地方可以使用支付宝付款?(可以√,不可以×)Which situation is allowed to use Alipay?

地方	可以	不可以	地方	可以	不可以
超市			出租车		
商场			公共汽车		
邮局			地铁站		
医院			图书馆		
学费			办签证		

2. 头脑风暴。Brainstorm.

说一说,除了支付宝、微信支付、Apple Pay,以后还有什么别的支付方式吗?你听说过人脸支付和指纹支付吗?你觉得这种支付方式怎么样?Discuss: Have you ever heard other new payment? Do you know face scan payment and fingerprint payment? What's your attitude?

(四)课后练习 After-class exercises

请帮助一个朋友或者家人注册一个支付宝账户。Please help a friend or a family member to register an Alipay account.

https://memberprod.alipay.com/account/reg/index.htm

课文翻译 Translation of the texts

Text A Alipay payment

Li Ming: Excuse me, how much money all together?

Salesgirl: 120 yuan, will you pay me through Alipay, cash or credit card?

Li Ming: I choose Alipay. Where can I scan?

Salesgirl: Please scan this QR code by your Alipay.

Li Ming: OK, done.

Salesgirl: Thanks, looking forward to your next coming.

Mark: I'd like to use Alipay, too. But I don't have an Alipay account.

Li Ming: You can register one on the internet; it will be more convenient to your life.

Mark: Do you think it is safe enough to use Alipay? Are there any risks? What if they deduct more money from your account?

Li Ming: Most of the Chinese are using Alipay or WeChat to pay at present. If you feel worried about the safety, you can set a payment password.

Mark: Good idea! Do you have time this afternoon? Could you help me to register one?

Li Ming: No problem, I will come to your room after one o'clock this afternoon; we can register it on computer.

Mark: All right! Thank you so much! See you afternoon.

Li Ming: See you.

Text B Sign up for an account

Mark: Good afternoon!

Li Ming: Good afternoon!

Mark: Please help me to register an Alipay account.

Li Ming: OK, let me open the computer firstly, and login the web www.alipay.com. Then we select the personal account. You come from Britain, right?

Mark: Yes, let me input my nationality and phone No. here.

Li Ming: You have to upload your passport, do you have a photo of it?

Mark: Got it, I have one in my E-mail box. Let me download at first.

Li Ming: Oh, the bank card number is also required.

Mark: Is any bank card OK?

Li Ming: You'd better input China's bank card number.

Mark: All down. What is the next step?

Li Ming: Let me check. Well, the next step is waiting for examining. Usually it needs 24 hours. We will know the result until tomorrow.

Mark: It's OK. I still have 100 yuan in my wallet. Yet the Chinese guys don't like to give small changes nowadays.

Li Ming: Yep, we are all used to use Alipay.

11 租房与买房
To rent and buy a house

话题导学
Guidance

你租过房吗？如果你在中国工作，你打算租房还是买房？

Have you rented a room? If you work in China, do you plan to rent or buy a house?

生词学习(一)
New words I

1. 听说 (tīngshuō)	*v.*	hear	听说她在学汉语
2. 租 (zū)	*v.*	rent	租房子；租金
3. 实习 (shíxí)	*v.*	practice	实习机会；实习期间
4. 加班 (jiābān)	*v.*	work overtime	周末加班；经常加班
5. 租金 (zūjīn)	*n.*	rent	交租金；租金很贵
6. 押 (yā)	*v.*	mortgage	押金；抵押
7. 付 (fù)	*v.*	pay	付钱；付学费
8. 理解 (lǐjiě)	*v.*	understand	阅读理解；不理解
9. 涨 (zhǎng)	*v.*	rise	涨工资；上涨

10. 西北风 (xī běi fēng) *n.* northwest wind 喝西北风；刮西北风

课文(一) 押一付三
Text A Charge a pair of three

安娜和马克聊租房。

安娜：马克，你好！

马克：安娜，你好！

安娜：听说你在外面租房住。

马克：是的。我现在在市区的公司实习，经常要加班，回来很晚，住在宿舍很不方便。

安娜：租金贵吗？

马克：一个月两千。押一付三。

安娜："押一付三"是什么意思？

马克：就是先交一个月的房租作为押金，同时还得一次交三个月的房租。

安娜：也就是说第一次要付四个月的房租。

马克：可以这么理解。而且，最近租金还在涨，昨天刚付了租金，现在我都快喝西北风了。

Ān nà hé Mǎ kè liáo zū fáng。(Anna and Mark is talking about renting a house.)

Ān nà：Mǎ kè，nǐ hǎo!

Mǎ kè：Ān nà，nǐ hǎo!

Ān nà：Tīng shuō nǐ zài wài miàn zū fáng zhù。

Mǎ kè：Shì de。Wǒ xiàn zài zài shì qū de gōng sī shí xí，jīng cháng yào jiā bān，huí lái hěn wǎn，zhù zài sù shè hěn bù fāng biàn。

Ān nà：Zū jīn guì ma?

Mǎ kè：Yí gè yuè liǎng qiān。Yā yī fù sān。

Ān nà："Yā yī fù sān" shì shí me yì si?

Mǎ kè：Jiù shì xiān jiāo yí ge yuè de fáng zū zuò wéi yā jīn，tóng shí hái děi yí cì jiāo sān ge yuè de fáng zū。

Ān nà：Yě jiù shì shuō dì yī cì yào fù sì ge yuè de fáng zū。

Mǎ kè：Kě yǐ zhè me lǐ jiě。Ér qiě，zuì jìn zū jīn hái zài zhǎng，zuó tiān gāng fù le zū jīn，xiàn zài wǒ dōu kuài hē xī běi fēng le。

根据课文(一)回答问题
Answer these questions according to the Text A

1. 安娜为什么要租房子?
2. "喝西北风"是什么意思?

生词学习(二)
New words II

1. 房价 (fáng jià) *n.* housing price　　高房价
2. 几乎 (jī hū) *adv.* almost　　几乎一样;几乎全对
3. 专家 (zhuān jiā) *n.* expert　　经济专家;教育专家
4. 继续 (jì xù) *v.* continue　　继续学习;继续进行
5. 毕业 (bì yè) *v.* graduate　　从工商大学毕业;毕业证书
6. 投资 (tóu zī) *v./n.* invest; investment　　投资房地产;投资领域
7. 欣赏 (xīn shǎng) *v.* appreciate　　欣赏音乐;欣赏美景
8. 压力 (yā lì) *n.* pressure　　压力很大;没有压力
9. 按揭 (àn jiē) *v.* mortgage　　按揭还款;按揭贷款
10. 分期 (fēn qī) *v.* by stages　　分期付款
11. 还 (huán) *v.* pay back　　还钱;还贷款

课文(二)　买房好,还是租房好?
Text B　Is it better to buy a house or to rent a house?

马克:听说最近杭州的房价也涨了不少。

安娜:下沙的房价就涨了几乎一倍。听专家分析,房价还要继续涨。

马克:我想毕业后在杭州买个房子,一方面是投资,另一方面也可以让我的家人来杭州住。这样他们每天都可以欣赏西湖的美景啦。

安娜:好主意!不过我打算毕业后在杭州继续租房子,因为买房子的压力太大了,我一下子拿不出那么多的钱。还是租房子好!

马克:买房子不用一下子付清所有的钱,你只要先付总房款的30%,余下的房款采用按揭的形式还款。

安娜:什么是按揭?

马克:就是分期付款的意思,你每个月还一点儿钱,这样压力就不大了。

安娜:太好了!

Mǎ kè: Tīng shuō zuì jìn Háng zhōu de fáng jià yě zhǎng le bú shǎo。

Ān nà: Xià shā de fáng jià jiù zhǎng le jǐ hū yí bèi。Tīng zhuān jiā fēn xī, fáng jià hái yào jì xù zhǎng。

Mǎ kè: Wǒ xiǎng bì yè hòu zài Háng zhōu mǎi ge fáng zi, yì fāng miàn shì tóu zī, lìng yī fāng miàn yě kě yǐ ràng wǒ de jiā rén lái háng zhōu zhù。Zhè yàng tā men měi tiān dōu kě yǐ xīn shǎng Xī hú de měi jǐng la。

Ān nà: Hǎo zhǔ yì! Bú guò wǒ dǎ suàn bì yè hòu zài Háng zhōu jì xù zū fáng zi, yīn wei mǎi fáng zi de yā lì tài dà le, wǒ yí xià zi ná bù chū nà me duō de qián。Hái shì zū fáng zi hǎo!

Mǎ kè: Mǎi fáng zi bú yòng yí xià zi fù qīng suǒ yǒu de qián, nǐ zhǐ yào xiān fù zǒng fáng kuǎn de bǎi fēn zhī sān shí, yú xià de fáng kuǎn cǎi yòng àn jiē de xíng shì huán kuǎn。

Ān nà: Shén me shì àn jiē?

Mǎ kè: Jiù shì fēn qī fù kuǎn de yì si, nǐ měi ge yuè huán yì diǎnr qián, zhè yàng yā lì jiù bú dà le。

Ān nà: Tài hǎo le!

根据课文(二)回答问题
Answer these questions according to the Text B

1. 马克打算毕业后做什么?
2. "按揭"是什么意思?

语言点
Language points

1. A还是B?

买房好,还是租房好?

"还是"表示选择,一般用在疑问句中。

"还是" means to choose, which is usually used in interrogative sentences.

(1)你喝茶还是喝咖啡?

(2)你去还是不去?

2. 一方面……,另一方面……

一方面是投资,另一方面也可以让我的家人来杭州住。

“一方面……,另一方面……”表示从两个方面来说明某种情况。

It indicates two aspects of a situation, which means “on the one hand..., on the other hand...”

(1)这样一方面可以激发孩子的学习兴趣,另一方面可以培养孩子的独立性。

(2)来中国学习汉语,一方面学得很快,另一方面,可以亲眼目睹中国的最新发展。

3. 也就是说

也就是说第一次要付四个月的房租。

“也就是说”的意思是“也可以这样理解,换一种说法”。

It means “that is to say”.

观察各地的城市治理创新,自下而上的参与越来越多,政府与社会的合作越来越多。也就是说,城市治理正从行政主导向着多元主体的治理结构转变。

4. 喝西北风

现在我都快喝西北风了。

“喝西北风”的意思是“没有东西吃”。

It means that one has nothing to eat。

妈妈说,不上班就只有喝西北风了。

综合练习 Comprehensive exercises

(一)熟读短语 Read the following phrases

1. 租房子　租汽车　租金
2. 几乎满分　几乎全错　几乎雷同
3. 继续学习　继续工作　继续上课
4. 欣赏风景　欣赏作品　欣赏音乐

(二)选词填空 Fill in the blanks

租　几乎　继续　涨　欣赏

1. 他们俩的试卷________雷同,老师很想知道原因。
2. 最近房价________得很快。
3. 他想________这套房子,因为离地铁很近。

4. ________美景能让人心情愉快。

5. 只有________学习汉语,我才能成为中国通。

(三)课堂练习 In-class exercises

1. 团队合作。Teamwork.

请你和你的同伴一起了解一下中国各大城市的房价,并和自己的国家做比较。

2. 头脑风暴。Brainstorm.

你们国家的年轻人一般选择租房还是买房?请详细说明。

(四)课后练习 After-class exercises

调查你的中国朋友,多少人选择买房?多少人选择租房?各有什么好处和坏处?

课文翻译 Translation of the texts

Text A　Charge a pair of three

Anna: Hello, Mark!

Mark: Hello, Anna!

Anna: I heard you live outside.

Mark: Yes. I am now working in an urban company. I often have to work overtime and come back late, so it is very inconvenient to stay in the dormitory.

Anna: Is the rent expensive?

Mark: Two thousand per month. I'll pay three.

Anna: What do you mean by paying three?

Mark: First, pay the rent for one month as a deposit, and pay three months' rent at the same time.

Anna: That means paying the rent for four months at the first time.

Mark: You can understand that. Besides, the rent is still rising recently. I just have paid the rent yesterday, and now I have no money left.

Text B　Is it better to buy a house or to rent a house?

Mark: I heard that house prices in Hangzhou have also risen a lot recently.

Anna: House prices in Xiasha District have almost doubled. Listen to expert's analysis, housing prices will continue to rise.

Mark: I want to buy a house in Hangzhou after graduation. On the one hand, it is an investment; on the other hand, it can let my family live in Hangzhou. So they can enjoy the beautiful scenery of the West Lake everyday.

Anna: Good idea! But I plan to rent a house in Hangzhou after graduation. Because the pressure to buy a house is too great, I can not afford to pay so much money at once. Better to rent a house!

Mark: You don't have to pay all the money at once to buy a house. You just have to pay 30% of the total mortgage in advance. The rest of the mortgage will be paid back.

Anna: What is a mortgage?

Mark: It means payment by installment. You pay a little money every month, so the pressure is not big.

Anna: Great!

12 在中国实习
To practice in China

话题导学 Guidance

你打算在中国实习还是回国实习?

Do you plan to practice in China or your country?

生词学习(一) New words I

1. 祝贺 (zhù hè) *v.* congratulate　　祝贺你;热烈祝贺
2. 正式 (zhèng shì) *adj.* formal　　正式工作;正式文件
3. 发布 (fā bù) *v.* release　　发布新闻;发布会
4. 招聘 (zhāo pìn) *v.* recruit　　招聘员工;招聘广告
5. 具体 (jù tǐ) *adj.* concrete　　具体内容;很具体
6. 业务 (yè wù) *n.* business　　业务范围;公司业务
7. 流程 (liú chéng) *n.* procedure　　流程图;业务流程
8. 着急 (zháo jí) *adj.* anxious　　很着急;别着急
9. 羡慕 (xiàn mù) *v.* admire　　羡慕别人;很羡慕

bù yǐ
10. 不已　*v.* go to a great extent　　激动不已

专有名词(Proper nouns)

Zhìlián zhāopìn
1. 智联招聘　Zhaopin Recruitment(the name of a company)

Ā lǐ bā bā
2. 阿里巴巴　Alibaba(the name of a company)

课文(一)　我在实习
Text A　I'm in the internship

玛丽和美玲在教室聊天。

玛丽:美玲,你好!

美玲:玛丽,你好!

玛丽:听说你找到了一份新工作。祝贺你!

美玲:谢谢! 不过不是正式的工作,现在只是实习。

玛丽:你是怎么找到这个实习机会的?

美玲:我在网上找到的。"智联招聘",你听说过吗?

玛丽:听说过,而且在地铁里常常可以看到他们公司的广告。

美玲:他们的网站上每天都会发布大量的招聘信息,其中有好多是招聘实习生的。

玛丽:太好了! 我也想试试。你在哪个公司实习?

美玲:阿里巴巴。

玛丽:哇,好棒呀! 那具体做什么呢?

美玲:我昨天刚去报到,经理让我先熟悉业务流程,不着急做具体的工作。

玛丽:有工资吗?

美玲:有,每月3000块,还有加班费。

玛丽:真是让人羡慕不已。

Mǎ lì hé Měi líng zài jiào shì liáo tian。(Mary is talking with Meiling in the classroom.)

Mǎ lì:Měi líng,nǐ hǎo!

Měi líng:Mǎ lì,nǐ hǎo!

Mǎ lì:Tīng shuō nǐ zhǎo dào le yí fèn xīn gōng zuò。Zhù hè nǐ!

Měi líng:Xiè xie! Bú guò bú shì zhèng shì de gōng zuò,xiàn zài zhǐ shì shí xí。

Mǎ lì:Nǐ shì zěn me zhǎo dào zhè ge shí xí jī huì de?

Měi líng:Wǒ zài wǎng shàng zhǎo dào de。“Zhì lián zhāo pìn”,nǐ tīng shuō guo ma?

Mǎ lì:Tīng shuō guo,ér qiě zài dì tiě lǐ cháng chang kě yǐ kàn dào tā men gōng sī de guǎng gào。

Měi líng:Tā men de wǎng zhàn shàng měi tiān dōu huì fā bù dà liàng de zhāo pìn xìn xī, qí zhōng yǒu hǎo duō shì zhāo pìn shí xí shēng de。

Mǎ lì:Tài hǎo le! Wǒ yě xiǎng shì shi。Nǐ zài nǎ ge gōng sī shí xí?

Měi líng:Ā lǐ bā bā。

Mǎ lì:Wa,hǎo bàng ya! Nà jù tǐ zuò shén me ne?

Měi líng:Wǒ zuó tiān gāng qù bào dào,jīng lǐ ràng wǒ xiān shú xī yè wù liú chéng,bú zháo jí zuò jù tǐ de gōng zuò。

Mǎ lì:Yǒu gōng zī ma?

Měi líng:Yǒu,měi yuè sān qiān kuài,hái yǒu jiā bān fèi。

Mǎ lì:Zhēn shì ràng rén xiàn mù bù yǐ。

根据课文(一)回答问题
Answer these questions according to the Text A

1. 美玲找到工作了吗?
2. 美玲实习有没有工资?

生词学习(二)
New words II

1.	jié shù 结束	*v.* finish	会议结束;学期结束
2.	gǎn jué 感觉	*v.* feel	感觉很难;感觉不舒服
3.	shòu yì fěi qiǎn 受益匪浅	*idm.* benefit a lot from…	让我受益匪浅
4.	shōu huò 收获	*v./n.* harvest;gains	收获粮食;很多收获
5.	kè hù 客户	*n.* customer	大客户;客户利益
6.	shàng dì 上帝	*n.* God	客户就是上帝
7.	tuán duì 团队	*n.* team	团队协作;团队精神
8.	hé zuò 合作	*v.* cooperate	一起合作;加强合作
9.	chuàng xīn 创新	*v./n.* innovate;innovation	不断创新;创新意识

10. 同事 tóng shì *n.* colleague　　新同事；很多同事

11. 提升 tí shēng *v.* improve　　提升水平；提升能力

课文(二) 受益匪浅
Text B Benefit a lot

玛丽和美玲在教室聊天。

玛丽：美玲，你好！

美玲：玛丽，你好！

玛丽：实习结束了吗？

美玲：昨天刚结束。

玛丽：感觉怎么样？

美玲：挺好的，通过这次实习，我受益匪浅，收获很多。

玛丽：有哪些收获呀？

美玲：首先，以客户为本，客户就是上帝；其次，团队合作，要与同事们合作；再次，创新工作方法；最后，我的汉语水平得到了很快的提升。

Mǎ lì hé Měi líng zài jiào shì liáo tiān。(Mary is talking with Meiling in the classroom.)

Mǎ lì:Měi líng,nǐ hǎo!

Měi líng:Mǎ lì,nǐ hǎo!

Mǎ lì:Shí xí jié shù le ma?

Měi líng:Zuó tiān gāng jié shù。

Mǎ lì:Gǎn jué zěn me yàng?

Měi líng:Tǐng hǎo de,tōng guò zhè cì shí xí,wǒ shòu yì fēi qiǎn,shōu huò hěn duō。

Mǎ lì:Yǒu nǎ xiē shōu huò ya?

Měi líng:Shǒu xiān,yǐ kè hù wéi běn,kè hù jiù shì shàng dì;qí cì,tuán duì hé zuò,yào yǔ tóng shì men hé zuò;zài cì,chuàng xīn gōng zuò fāng fǎ;zuì hòu,wǒ de hàn yǔ shuǐ píng dé dào le hěn kuài de tí shēng。

根据课文(二)回答问题
Answer these questions according to the Text B

1. 美玲实习得怎么样？
2. 美玲有哪些收获？

语言点 Language points

1. 是……的

你是怎么找到这个实习机会的?

"是……的"表示强调。The structure "是……的……" indicates emphasis.

(1)我是昨天来杭州的。

(2)她是坐飞机来中国的。

2. 首先,……其次,……再次,……最后,……

首先,以客户为本,客户就上帝;其次,团队合作,要与同事们合作;再次,创新工作方法;最后,我的汉语水平得到了很快的提升。

"首先……;其次……;再次……;最后……"表示相关句子的先后次序。

It means "Firstly... Secondly... Thirdly... Finally...".

3.挺……的

挺好的,通过这次实习,我受益匪浅,收获很多。

在汉语中,程度副词"挺"一般和"的"一起使用。

In Chinese, the degree adverb "挺" is usually used together with "的".

今天风挺大的,外边挺冷的。

综合练习 Comprehensive exercises

(一)熟读短语 Read the following phrases

1. 正式的工作　正式的比赛　正式的会谈
2. 发布新闻　发布命令　发布消息
3. 实习结束　工作结束　学习结束
4. 提升能力　提升品质　提升职位

(二)选词填空 Fill in the blanks

正式　发布　结束　提升　受益匪浅

1. 这次实习让我________。
2. 在中国的学习就要________了。
3. 中国政府通过电视和网络________了这个新闻。
4. 只有不断________品质,才能吸引更多的消费者。
5. 现在我还没找到________的工作,有点儿着急。

(三)课堂练习 In-class exercises

1. 团队合作。Teamwork.

   请你和你的同伴尝试在网上找实习的岗位。

2. 头脑风暴。Brainstorm.

   你觉得是在中国实习好,还是在回国实习好?

(四)课后练习 After-class exercises

通过各种渠道,发现3个以上的实习机会,搞清楚实习地点、具体工作、薪酬待遇、招聘方式。

课文翻译 Translation of the texts

Text A I'm in the internship

Mary: Hello, Meiling!

Meiling: Hello, Mary!

Mary: I heard that you have found a new job. Congratulations!

Meiling: Thank you! But it's not a formal job. It's just an internship.

Mary: How did you find this internship opportunity?

Meiling: I found it on the internet. "Zhaopin Recruitment", have you heard of it?

Mary: Yes, and you can often see their company's advertisements in the subway.

Meiling: Their website publishes a lot of recruitment information every day, many of which are interns.

Mary: Great! I also want to try. Which company do you work for?

Meiling: Alibaba.

Mary: Wow, great! So what exactly does it do?

Meiling: I just went to report yesterday. The manager let me familiarize myself with the business process and do not rush to do specific work.

Mary: Is there any salary?

Meiling: Yes, It's 3,000 yuan per month and overtime pay.

Mary: I'm so jealous of you.

Text B Benefit a lot

Mary: Hello, Meiling!

Meiling: Hello, Mary!

Mary: Is the internship finished?

Meiling: Yesterday just ended.

Mary: How do you feel?

Meiling: Very good. Through this internship, I benefits a lot and gains a lot.

Mary: What are the gains?

Meiling: First of all, customer-oriented, customer God; secondly, teamwork, to cooperate with colleagues; thirdly, innovative working methods; finally, my Chinese level has been rapidly improved.

13 请喝茶
Please drink tea

话题导学
Guidance

你喝过中国茶吗？你知道中国茶叶有哪些种类吗？每种茶叶中最好的茶是什么？你喜欢中国茶吗？

Have you ever had Chinese tea? Do you know what kinds of Chinese tea are? What is the best tea in each kind of tea? Do you like Chinese tea?

生词学习(一)
New words I

1. 真 (zhēn) *adj.* true　　真实；真正
2. 绿茶 (lǜ chá) *n.* green tea　　买绿茶；制作绿茶
3. 倒 (dào) *v.* pour　　倒水；倒垃圾
4. 种 (zhòng) *v.* plant　　种树；种花
5. 机会 (jī huì) *n.* opportunity　　好机会；难得的机会
6. 趁 (chèn) *prep.* while　　趁热吃；趁热打铁
7. 热 (rè) *adj.* hot　　热水；天气很热

专有名词(Proper nouns)

1. 龙井(lóngjǐng) Longjing Tea
2. 西湖龙井(Xī hú lóngjǐng) the West Lake Dragon Well Tea

课文(一) 请喝茶
Text A Have some tea, please

安娜和马克在房间里聊天。

安娜:马克,你好!

马克:安娜,你好!

安娜:请坐,请喝茶。

马克:这茶真好喝,是什么茶?

安娜:西湖龙井,中国最好的绿茶。

马克:茶叶的名字也很好听,是在西湖里种的吗?

安娜:那倒不是,西湖龙井绿茶种在西湖附近的龙井村。那儿不仅风景好,更重要的是绿茶好!

马克:有机会一起去看看吧。

安娜:好啊! 喝茶要趁热,冷了就不好喝了,快喝吧!

马克:好的,味道好极了。

Ān nà hé Mǎ kè zài fáng jiān lǐ liáo tiān。(Anna is talking with Mark in the room.)

Ān nà:Mǎ kè,nǐ hǎo!

Mǎ kè:Ān nà,nǐ hǎo!

Ān nà:Qǐng zuò,qǐng hē chá。

Mǎ kè:Zhè chá zhēn hǎo hē,shì shén me chá?

Ān nà:Xī hú Lóng jǐng,Zhōng guó zuì hǎo de lǜ chá。

Mǎ kè:Chá yè de míng zì yě hěn hǎo tīng,shì zài Xī hú li zhòng de ma?

Ān nà:Nà dào bú shì,Xī hú Lóng jǐng lǜ chá zhòng zài Xī hú fù jìn de Lóng jǐng cūn。Nàr bú jǐn fēng jǐng hǎo,gèng zhòng yào de shì lǜ chá hǎo!

Mǎ kè:Yǒu jī huì yì qǐ qù kàn kan ba。

Ān nà:Hǎo a! Hē chá yào chèn rè,lěng le jiù bù hǎo hē le,kuài hē ba!

Mǎ kè:Hǎo de,wèi dao hǎo jí le。

根据课文(一)回答问题
Answer these questions according to the Text A

1. 最好的绿茶是什么?
2. 西湖龙井是一个地方吗?

生词学习(二)
New words II

1. 推荐	tuī jiàn	*v.* recommend	推荐人选;推荐信
2. 根据	gēn jù	*prep.* according to	根据天气;根据时间来安排
3. 定	dìng	*v.* decide	定时间;决定
4. 饮	yǐn	*v.* drink	饮酒;饮茶
5. 花茶	huā chá	*n.* flower tea	买花茶;制作花茶
6. 乌龙茶	wū lóng chá	*n.* oolong tea	买乌龙茶;制作乌龙茶
7. 红茶	hóng chá	*n.* black tea	买红茶;制作红茶
8. 便宜	pián yi	*adj.* cheap	价格便宜;很便宜
9. 味道	wèi dào	*n.* taste	味道不错;各种味道

专有名词(Proper nouns)

1. 祁门红茶 (qí mén hóng chá) Qimen Black Tea
2. 联华超市 (lián huá chāo shì) Lianhua Supermarket

课文(二) 哪种茶好?
Text B Which tea is better?

安娜和马克在房间里聊天。

安娜:马克,你好!

马克:安娜,你好!

安娜:我想给我的朋友送点中国的茶叶,你能帮我推荐一下吗?

马克:绿茶当属西湖龙井最好;红茶的话,我推荐祁门红茶;乌龙茶,我觉得铁观音不错。

安娜:那我应该买哪种茶叶呢?

马克:这要根据季节来定,春饮花茶,夏饮绿茶,秋饮乌龙茶,冬饮红茶。

安娜:我的国家现在是夏季,那我就买些绿茶送给我的朋友。

马克:可以去联华超市买哦。那儿的绿茶不仅便宜,味道也很不错。

Ān nà hé Mǎ kè zài fáng jiān lǐ liáo tiān。(Anna is talking with Mark in the room.)

Ān nà:Mǎ kè,nǐ hǎo!

Mǎ kè:Ān nà,nǐ hǎo!

Ān nà:Wǒ xiǎng gěi wǒ de péng you sòng diǎn Zhōng guó de chá yè,nǐ néng bāng wǒ tuī jiàn yí xià ma?

Mǎ kè:Lǜ chá dāng shǔ Xī hú lóng jǐng zuì hǎo;hóng chá de huà,wǒ tuī jiàn qí mén hóng chá;wū lóng chá,wǒ júe de tiě guān yīn bú cuò。

Ān nà:Nà wǒ yīng gāi mǎi nǎ zhǒng chá yè ne?

Mǎ kè:Zhè yào gēn jù jì jiē lái dìng,chūn yǐn huā chá,xià yǐn lǜ chá,qiū yǐn wū lóng chá,dōng yǐn hóng chá。

Ān nà:Wǒ de guó jiā xiàn zài shì xià jì,nà wǒ jiù mǎi xiē lǜ chá sòng gěi wǒ de péng you。

Mǎ kè:Kě yǐ qù lián huá chāo shì mǎi o。Nàr de lǜ chá bú jǐn pián yi,wèi dao yě hěn bú cuò。

根据课文(二)回答问题
Answer these questions according to the Text B

1. 铁观音属于哪种茶?
2. 什么季节喝绿茶好?

语言点
Language points

1. ……极了

味道好极了。

“极了”表示相当高的程度。

The structure “极了……” indicates extremely.

(1)她的汉语说得好极了。

(2)西湖美极了。

2. ……的话

红茶的话，我推荐祁门红茶。

“的话”表示“如果”的意思。

The structure “……的话” is the meaning of “if”.

(1)来杭州旅游的话，你一定要去西湖。

(2)吃正宗烤鸭的话，最好去全聚德。

3. 倒

那倒不是。

“倒”表示跟意料相反。

It means contrary to expectation.

屋子不大，收拾得倒还挺干净的。

4. 呢

那我应该买哪种茶叶呢？

“呢”用于强调问题。

It is used to emphasize problems.

(1)他去哪里了呢？

(2)现在怎么办呢？

综合练习 Comprehensive exercises

(一)熟读短语 Read the following phrases

1. 真的　真正　真好
2. 种花　种树　种植
3. 根据情况　根据季节　根据价格
4. 饮水　饮用　饮酒

(二)选词填空 Fill in the blanks

真　种　根据　推荐　趁

1. 今天________热，气温高达 40 度。
2. 茶要________热喝，冷了就不好喝。
3. ________她现在的汉语水平，要通过 HSK6 级几乎不可能。
4. 请帮我________合适的人选。
5. 这是我去年________的树。

(三)课堂练习 In-class exercises

1. 团队合作。Teamwork.

   请你和你的同伴一起了解一下中国各个地方代表性的茶叶。

2. 头脑风暴。Brainstorm.

   你们国家的人喝茶吗?你们喝的茶以及喝茶的习俗跟中国有什么不一样吗?what difference are the tea customs in China and in your country?

(四)课后练习 After-class exercises

去一趟龙井村,问一问村民或者路人,为什么他们都喜欢喝龙井茶?Visiting the dragon well village, asking the people why they love drinking dragon well tea so much?

课文翻译 Translation of the texts

Text A　Have some tea, please

Anna: Hello, Mark!

Mark: Hello, Anna!

Anna: Please have a seat. Please have some tea.

Mark: This tea is really good. What kind of tea is it?

Anna: The West Lake Dragon Well Tea, China's best green tea.

Mark: The name of the tea is also very pleasant to hear. Is it planted in the West Lake?

Anna: That's not true. West Lake Longjing green tea is planted in Longjing village near the West Lake. Not only is the scenery good, but more importantly, the green tea is good.

Mark: Have a chance to go and have a look.

Anna: OK! It tastes good while it is hot. Drink it!

Mark: Yes, it tastes great.

Text B　Which tea is better?

Anna: Hello, Mark!

Mark: Hello, Anna!

Anna: I want to send some Chinese tea to my friend. Can you recommend it for me?

Mark: Green tea is the best in Longjing, West Lake. If black tea is used, I recommend Qimen Black Tea. Oolong tea, I think Tieguanyin is good.

Anna: what kind of tea should I buy?

Mark: It depends on the season, spring scented tea, summer green tea, autumn Oolong tea and winter black tea.

Anna: My country is summer now, so I'll buy some green tea for my friends.

Mark: You can go to Lianhua Supermarket to buy it. It's not only cheap, but also delicious.

14 报名参加 HSK
Sign up for HSK

话题导学 Guidance

你考过 HSK 吗？什么时候可以报名？怎么报名？如何付报名费？

Have you ever tested HSK? When can I sign up? How do I sign up? How do I pay the registration fee?

生词学习(一) New words I

1. kǎo chá 考查 *v.* check —— 考查能力；考查知识
2. yùn yòng 运用 *v.* put to use —— 运用汉语；运用新技术
3. jiāo jì 交际 *v./n.* communicate/communication —— 进行交际；交际能力
4. kǎo 考 *v.* take an examination —— 高考；考研
5. lē 了 *aux.* (used after a verb or an adjective to indicate the completion of an action) —— 吃了；饱了
6. tīng lì 听力 *n.* listening —— 听力考试；听力理解
7. yuè dú 阅读 *n.* reading —— 阅读考试；阅读理解
8. xiě zuò 写作 *n.* writing —— 写作考试；写作能力

zǒng fēn
9. 总分 *n.* total points　　总分 100 分

zuì zhōng
10. 最终 *adv.* finally　　最终通过考试;最终获得冠军

hái shì
11. 还是 *adv.* unexpectedly　　还是通过考试了

tōng guò
12. 通过 *v.* pass　　通过考试;通过答辩

lì hai
13. 厉害 *adj.* excellent　　很厉害;太厉害了

专有名词(Proper noun)

hàn yǔ shuǐ píng kǎo shì
HSK 汉语水平考试

课文(一) 太厉害了
Text A You are excellent

玛丽和美玲在教室聊天。

玛丽:美玲,你好!

美玲:玛丽,你好!

玛丽:你知不知道 HSK?

美玲:当然,HSK 就是汉语水平考试,是一项国际标准化考试,考查汉语非第一语言的考生运用汉语进行交际的能力。

玛丽:你考过 HSK 吗?

美玲:上学期考的。

玛丽:你考的是哪一级呀?

美玲:六级。

玛丽:考了多少分?

美玲:听力 90 分,阅读 90 分,写作只得了 60 分。总分 240 分。最终还是通过了。

玛丽:太厉害了。祝贺你!

美玲:谢谢!

Mǎ lì hé Měi líng zài jiào shì liáo tiān。(Marie is talking with Meiling in the classroom.)

Mǎ lì:Měi líng,nǐ hǎo!

Měi líng:Mǎ lì,nǐ hǎo!

Mǎ lì:Nǐ zhī bu zhī dào HSK?

Měi líng: Dāng rán, HSK jiù shì hàn yǔ shuǐ píng kǎo shì, shì yí xiàng guó jì biāo zhǔn huà kǎo shì, kǎo chá hàn yǔ fēi dì yī yǔ yán de kǎo shēng yùn yòng hàn yǔ jìn xíng jiāo jì de néng lì。

Mǎ lì: Nǐ kǎo guo HSK ma?

Měi líng: Shàng xué qī kǎo de。

Mǎ lì: Nǐ kǎo de shì nǎ yī jí ya?

Měi líng: Liù jí。

Mǎ lì: Kǎo le duō shǎo fēn?

Měi líng: Tīng lì jiǔ shí fēn, yuè dú jiǔ shí fēn, xiě zuò zhǐ dé le liù shí fēn。Zǒng fēn èr bǎi sì shí fēn。Zuì zhōng hái shì tōng guò le。

Mǎ lì: Tài lì hai le。Zhù hè nǐ!

Měi líng: Xiè xie!

根据课文(一)回答问题
Answer these questions according to the Text A

1. 美玲通过了 HSK 吗?
2. 美玲的分数高不高?

生词学习(二)
New words II

1. bào míng 报名 *v.* sign up 报名参加考试;报名学习汉语
2. yǐng xiǎng 影响 *v.* affect 影响学习;影响社会发展
3. wǎng kǎo 网考 *n.* examination on the internet 参加网考
4. jiàn pán 键盘 *n.* keyboard 敲键盘;蓝牙键盘
5. shǔ biāo 鼠标 *n.* mouse 移动鼠标;换鼠标
6. shì hé 适合 *v.* fit 适合生活;适合学习

课文(二) 我想报名考 HSK
Text B I want to sign up for HSK

玛丽和美玲在教室聊天。

玛丽:美玲,你好!

美玲:玛丽,你好!

玛丽：我想考 HSK，你知道怎么报名参加考试吗？

美玲：现在报名很方便，先登录汉语考试服务网 www.chinesetest.cn，然后注册用户，接下来选择考点和考试时间，上传考生照片，最后通过网上银行支付考试费用。

玛丽：我的汉字写得不太好，不会影响考试结果吧？

美玲：那你可以选择网考，就是使用电脑考试，用键盘、鼠标输入作答。

玛丽：太适合我了！

Mǎ lì hé Měi líng zài jiào shì liáo tiān。(Marie is talking with Meiling in the classroom.)

Mǎ lì：Měi líng，nǐ hǎo！

Měi líng：Mǎ lì，nǐ hǎo！

Mǎ lì：Wǒ xiǎng kǎo HSK，nǐ zhī dao zěn me bào míng cān jiā kǎo shì ma？

Měi líng：Xiàn zài bào míng hěn fāng biàn，xiān dēng lù hàn yǔ kǎo shì fú wù wǎng www.chinesetest.cn，rán hòu zhù cè yòng hù，jiē xià lai xuǎn zé kǎo diǎn hé kǎo shì shí jiān，shàng chuán kǎo shēng zhào piàn，zuì hòu tōng guò wǎng shàng yín háng zhī fù kǎo shì fèi yòng。

Mǎ lì：Wǒ de hàn zì xiě de bú tài hǎo，bú huì yǐng xiǎng kǎo shì jié guǒ ba？

Měi líng：Nà nǐ kě yǐ xuǎn zé wǎng kǎo，jiù shì shǐ yòng diàn nǎo kǎo shì，yòng jiàn pán、shǔ biāo shū rù zuò dá。

Mǎ lì：Tài shì hé wǒ le！

根据课文(二)回答问题
Answer these questions according to the Text B

1. 怎么报名参加 HSK？
2. HSK 有网考吗？

语言点
Language points

1. 还是$_2$

最终还是通过了。

“还是”表示意料之外。

“还是” indicates unexpectedly.

(1)他还是大学生呢，连这个字都不认识。

(2)这么高的山，她还是爬上去了。

2. 正反问(知不知道)

你知不知道 HSK?

"知不知道"与"知道……吗"意思相同。此类格式为"*v*.不 *v*.",表示正反问。

It means "know or not". This format is "*v*.不 *v*.", which means positive and negative questions.

(1)明天你去不去杭州?

(2)他喜不喜欢你?

3. 情态补语

我的汉字写得不太好,不会影响考试结果吧?

"*v*.+得+*adj*."结构表达了说话者对一个动作结果或者状态的评论。

It explains one's view or opinion about how something is done.

(1)她穿得很漂亮。

(2)他学得很好。

"吧"用在句末,使原来的提问带有揣测和估计的意味。

"吧" should be placed at the end of a declarative sentence, to confirm his or her presumption.

(1)你是外国人吧?

(2)她回国了吧?

综合练习 Comprehensive exercises

(一)熟读短语 Read the following phrases

1.考 HSK　考研究生　考大学

2.吃过烤鸭　来过杭州　看过电影

3.参加考试　参加活动　参加比赛

4.适合学习　适合运动　适合工作

(二)选词填空 Fill in the blanks

考　适合　过　参加　还是

1. 虽然我只学习了一个月,但我_______通过了考试。

2. 这个工作_______年轻人做。

3. 要想进入这所大学学习商务汉语专业,必须_______入学考试。

4. 十年前她来_______杭州。

5. 他_______上了研究生,家里人都很开心。

(三)课堂练习 In-class exercises

1. 团队合作。Teamwork.

请你和你的同伴一起了解一下 HSK 考试的流程。

2. 头脑风暴。Brainstorm.

你会参加 HSK 考试吗？如果参加,请说一说如何准备;如果不参加,说说为什么？

(四)课后练习 After-class exercises

问一下身边考过 HSK 的朋友,为什么他们要参加考试？HSK 考试中最难的是什么？

Why did some of your friends take part in the exam? which is the most difficult part in the exam?

课文翻译 Translation of the texts

Text A　You are excellent!

Marie: Hello, Mei Ling!

Mei Ling: Hello, Marie!

Marie: Do you know HSK?

Meiling: Of course, HSK is the Chinese proficiency test. It is an international standardized test to test the ability of non-native speakers to communicate in Chinese.

Marie: Have you ever tested HSK?

Mei Ling: The last semester.

Marie: What grade did you take?

Mei Ling: Grade six.

Marie: How many points did you get?

Mei Ling: 90 points in listening, 90 points in reading, and 60 points in writing. The total score is 240 points. Finally passed.

Marie: That's amazing. Congratulations!

Mei Ling: Thank you!

Text B　I want to sign up for HSK

Marie: Hello, Mei Ling!

Mei Ling: Hello, Marie!

Marie: I want to sign up for HSK. Do you know how to sign up for the examination?

Meiling: Now it's very convenient to sign up. First, go to **www. chinesetest. cn**, then register the user, then choose the exam level and time, upload the photos of the candidates, and finally pay the exam fee through the online bank.

Marie: I can't write Chinese characters very well. Will it not affect the result of the examination?

Mei Ling: Then you can choose the no line test, that is, use keyboard and mouse to input your answers.

Marie: That suits me perfectly.

15 G20 杭州峰会
G20 Hangzhou summit

话题导学
Guidance

你听说过 G20 杭州峰会吗？能说一说这次峰会的特点吗？

Do you know about the G20 summit in Hangzhou? Can you talk about the characteristics of this summit?

生词学习(一)
New words I

1. 峰会 (fēng huì)	*n.* summit	举行峰会；杭州峰会
2. 主题 (zhǔ tí)	*n.* theme	确定主题；修改主题
3. 构建 (gòu jiàn)	*v.* establish	构建人类命运共同体
4. 活力 (huó lì)	*n.* vitality	充满活力；活力四射
5. 联动 (lián dòng)	*v.* chain affect	上下联动；内外联动
6. 包容 (bāo róng)	*n.* inclusiveness	相互包容；包容彼此
7. 嘉宾 (jiā bīn)	*n.* distinguished guest	与会嘉宾；邀请嘉宾
8. 主持 (zhǔ chí)	*v.* preside	主持会议；主持人

9. 开展 (kāi zhǎn) *v.* carry out 开展比赛;开展活动

10. 接触 (jiē chù) *v.* come into contact with 接触中国人;接触社会

11. 交流 (jiāo liú) *v.* exchange 交流体会;分享交流

12. 精彩 (jīng cǎi) *adj.* wonderful 非常精彩;精彩的演出

13. 盛大 (shèng dà) *adj.* grand 盛大的晚会;盛大举行

课文(一) G20杭州峰会
Text A G20 summit in Hangzhou

安娜和马克在教室聊杭州的G20峰会。

安娜:马克,你好!

马克:安娜,你好!

安娜:你知道G20杭州峰会吗?

马克:当然知道了。2016年9月4日至5日在中国杭州召开了G20峰会。

安娜:峰会的主题是什么?

马克:峰会的主题是“构建创新、活力、联动、包容的世界经济”。

安娜:有多少领导参加?

马克:二十国集团成员、八个嘉宾国领导人,以及七个国际组织负责人与会。中国国家主席习近平主持了二十国集团领导人杭州峰会,开展了五十三场活动,并同其他来宾进行接触和交流。

安娜:峰会开得成功吗?

马克:峰会发表了《二十国集团领导人杭州峰会公报》和二十八份具体成果文件。峰会开得很成功。

安娜:你了解的真不少。

马克:还有峰会的文艺演出“最忆是杭州”也非常精彩。

安娜:我还没看过呢。

马克:那你可要看一下。你可以在网上看,也可以去现场看。这场盛大的演出,从2017年五一开始就在西湖边天天上演。

安娜:精彩不容错过,我一定要去看一下。

Ān nà hé Mǎ kè zài jiào shì liáo Háng zhōu de G20 fēng huì。(Anna is talking with Mark about G20 summit in Hangzhou in the classroom.)

Ān nà:Mǎ kè,nǐ hǎo!

Mǎ kè:Ān nà,nǐ hǎo!

Ān nà:Nǐ zhī dao G20 háng zhōu fēng huì ma?

Mǎ kè:Dāng rán zhī dao le。2016 nián jiǔ yuè sì rì zhì wǔ rì zài Zhōng guó Háng zhōu zhào kāi le G20 fēng huì。

Ān nà:Fēng huì de zhǔ tí shì shén me?

Mǎ kè:Fēng huì de zhǔ tí shì "gòu jiàn chuàng xīn、huó lì、lián dòng、bāo róng de shì jiè jīng jì"。

Ān nà:Yǒu duō shao lǐng dǎo cān jiā?

Mǎ kè:Èr shí guó jí tuán chéng yuán、bā ge jiā bīn guó lǐng dǎo rén,yǐ jí qī ge guó jì zǔ zhī fù zé rén yù huì。Zhōng guó guó jiā zhǔ xí xí jìn píng zhǔ chí le èr shí guó jí tuán lǐng dǎo rén Háng zhōu fēng huì,kāi zhǎn le wǔ shí sān chǎng huó dòng,bìng tóng qí tā lái bīn jìn xíng jiē chù hé jiāo liú。

Ān nà:Fēng huì kāi de chéng gōng ma?

Mǎ kè:Fēng huì fā biǎo le《èr shí guó jí tuán lǐng dǎo rén Háng zhōu fēng huì gōng bào》hé èr shí bā fèn jù tǐ chéng guǒ wén jiàn。Fēng huì kāi de hěn chéng gōng。

Ān nà:Nǐ lǐao jiě de zhēn bù shǎo。

Mǎ kè:Hái yǒu fēng huì de wén yì yǎn chū "zuì yì shì Háng zhōu" yě fēi cháng jīng cǎi。

Ān nà:Wǒ hái méi kàn guò ne。

Mǎ kè:Nà nǐ kě yào kàn yí xià。Nǐ kě yǐ zài wǎng shang kàn,yě kě yǐ qù xiàn chǎng kàn。Zhè chǎng shèng dà de yǎn chū,cóng èr líng yī qī nián wǔ yī kāi shǐ jiù zài xī hú biān tiān tiān shàng yǎn。

Ān nà:Jīng cǎi bú róng cuò guò,wǒ yí dìng yào qù kàn yí xia。

根据课文(一)回答问题
Answer these questions according to the Text A

1. G20 杭州峰会什么时候召开的?
2. 峰会开得怎么样?

生词学习(二)
New words II

1. 创意 (chuàng yì) *n.* creativity　　富有创意;创意十足

2.	huì biāo 会标	*n.* symbol of an event	制作会标;设计会标
3.	jiè shào 介绍	*v.* introduce	介绍公司;介绍人
4.	xiàn tiáo 线条	*n.* line	画线条;一根线条
5.	miáo huì 描绘	*v.* depict	描绘图画;描绘画卷
6.	lún kuò 轮廓	*n.* outline	人物轮廓;景物轮廓
7.	yù yì 寓意	*v.*/*n.* imply;implication	寓意丰富;解读寓意
8.	gòng yíng 共赢	*v.* win together	互利共赢;合作共赢
9.	hù lián hù tōng 互联互通	*v.* interconnect	
10.	xié zuò 协作	*v.* collaborate	相互协作;协作发展
11.	yìn zhāng 印章	*n.* seal	制作印章;一枚印章
12.	zhāng xiǎn 彰显	*v.* display	彰显特色;彰显优势
13.	nèi hán 内涵	*n.* connotation	内涵丰富;有内涵
14.	hū yìng 呼应	*v.* act in cooperation with each other	首尾呼应
15.	yùn wèi 韵味	n. flavour	独特韵味;韵味十足
16.	gài kuò 概括	*v.* generalize	概括大意;进行概括

课文(二) 富有创意的会标
Text B The logo of the G20 Hangzhou summit is very creative

安娜和马克都觉得G20峰会的会标很有创意。

安娜:马克,你好!

马克:安娜,你好!

安娜:G20峰会的会标很有意思,你能介绍一下吗?

马克:2016年G20峰会会标图案,用20根线条,描绘出一个桥形轮廓。

安娜:桥梁的寓意是什么?

马克:桥梁寓意着G20已成为全球经济增长之桥、国际社会合作之桥、面向未来的共赢之桥。

安娜：互联网也是一座桥，对吧？

马克：是啊，桥梁线条形似光纤，寓意信息时代的互联互通。

安娜：图案中 G20 的“0”有什么特别的含义？

马克：图案中 G20 的“0”体现了各国团结、协作的精神。

安娜：图案中还有“中国”这两个汉字的印章。

马克：中文印章彰显了中国传统文化内涵，与英文 CHINA 相呼应。

安娜：如此看来，用“西湖元素、杭州特色、江南韵味、中国气派和世界大同”来概括 G20 杭州峰会的会标最合适不过了。

Ān nà hé Mǎ kè dōu jué de G20 fēng huì de huì biāo hěn yǒu chuàng yì。(Anna and Mark both thought the G20 summit bid was creative.)

Ān nà:Mǎ kè,nǐ hǎo!

Mǎ kè:Ān nà,nǐ hǎo!

Ān nà:G20 fēng huì de huì biāo hěn yǒu yì si,nǐ néng jiè shào yí xià ma?

Mǎ kè:2016 nián G20 fēng huì huì biāo tú àn,yòng èr shí gēn xiàn tiáo,miáo huì chū yí ge qiáo xíng lún kuò。

Ān nà:Qiáo liáng de yù yì shì shén me?

Mǎ kè:Qiáo liáng yù yì zhe G20 yǐ chéng wéi quán qiú jīng jì zēng zhǎng zhī qiáo、guó jì shè huì hé zuò zhī qiáo、miàn xiàng wèi lái de gòng yíng zhī qiáo。

Ān nà:Hù lián wǎng yě shì yí zuò qiáo,duì ba?

Mǎ kè:Shì a,qiáo liáng xiàn tiáo xíng sì guāng xiān,yù yì xìn xī shí dài de hù lián hù tōng。

Ān nà:Tú àn zhōng G20 de “líng” yǒu shén me tè bié de hán yì?

Mǎ kè:Tú àn zhōng G20 de “líng” tǐ xiàn le gè guó tuán jié、xié zuò de jīng shén。

Ān nà:Tú àn zhōng hái yǒu “Zhōng guó” zhè liǎng ge hàn zì de yìn zhāng。

Mǎ kè:Zhōng wén yìn zhāng zhāng xiǎn le Zhōng guó chuán tǒng wén huà nèi hán,yǔ yīng wén CHINA xiàng hū yìng。

Ān nà:Rú cǐ kàn lái,yòng “Xī hú yuán sù、Háng zhōu tè sè、Jiāng nán yùn wèi、Zhōng guó qì pài hé shì jiè dà tóng” lái gài kuò G20 háng zhōu fēng huì de huì biāo zuì hé shì bú guò le。

根据课文(二)回答问题
Answer these questions according to the Text B

1. 为什么说 G20 杭州峰会会标富有创意？

2. 会标上的“桥”有什么寓意?

语言点 Language points

1. 最……不过

用“西湖元素、杭州特色、江南韵味、中国气派和世界大同”来概括最合适不过了。

“最……不过”意思是“最”。

The structure “最……不过” means the most.

2. 进行

中国国家主席习近平主持了二十国集团领导人杭州峰会,开展了五十三场活动,并同其他来宾进行了接触和交流。

动词“进行”表示“从事(某种活动)”,后可接动词。

It means to engage in certain activities, followed by verbs.

(1)他们正在进行讨论。

(2)会议正在进行。

3. 可

那你可要看一下。

“可”表示强调。

It is used to express emphasis.

(1)杭州可美了。

(2)冬天可冷啦。

综合练习 Comprehensive exercises

(一)熟读短语 Read the following phrases

开展活动　开展学习　开展工作

精彩演出　精彩演讲　十分精彩

介绍同事　介绍大学　介绍公司

描绘蓝图　描绘画卷　精心描绘

(二)选词填空 Fill in the blanks

精彩　了　过　共赢　开展

1. 最近学校________了很多文化活动,同学们都很感兴趣。

2. 三年前她去________长城。

3. 21 世纪我们必须加强合作，才能________。

4. 今天的晚会真的非常________。

5. 我学________一年多汉语，还想继续学。

(三)课堂练习 In-class exercises

1. 团队合作。Teamwork.

请你和你的同伴一起了解一下每届 G20 峰会的主题。

2. 头脑风暴。Brainstorm.

G20 峰会在杭州召开，对杭州有什么好处？

(四)课后练习 After-class exercises

找到 5 个与 G20 峰会有关的地方，说说在哪里？跟 G20 有什么关系？现在有什么不一样了？

课文翻译 Translation of the texts

Text A G20 summit in Hangzhou

Anna: Hello, Mark!

Mark: Hello, Anna!

Anna: Do you know the G20 summit in Hangzhou?

Mark: Of course. G20 summit was held in Hangzhou, China from September 4th to 5th, 2016.

Anna: What is the theme of the summit?

Mark: The theme of the summit is "building a world economy with innovation, vitality, interaction and inclusiveness".

Anna: How many leaders are there?

Mark: There are 20 members, leaders of 8 distinguished guests and 7 heads of international organizations attending the meeting. Chinese President Xi Jinping chaired the G20 Hangzhou Summit held 53 events and held contacts and exchanges with other guests.

Anna: Did the summit succeed?

Mark: The summit issued the Hangzhou Summit Bulletin of the G20 leaders and 28 specific outcome documents. The summit was a success.

Anna: You know a lot.

Mark: There is also a summit performance. "The Most memory of Hangzhou" is also very exciting.

Anna: I haven't seen it yet.

Mark: Then you can see. You can see it online, or you can see it on the spot. This grand performance has been staged every day since May 1st on the side of the West Lake.

Anna: Wonderful, not to be missed. I must go and have a look.

Text B The logo of the G20 Hangzhou summit is creative

Anna: Hello, Mark!

Mark: Hello, Anna!

Anna: The logo of the G20 summit is very interesting. Can you introduce it?

Mark: 2016 G20 summit logo design is showed by 20 lines, depicting a bridge outline.

Anna: What is the meaning of bridges?

Mark: The bridge implies that the G20 has become a bridge of global economic growth, of international cooperation, and of a win-win future.

Anna: The internet is also a bridge, isn't it?

Mark: Yes, the lines of the bridge are similar to optical fiber, which means the interconnection and interconnection of the information age.

Anna: What is the special meaning of the "0" of G20 in the design?

Mark: The "0" of G20 reflects the spirit of solidarity and cooperation among different countries.

Anna: There are also the seals of the two Chinese characters of "中国" in the pattern.

Mark: Chinese seal highlights Chinese traditional culture and echoes with English CHINA.

Anna: So it seems most appropriate to generalize the G20 Hangzhou Summit's symbols with "West Lake elements, Hangzhou characteristics, Jiangnan flavor, Chinese style and world harmony".

生词表 New words

A
唉 3
爱情 5
APP 6
安排 8
按揭 11
阿里巴巴 12

B
表演 1
巴西 1
表示 2
白天 3
保暖 3
保留 4
半价 4
部分 5
比如说 5
本来 6
百度地图 7
办 8
抱歉 9
帮助 9
步 10
毕业 11
不已 12
报名 14
包容 15

C
春节 1
城市 1
除了 1
成都 1
参加 2
成熟 3
除了 6
出现 6
查 7
次 8
成为 9
聪明 9
创新 12
趁 13
创意 15

D
等 1
东南 1
大象 1
担心 1
导游 1
度 3
都 3
段 3
大概 3
多云 3
大衣 4
订单 4
但是 4
得 5
当 5
单车 6
当然 6
到处 6
电动车 6
对 7
地址 7
锻炼 8
带 8
大厅 8
达人 8
电影 9
登录 10
等待 10
倒 13
定 13

E
俄罗斯娃娃 1
俄罗斯 1
二维码 6

F
伏特加 1
风景 2
风 2
付钱 4
发票 4
方便 5
发生 5
附近 7
非常 7
放 8
方法 9
风险 10

编写说明

本教材为带有商务元素的初级汉语口语系列教材，共三册，本册为第三册。本册使用对象为已学习一学年、周课时在3课时左右的汉语学习者，学习者可用汉语就熟悉的日常话题进行简单的交流，达到初级汉语优等水平。

本教材的特点是，将日常口语交流与商务情境相结合，使学生在学习该课程后，能用汉语解决日常学习、生活中的基本问题，也能在商务场合进行基本的口语交流。相比较于北京外国语大学出版社、北京大学出版社等出版的教材，本教材在内容、情境设置上力求贴合南方院校，尤其是在浙学生的学习环境。在人物背景设置上，相较于以往语言进修生教材中主要人物来自欧美、日韩等国，本教材在此基础上增设了亚洲其他国家及非洲国家等人物背景，以符合目前进修生背景多样化的实际情况，使得来自不同国家和地区的学习者更有亲切感。

本册共设15课，在话题上，主要涉及商务元素，考虑学生生活实际，也有若干篇课文以校园生活为背景，以帮助学生提高在校园生活的语言运用能力。主题包含身份介绍、时间日期、天气、购物、地址介绍、交通方式、用餐、兴趣爱好、职业介绍、去银行、住宿、工作、娱乐等方面。

在结构上，每课都设有“话题导学”，每个问题都有英文翻译，以帮助学生更好地了解新课内容，做好学习热身。在生词部分，除了列举词性和英文翻译，还列举了相关常用短语，以帮助学生更好地掌握词汇的用法。为保证教材使用的实用性和有效性，适当照顾各层级学生的水平及课时多寡的需要，每课设有2篇比较简短的课文，在内容上侧重该课话题的不同方面，教师可根据学生学习接受能力和学时，使用2篇或选择其中1篇安排教学。每课有3—6个语言点解释，为便于学习者更好地理解，各语言点后有2—3个例句。核心句部分，要求学生熟练朗读，最好能脱口而出。

本教材的综合练习部分，以读、说等口语练习的形式为主，也有部分书面练习和社会实践练习。

由于本教材为口语教材，教师可根据实际需要和课程要求，为学生补充适当的汉字书写辅助练习，以帮助初级汉语学习者提高汉字的认读、书写能力，从而促使学生更好地掌握所学词汇等，顺利进入更高程度的汉语学习。

在编写安排上，孙鹏飞老师负责本册的统稿、样课的编写及框架的制定。其中，第1,2,3,4,6课由孙鹏飞老师编写；第5,7,8,9,10课由许飞燕老师编写；第11,12,13,14,15课由赵军老师编写。编写人员均为一线教师，为编写适合学生实际需要的教材，在上课之余认真思考，付出了较多的心血。但因水平和时间所限，恐有疏漏，敬请方家指正。

编者

2019年6月

透过案例
学公路工程计量与计价

杨建宏　陈志强　编著
王云江　　　　　主审

中国建材工业出版社

图书在版编目（CIP）数据

透过案例学公路工程计量与计价/杨建宏，陈志强编著．—北京：中国建材工业出版社，2011.4（2024.1 重印）

ISBN 978-7-80227-905-6

Ⅰ.①透… Ⅱ.①杨… ②陈… Ⅲ.①道路工程-工程造价 Ⅳ.①U415.13

中国版本图书馆 CIP 数据核字（2011）第 022899 号

内 容 提 要

全书共六章。主要内容包括公路工程造价组成与计算、公路工程工程量清单、路基工程计量与计价、路面工程计量与计价、桥涵工程计量与计价和隧道工程计量与计价。在各章中均有大量的计算例题并列举了完整的工程计价实例，而且还完整地演示了定额计量与计价、工程量清单计量与计价的过程和具体方法。本书具有内容翔实、通俗易懂、实例具体、可操作性强等特点。

本书适用于公路工程造价管理人员使用，也可作为大中专道路桥梁工程技术专业及工程造价管理专业的教材。

透过案例学公路工程计量与计价

杨建宏　陈志强　编著

王云江　　　　主审

出版发行：中国建材工业出版社

地　　址：北京市海淀区三里河路 11 号

邮　　编：100831

经　　销：全国各地新华书店

印　　刷：北京雁林吉兆印刷有限公司

开　　本：787mm×1092mm　1/16

印　　张：22

字　　数：542 千字

版　　次：2011 年 4 月第 1 版

印　　次：2024 年 1 月第 4 次

书　　号：ISBN 978-7-80227-905-6

定　　价：68.00 元

本社网址：www.jccbs.com，微信公众号：zgjcgycbs

请选用正版图书，采购、销售盗版图书属违法行为

前　言

本书是丛书《透过案例学工程计量与计价》之一。本书结合中华人民共和国交通部颁发的《公路工程预算定额》(JTGT B06—02—2007)、《公路工程机械台班费用定额》(JTGT B06—03—2007)、《公路工程基本建设项目概算预算编制办法》(JTG B06—2007)、《公路工程标准施工招标文件》(2009年版),以及《公路工程工程量清单计量规则》进行编写,将理论和实践相结合、文字与图表相结合,工程量计算方法、定额应用与实例相结合。

全书共六章。其中第一章公路工程造价组成与计算、第二章公路工程工程量清单、第三章路基工程计量与计价、第四章路面工程计量与计价、第五章桥涵工程计量与计价、第六章隧道工程计量与计价。本书由杨建宏、陈志强编著,王云江主审,编写人员有董海东、应小平、余茂华、李洋、蒙媛、施晓丽、刘建锋。

为突出本书的实用性、科学性和可操作性,在各章中均有大量的计算例题。在路基工程、路面工程、桥涵工程、隧道工程、防护工程各章中均列举了完整的工程计价实例(包括施工图),而且完整地演示了定额计量与计价、工程量清单计量与计价的过程和具体方法,读者在学习后能清楚地了解两种计价方法的编制知识。

本书具有内容翔实、通俗易懂、实例具体、可操作性强等特点,适用于公路工程造价管理人员学习使用,也可作为大中专道路桥梁工程技术专业及工程造价管理专业的教材。

限于编者的水平,书中难免有不妥与疏漏之处,恳请读者批评指正。

编　者

2011.1